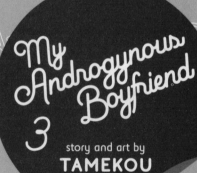

My Androgynous Boyfriend
3

story and art by
TAMEKOU

CHARACTERS

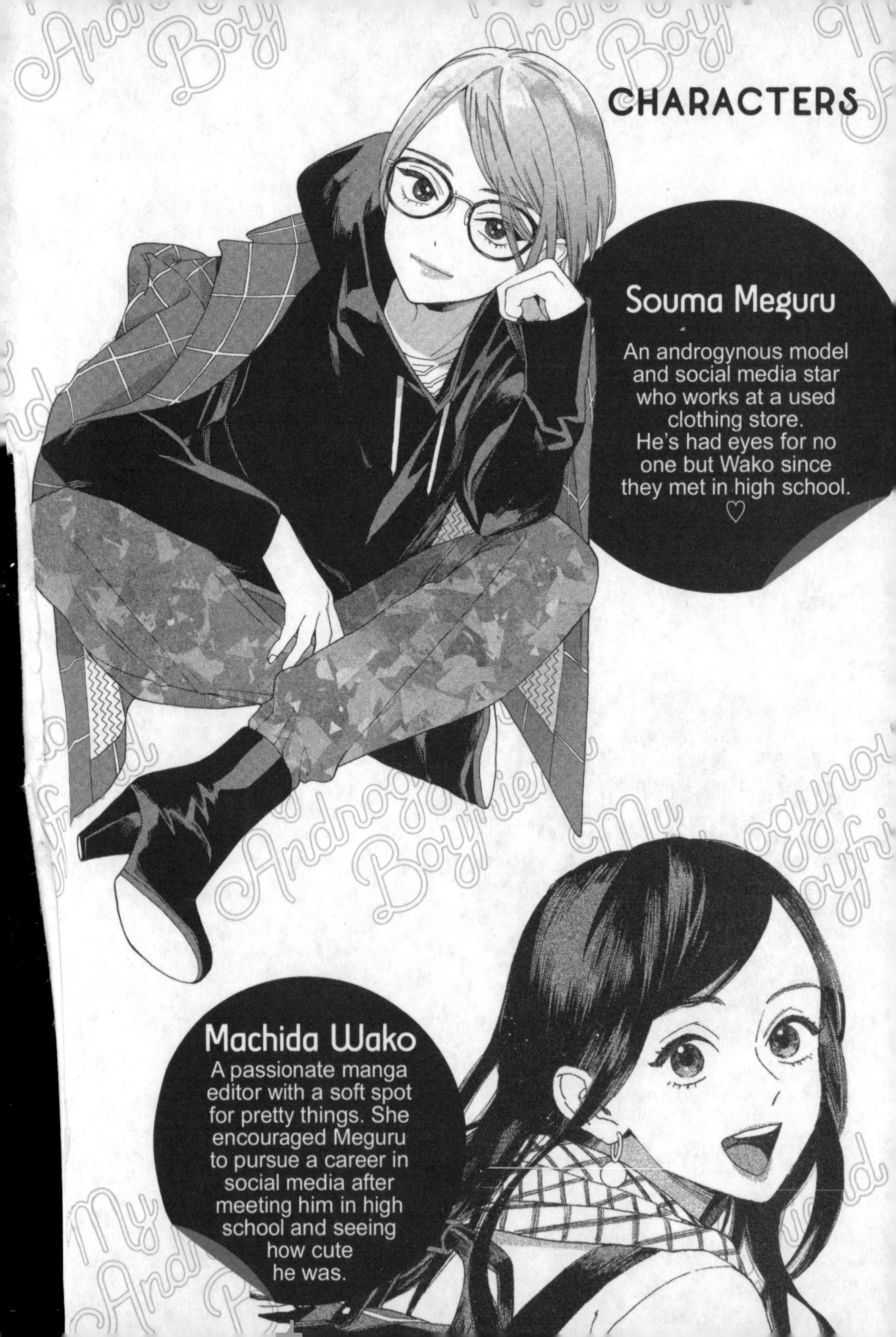

Souma Meguru

An androgynous model and social media star who works at a used clothing store. He's had eyes for no one but Wako since they met in high school. ♡

Machida Wako

A passionate manga editor with a soft spot for pretty things. She encouraged Meguru to pursue a career in social media after meeting him in high school and seeing how cute he was.

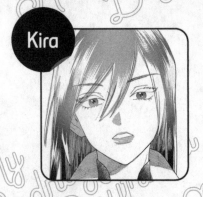

Kira

A model at the same agency as Meguru. This unique, androgynous man only pays attention to beautiful things.

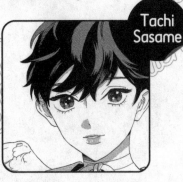

Tachi Sasame

An androgynous model, and Meguru's partner in the Unicorn Boys. He wants to be courageous and powerful like his bro.

Kanzaki Noboru

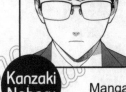

Manager for Meguru, Sasame, and Kira.

Kondo Kaoru

Manga artist edited by Wako. Fan of Unicorn Boys.

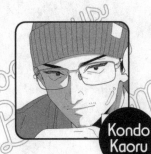

Wako's boss

Managing Editor

STORY

From his makeup to his fingernails, Meguro is a hundred percent adorable—and androgynous! However, his girlfriend Wako is an ordinary office worker. She's his biggest fan, and he's always trying to better himself for her. This is the story of their sweet, love-filled life! ♡

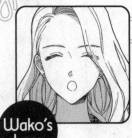

CONTENTS

The Twenty-First One

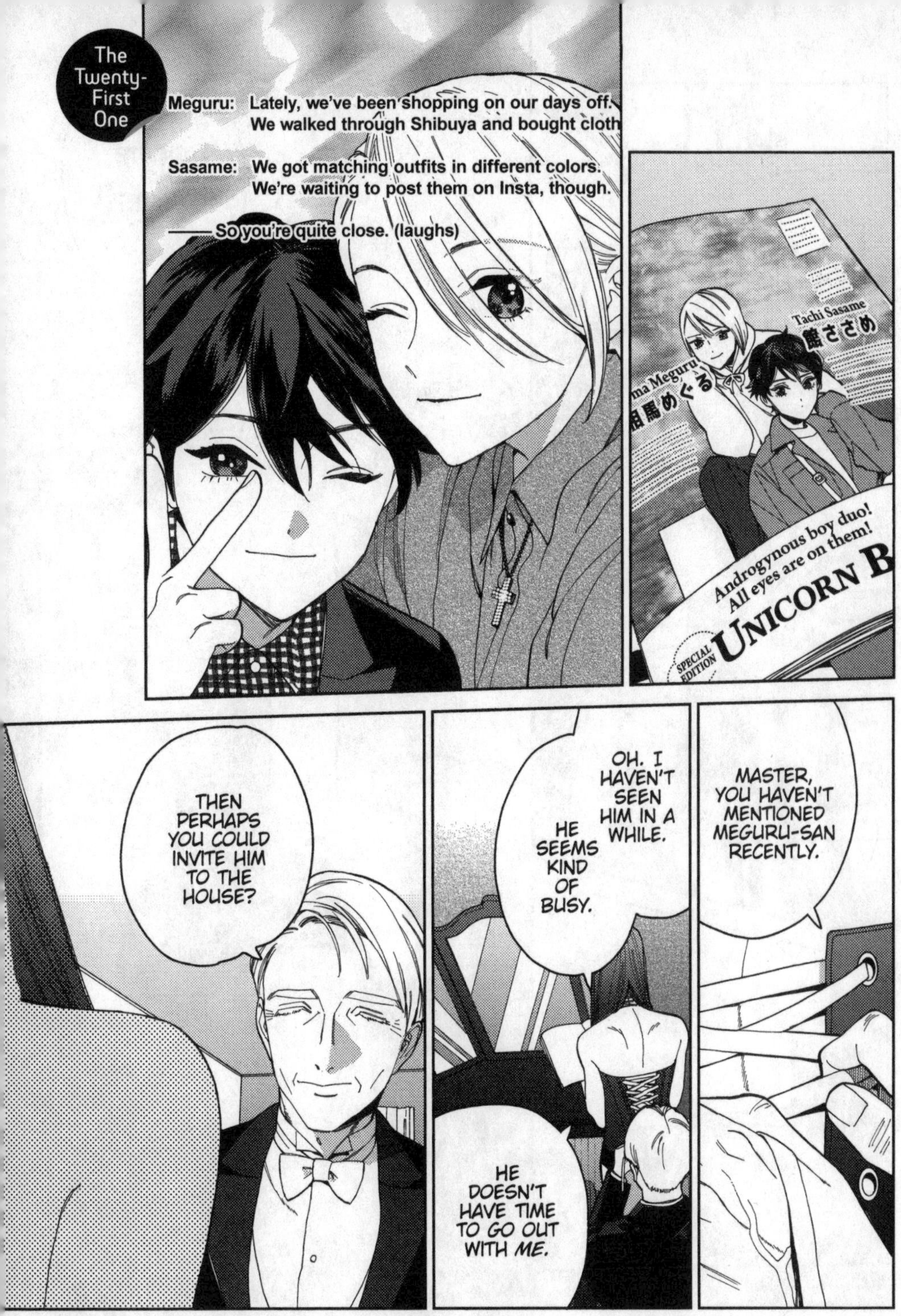
Tachi Sasame
舘ささめ
Androgynous boy duo! All eyes are on them!
SPECIAL EDITION
UNICORN B
Meguru: Lately, we've been shopping on our days off. We walked through Shibuya and bought cloth
Sasame: We got matching outfits in different colors. We're waiting to post them on Insta, though.
—— So you're quite close. (laughs)
MASTER, YOU HAVEN'T MENTIONED MEGURU-SAN RECENTLY.
OH. I HAVEN'T SEEN HIM IN A WHILE.
HE SEEMS KIND OF BUSY.
HE DOESN'T HAVE TIME TO GO OUT WITH *ME*.
THEN PERHAPS YOU COULD INVITE HIM TO THE HOUSE?

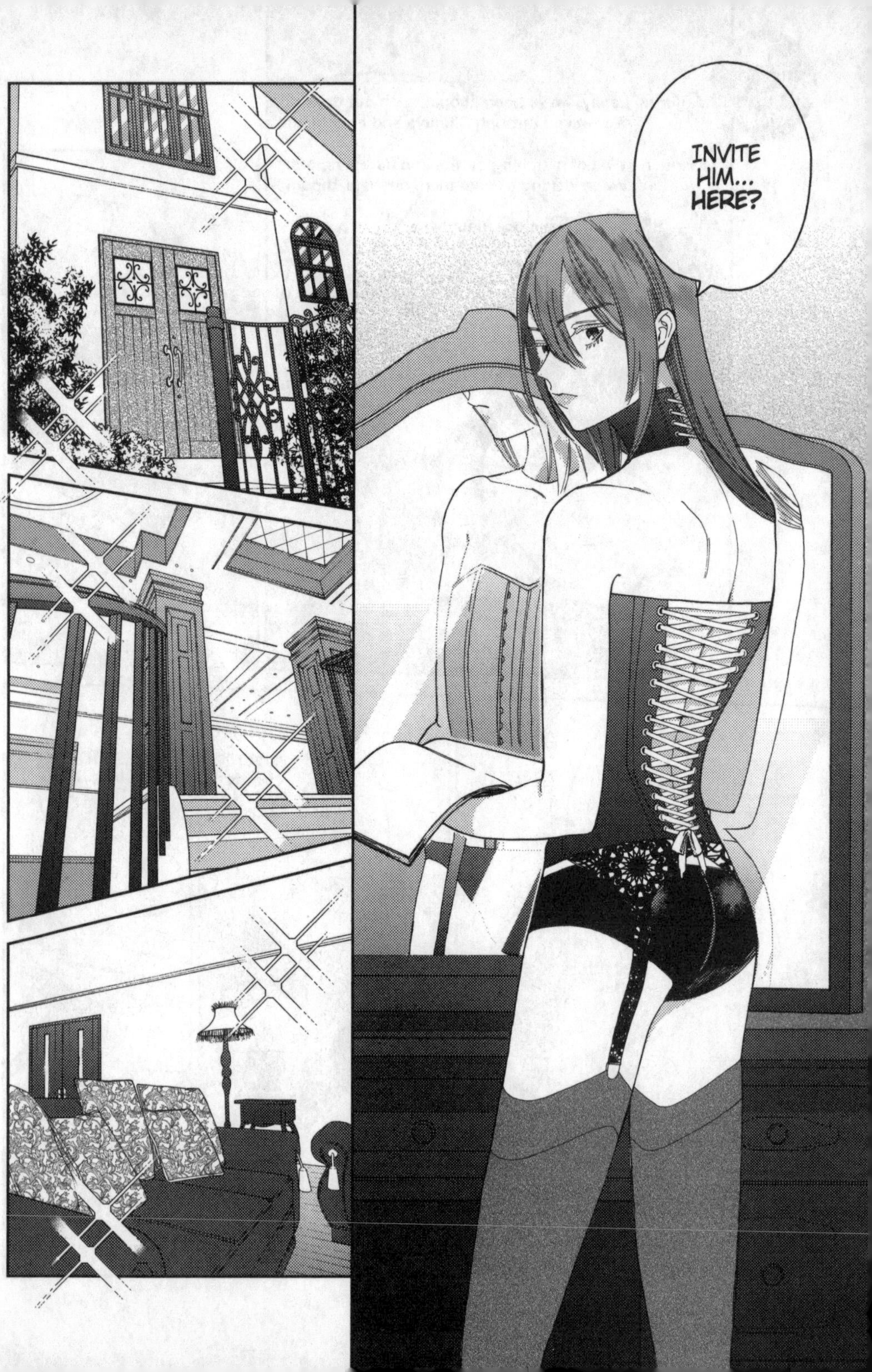
INVITE HIM... HERE?

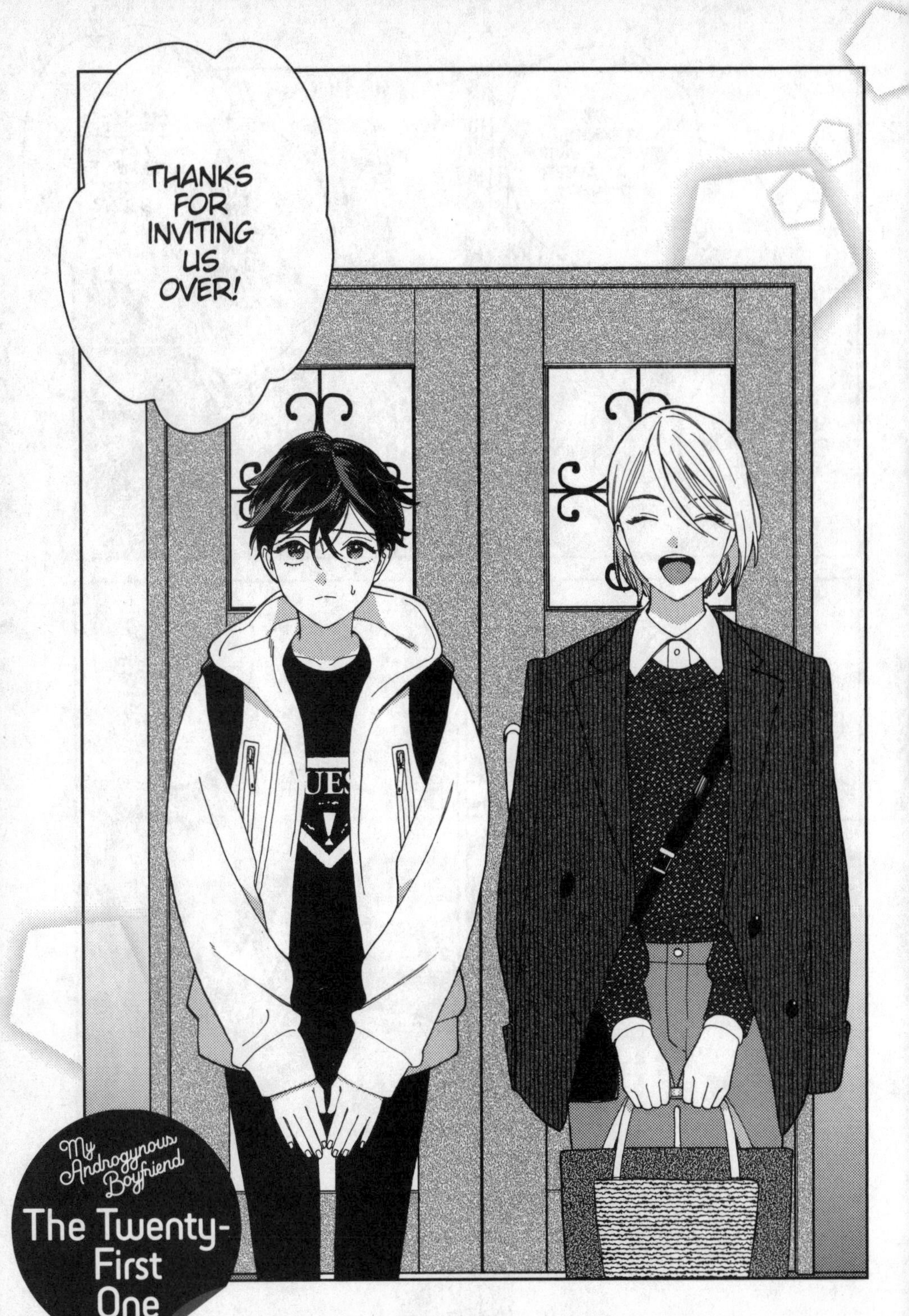
THANKS FOR INVITING US OVER!
My Androgynous Boyfriend
The Twenty-First One

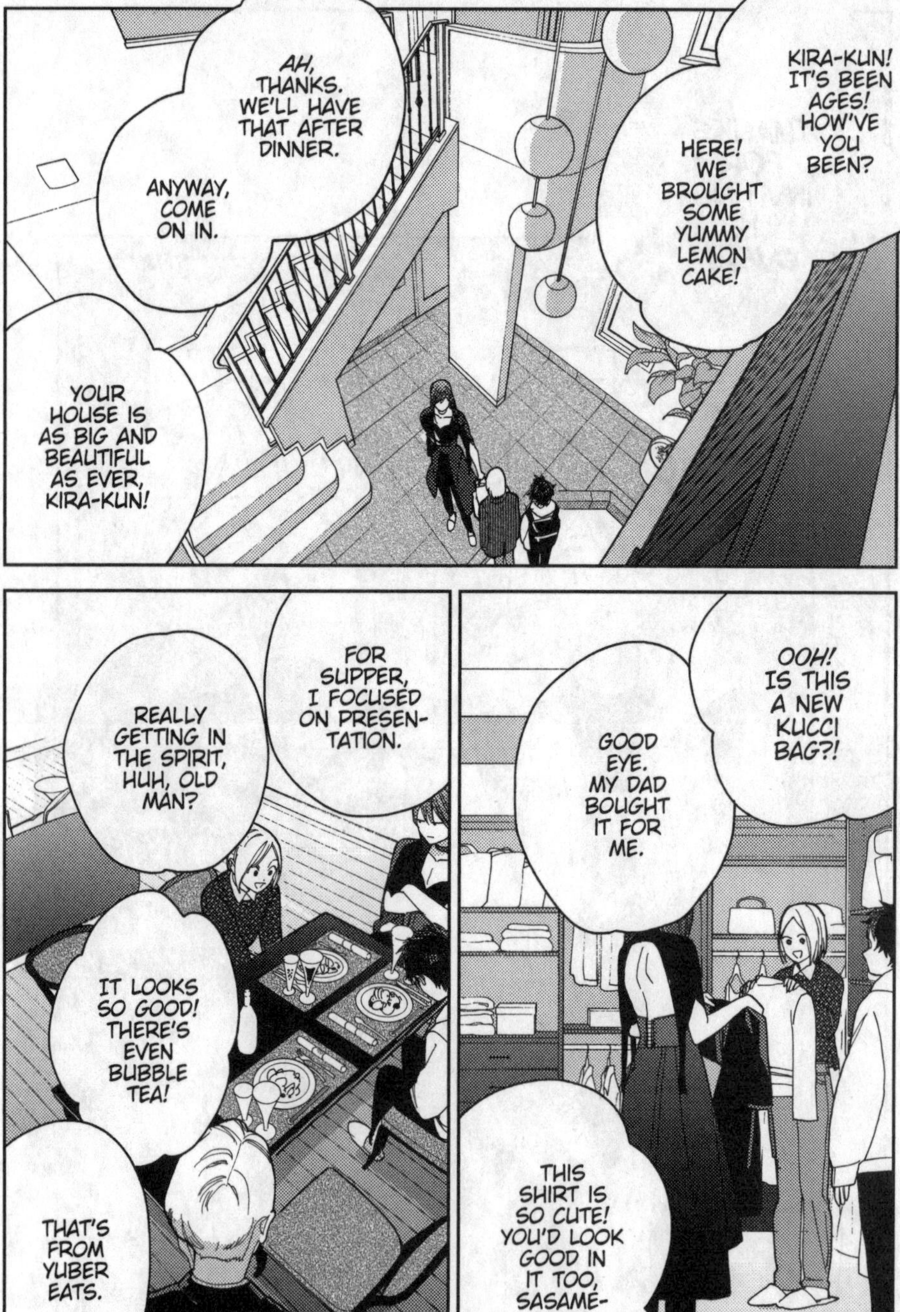
KIRA-KUN! IT'S BEEN AGES! HOW'VE YOU BEEN?
HERE! WE BROUGHT SOME YUMMY LEMON CAKE!
AH, THANKS. WE'LL HAVE THAT AFTER DINNER.
ANYWAY, COME ON IN.
YOUR HOUSE IS AS BIG AND BEAUTIFUL AS EVER, KIRA-KUN!
OOH! IS THIS A NEW KUCCI BAG?!
GOOD EYE. MY DAD BOUGHT IT FOR ME.
THIS SHIRT IS SO CUTE! YOU'D LOOK GOOD IN IT TOO, SASAME-KUN!
FOR SUPPER, I FOCUSED ON PRESENTATION.
REALLY GETTING IN THE SPIRIT, HUH, OLD MAN?
IT LOOKS SO GOOD! THERE'S EVEN BUBBLE TEA!
THAT'S FROM YUBER EATS.

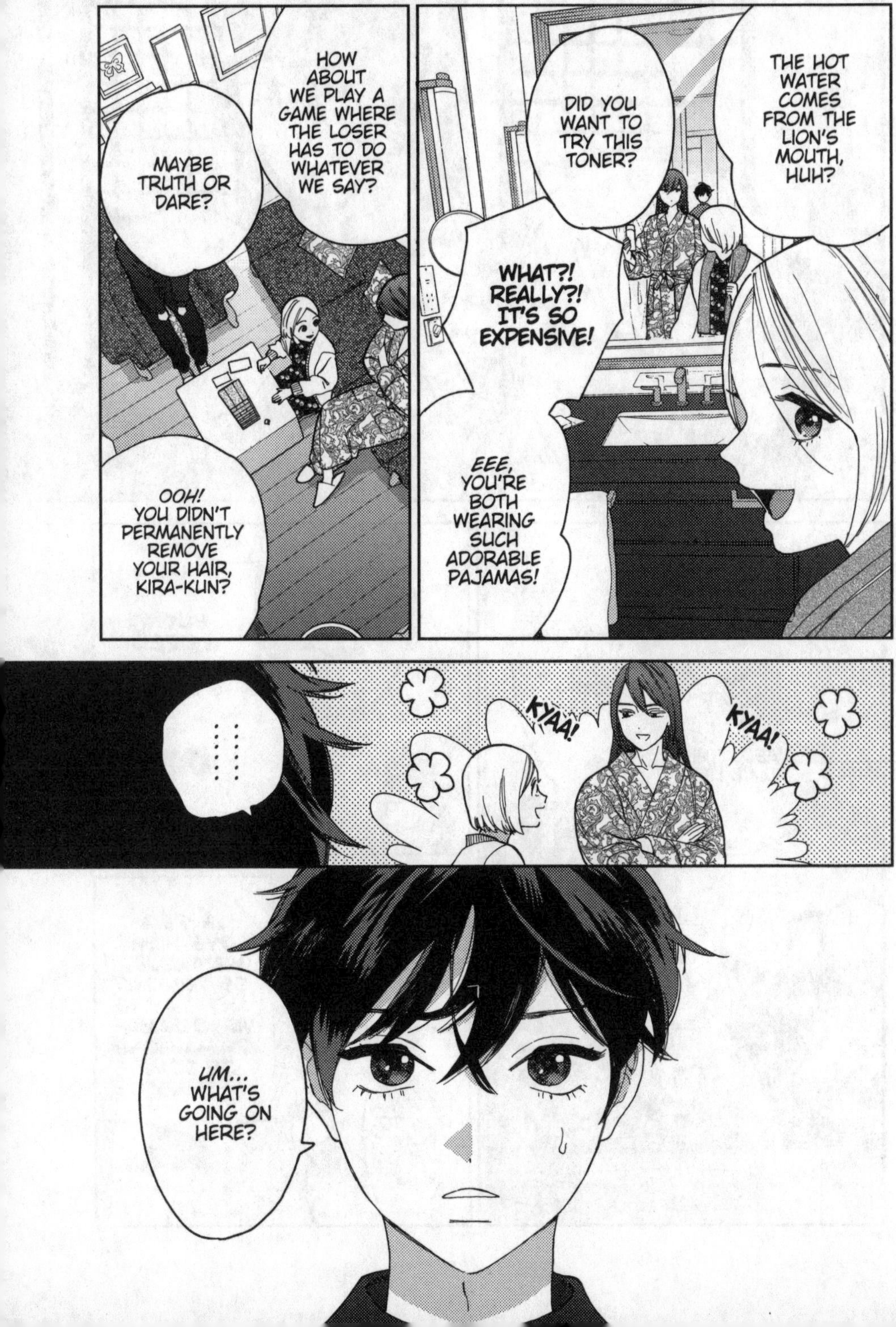
THE HOT WATER COMES FROM THE LION'S MOUTH, HUH?
DID YOU WANT TO TRY THIS TONER?
WHAT?! REALLY?! IT'S SO EXPENSIVE!
EEE, YOU'RE BOTH WEARING SUCH ADORABLE PAJAMAS!
HOW ABOUT WE PLAY A GAME WHERE THE LOSER HAS TO DO WHATEVER WE SAY?
MAYBE TRUTH OR DARE?
OOH! YOU DIDN'T PERMANENTLY REMOVE YOUR HAIR, KIRA-KUN?
KYAA!
KYAA!
......
UM... WHAT'S GOING ON HERE?

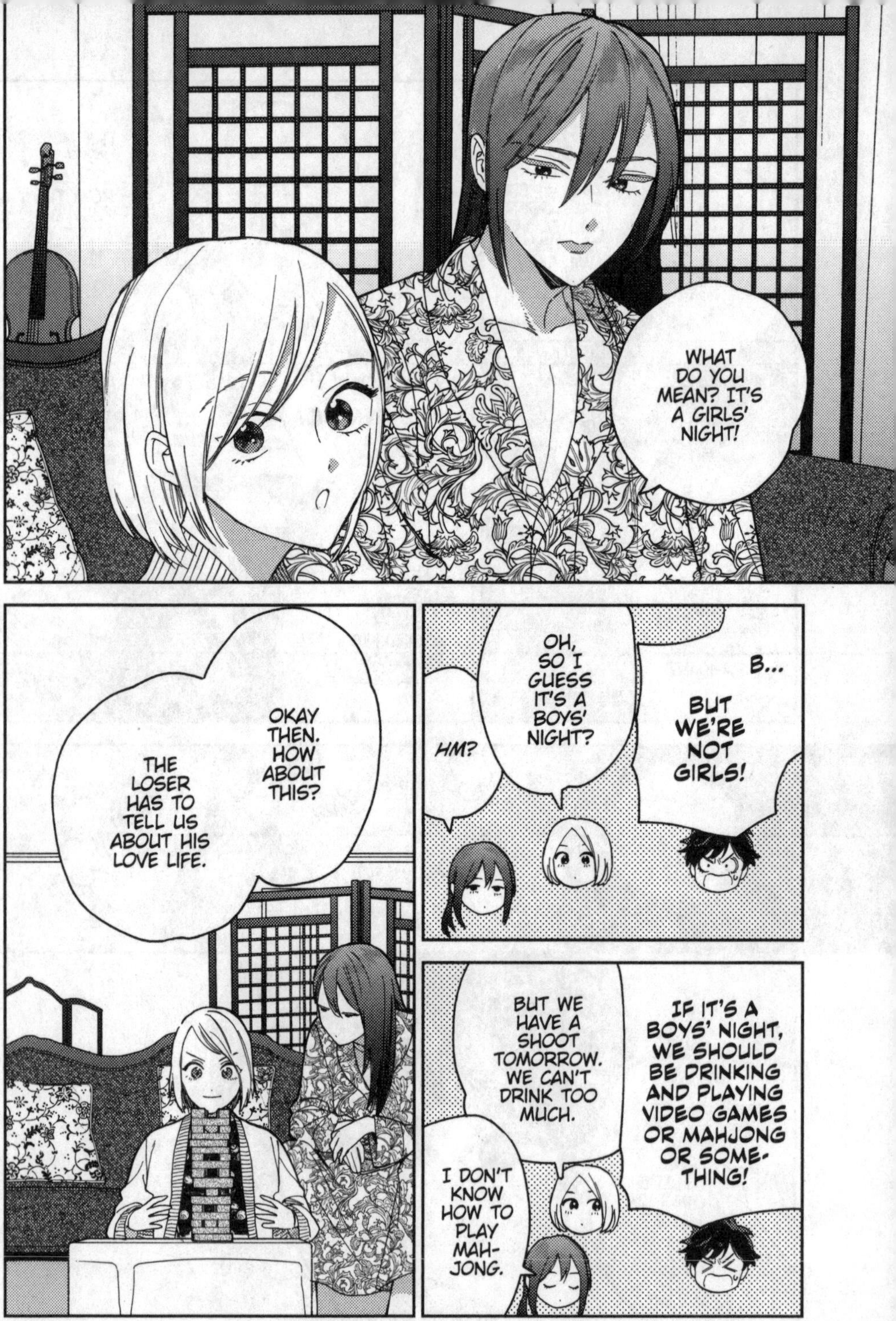
WHAT DO YOU MEAN? IT'S A GIRLS' NIGHT!
B...
BUT WE'RE NOT GIRLS!
OH, SO I GUESS IT'S A BOYS' NIGHT?
HM?
IF IT'S A BOYS' NIGHT, WE SHOULD BE DRINKING AND PLAYING VIDEO GAMES OR MAHJONG OR SOME-THING!
BUT WE HAVE A SHOOT TOMORROW. WE CAN'T DRINK TOO MUCH.
I DON'T KNOW HOW TO PLAY MAH-JONG.
OKAY THEN. HOW ABOUT THIS?
THE LOSER HAS TO TELL US ABOUT HIS LOVE LIFE.

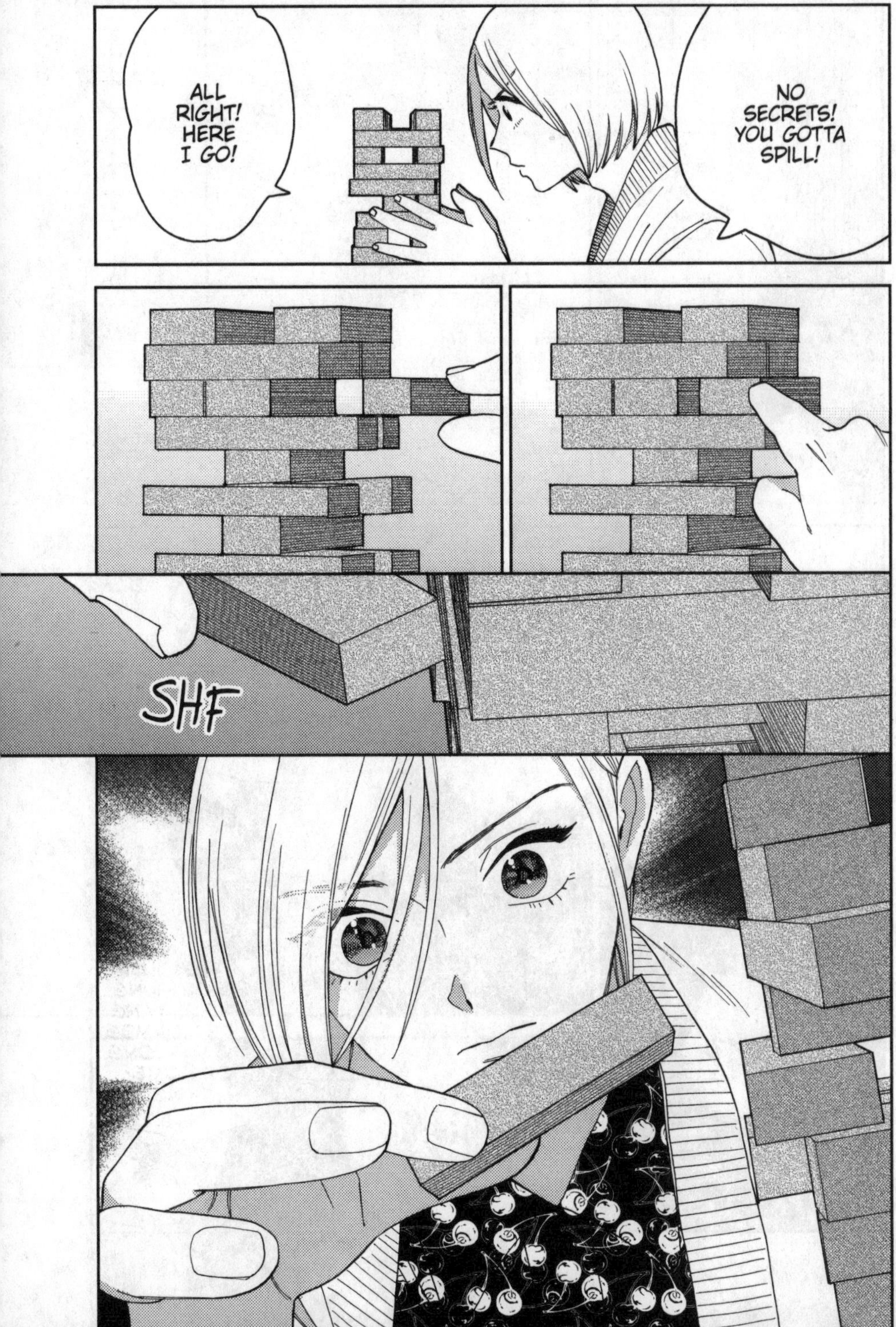
NO SECRETS! YOU GOTTA SPILL!
ALL RIGHT! HERE I GO!
SHF

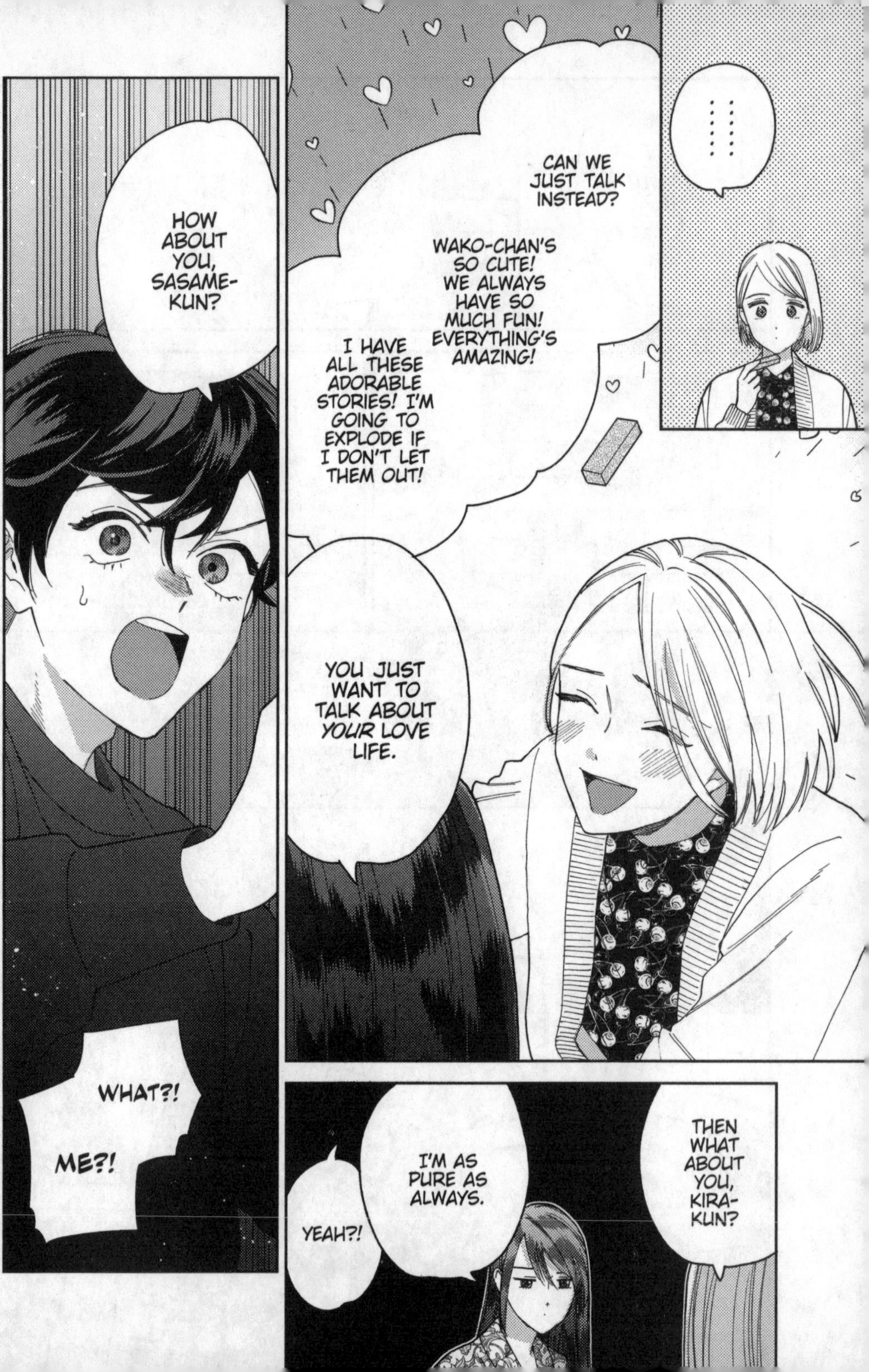
……
CAN WE JUST TALK INSTEAD?
WAKO-CHAN'S SO CUTE! WE ALWAYS HAVE SO MUCH FUN! EVERYTHING'S AMAZING!
I HAVE ALL THESE ADORABLE STORIES! I'M GOING TO EXPLODE IF I DON'T LET THEM OUT!
YOU JUST WANT TO TALK ABOUT *YOUR* LOVE LIFE.
THEN WHAT ABOUT YOU, KIRA-KUN?
I'M AS PURE AS ALWAYS.
YEAH?!
HOW ABOUT YOU, SASAME-KUN?
WHAT?!
ME?!

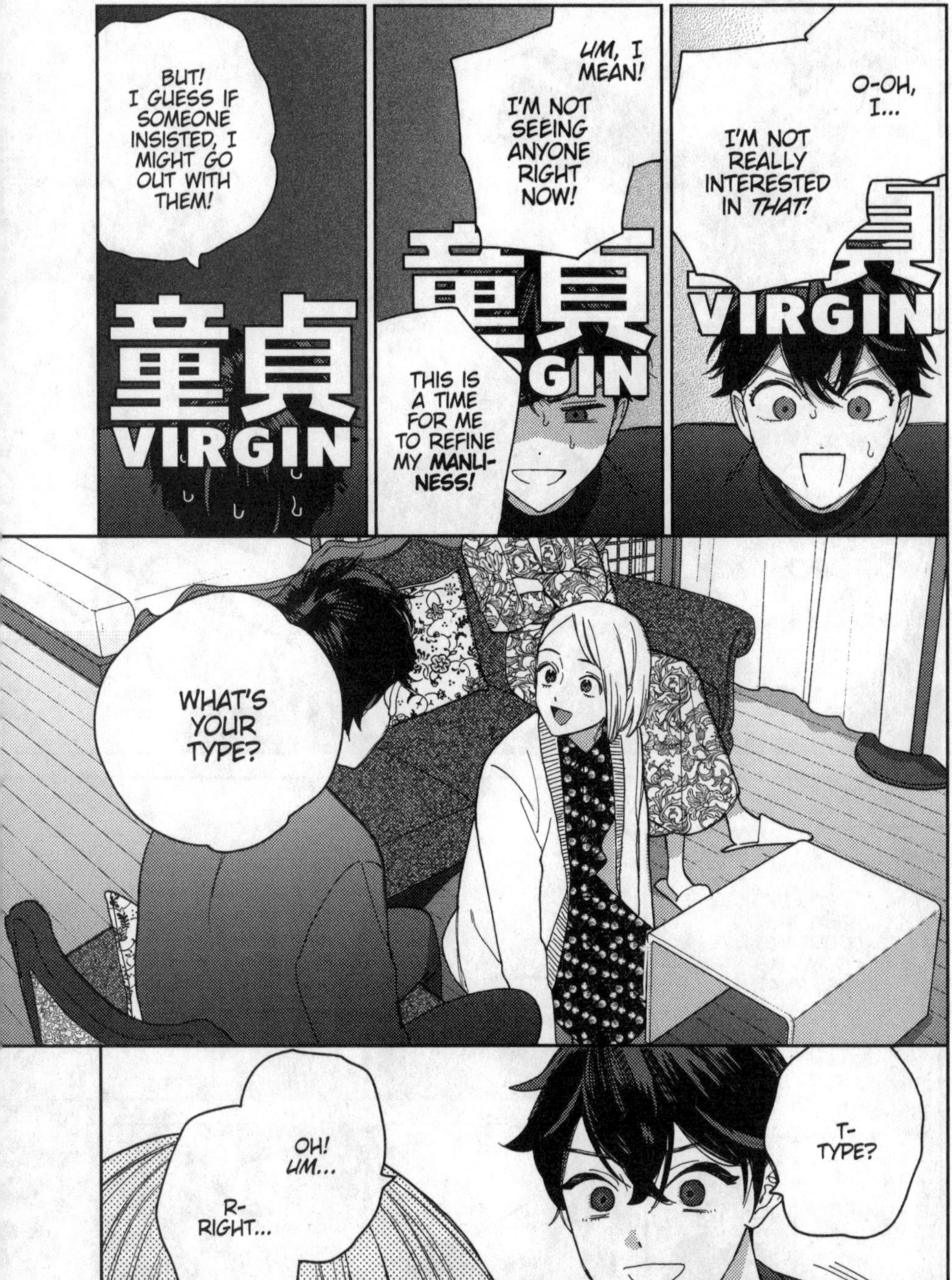
O-OH, I...
I'M NOT REALLY INTERESTED IN *THAT!*
VIRGIN
UM, I MEAN!
I'M NOT SEEING ANYONE RIGHT NOW!
童貞
THIS IS A TIME FOR ME TO REFINE MY **MANLINESS!**
BUT! I GUESS IF SOMEONE INSISTED, I MIGHT GO OUT WITH THEM!
童貞
VIRGIN
WHAT'S YOUR TYPE?
T-TYPE?
OH! UM...
R-RIGHT...

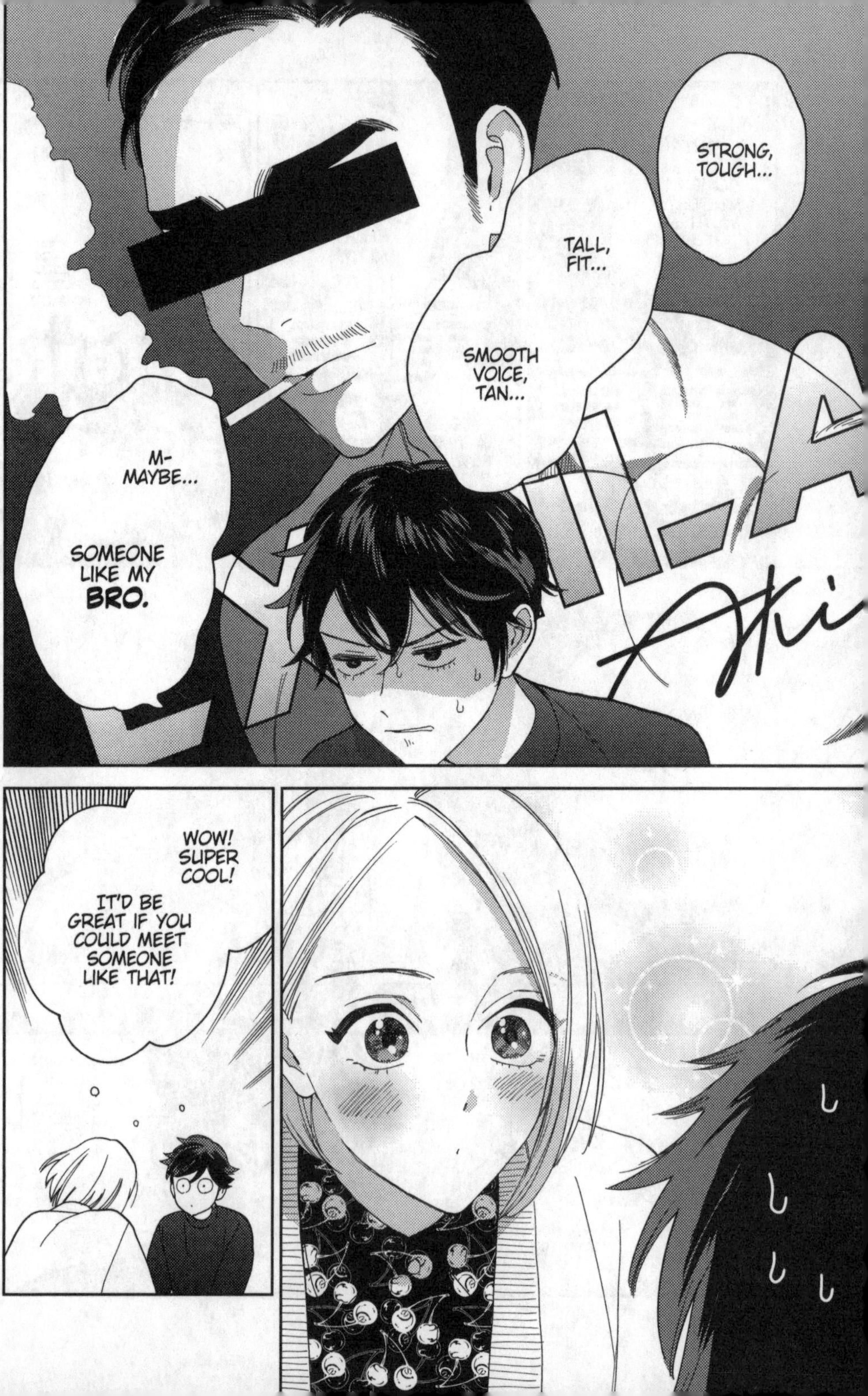
STRONG, TOUGH...
TALL, FIT...
SMOOTH VOICE, TAN...
M- MAYBE... SOMEONE LIKE MY **BRO.**
WOW! SUPER COOL! IT'D BE GREAT IF YOU COULD MEET SOMEONE LIKE THAT!

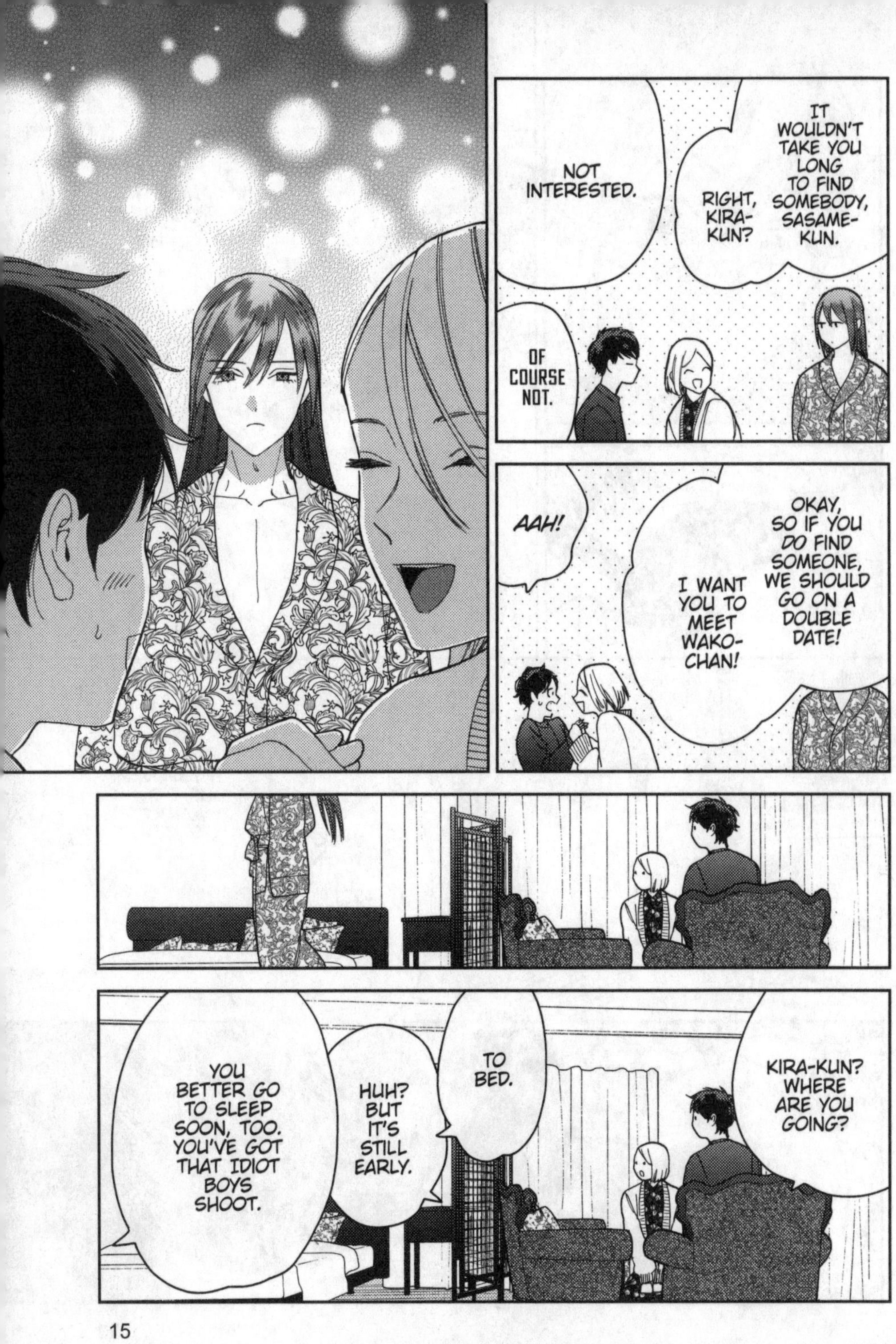
IT WOULDN'T TAKE YOU LONG TO FIND SOMEBODY, SASAME-KUN.
RIGHT, KIRA-KUN?
NOT INTERESTED.
OF COURSE NOT.
OKAY, SO IF YOU *DO* FIND SOMEONE, WE SHOULD GO ON A DOUBLE DATE!
I WANT YOU TO MEET WAKO-CHAN!
AAH!
KIRA-KUN? WHERE ARE YOU GOING?
TO BED.
HUH? BUT IT'S STILL EARLY.
YOU BETTER GO TO SLEEP SOON, TOO. YOU'VE GOT THAT IDIOT BOYS SHOOT.

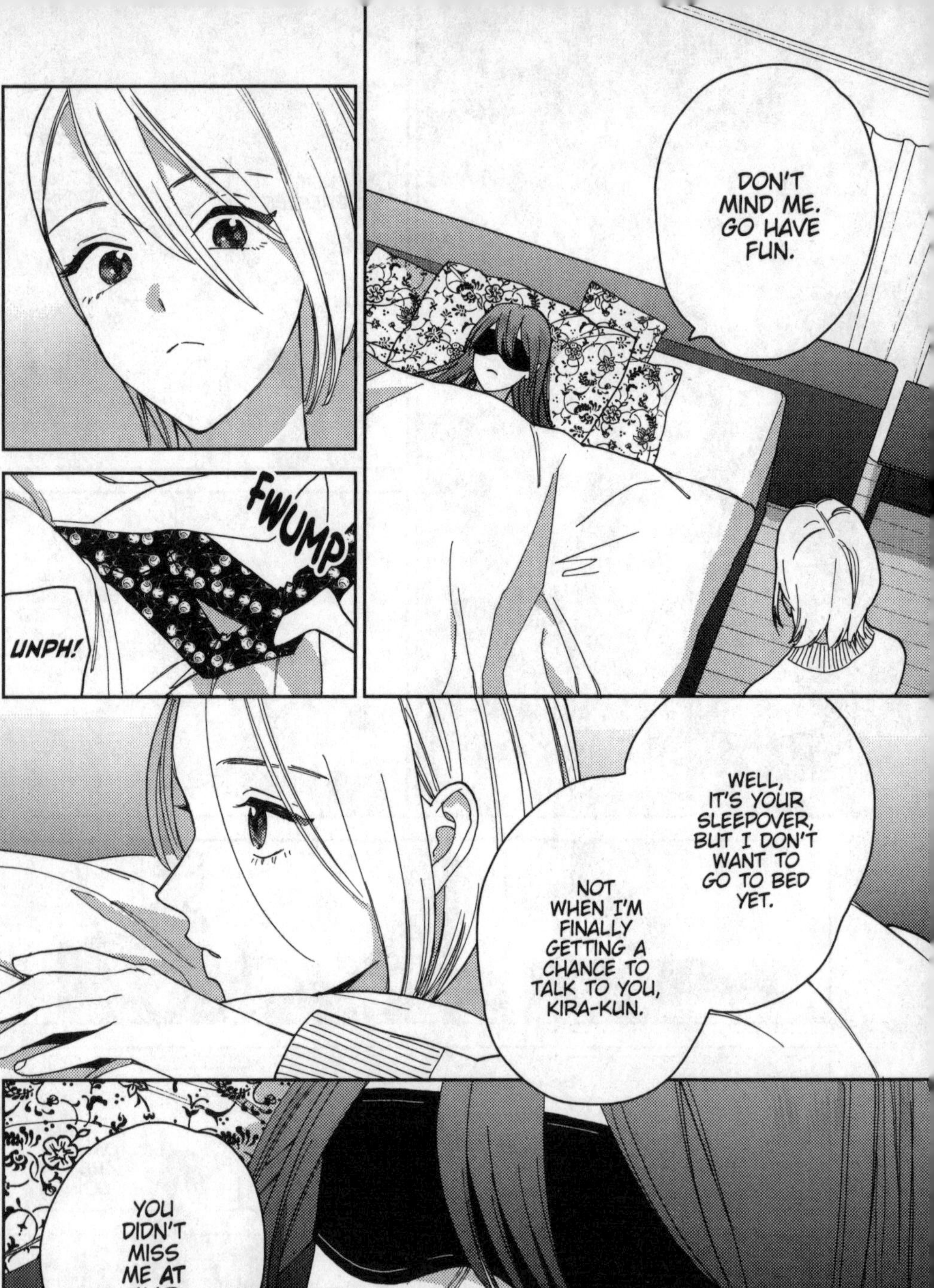
DON'T MIND ME. GO HAVE FUN.
FWUMP
UNPH!
WELL, IT'S YOUR SLEEPOVER, BUT I DON'T WANT TO GO TO BED YET.
NOT WHEN I'M FINALLY GETTING A CHANCE TO TALK TO YOU, KIRA-KUN.
YOU DIDN'T MISS ME AT ALL?

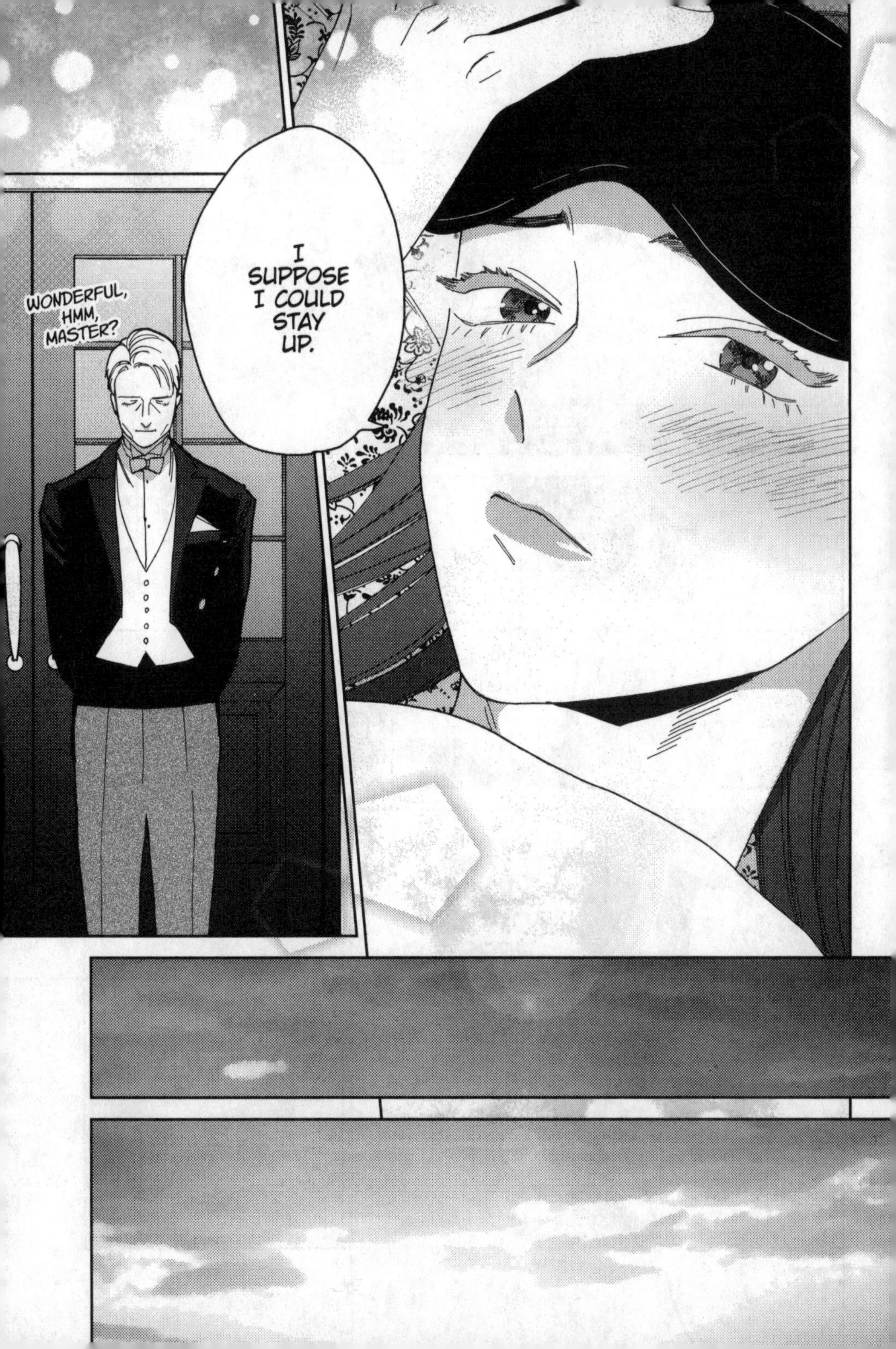
I SUPPOSE I COULD STAY UP.
WONDERFUL, HMM, MASTER?

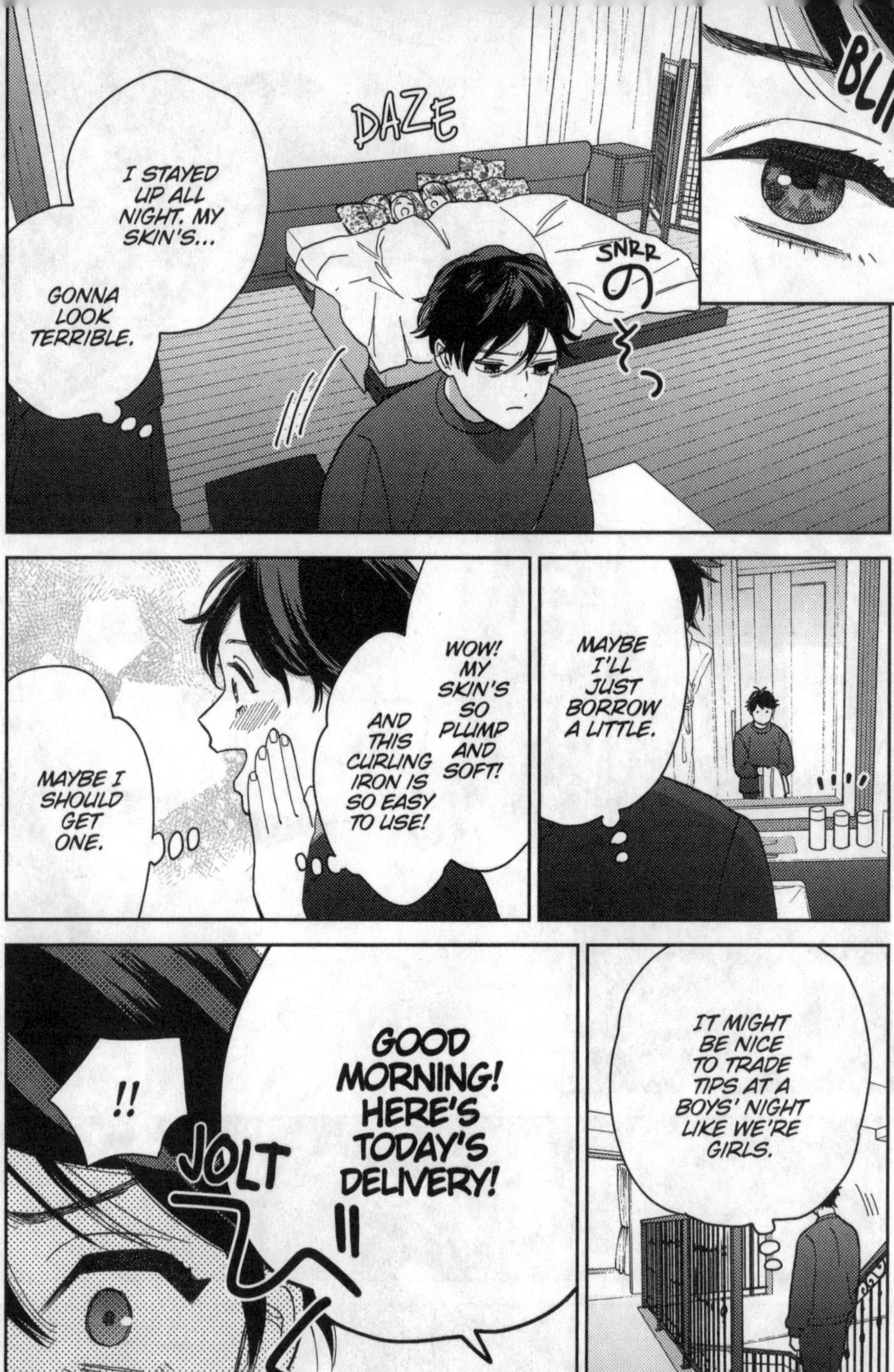
BLINK
DAZE
SNRR
I STAYED UP ALL NIGHT. MY SKIN'S...
GONNA LOOK TERRIBLE.
MAYBE I'LL JUST BORROW A LITTLE.
WOW! MY SKIN'S SO PLUMP AND SOFT!
AND THIS CURLING IRON IS SO EASY TO USE!
MAYBE I SHOULD GET ONE.
IT MIGHT BE NICE TO TRADE TIPS AT A BOYS' NIGHT LIKE WE'RE GIRLS.
GOOD MORNING! HERE'S TODAY'S DELIVERY!!
!!
JOLT

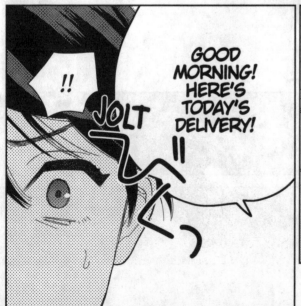

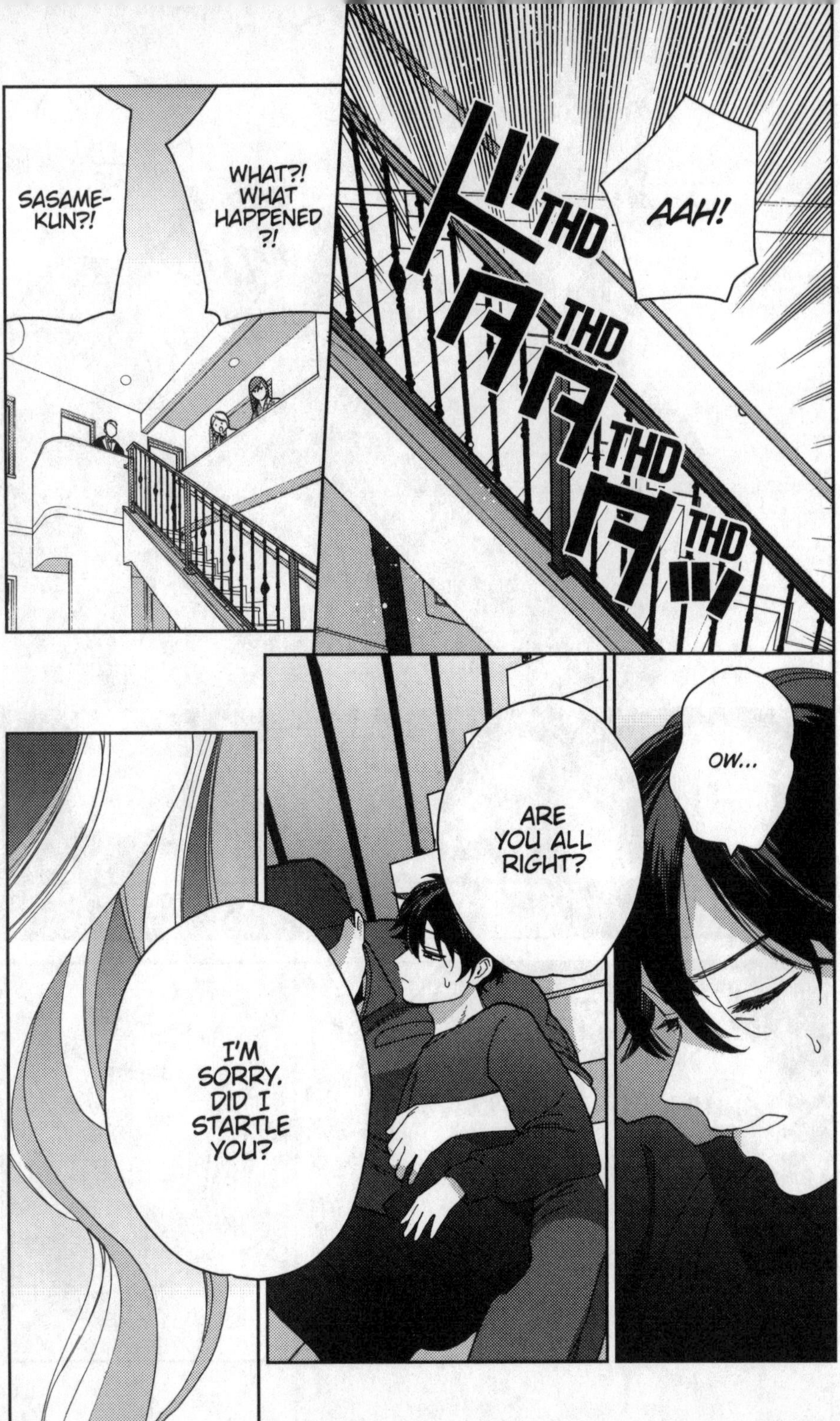
AAH!
THD THD THD THD
WHAT?! WHAT HAPPENED ?!
SASAME-KUN?!
OW...
ARE YOU ALL RIGHT?
I'M SORRY. DID I STARTLE YOU?

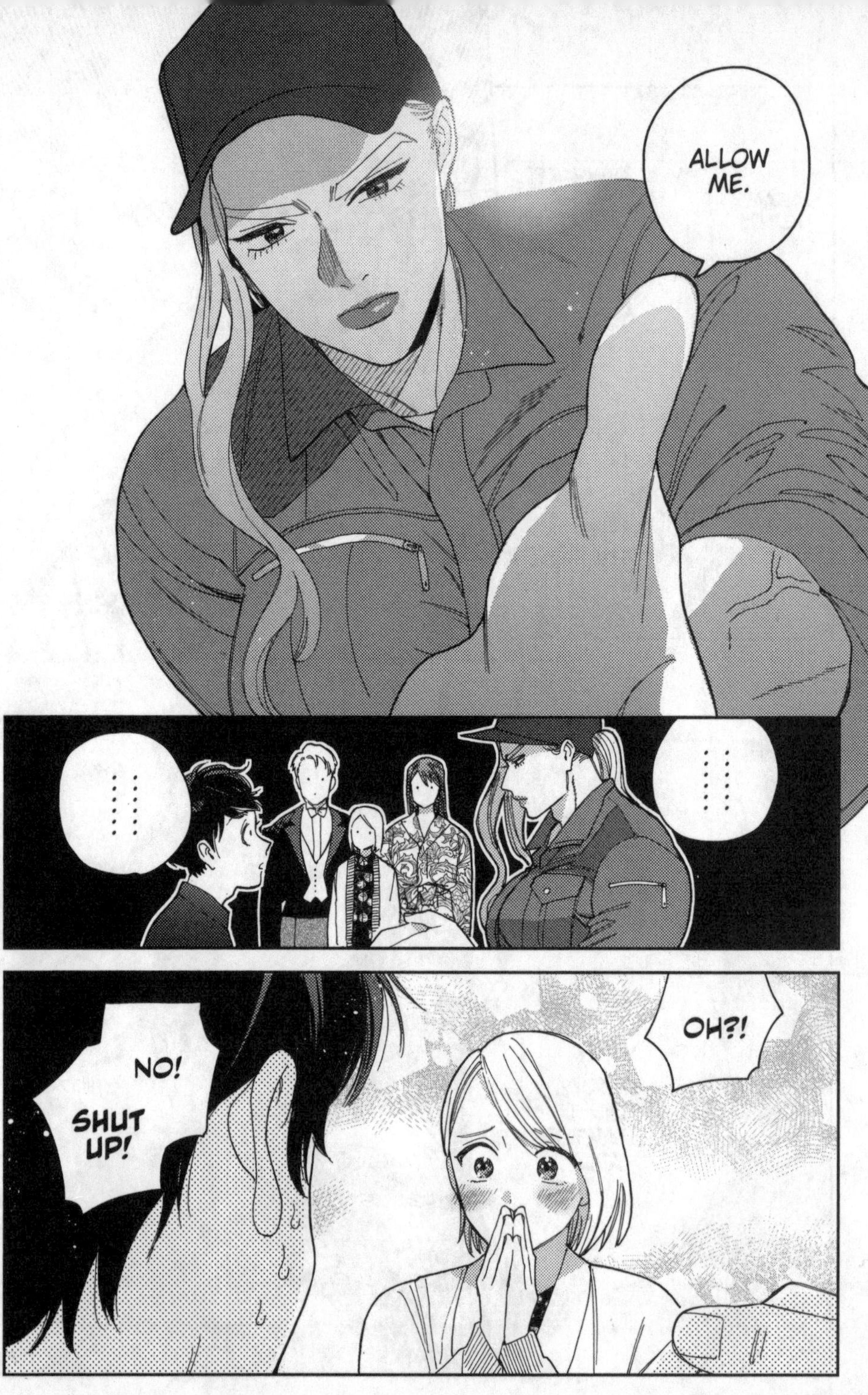

ALLOW ME.
......
......
OH?!
NO!
SHUT UP!

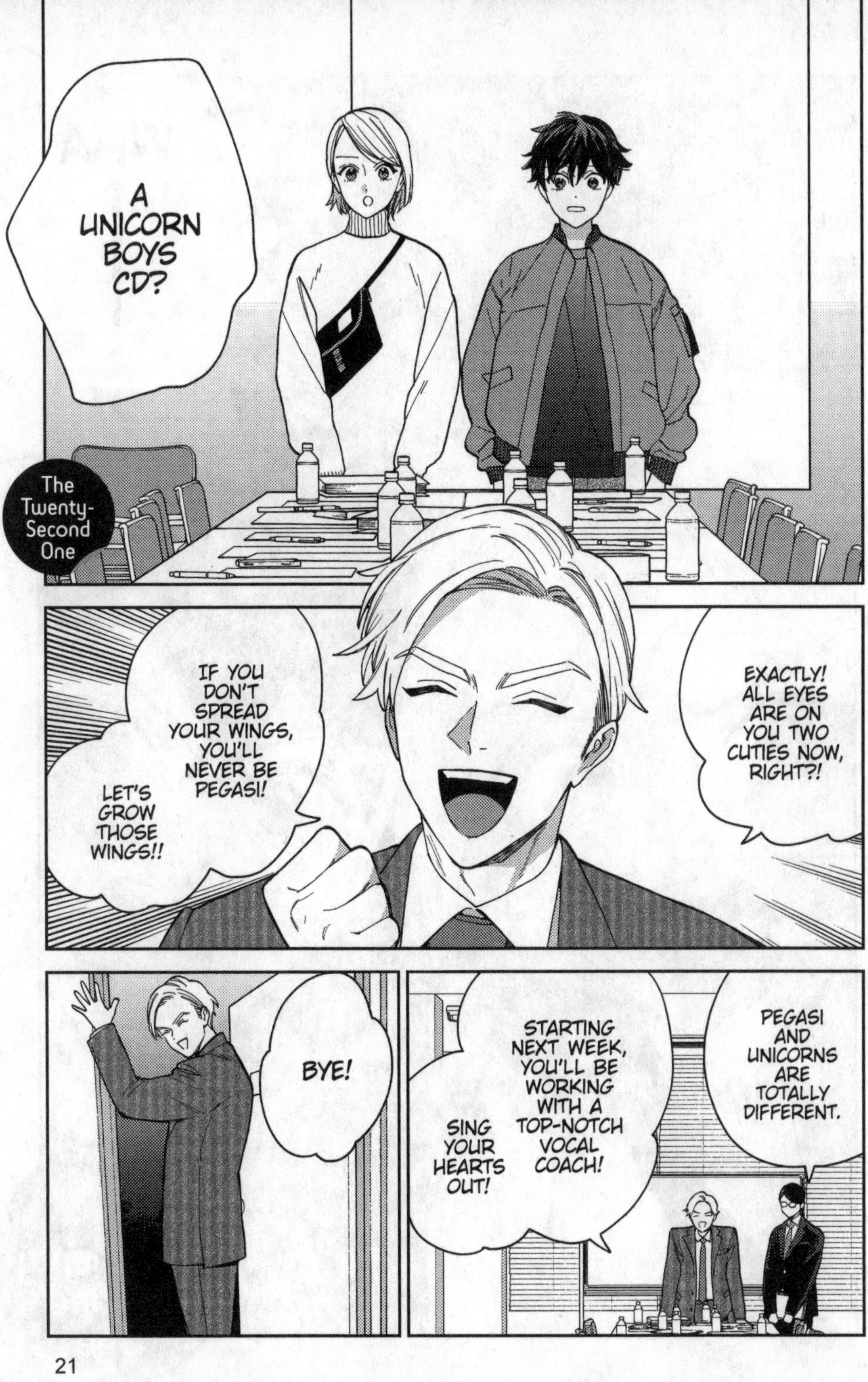
The Twenty-Second One
A UNICORN BOYS CD?
EXACTLY! ALL EYES ARE ON YOU TWO CUTIES NOW, RIGHT?!
IF YOU DON'T SPREAD YOUR WINGS, YOU'LL NEVER BE PEGASI!
LET'S GROW THOSE WINGS!!
PEGASI AND UNICORNS ARE TOTALLY DIFFERENT.
STARTING NEXT WEEK, YOU'LL BE WORKING WITH A TOP-NOTCH VOCAL COACH!
SING YOUR HEARTS OUT!
BYE!

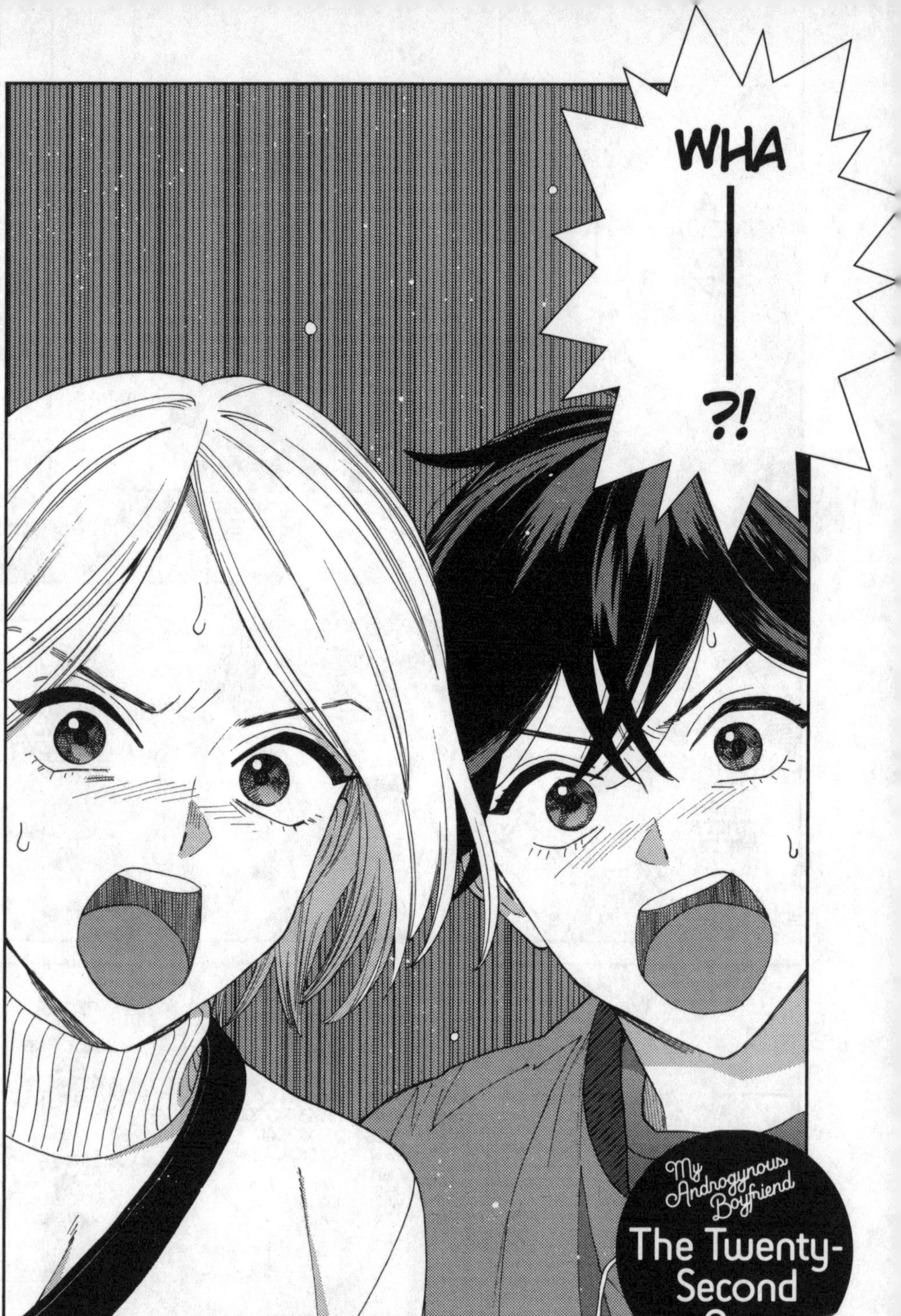
WHA—?!
My Androgynous Boyfriend
The Twenty-Second One

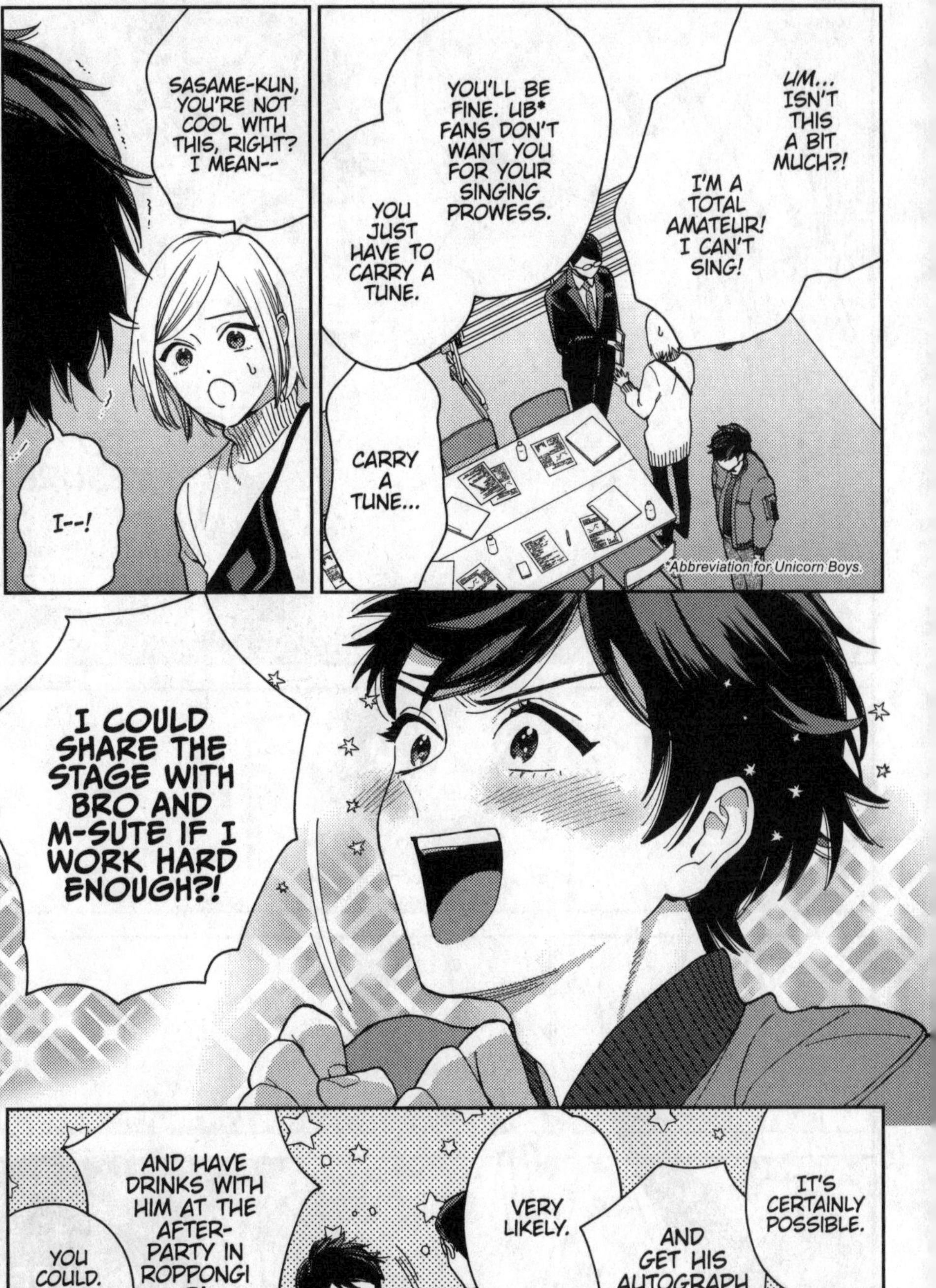
UM... ISN'T THIS A BIT MUCH?!
I'M A TOTAL AMATEUR! I CAN'T SING!
YOU'LL BE FINE. UB* FANS DON'T WANT YOU FOR YOUR SINGING PROWESS.
YOU JUST HAVE TO CARRY A TUNE.
CARRY A TUNE...
*Abbreviation for Unicorn Boys.
SASAME-KUN, YOU'RE NOT COOL WITH THIS, RIGHT? I MEAN--
I--!
I COULD SHARE THE STAGE WITH BRO AND M-SUTE IF I WORK HARD ENOUGH?!
IT'S CERTAINLY POSSIBLE.
AND GET HIS AUTOGRAPH?!
VERY LIKELY.
AND HAVE DRINKS WITH HIM AT THE AFTER-PARTY IN ROPPONGI?!
YOU COULD. ABSOLUTELY.

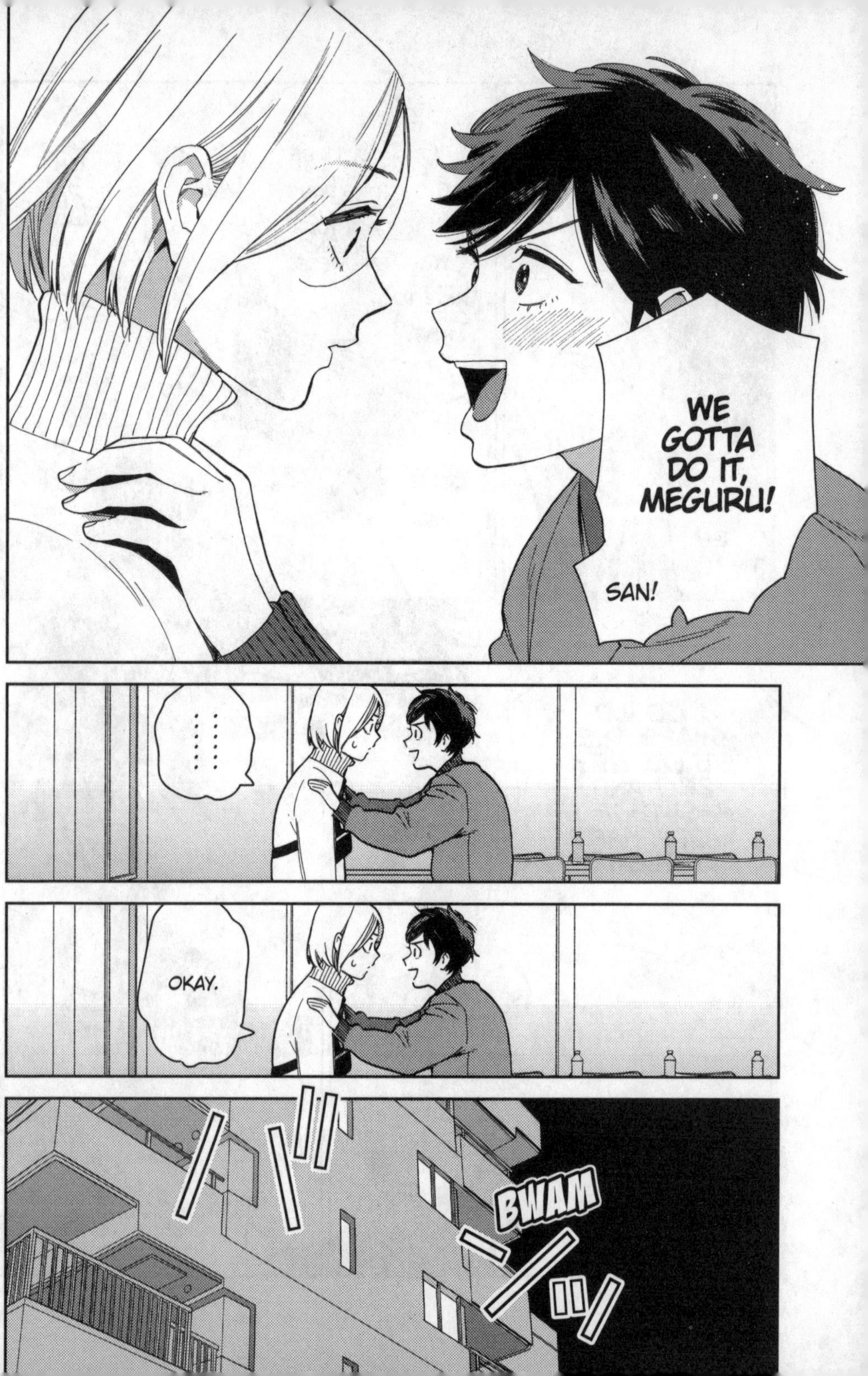
WE GOTTA DO IT, MEGURU!
SAN!
......
OKAY.
BWAM

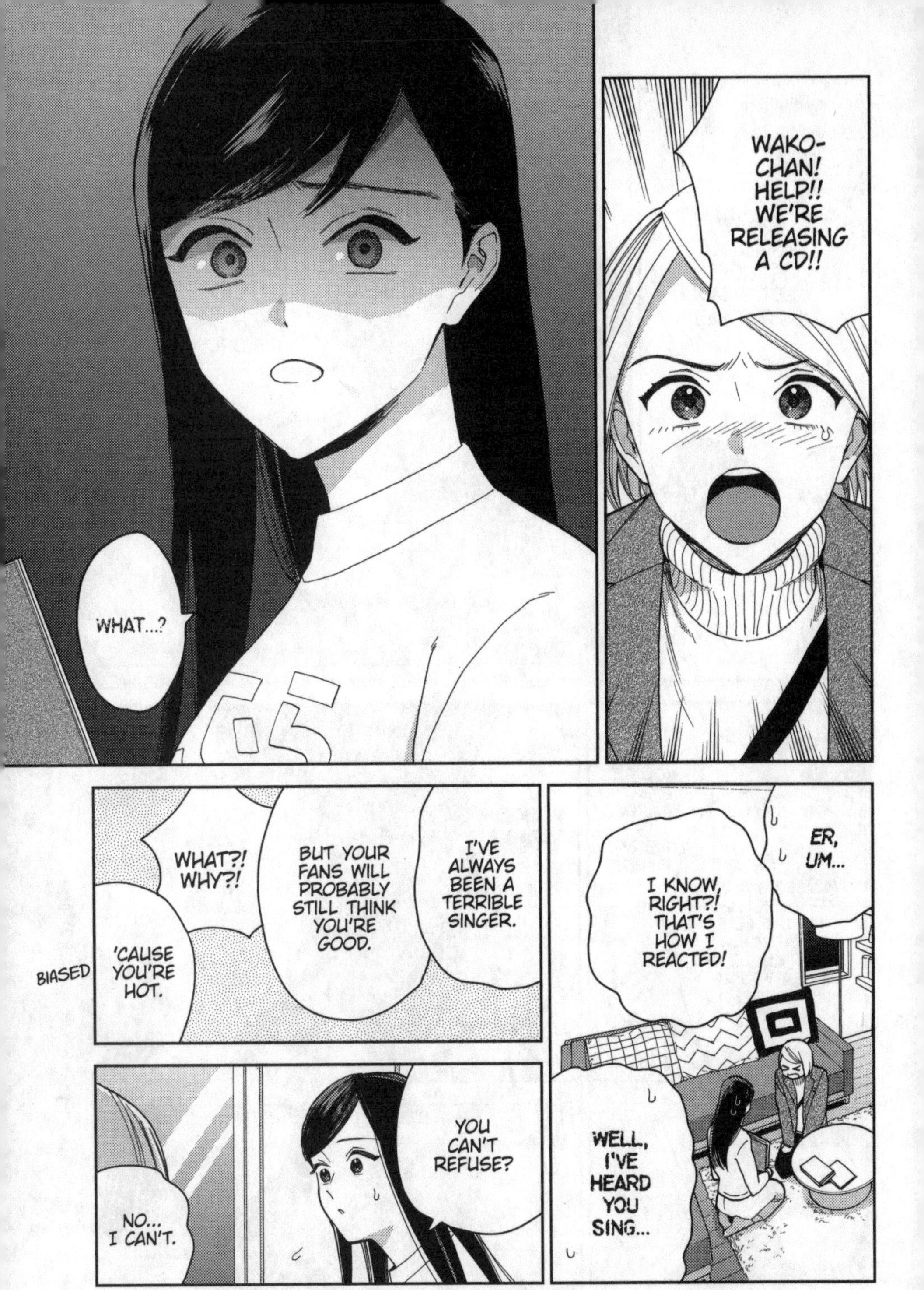
WAKO-CHAN! HELP!! WE'RE RELEASING A CD!!
WHAT...?
ER, UM...
I KNOW, RIGHT?! THAT'S HOW I REACTED!
WELL, I'VE HEARD YOU SING...
I'VE ALWAYS BEEN A TERRIBLE SINGER.
BUT YOUR FANS WILL PROBABLY STILL THINK YOU'RE GOOD.
WHAT?! WHY?!
'CAUSE YOU'RE HOT.
BIASED
YOU CAN'T REFUSE?
NO... I CAN'T.

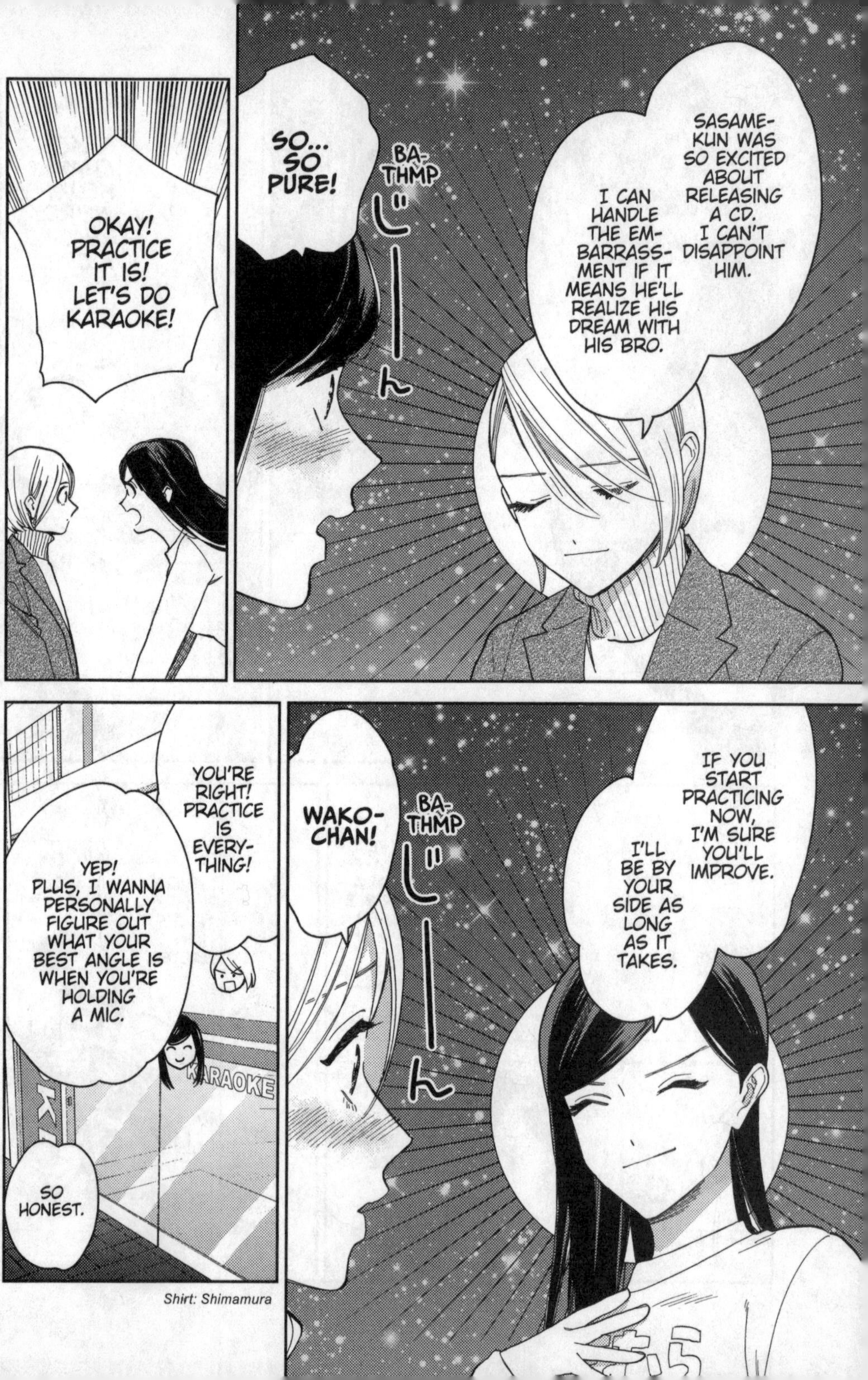
SASAME-KUN WAS SO EXCITED ABOUT RELEASING A CD. I CAN'T DISAPPOINT HIM.
I CAN HANDLE THE EMBARRASSMENT IF IT MEANS HE'LL REALIZE HIS DREAM WITH HIS BRO.
BA-THMP
じーん
SO... SO PURE!
OKAY! PRACTICE IT IS! LET'S DO KARAOKE!
IF YOU START PRACTICING NOW, I'M SURE YOU'LL IMPROVE.
I'LL BE BY YOUR SIDE AS LONG AS IT TAKES.
BA-THMP
じーん
WAKO-CHAN!
YOU'RE RIGHT! PRACTICE IS EVERYTHING!
YEP! PLUS, I WANNA PERSONALLY FIGURE OUT WHAT YOUR BEST ANGLE IS WHEN YOU'RE HOLDING A MIC.
KARAOKE
SO HONEST.

Shirt: Shimamura

THEY CHANGED CLOTHES.

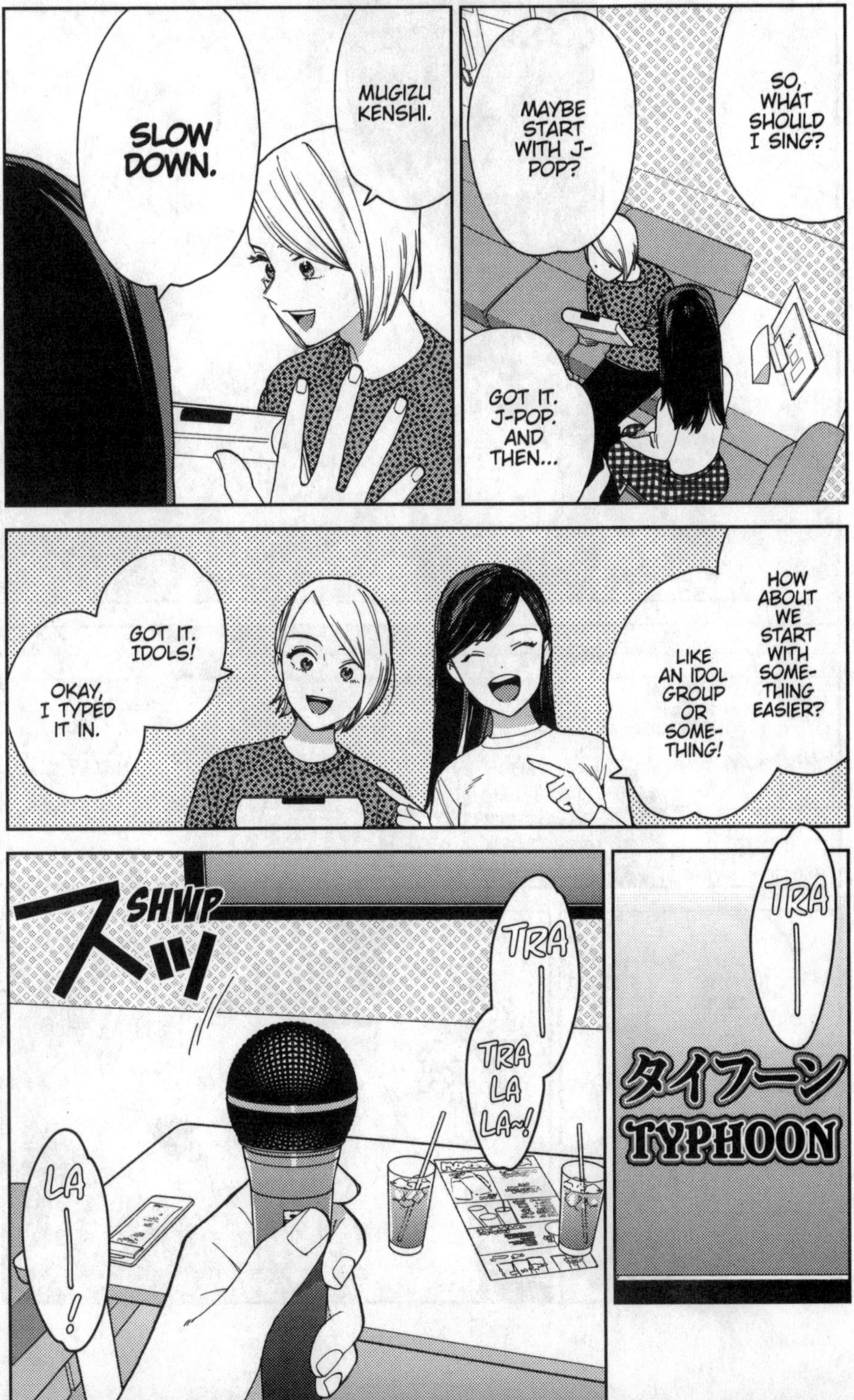

SO, WHAT SHOULD I SING?
MAYBE START WITH J-POP?
GOT IT. J-POP. AND THEN...
MUGIZU KENSHI.
SLOW DOWN.
HOW ABOUT WE START WITH SOME-THING EASIER?
LIKE AN IDOL GROUP OR SOME-THING!
GOT IT. IDOLS!
OKAY, I TYPED IT IN.
TRA—
タイフーン
TYPHOON
スッ
SHWP
TRA—
TRA LA LA~!
LA—!

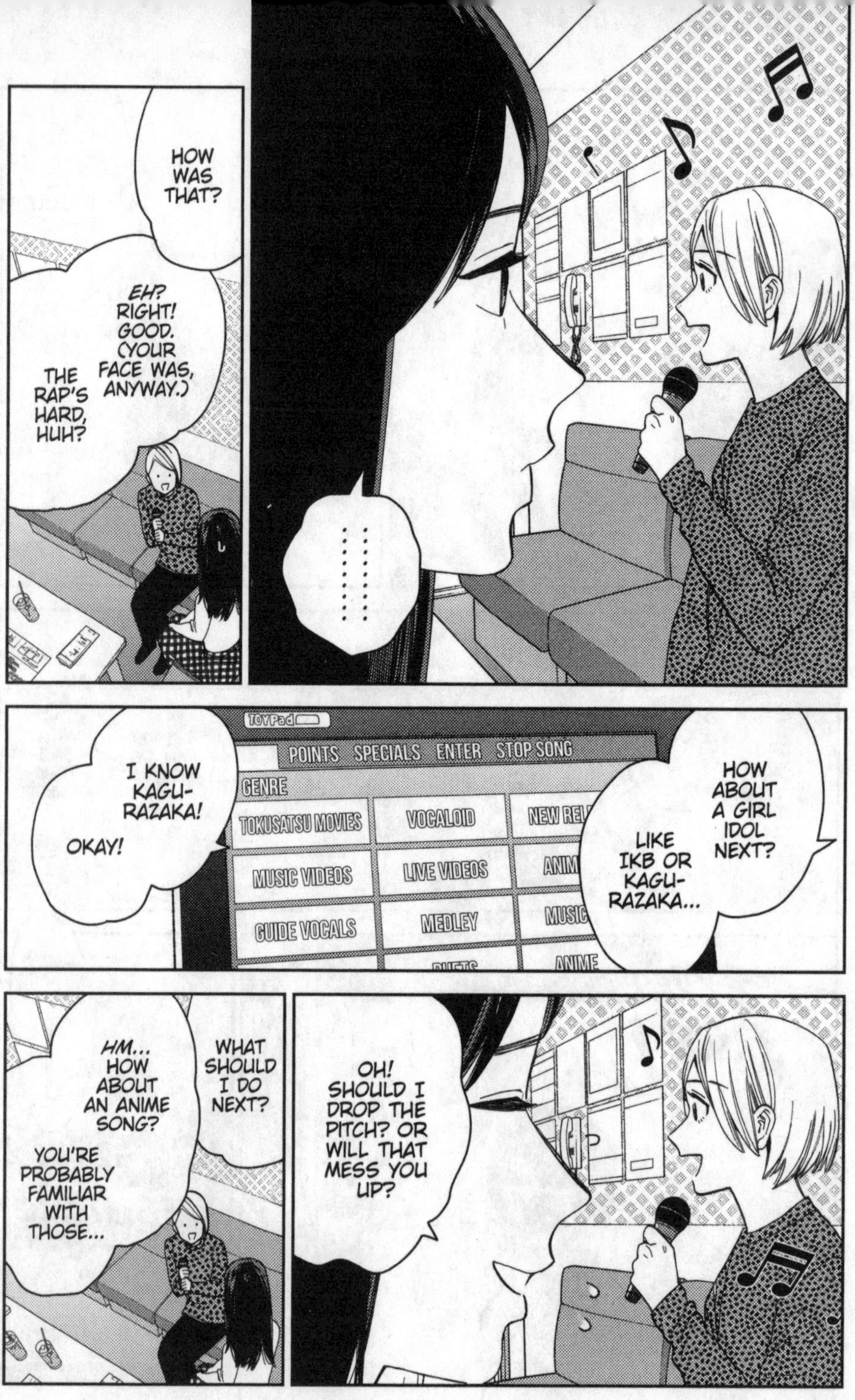
......
HOW WAS THAT?
EH? RIGHT! GOOD. (YOUR FACE WAS, ANYWAY.)
THE RAP'S HARD, HUH?
HOW ABOUT A GIRL IDOL NEXT?
LIKE IKB OR KAGURAZAKA...
TOYPad
POINTS SPECIALS ENTER STOP SONG
GENRE
TOKUSATSU MOVIES
VOCALOID
MUSIC VIDEOS
LIVE VIDEOS
GUIDE VOCALS
MEDLEY
I KNOW KAGURAZAKA!
OKAY!
OH! SHOULD I DROP THE PITCH? OR WILL THAT MESS YOU UP?
WHAT SHOULD I DO NEXT?
HM... HOW ABOUT AN ANIME SONG?
YOU'RE PROBABLY FAMILIAR WITH THOSE...

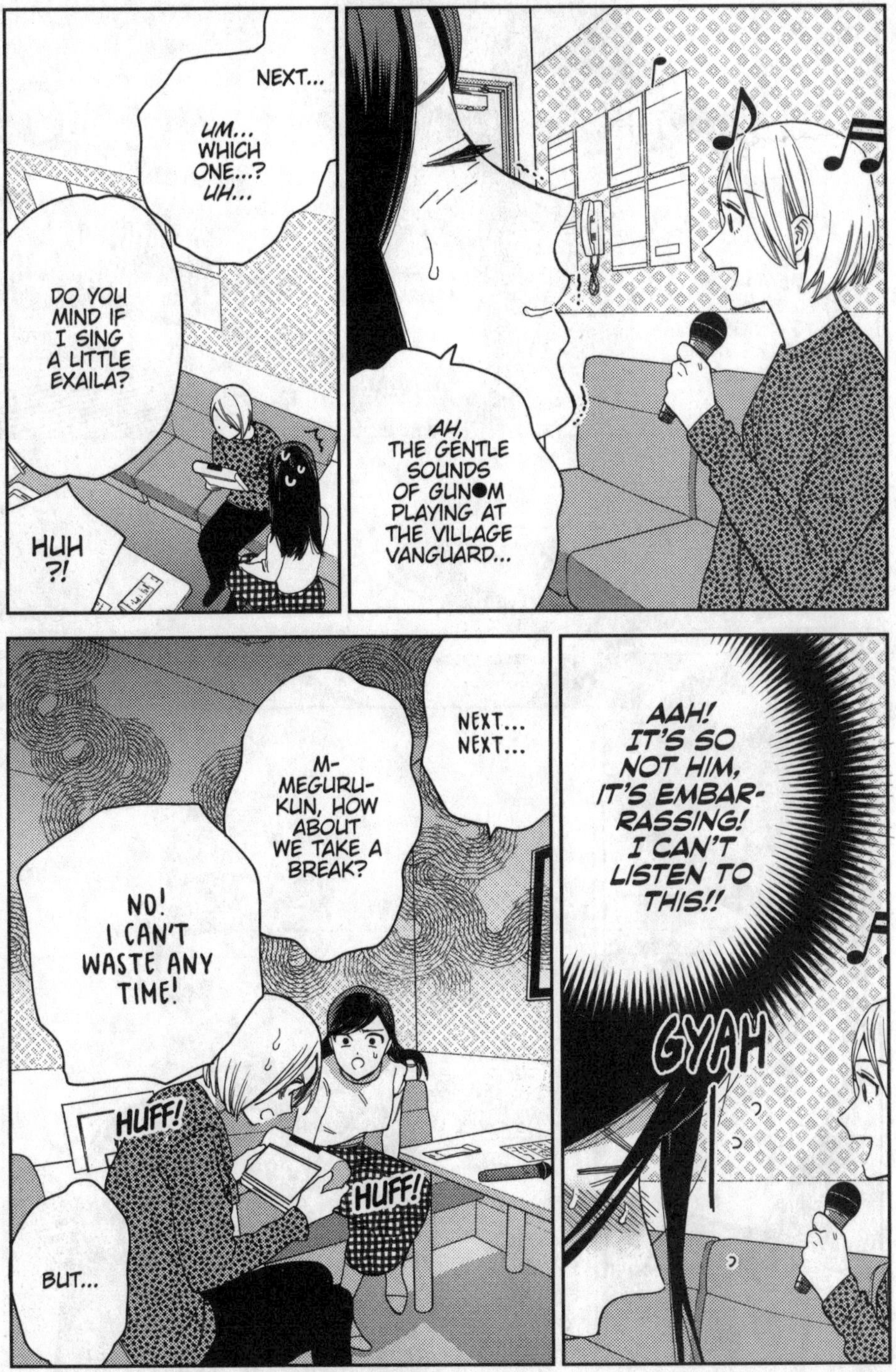
AH, THE GENTLE SOUNDS OF GUN●M PLAYING AT THE VILLAGE VANGUARD...
NEXT...
UM... WHICH ONE...? UH...
DO YOU MIND IF I SING A LITTLE EXAILA?
HUH ?!
AAH! IT'S SO NOT HIM, IT'S EMBAR-RASSING! I CAN'T LISTEN TO THIS!!
GYAH
NEXT... NEXT...
M-MEGURU-KUN, HOW ABOUT WE TAKE A BREAK?
NO! I CAN'T WASTE ANY TIME!
HUFF!
HUFF!
BUT...

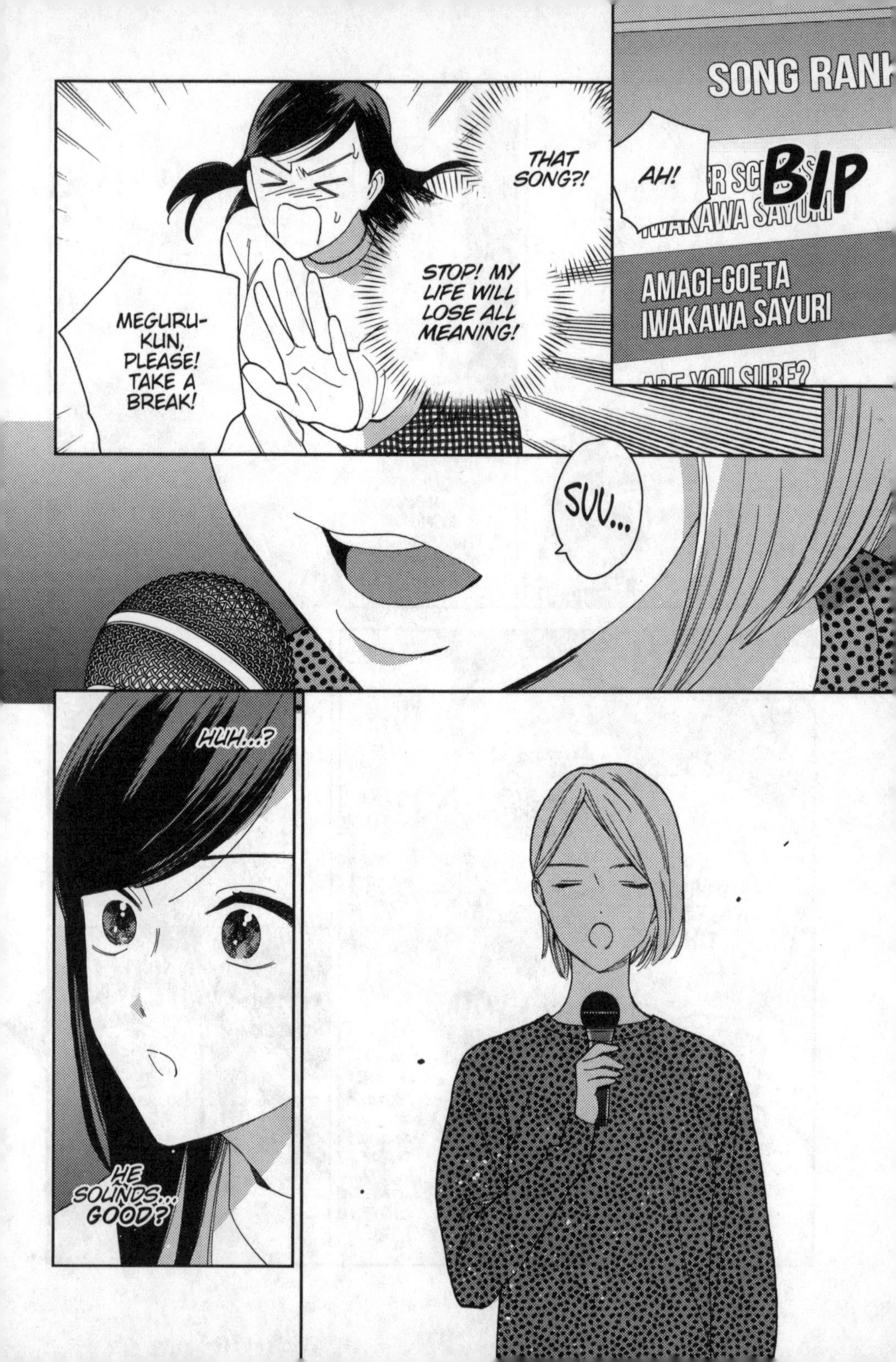
SONG RANK
AH!
BIP
AMAGI-GOETA
IWAKAWA SAYURI
THAT SONG?!
STOP! MY LIFE WILL LOSE ALL MEANING!
MEGURU-KUN, PLEASE! TAKE A BREAK!
SUU...
HUH...?
HE SOUNDS... GOOD?

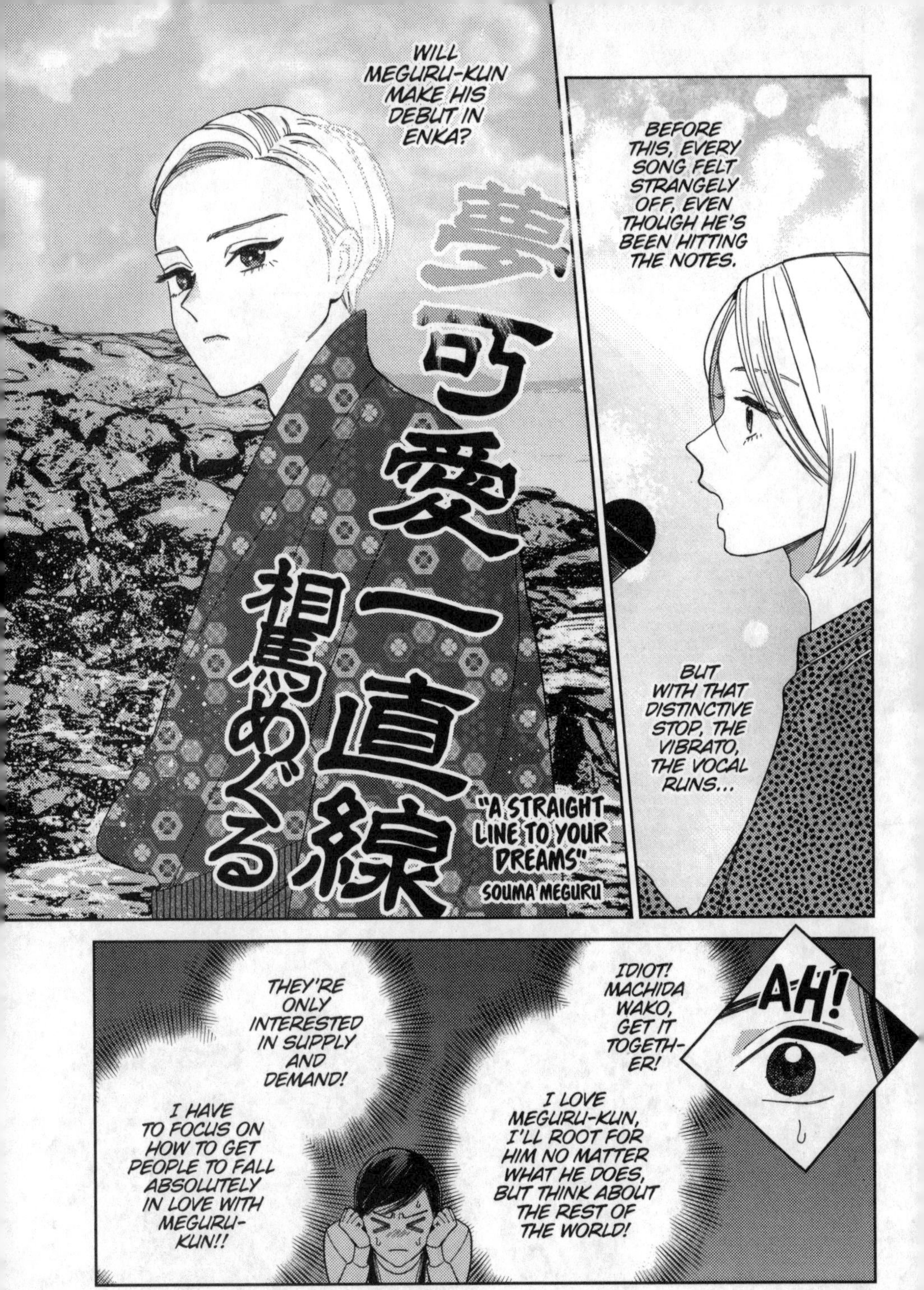
BEFORE THIS, EVERY SONG FELT STRANGELY OFF, EVEN THOUGH HE'S BEEN HITTING THE NOTES.
BUT WITH THAT DISTINCTIVE STOP, THE VIBRATO, THE VOCAL RUNS...
WILL MEGURU-KUN MAKE HIS DEBUT IN ENKA?
夢乃愛一直線
相馬めぐる
"A STRAIGHT LINE TO YOUR DREAMS"
SOUMA MEGURU
AH!
IDIOT! MACHIDA WAKO, GET IT TOGETH-ER!
THEY'RE ONLY INTERESTED IN SUPPLY AND DEMAND!
I LOVE MEGURU-KUN, I'LL ROOT FOR HIM NO MATTER WHAT HE DOES, BUT THINK ABOUT THE REST OF THE WORLD!
I HAVE TO FOCUS ON HOW TO GET PEOPLE TO FALL ABSOLUTELY IN LOVE WITH MEGURU-KUN!!

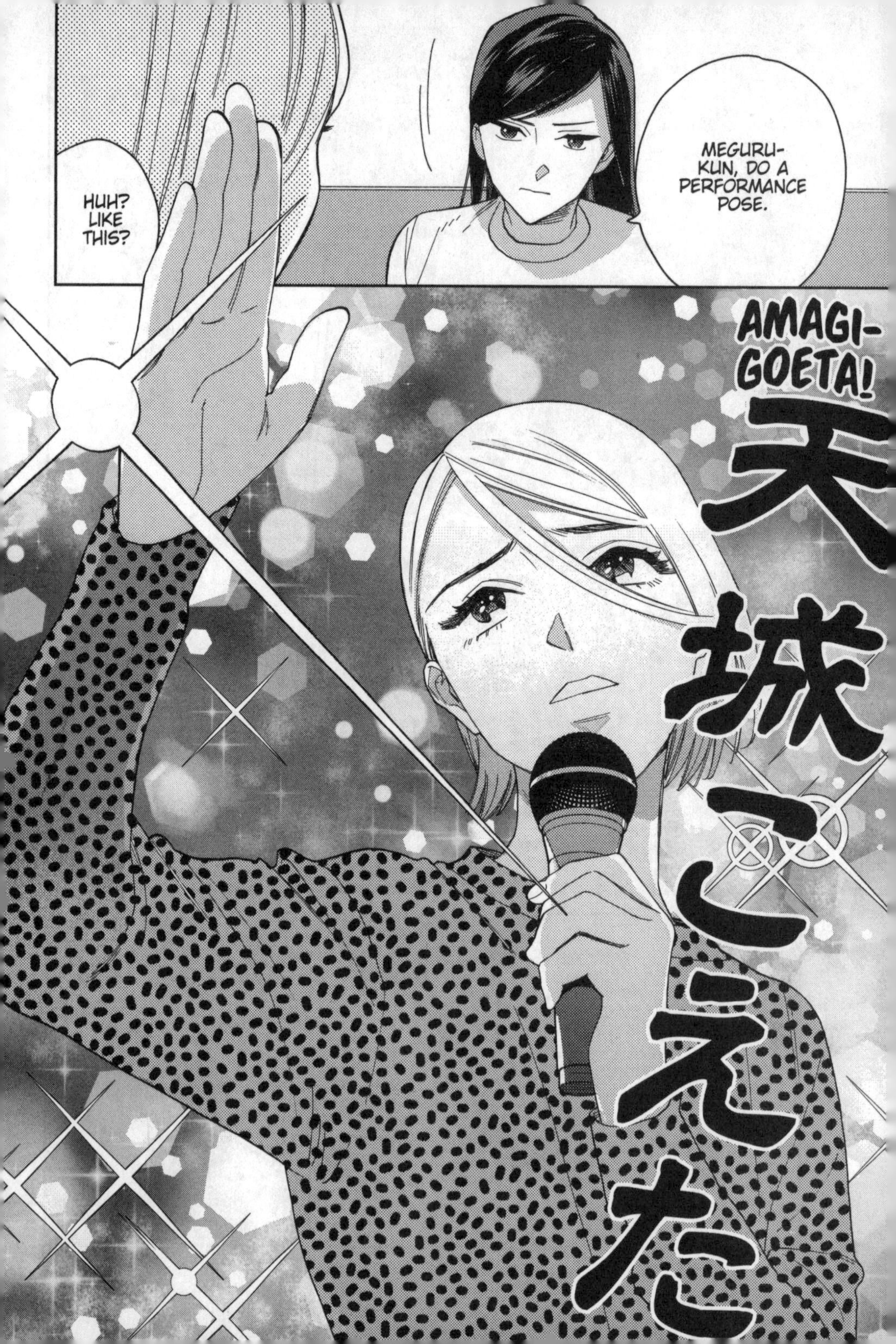
MEGURU-KUN, DO A PERFORMANCE POSE.
HUH? LIKE THIS?
AMAGI-GOETA!
天城こえた

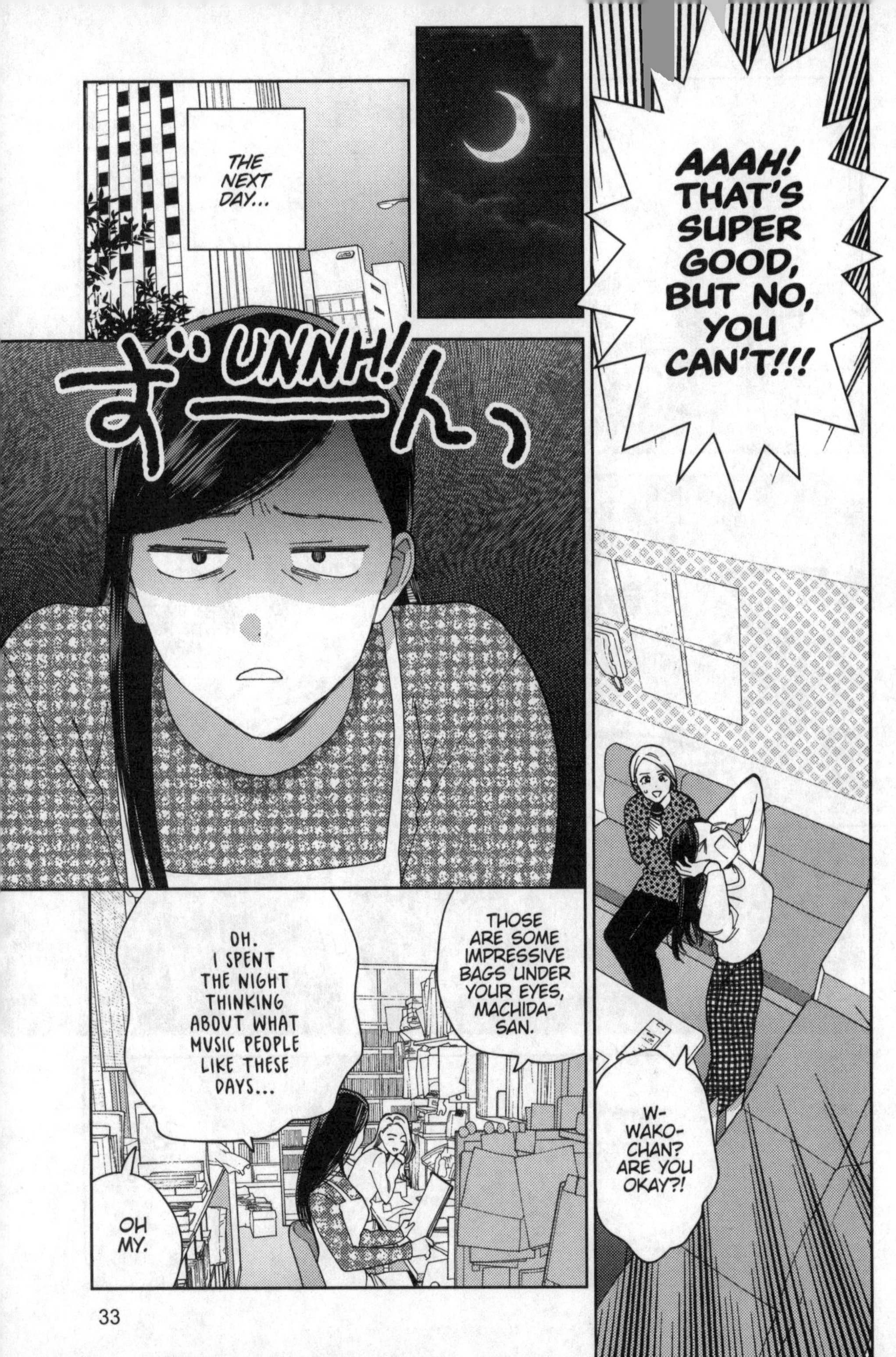
AAAH! THAT'S SUPER GOOD, BUT NO, YOU CAN'T!!!
W-WAKO-CHAN? ARE YOU OKAY?!
THE NEXT DAY...
すーーん UNNH!
THOSE ARE SOME IMPRESSIVE BAGS UNDER YOUR EYES, MACHIDA-SAN.
OH. I SPENT THE NIGHT THINKING ABOUT WHAT MUSIC PEOPLE LIKE THESE DAYS...
OH MY.

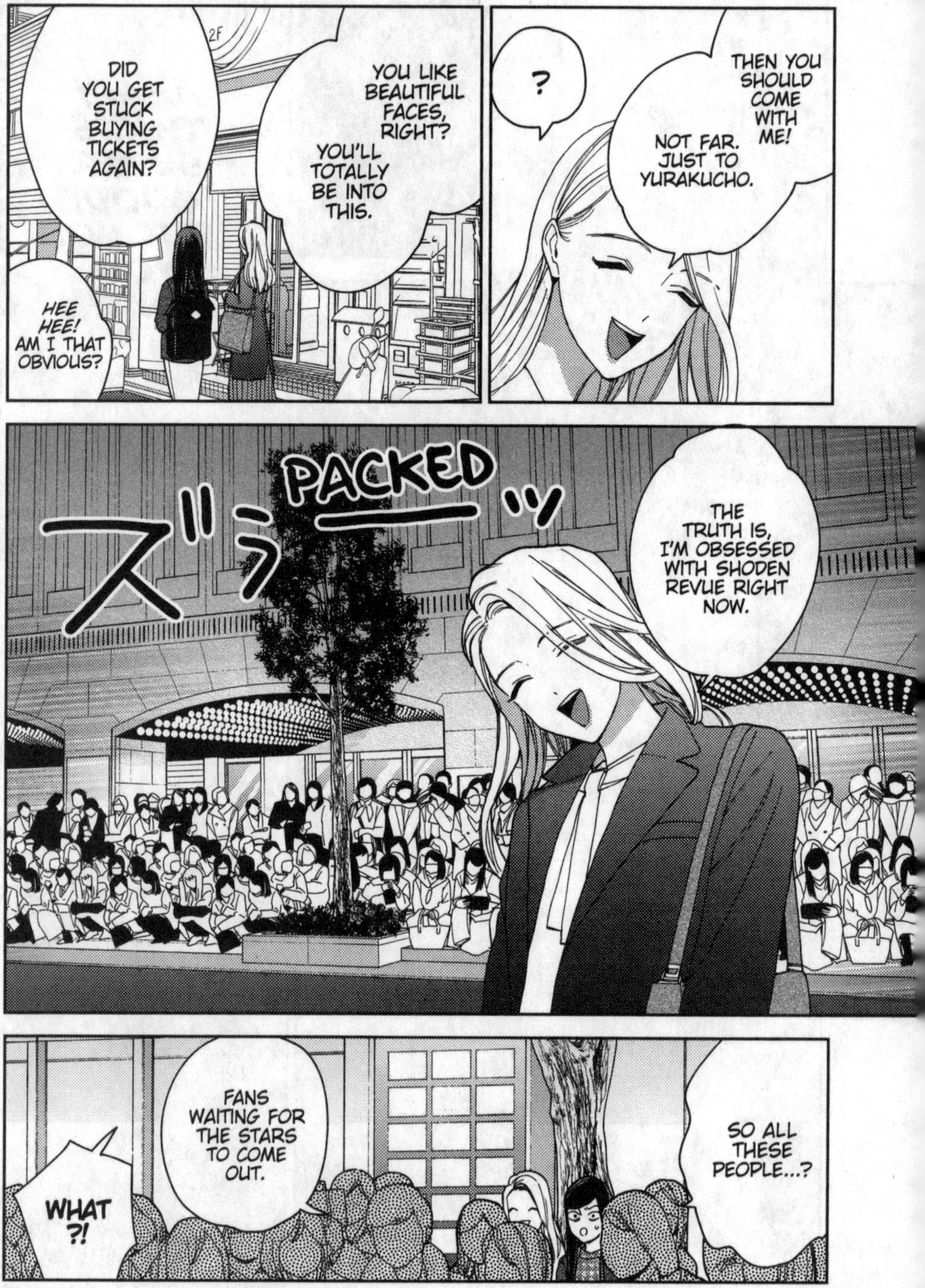
?
THEN YOU SHOULD COME WITH ME!
NOT FAR. JUST TO YURAKUCHO.
YOU LIKE BEAUTIFUL FACES, RIGHT?
YOU'LL TOTALLY BE INTO THIS.
DID YOU GET STUCK BUYING TICKETS AGAIN?
2F
HEE HEE! AM I THAT OBVIOUS?
THE TRUTH IS, I'M OBSESSED WITH SHODEN REVUE RIGHT NOW.
PACKED
ズラーッ
SO ALL THESE PEOPLE...?
FANS WAITING FOR THE STARS TO COME OUT.
WHAT ?!

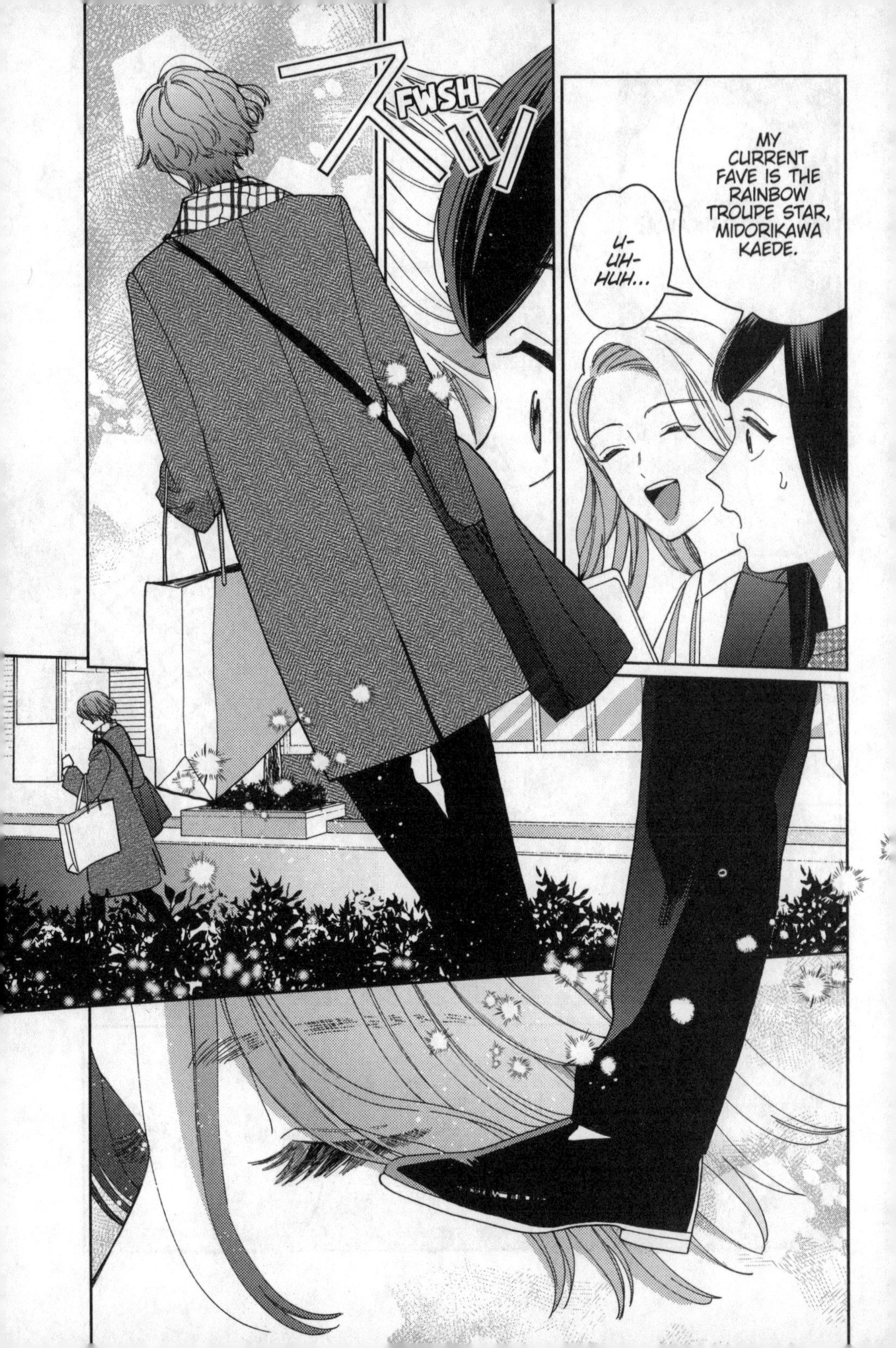
MY CURRENT FAVE IS THE RAINBOW TROUPE STAR, MIDORIKAWA KAEDE.
U-UH-HUH...
FWSH

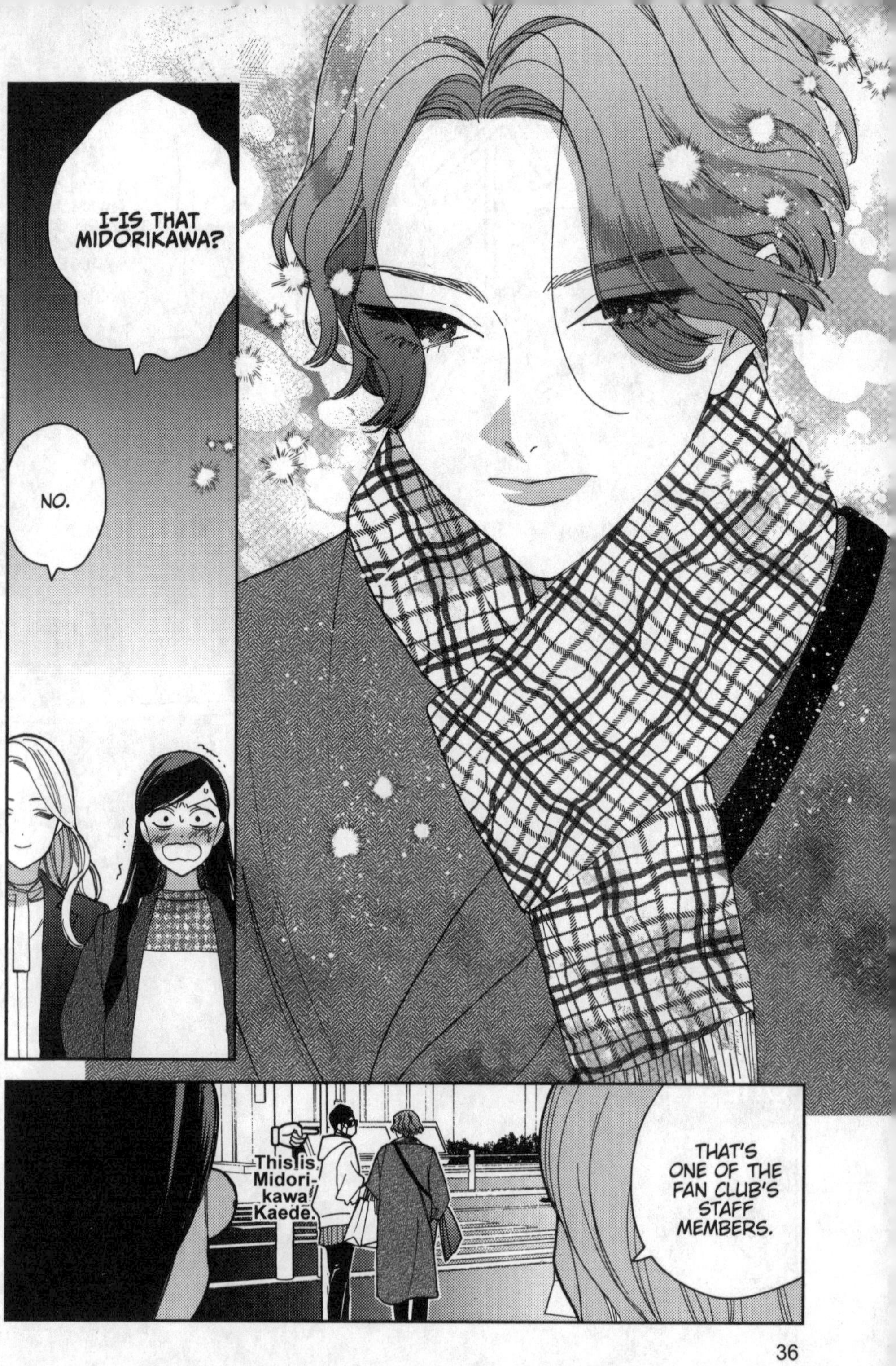
I-IS THAT MIDORIKAWA?
NO.
THAT'S ONE OF THE FAN CLUB'S STAFF MEMBERS.
This is Midorikawa Kaede.

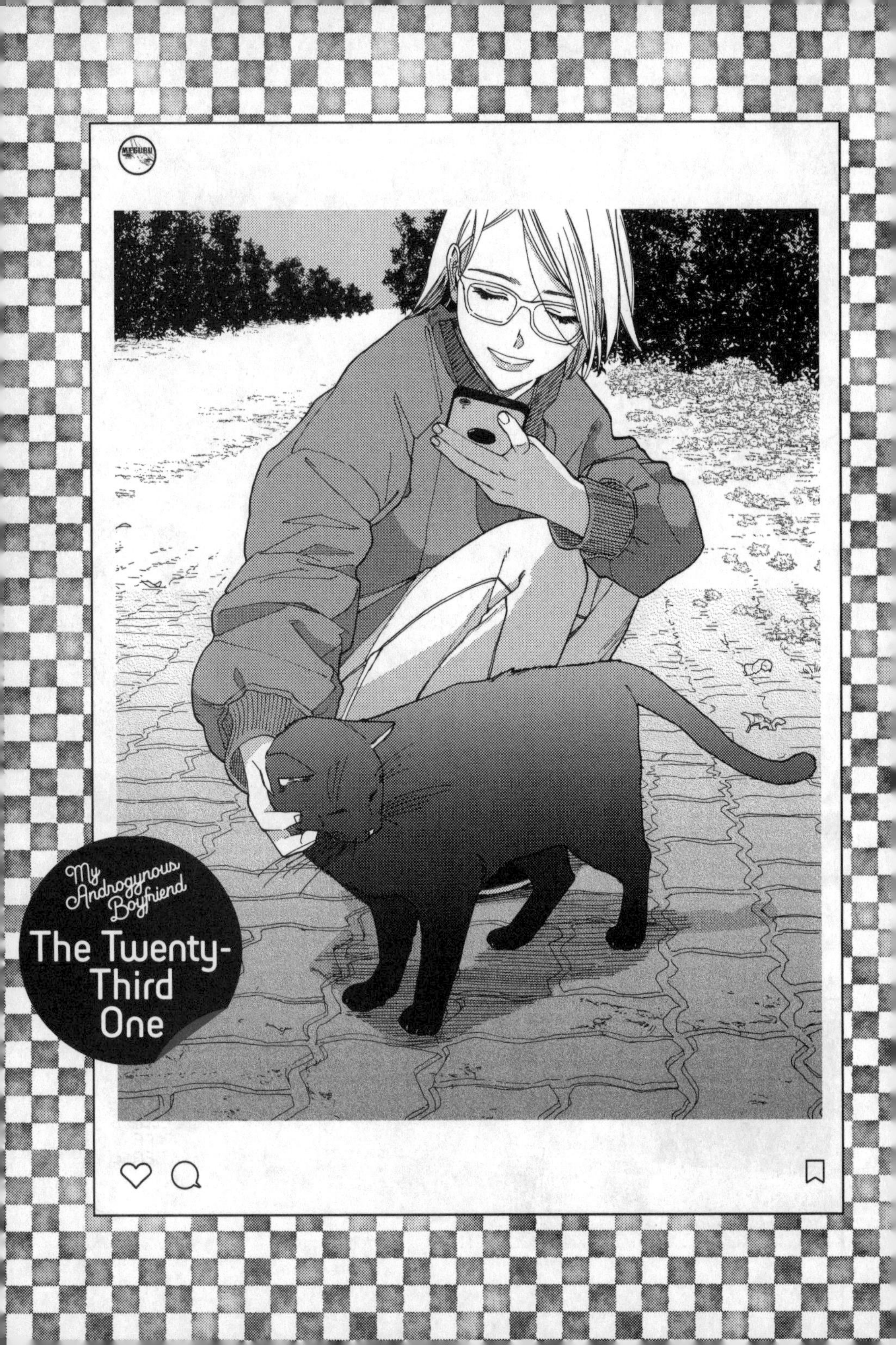
MEGURU
My Androgynous Boyfriend
The Twenty-Third One

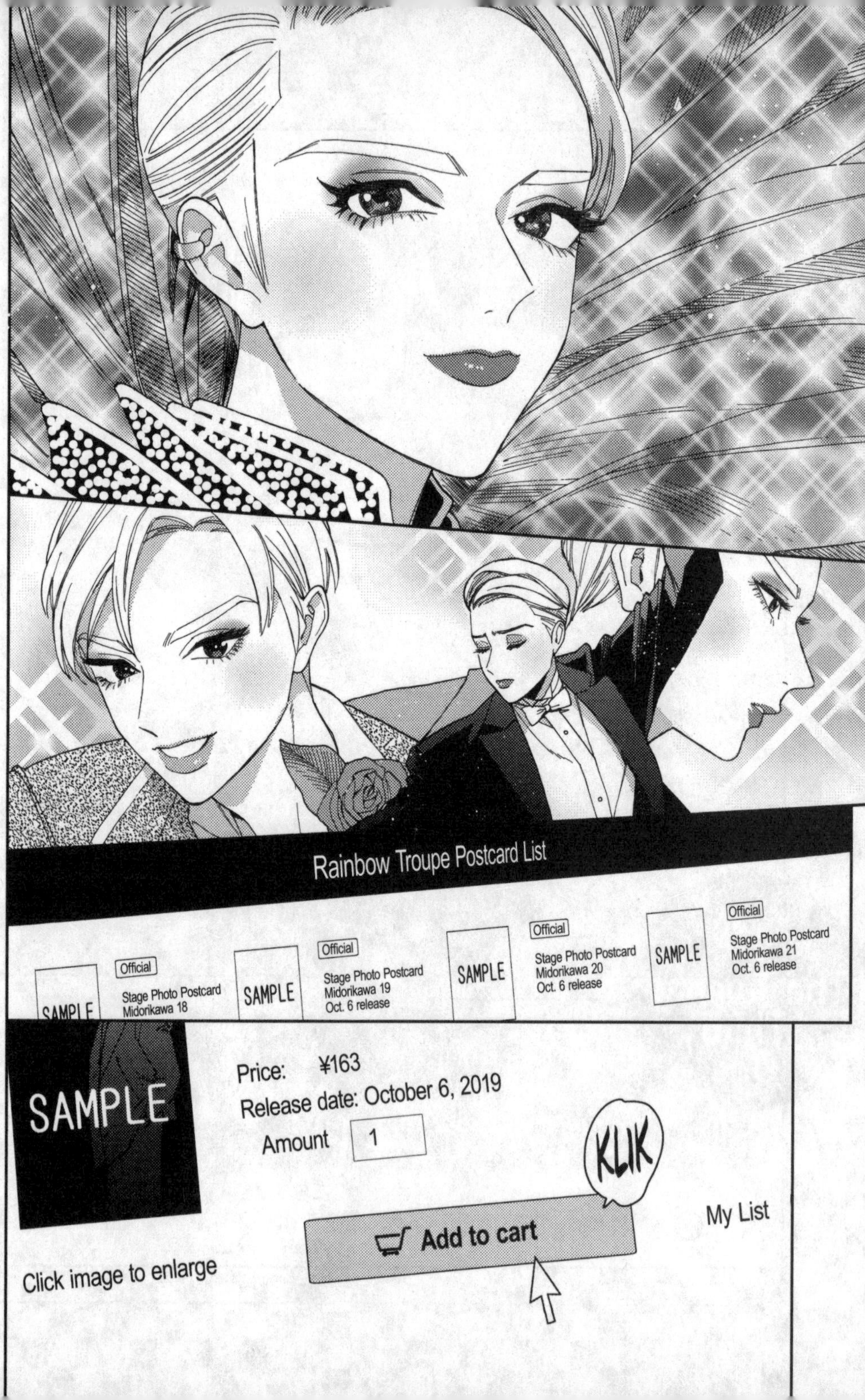

Rainbow Troupe Postcard List
Official
Stage Photo Postcard
Midorikawa 18
SAMPLE
Official
Stage Photo Postcard
Midorikawa 19
Oct. 6 release
SAMPLE
Official
Stage Photo Postcard
Midorikawa 20
Oct. 6 release
SAMPLE
Official
Stage Photo Postcard
Midorikawa 21
Oct. 6 release
SAMPLE
SAMPLE
Click image to enlarge
Price: ¥163
Release date: October 6, 2019
Amount 1
KLIK
Add to cart
My List

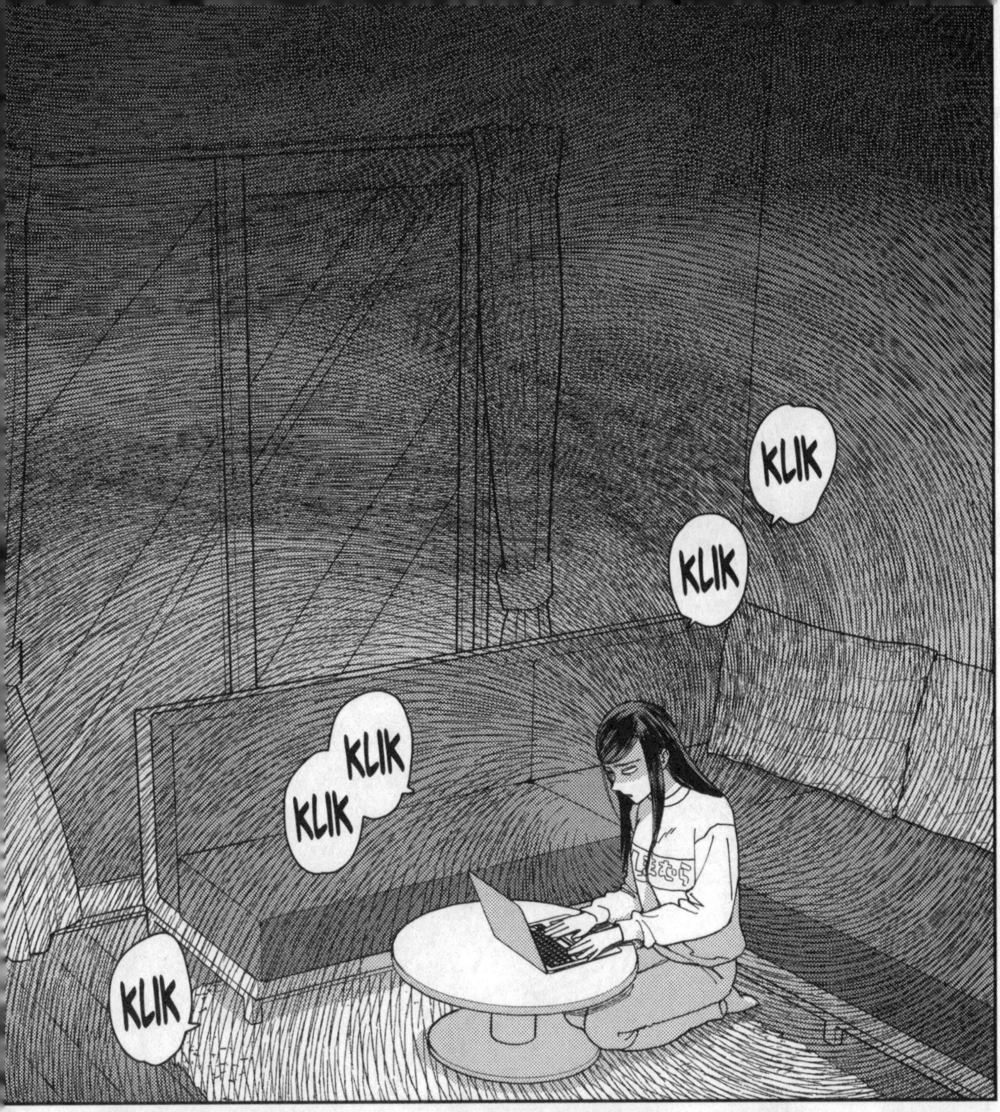
KLIK
KLIK
KLIK
KLIK
KLIK

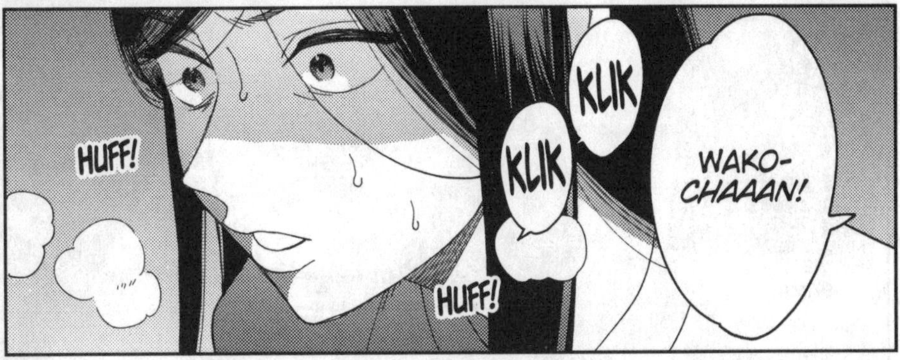
WAKO-CHAAAN!
KLIK
KLIK
HUFF!
HUFF!

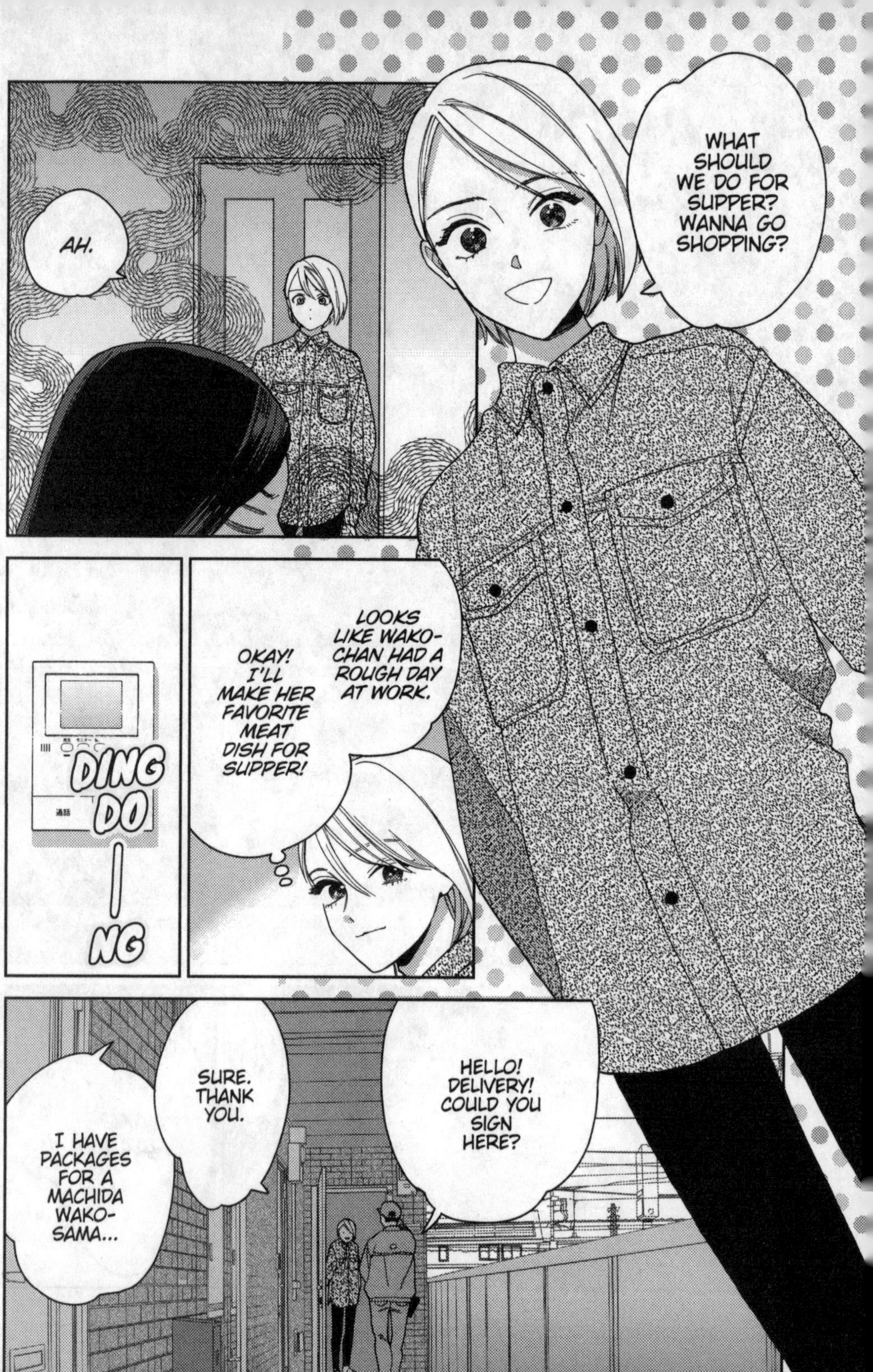
WHAT SHOULD WE DO FOR SUPPER? WANNA GO SHOPPING?
AH.
LOOKS LIKE WAKO-CHAN HAD A ROUGH DAY AT WORK.
OKAY! I'LL MAKE HER FAVORITE MEAT DISH FOR SUPPER!
DING DO-I-NG
HELLO! DELIVERY! COULD YOU SIGN HERE?
SURE. THANK YOU.
I HAVE PACKAGES FOR A MACHIDA WAKO-SAMA...

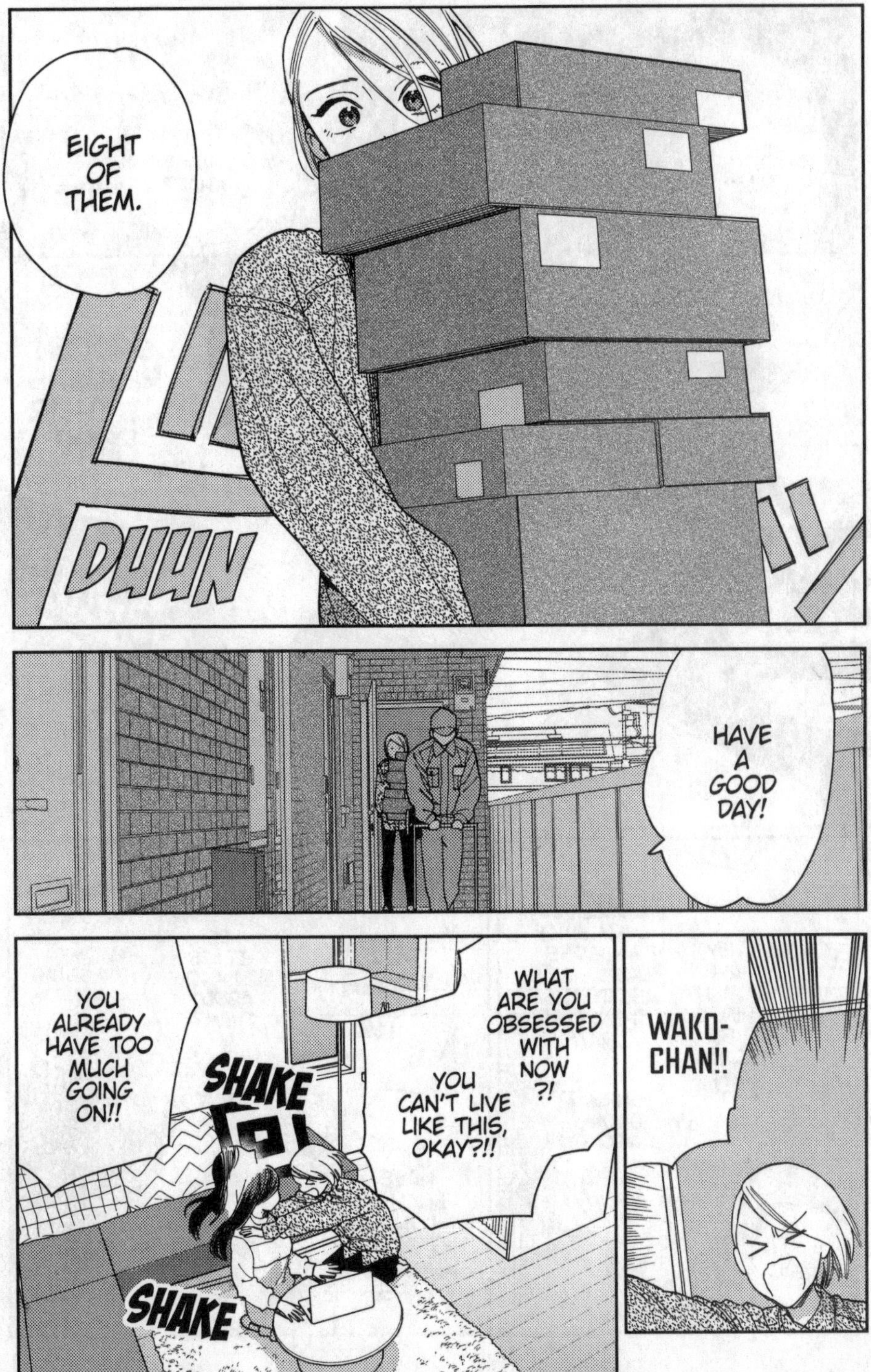
EIGHT OF THEM.
DUUN
HAVE A GOOD DAY!
WAKO-CHAN!!
WHAT ARE YOU OBSESSED WITH NOW?!
YOU CAN'T LIVE LIKE THIS, OKAY?!!
YOU ALREADY HAVE TOO MUCH GOING ON!!
SHAKE
SHAKE

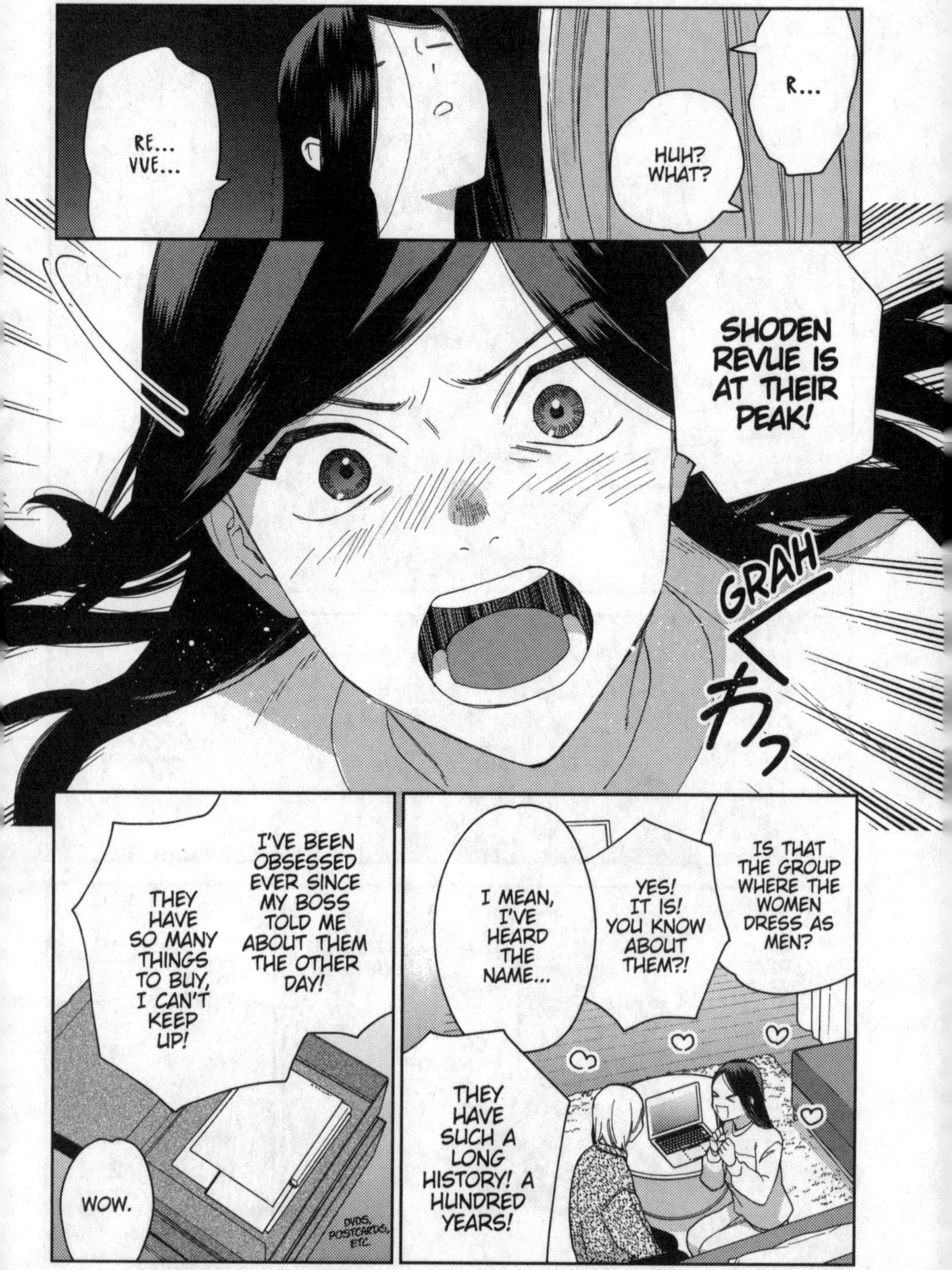
R...
HUH? WHAT?
RE... VUE...
SHODEN REVUE IS AT THEIR PEAK!
GRAH
わっ
IS THAT THE GROUP WHERE THE WOMEN DRESS AS MEN?
YES! IT IS! YOU KNOW ABOUT THEM?!
I MEAN, I'VE HEARD THE NAME...
THEY HAVE SUCH A LONG HISTORY! A HUNDRED YEARS!
I'VE BEEN OBSESSED EVER SINCE MY BOSS TOLD ME ABOUT THEM THE OTHER DAY!
THEY HAVE SO MANY THINGS TO BUY, I CAN'T KEEP UP!
WOW.
DVDS, POSTCARDS, ETC.

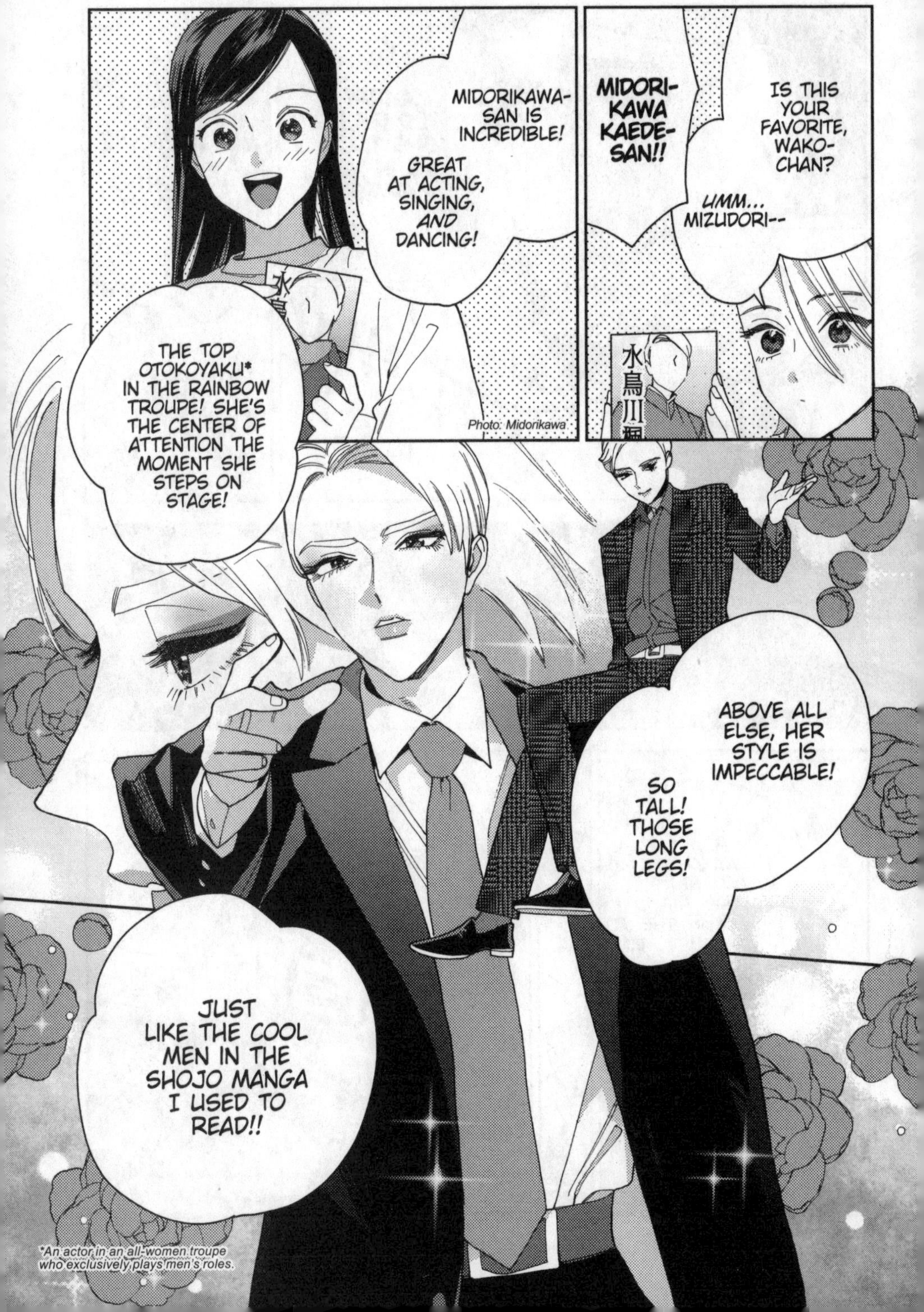
IS THIS YOUR FAVORITE, WAKO-CHAN?
UMM... MIZUDORI--
MIDORI-KAWA KAEDE-SAN!!
MIDORIKAWA-SAN IS INCREDIBLE!
GREAT AT ACTING, SINGING, AND DANCING!
Photo: Midorikawa
THE TOP OTOKOYAKU* IN THE RAINBOW TROUPE! SHE'S THE CENTER OF ATTENTION THE MOMENT SHE STEPS ON STAGE!
ABOVE ALL ELSE, HER STYLE IS IMPECCABLE!
SO TALL! THOSE LONG LEGS!
JUST LIKE THE COOL MEN IN THE SHOJO MANGA I USED TO READ!!

*An actor in an all-women troupe who exclusively plays men's roles.

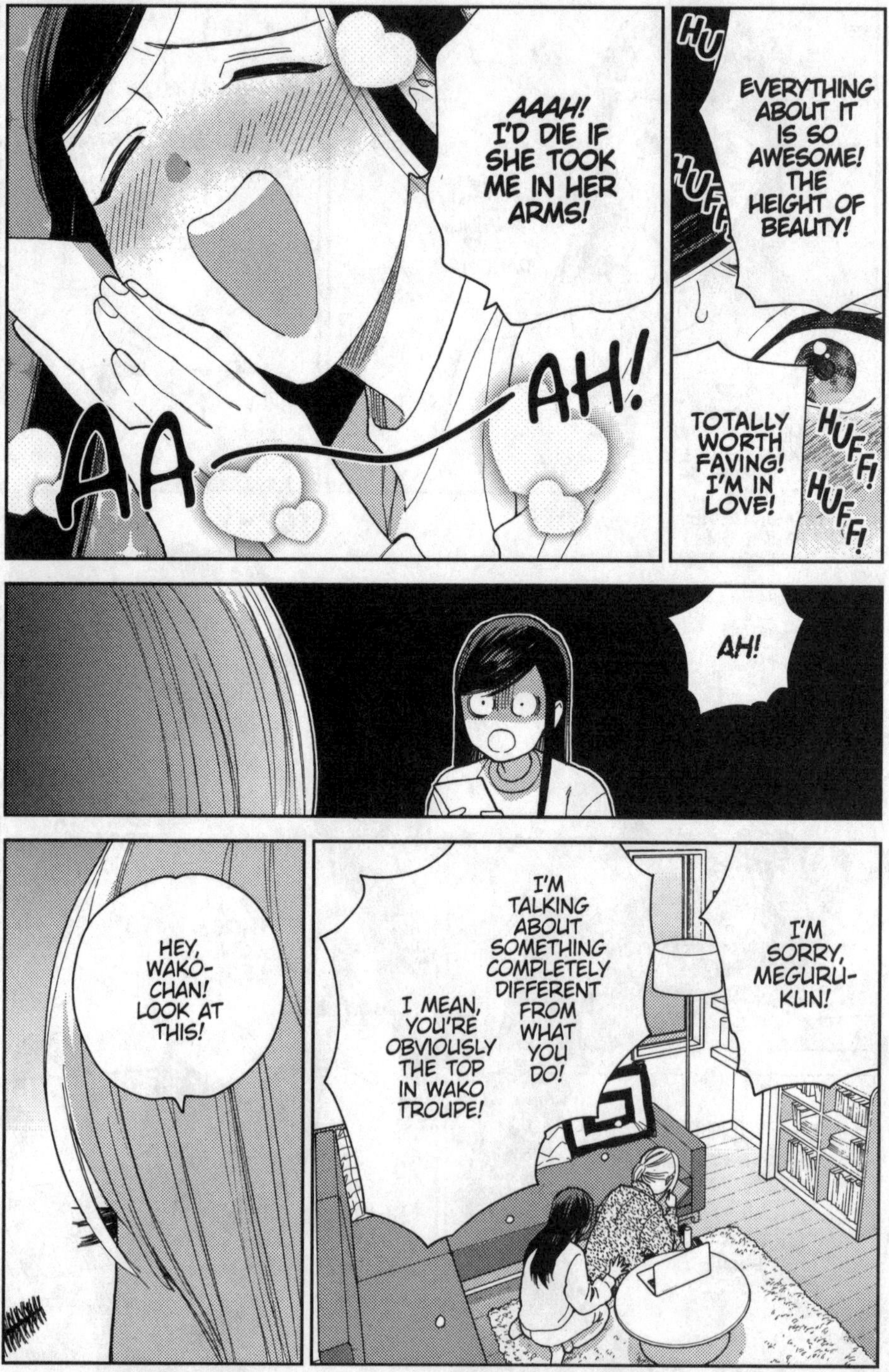
HU
HUFF
EVERYTHING ABOUT IT IS SO AWESOME! THE HEIGHT OF BEAUTY!
TOTALLY WORTH FAVING! I'M IN LOVE!
HUFF! HUFF!
AAAH! I'D DIE IF SHE TOOK ME IN HER ARMS!
AA—AH!
AH!
I'M SORRY, MEGURU-KUN!
I'M TALKING ABOUT SOMETHING COMPLETELY DIFFERENT FROM WHAT YOU DO!
I MEAN, YOU'RE OBVIOUSLY THE TOP IN WAKO TROUPE!
HEY, WAKO-CHAN! LOOK AT THIS!

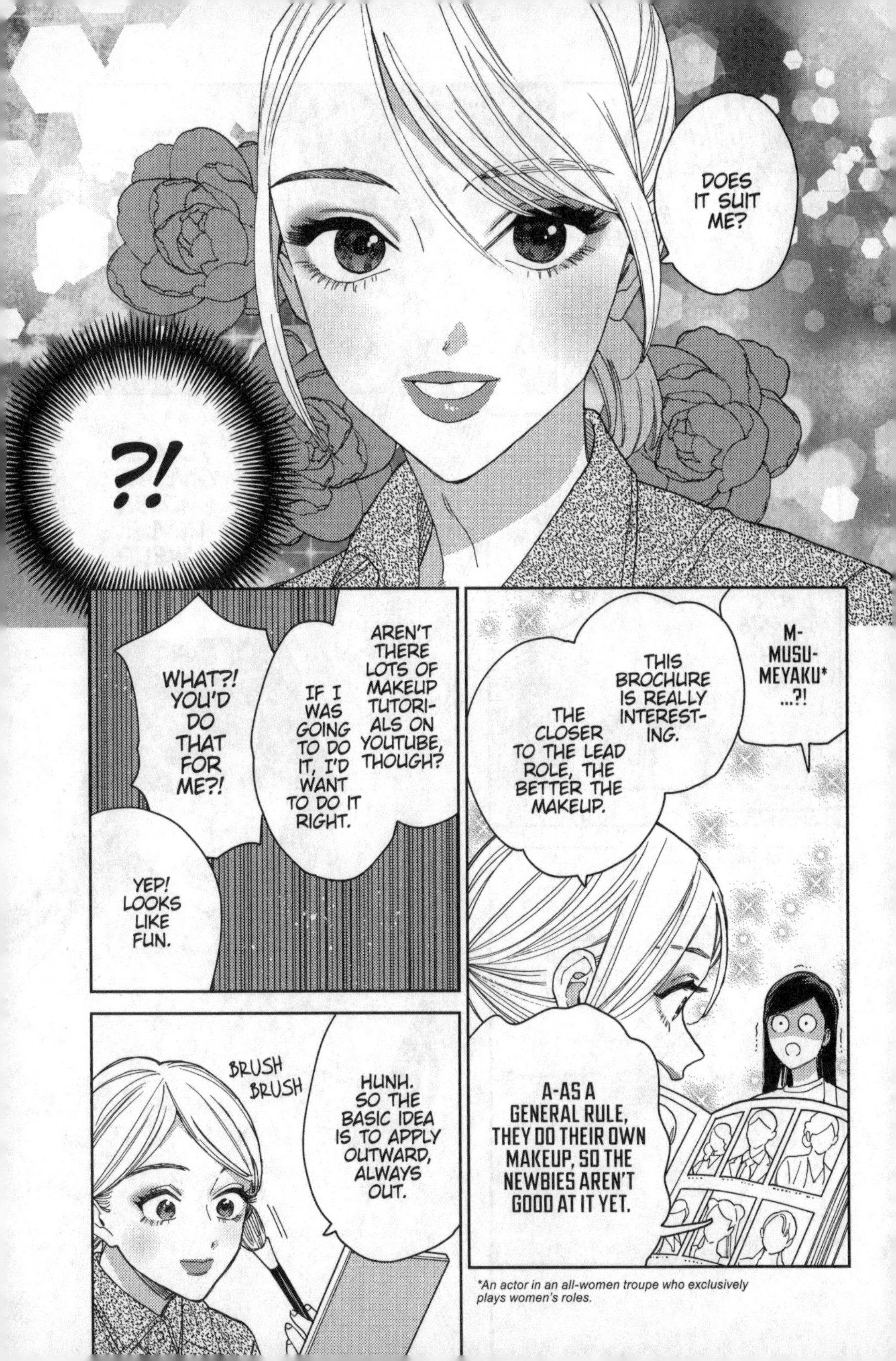
DOES IT SUIT ME?
?!
M-MUSUMEYAKU* ...?!
THIS BROCHURE IS REALLY INTERESTING.
THE CLOSER TO THE LEAD ROLE, THE BETTER THE MAKEUP.
A-AS A GENERAL RULE, THEY DO THEIR OWN MAKEUP, SO THE NEWBIES AREN'T GOOD AT IT YET.
AREN'T THERE LOTS OF MAKEUP TUTORIALS ON YOUTUBE, THOUGH?
IF I WAS GOING TO DO IT, I'D WANT TO DO IT RIGHT.
WHAT?! YOU'D DO THAT FOR ME?!
YEP! LOOKS LIKE FUN.
HUNH. SO THE BASIC IDEA IS TO APPLY OUTWARD, ALWAYS OUT.
BRUSH BRUSH

*An actor in an all-women troupe who exclusively plays women's roles.

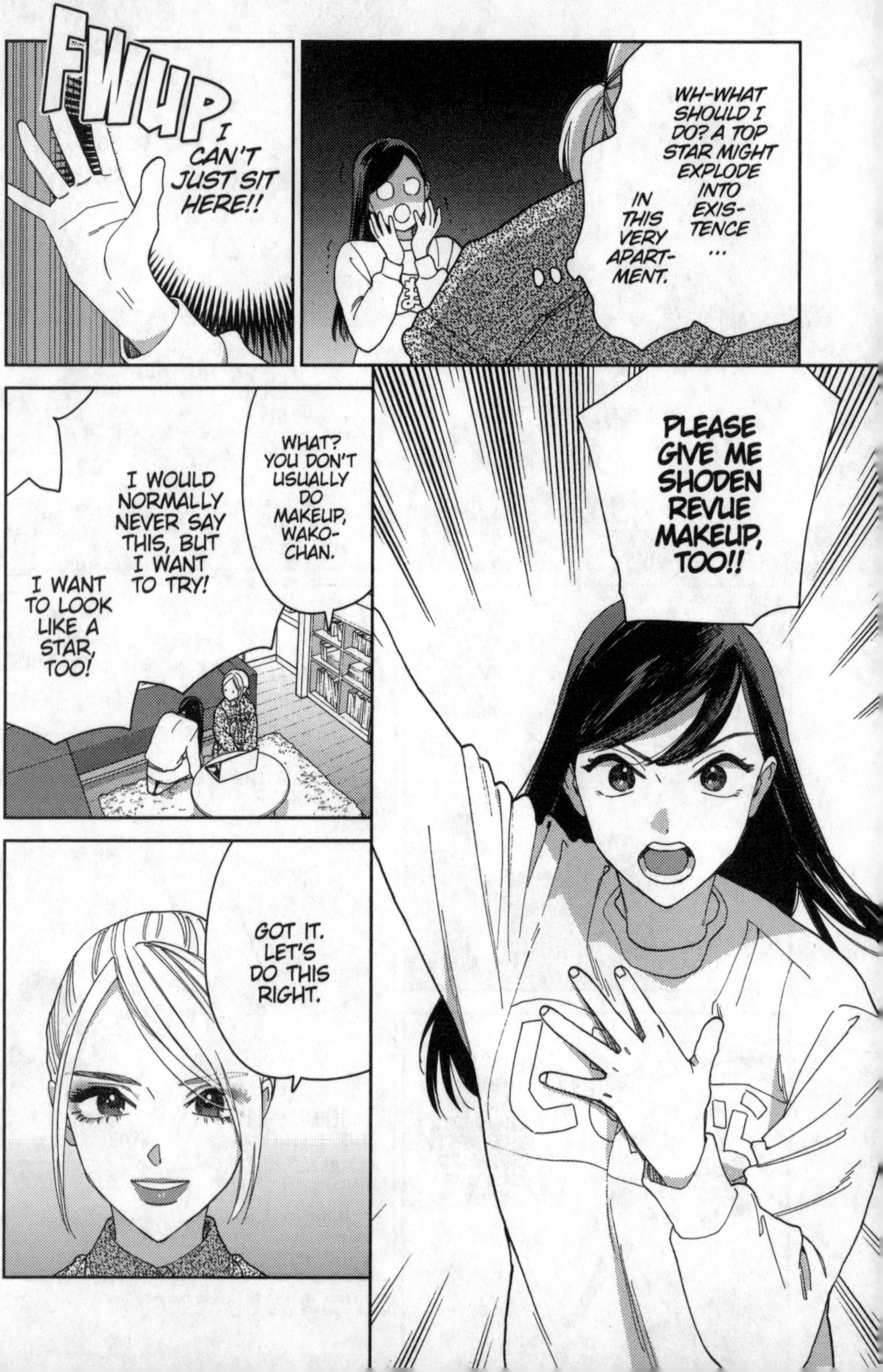
WH-WHAT SHOULD I DO? A TOP STAR MIGHT EXPLODE INTO EXIS-TENCE...
IN THIS VERY APART-MENT.
FWUP
I CAN'T JUST SIT HERE!!
PLEASE GIVE ME SHODEN REVUE MAKEUP, TOO!!
WHAT? YOU DON'T USUALLY DO MAKEUP, WAKO-CHAN.
I WOULD NORMALLY NEVER SAY THIS, BUT I WANT TO TRY!
I WANT TO LOOK LIKE A STAR, TOO!
GOT IT. LET'S DO THIS RIGHT.

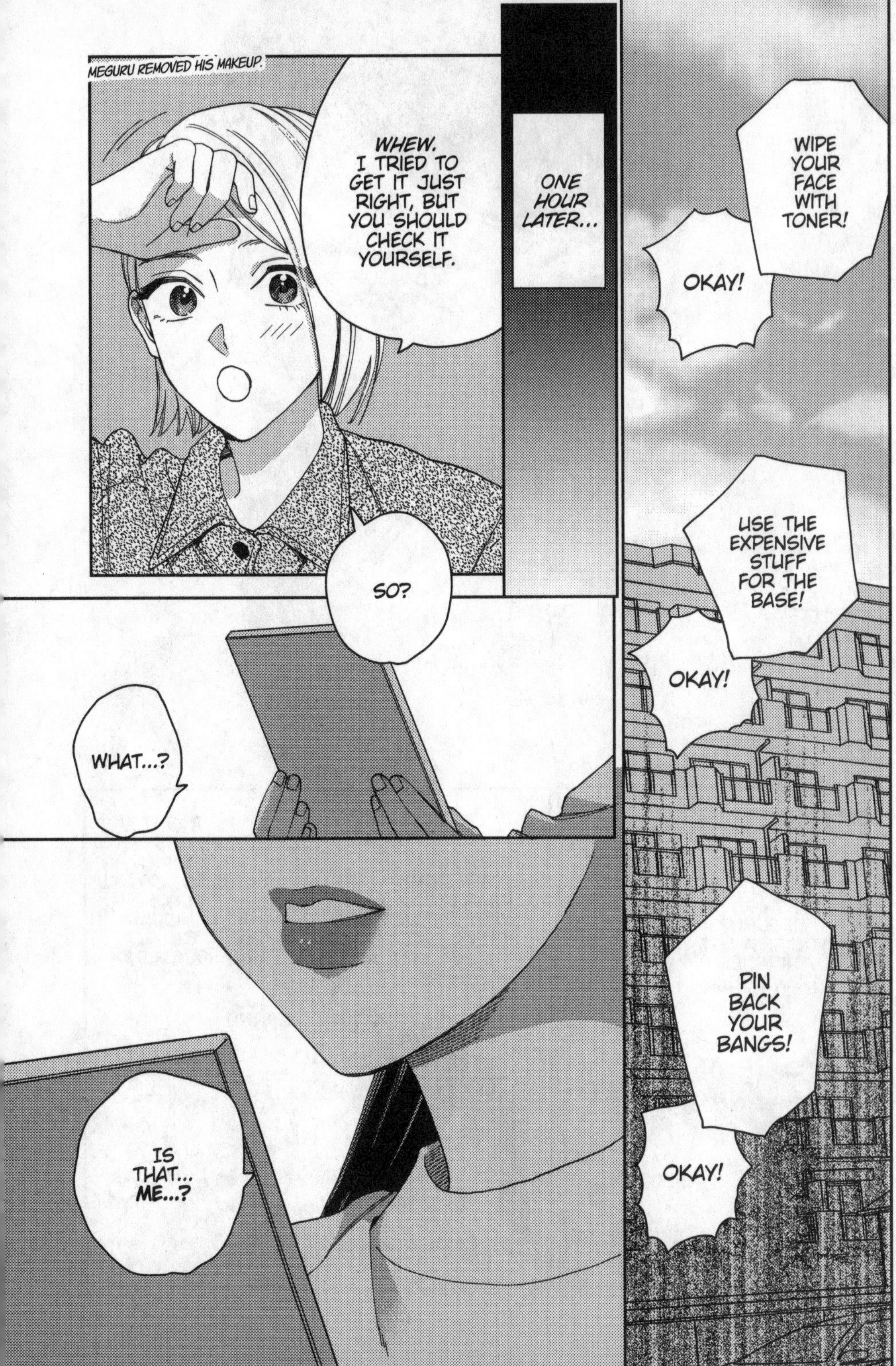

WIPE YOUR FACE WITH TONER!
OKAY!
USE THE EXPENSIVE STUFF FOR THE BASE!
OKAY!
PIN BACK YOUR BANGS!
OKAY!
ONE HOUR LATER...
WHEW. I TRIED TO GET IT JUST RIGHT, BUT YOU SHOULD CHECK IT YOURSELF.
MEGURU REMOVED HIS MAKEUP.
SO?
WHAT...?
IS THAT... ME...?

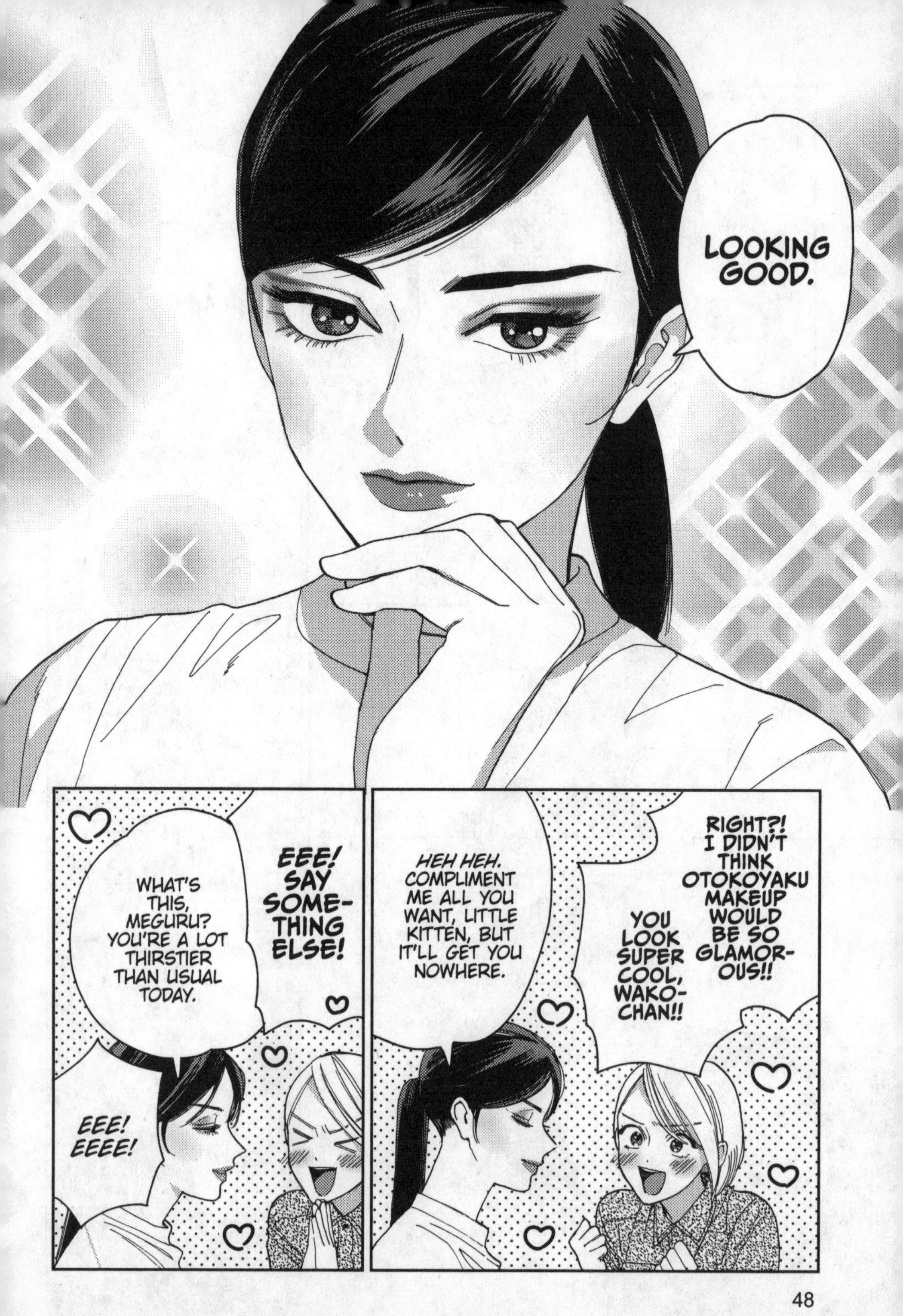
LOOKING GOOD.
RIGHT?! I DIDN'T THINK OTOKOYAKU MAKEUP WOULD BE SO GLAMOROUS!!
YOU LOOK SUPER COOL, WAKO-CHAN!!
HEH HEH. COMPLIMENT ME ALL YOU WANT, LITTLE KITTEN, BUT IT'LL GET YOU NOWHERE.
EEE! SAY SOMETHING ELSE!
WHAT'S THIS, MEGURU? YOU'RE A LOT THIRSTIER THAN USUAL TODAY.
EEE! EEEE!

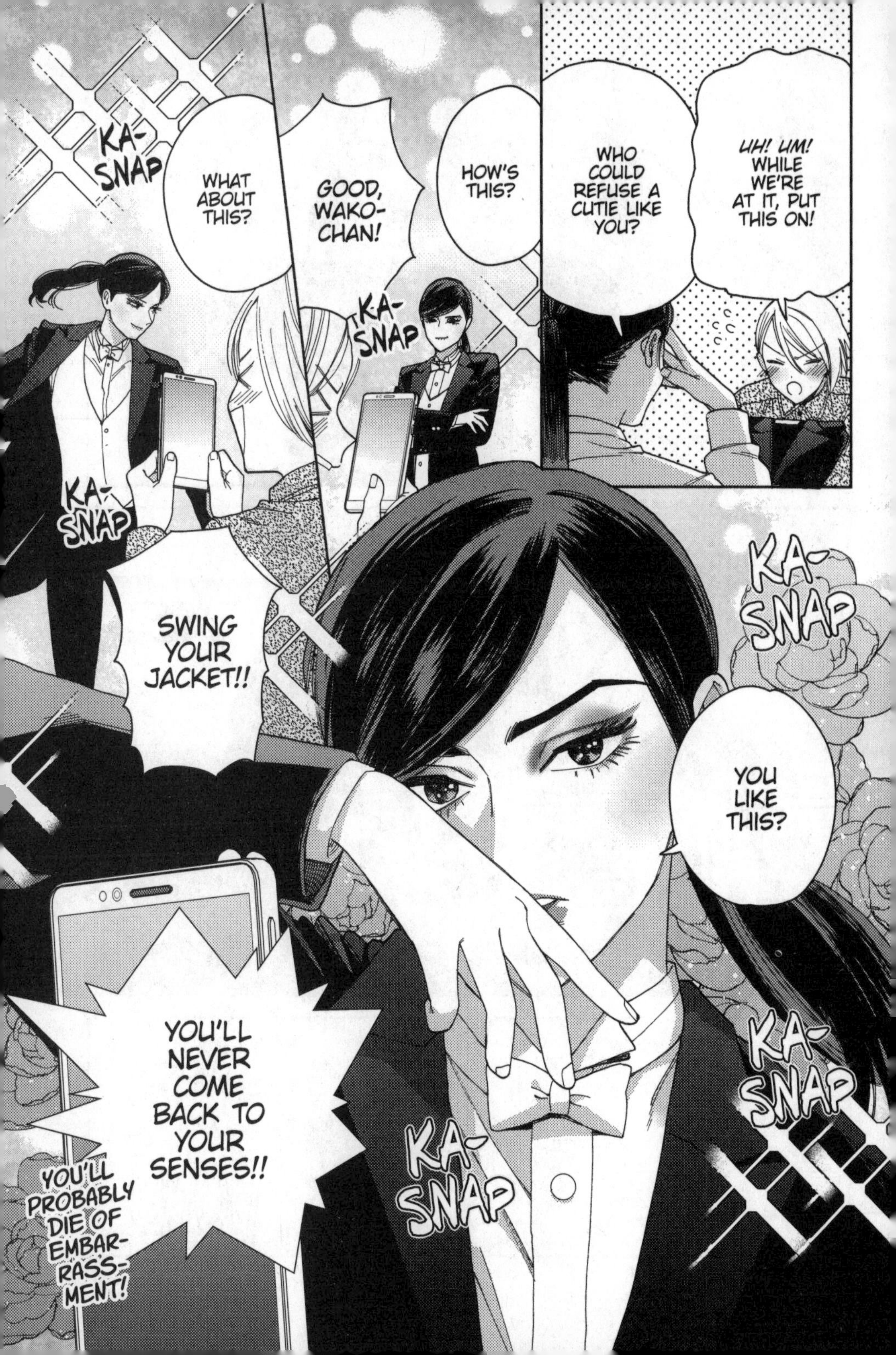
UH! UM! WHILE WE'RE AT IT, PUT THIS ON!
WHO COULD REFUSE A CUTIE LIKE YOU?
HOW'S THIS?
GOOD, WAKO-CHAN!
KA-SNAP
KA-SNAP
WHAT ABOUT THIS?
KA-SNAP
SWING YOUR JACKET!!
KA-SNAP
YOU LIKE THIS?
KA-SNAP
KA-SNAP
YOU'LL NEVER COME BACK TO YOUR SENSES!!
YOU'LL PROBABLY DIE OF EMBAR-RASS-MENT!

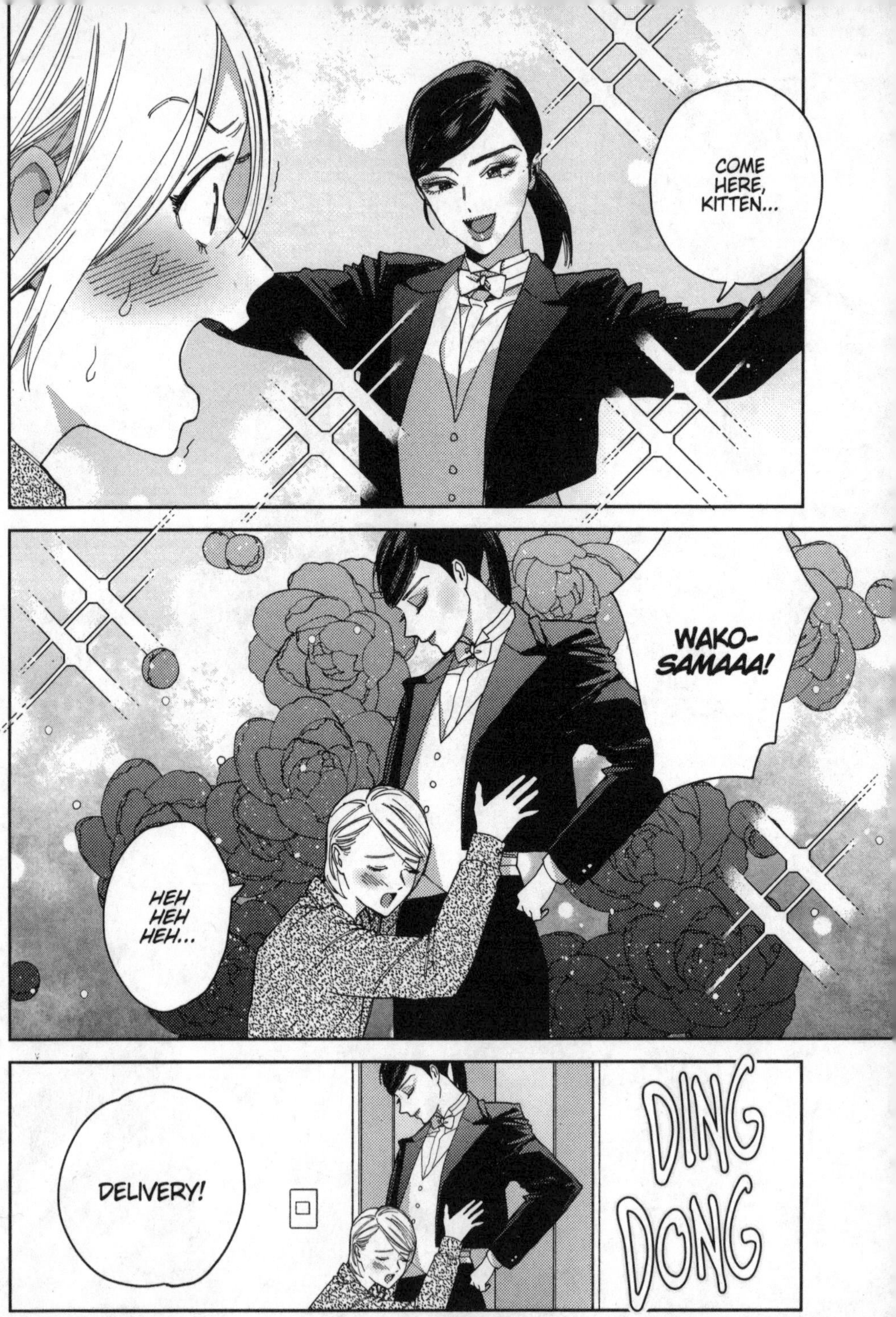
COME HERE, KITTEN...
WAKO-SAMAAA!
HEH HEH HEH...
DING DONG
DELIVERY!

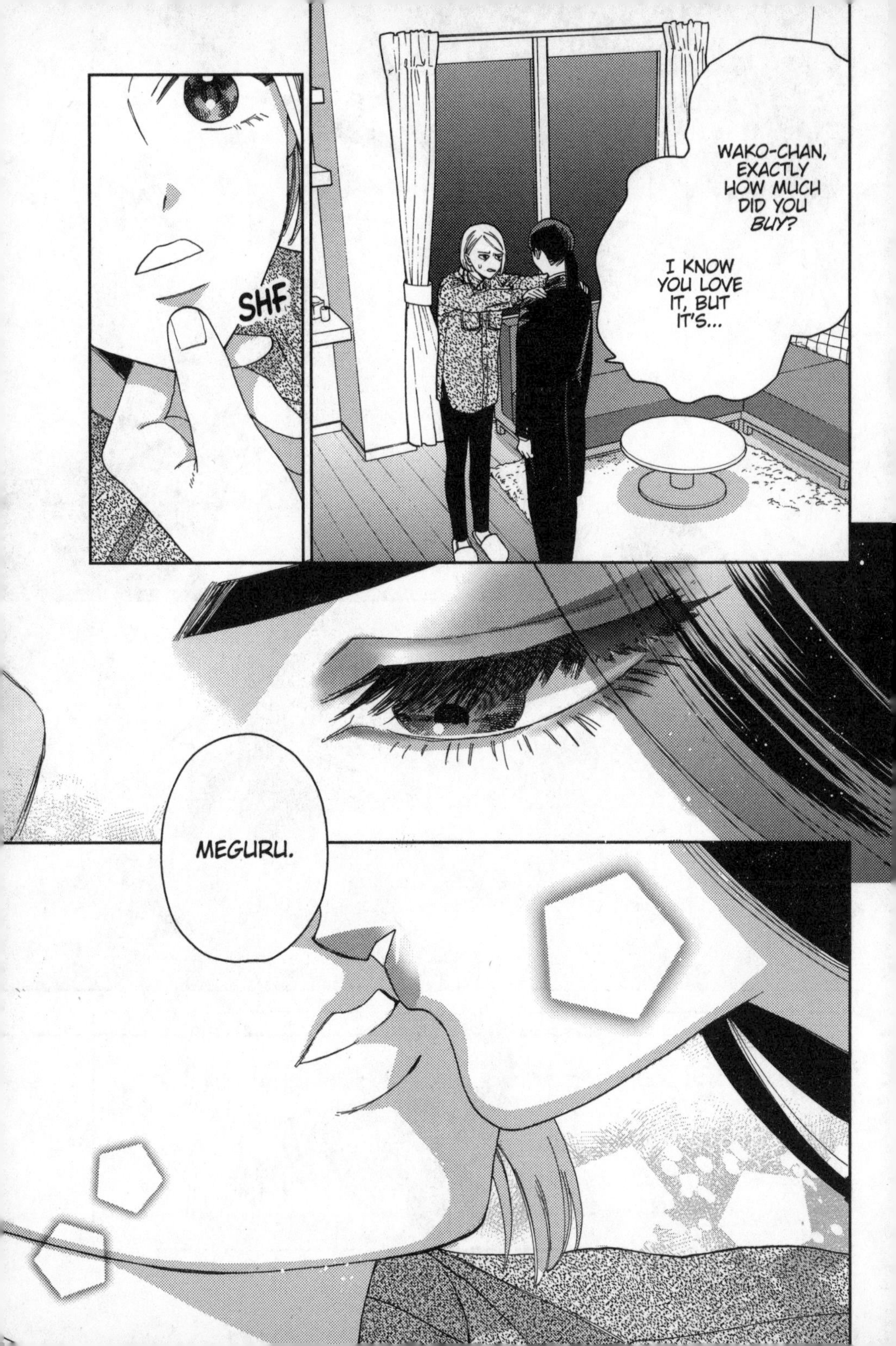
WAKO-CHAN, EXACTLY HOW MUCH DID YOU *BUY*?
I KNOW YOU LOVE IT, BUT IT'S...
SHF
MEGURU.

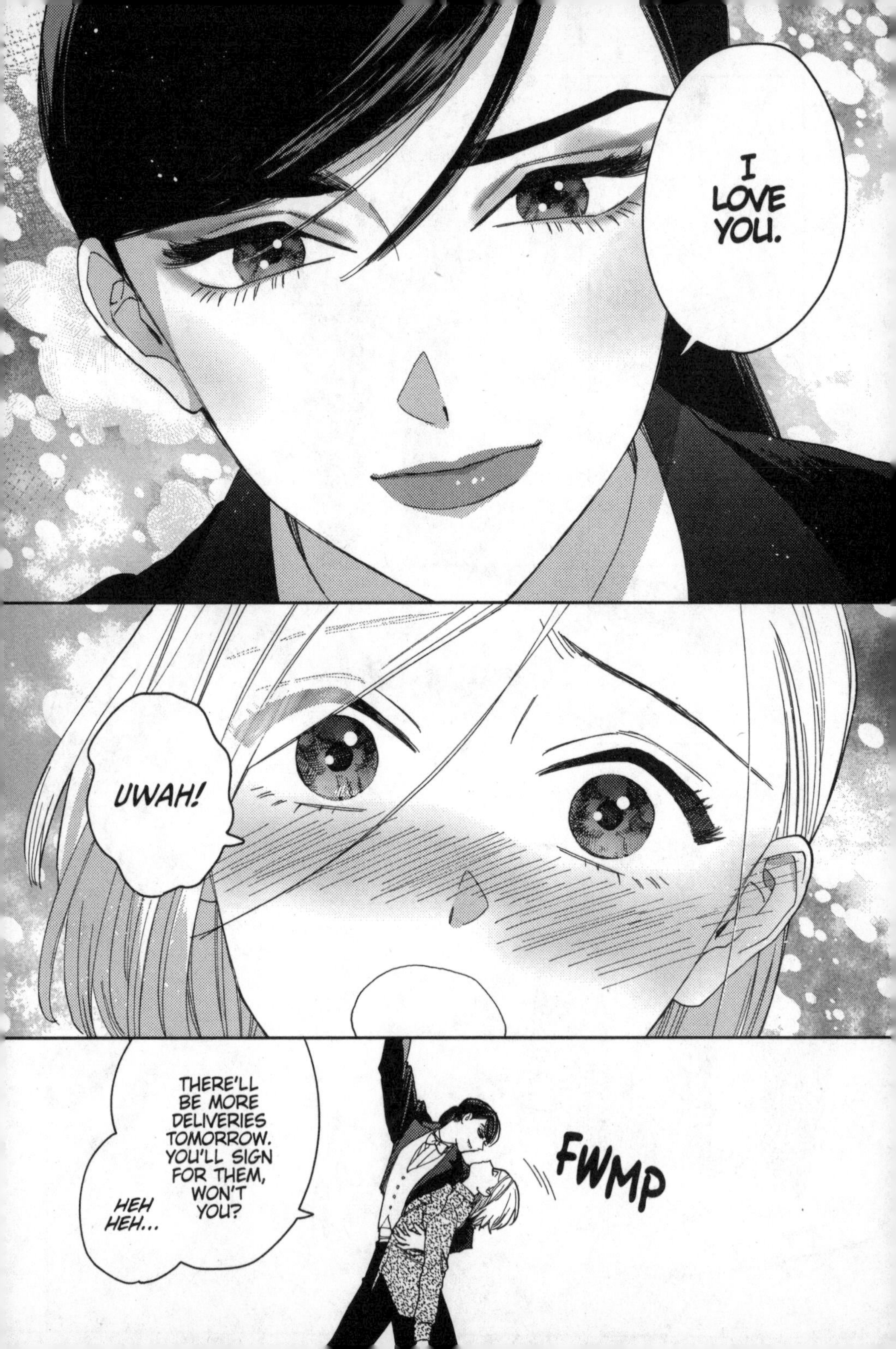
I LOVE YOU.
UWAH!
THERE'LL BE MORE DELIVERIES TOMORROW. YOU'LL SIGN FOR THEM, WON'T YOU?
HEH HEH...
FWMP

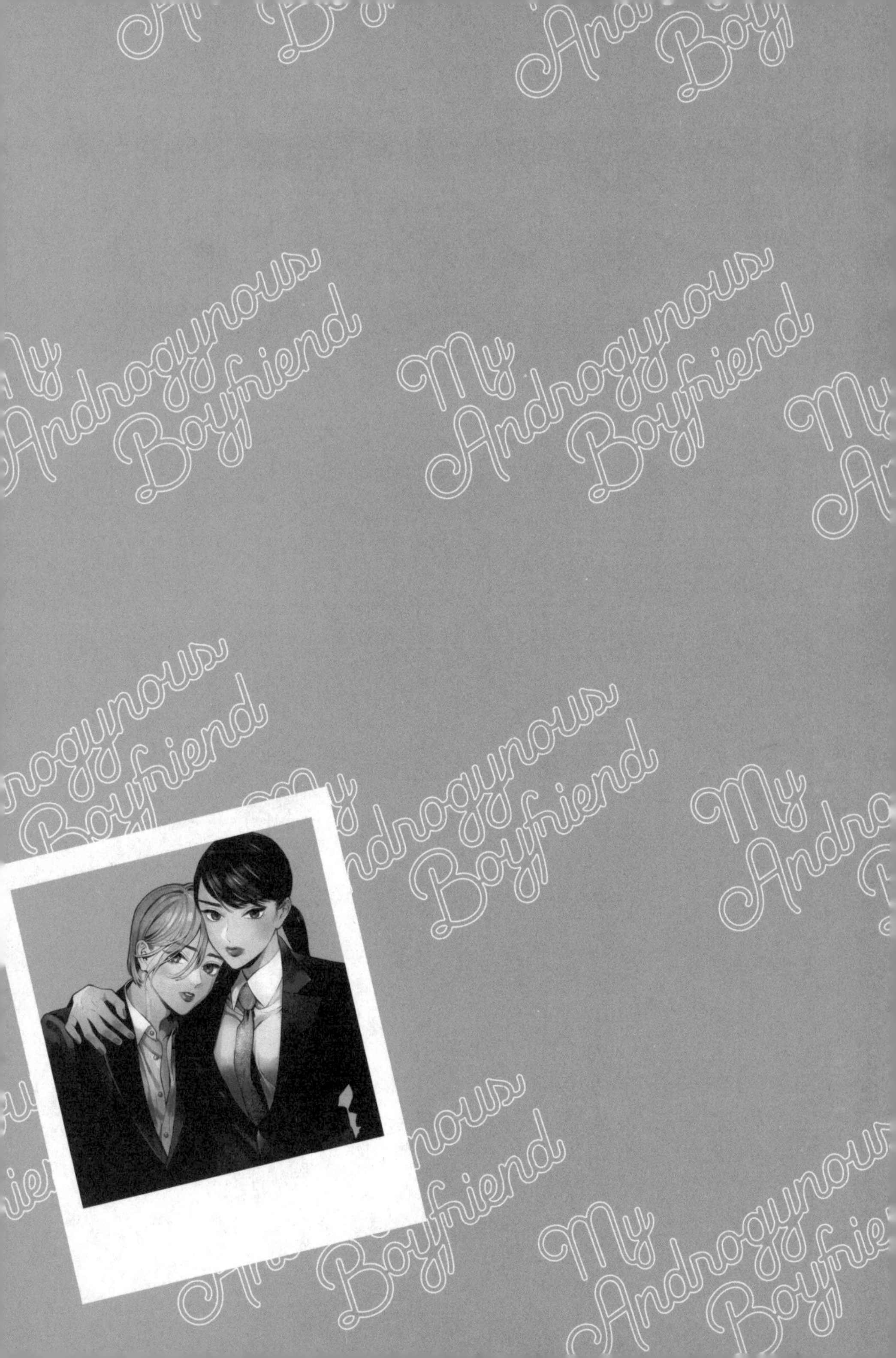
My Androgynous Boyfriend

My Androgynous Boyfriend

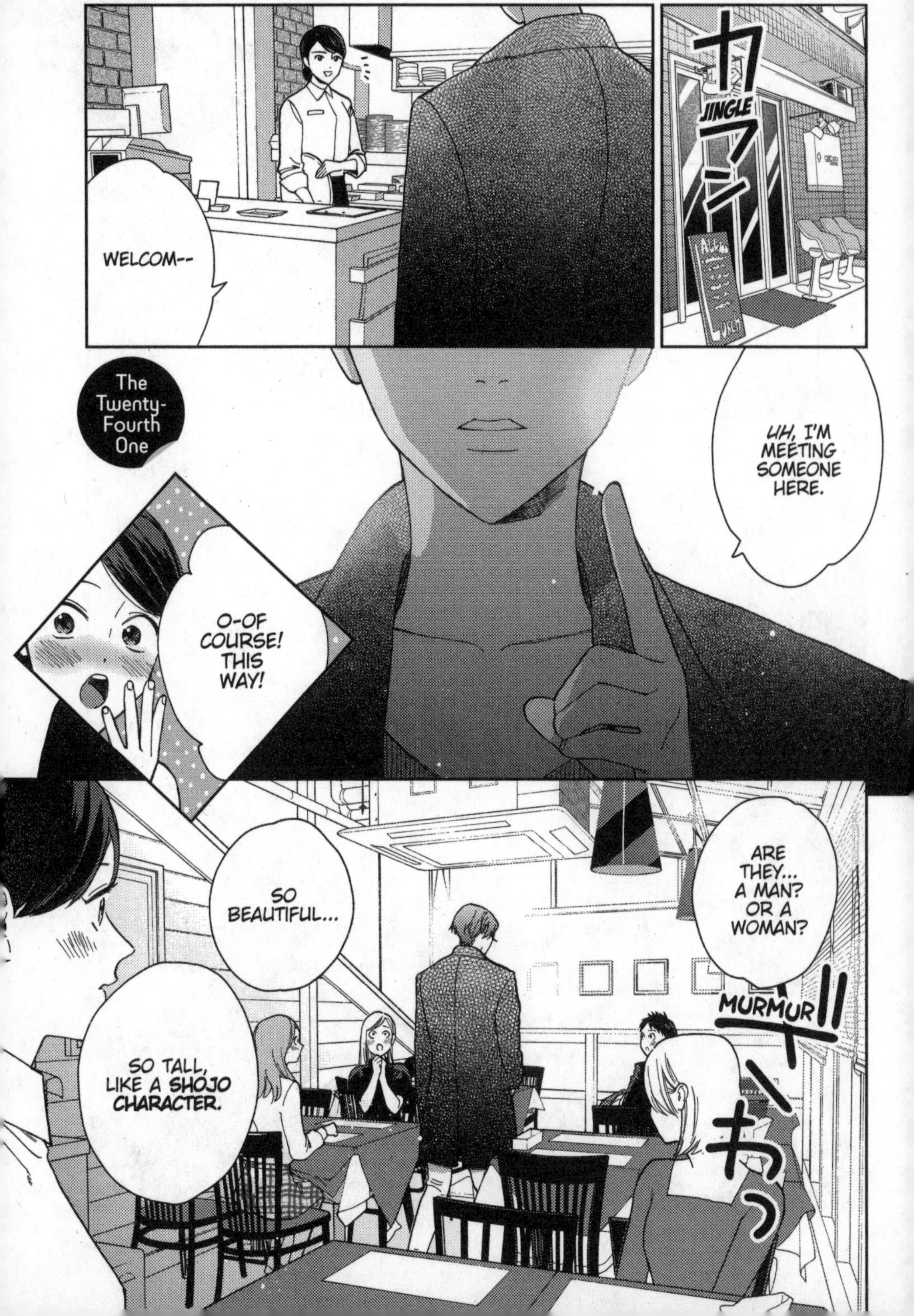

JINGLE
カラン
WELCOM--
The Twenty-Fourth One
UH, I'M MEETING SOMEONE HERE.
O-OF COURSE! THIS WAY!
ARE THEY... A MAN? OR A WOMAN?
MURMUR
SO BEAUTIFUL...
SO TALL, LIKE A SHOJO CHARACTER.

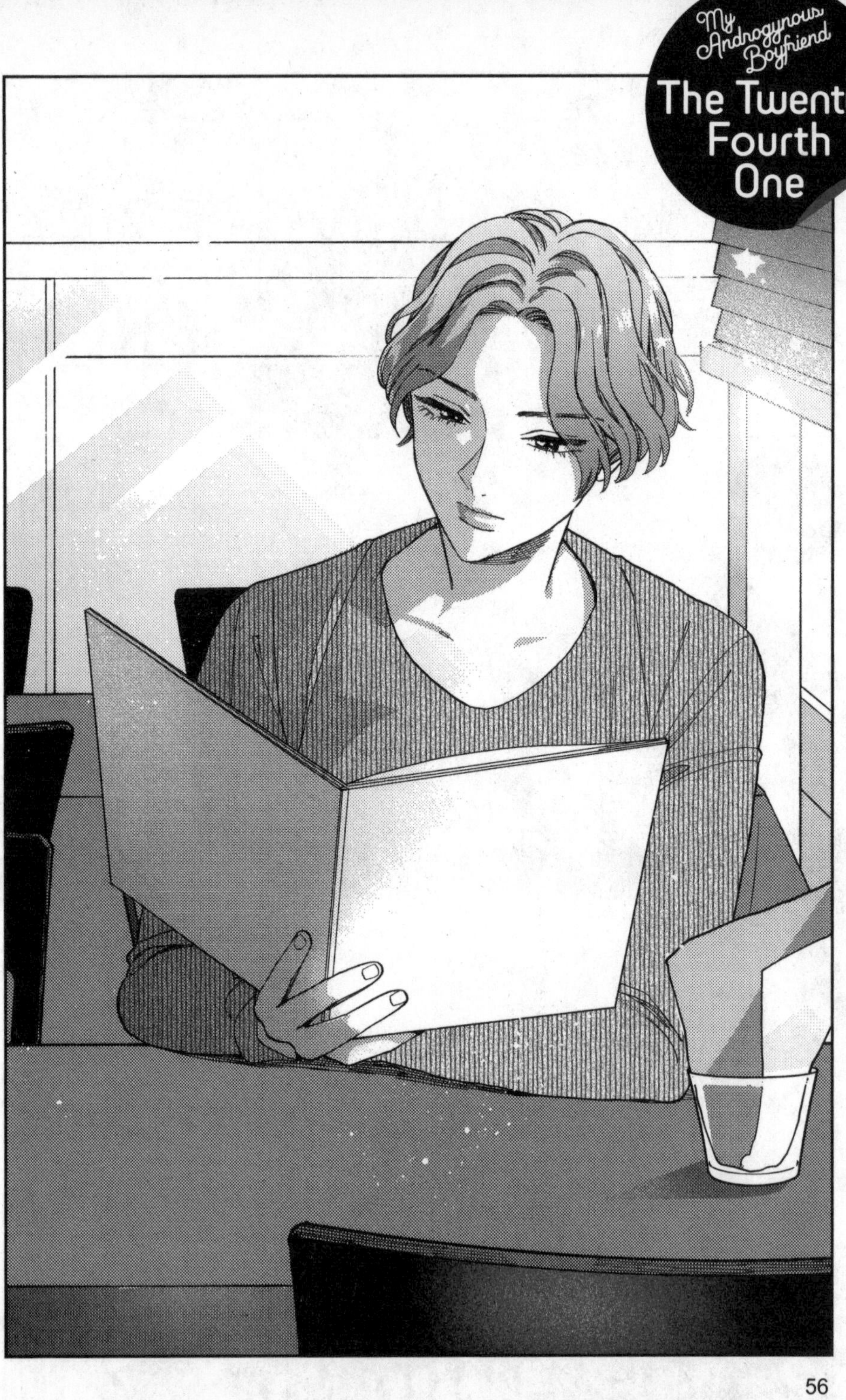
My Androgynous Boyfriend
The Twenty-Fourth One

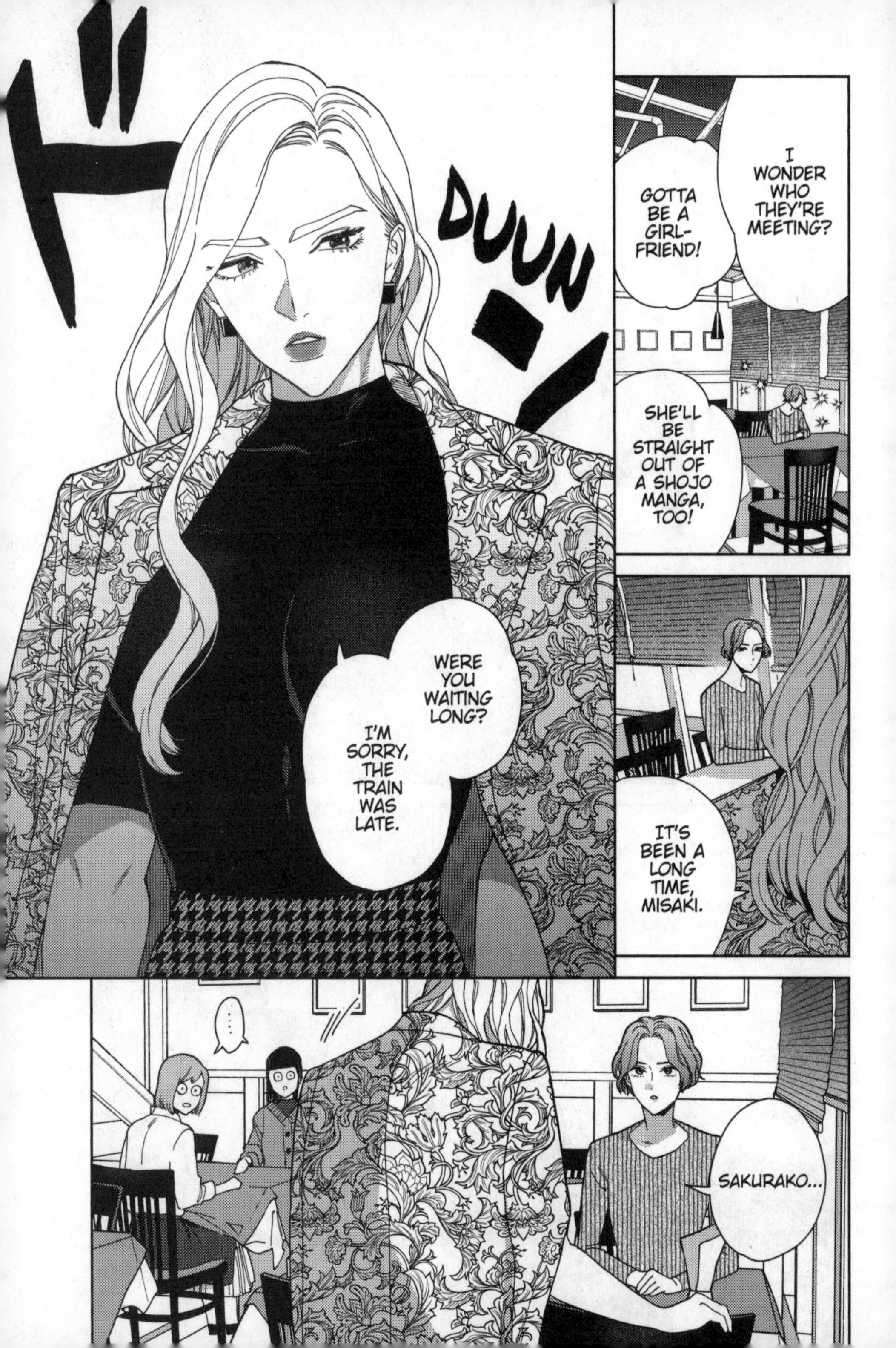
I WONDER WHO THEY'RE MEETING?
GOTTA BE A GIRL-FRIEND!
SHE'LL BE STRAIGHT OUT OF A SHOJO MANGA, TOO!
IT'S BEEN A LONG TIME, MISAKI.
DUUN
WERE YOU WAITING LONG?
I'M SORRY, THE TRAIN WAS LATE.
SAKURAKO...
...

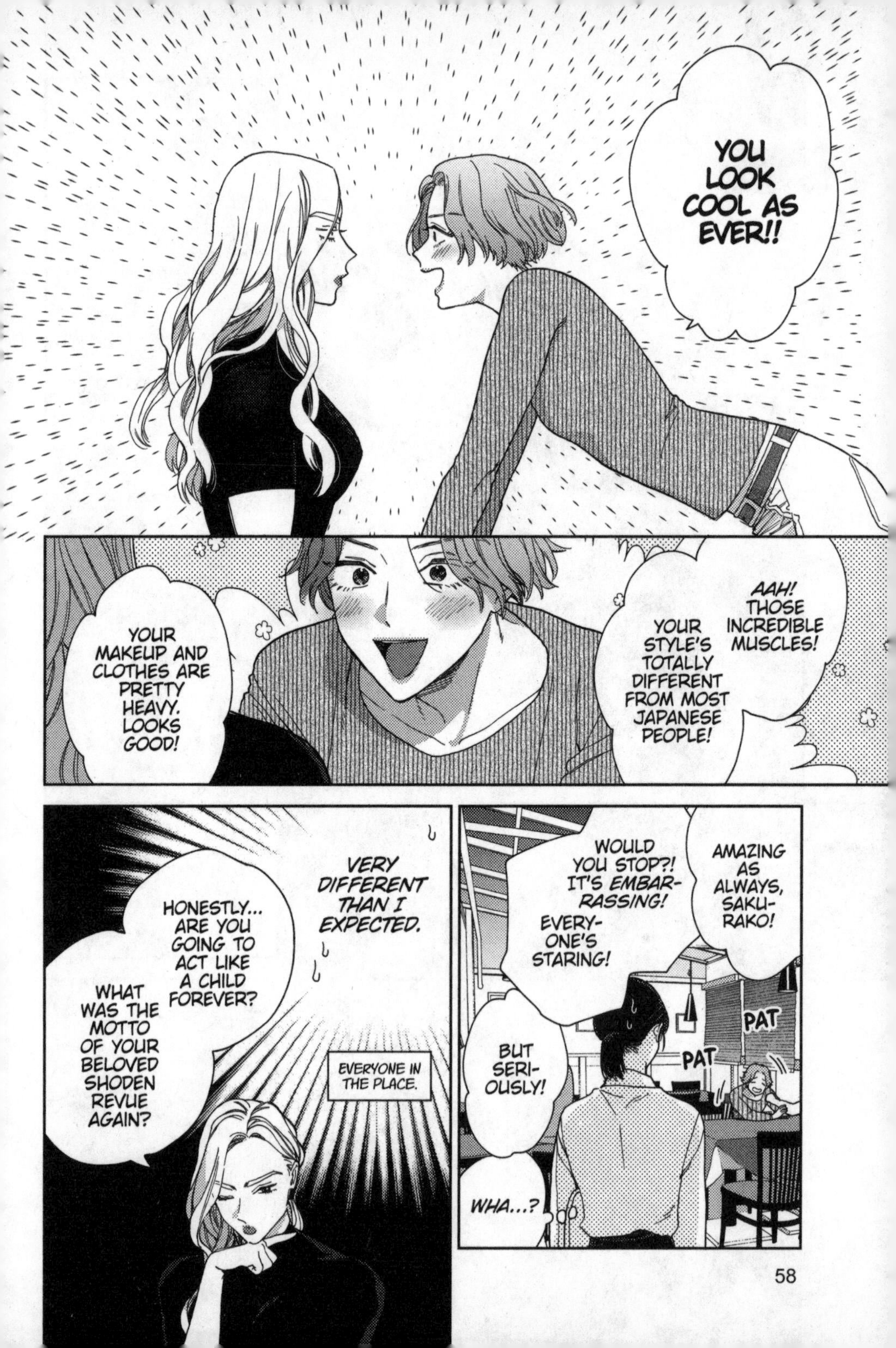
YOU LOOK COOL AS EVER!!
AAH! THOSE INCREDIBLE MUSCLES!
YOUR STYLE'S TOTALLY DIFFERENT FROM MOST JAPANESE PEOPLE!
YOUR MAKEUP AND CLOTHES ARE PRETTY HEAVY. LOOKS GOOD!
AMAZING AS ALWAYS, SAKURAKO!
WOULD YOU STOP?! IT'S EMBARRASSING!
EVERYONE'S STARING!
PAT
PAT
BUT SERIOUSLY!
WHA...?
VERY DIFFERENT THAN I EXPECTED.
EVERYONE IN THE PLACE.
HONESTLY... ARE YOU GOING TO ACT LIKE A CHILD FOREVER?
WHAT WAS THE MOTTO OF YOUR BELOVED SHODEN REVUE AGAIN?

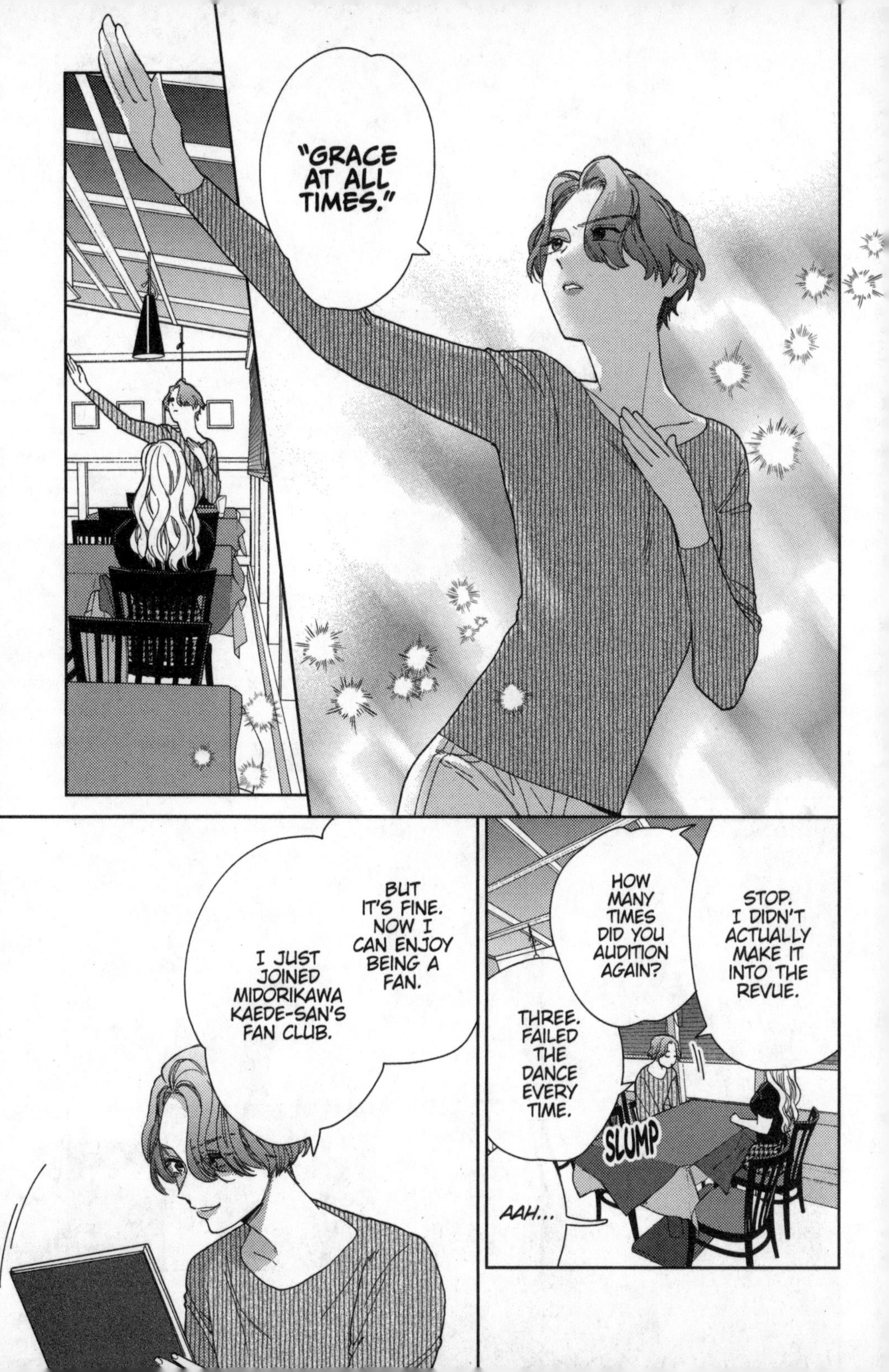
"GRACE AT ALL TIMES."
STOP. I DIDN'T ACTUALLY MAKE IT INTO THE REVUE.
HOW MANY TIMES DID YOU AUDITION AGAIN?
THREE. FAILED THE DANCE EVERY TIME.
SLUMP
AAH...
BUT IT'S FINE. NOW I CAN ENJOY BEING A FAN.
I JUST JOINED MIDORIKAWA KAEDE-SAN'S FAN CLUB.

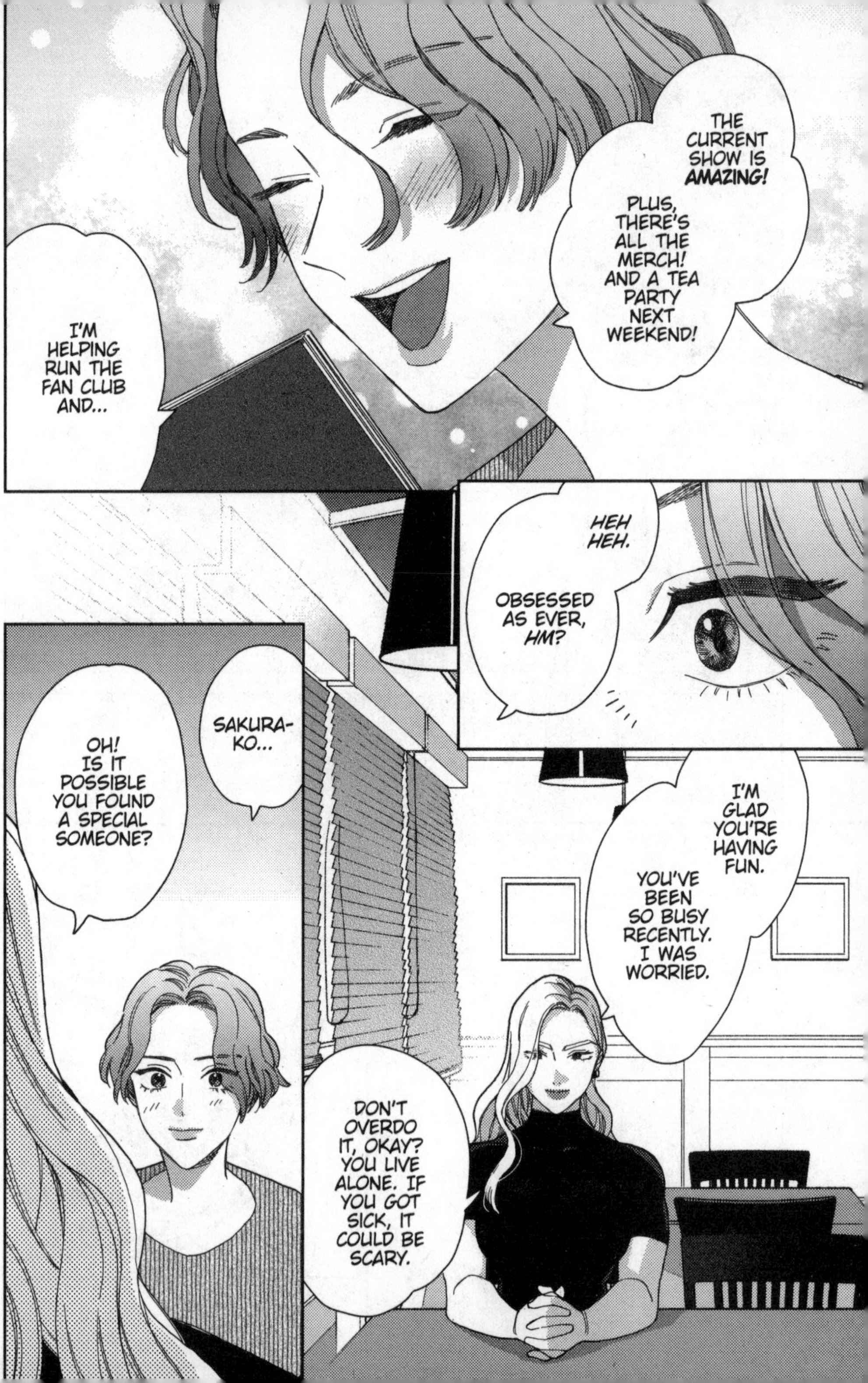
THE CURRENT SHOW IS **AMAZING!**
PLUS, THERE'S ALL THE MERCH! AND A TEA PARTY NEXT WEEKEND!
I'M HELPING RUN THE FAN CLUB AND...
HEH HEH.
OBSESSED AS EVER, *HM?*
I'M GLAD YOU'RE HAVING FUN.
YOU'VE BEEN SO BUSY RECENTLY. I WAS WORRIED.
DON'T OVERDO IT, OKAY? YOU LIVE ALONE. IF YOU GOT SICK, IT COULD BE SCARY.
SAKURA-KO...
OH! IS IT POSSIBLE YOU FOUND A SPECIAL SOMEONE?

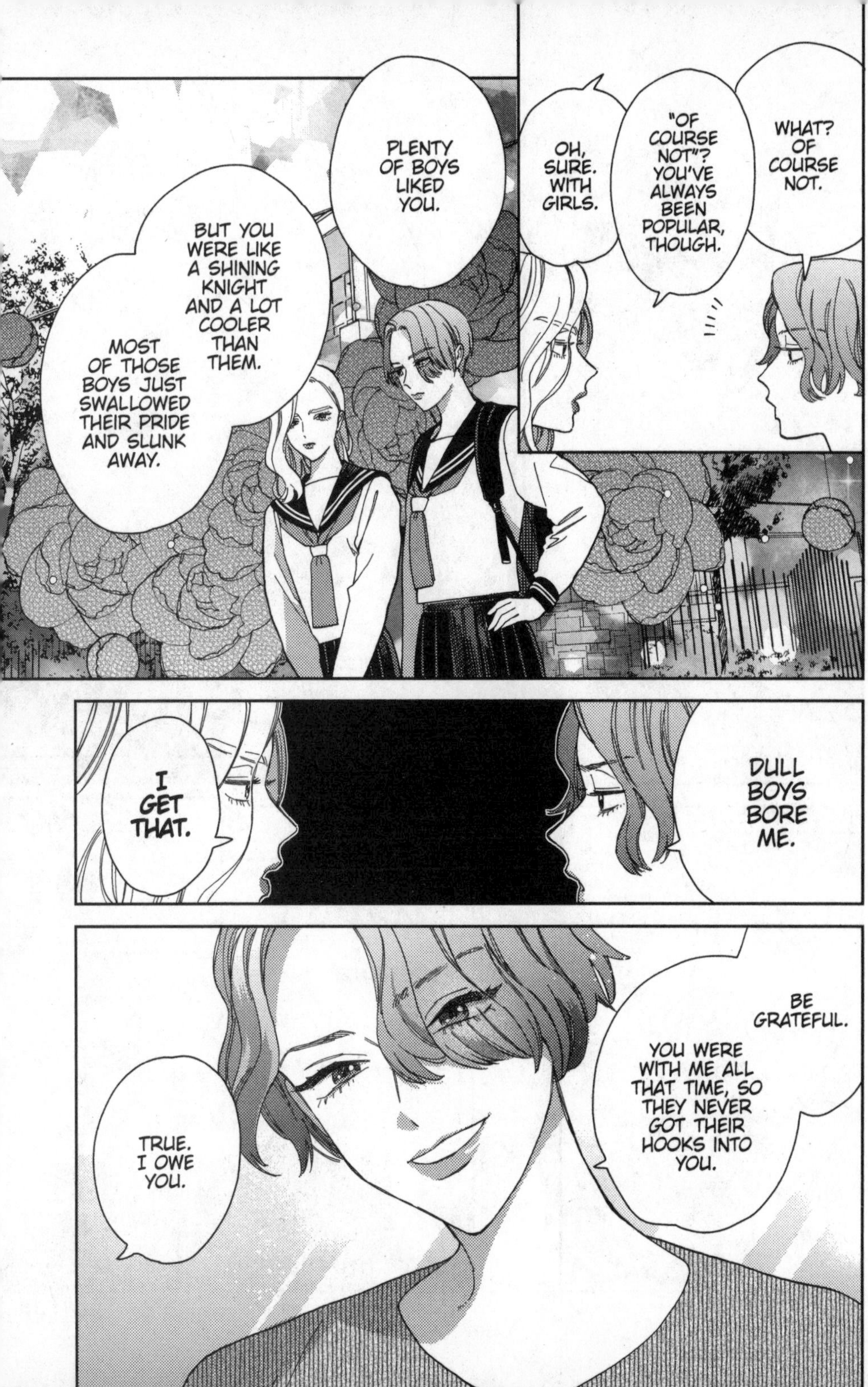
WHAT? OF COURSE NOT.
"OF COURSE NOT"? YOU'VE ALWAYS BEEN POPULAR, THOUGH.
OH, SURE. WITH GIRLS.
PLENTY OF BOYS LIKED YOU.
BUT YOU WERE LIKE A SHINING KNIGHT AND A LOT COOLER THAN THEM.
MOST OF THOSE BOYS JUST SWALLOWED THEIR PRIDE AND SLUNK AWAY.
DULL BOYS BORE ME.
I GET THAT.
BE GRATEFUL.
YOU WERE WITH ME ALL THAT TIME, SO THEY NEVER GOT THEIR HOOKS INTO YOU.
TRUE. I OWE YOU.

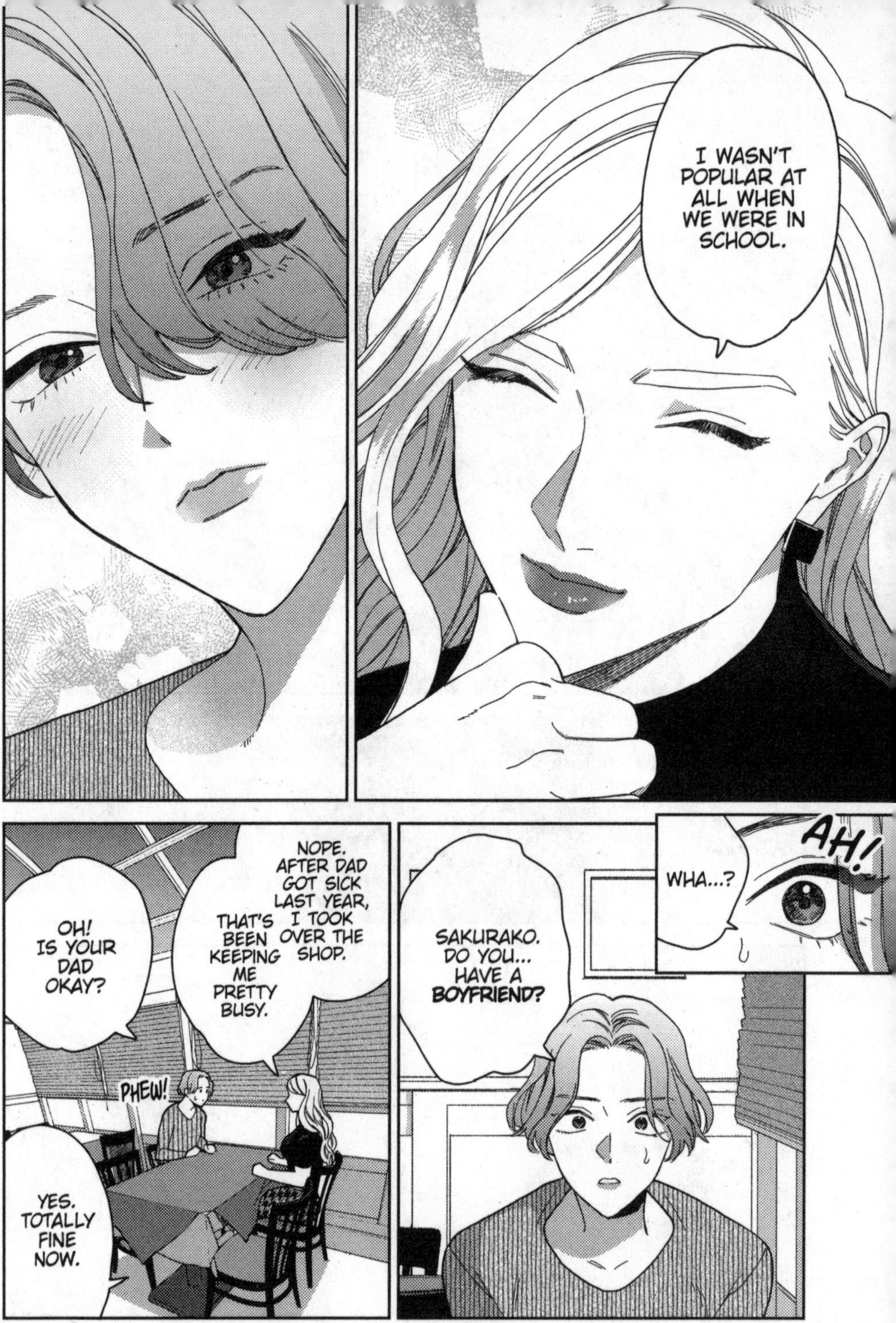
I WASN'T POPULAR AT ALL WHEN WE WERE IN SCHOOL.
AH!
WHA...?
SAKURAKO. DO YOU... HAVE A BOYFRIEND?
NOPE. AFTER DAD GOT SICK LAST YEAR, I TOOK OVER THE SHOP.
THAT'S BEEN KEEPING ME PRETTY BUSY.
OH! IS YOUR DAD OKAY?
PHEW!
YES. TOTALLY FINE NOW.

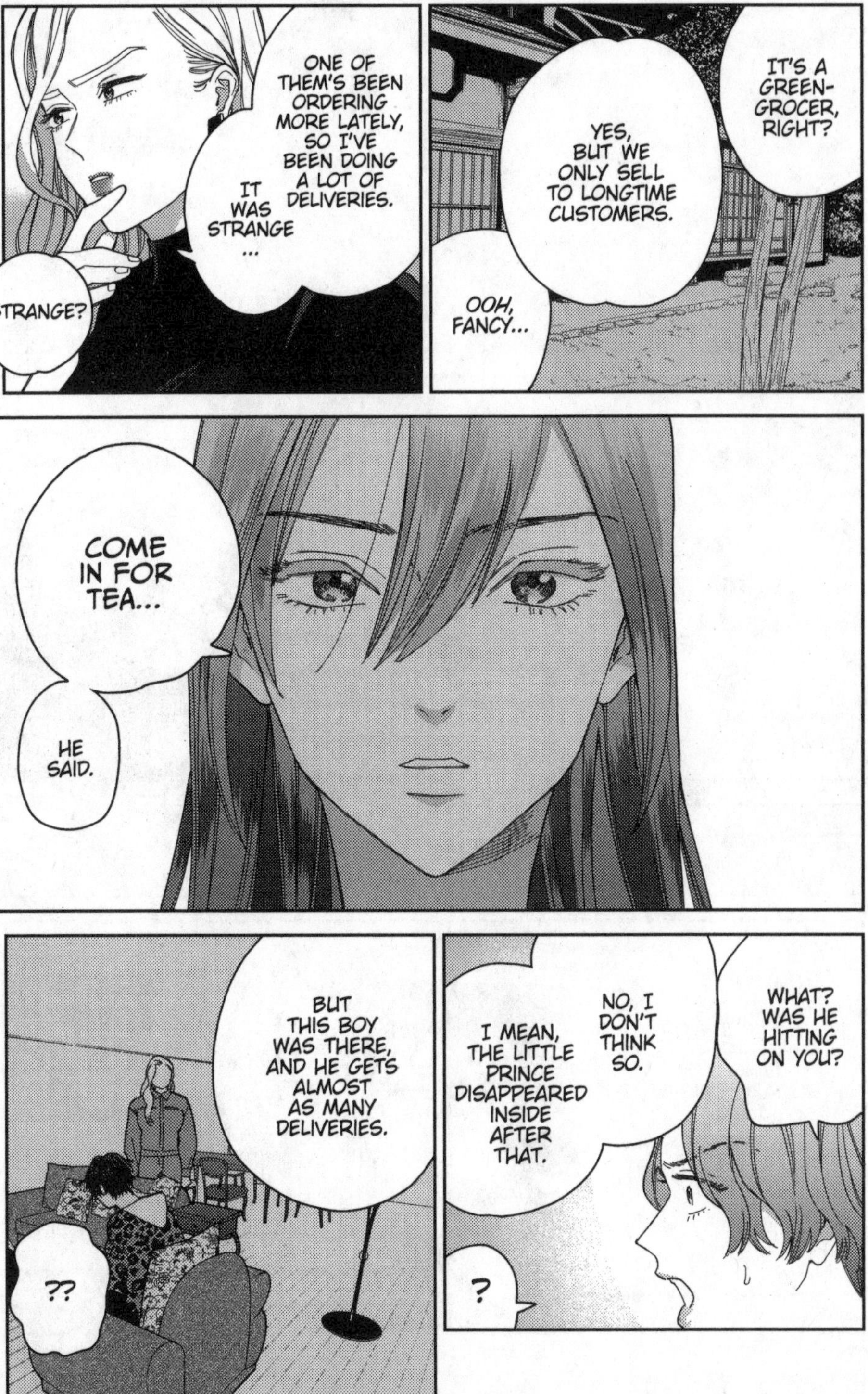
IT'S A GREEN-GROCER, RIGHT?
YES, BUT WE ONLY SELL TO LONGTIME CUSTOMERS.
OOH, FANCY...
ONE OF THEM'S BEEN ORDERING MORE LATELY, SO I'VE BEEN DOING A LOT OF DELIVERIES.
IT WAS STRANGE ...
STRANGE?
COME IN FOR TEA...
HE SAID.
WHAT? WAS HE HITTING ON YOU?
NO, I DON'T THINK SO.
I MEAN, THE LITTLE PRINCE DISAPPEARED INSIDE AFTER THAT.
?
BUT THIS BOY WAS THERE, AND HE GETS ALMOST AS MANY DELIVERIES.
??

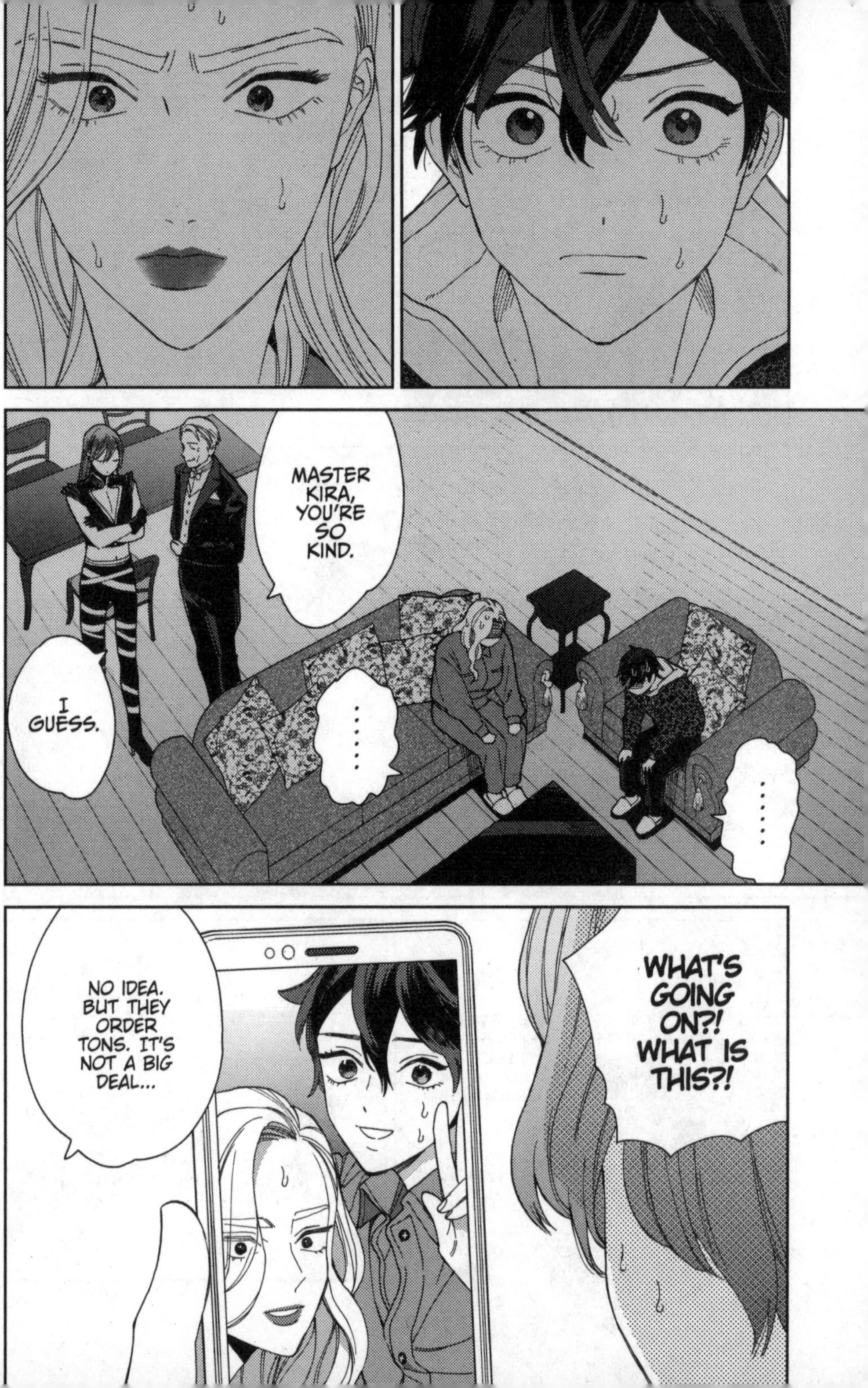
MASTER KIRA, YOU'RE SO KIND.
......
......
I GUESS.
WHAT'S GOING ON?! WHAT IS THIS?!
NO IDEA. BUT THEY ORDER TONS. IT'S NOT A BIG DEAL...

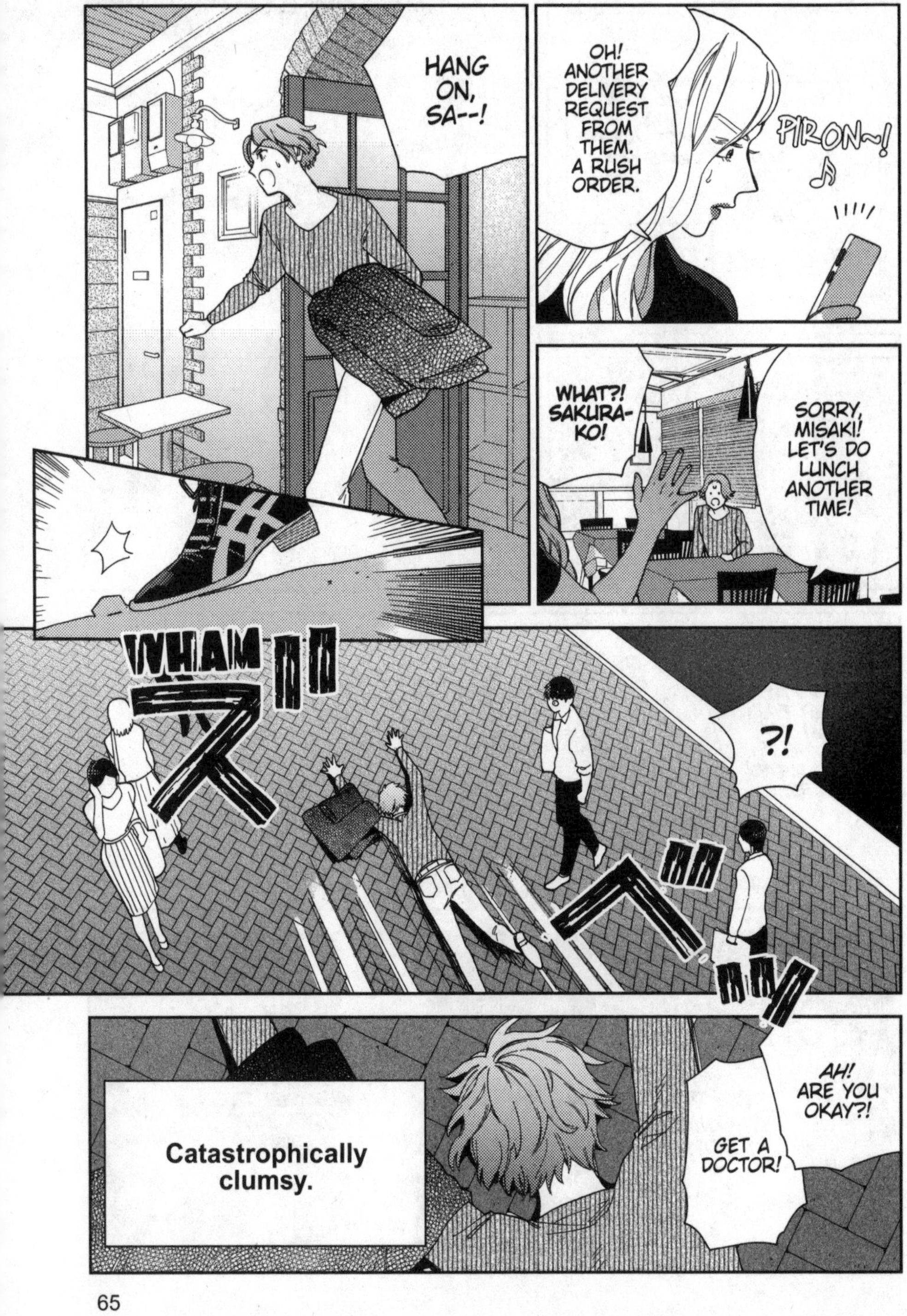
OH! ANOTHER DELIVERY REQUEST FROM THEM. A RUSH ORDER.
PIRON~! ♪
SORRY, MISAKI! LET'S DO LUNCH ANOTHER TIME!
WHAT?! SAKURA-KO!
HANG ON, SA--!
WHAM!!
?!
AH! ARE YOU OKAY?!
GET A DOCTOR!
Catastrophically clumsy.

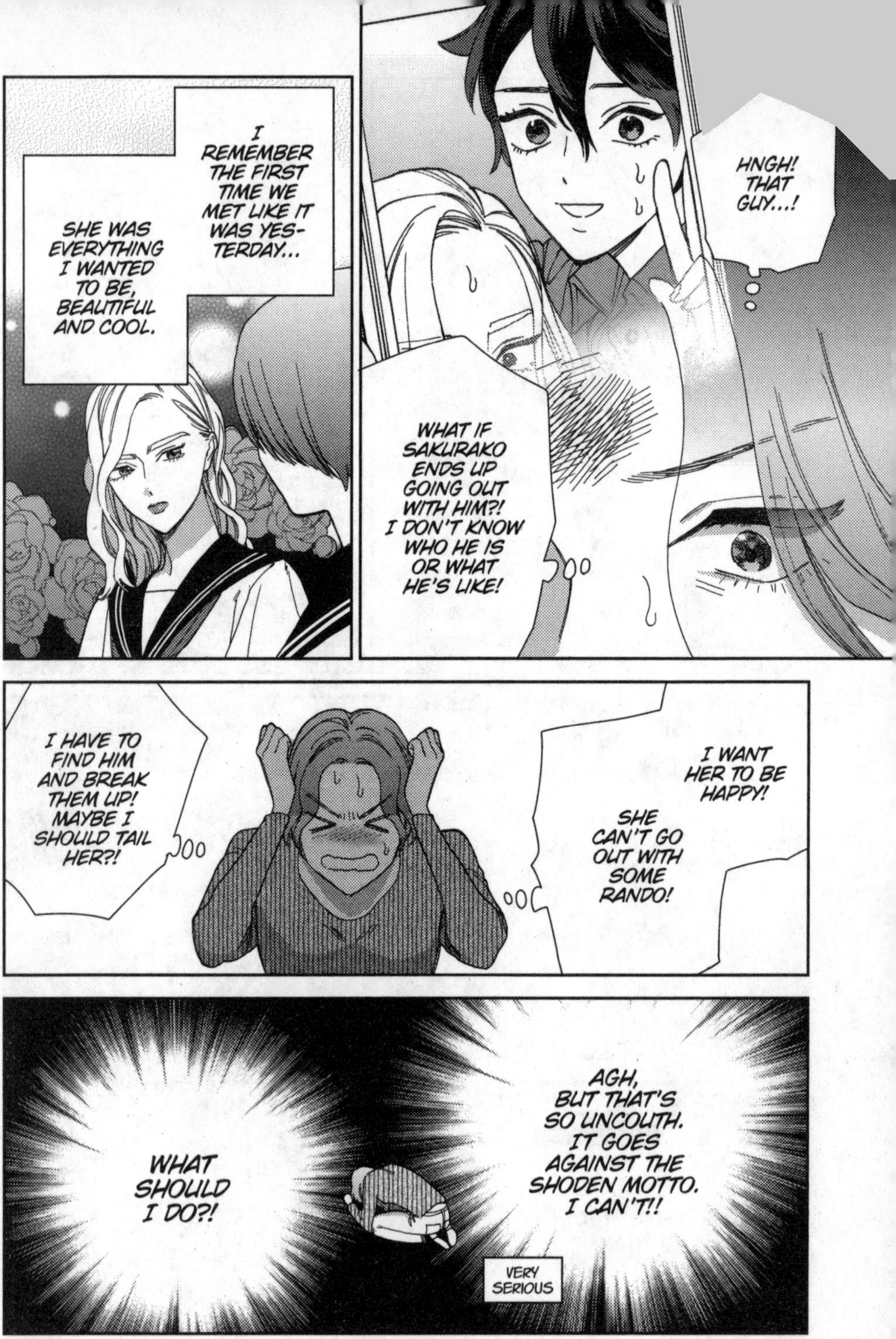
HNGH! THAT GUY...!
WHAT IF SAKURAKO ENDS UP GOING OUT WITH HIM?! I DON'T KNOW WHO HE IS OR WHAT HE'S LIKE!
I REMEMBER THE FIRST TIME WE MET LIKE IT WAS YES-TERDAY...
SHE WAS EVERYTHING I WANTED TO BE, BEAUTIFUL AND COOL.
I WANT HER TO BE HAPPY!
SHE CAN'T GO OUT WITH SOME RANDO!
I HAVE TO FIND HIM AND BREAK THEM UP! MAYBE I SHOULD TAIL HER?!
AGH, BUT THAT'S SO UNCOUTH. IT GOES AGAINST THE SHODEN MOTTO. I CAN'T!!
WHAT SHOULD I DO?!
VERY SERIOUS

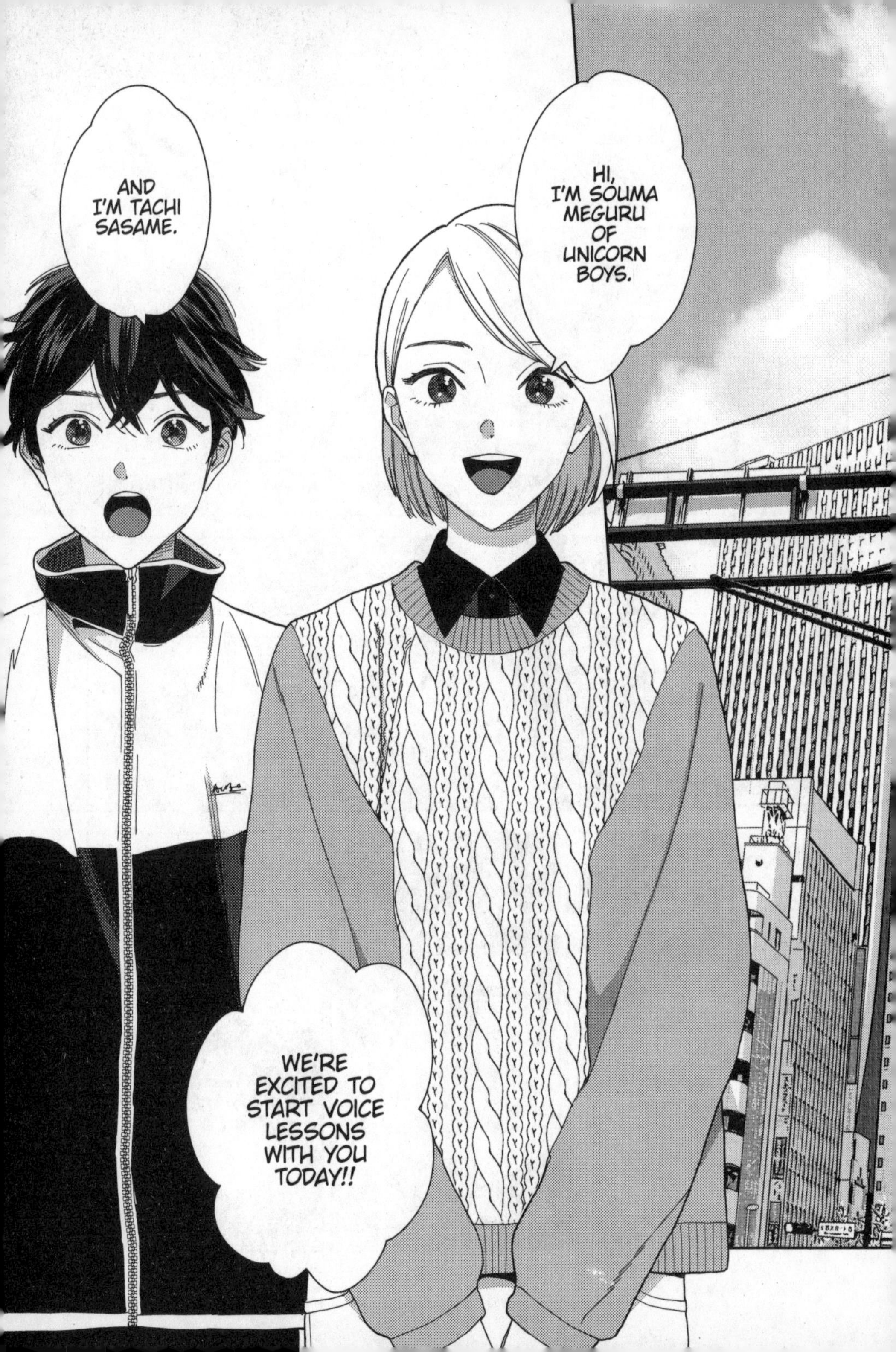
HI, I'M SOUMA MEGURU OF UNICORN BOYS.
AND I'M TACHI SASAME.
WE'RE EXCITED TO START VOICE LESSONS WITH YOU TODAY!!

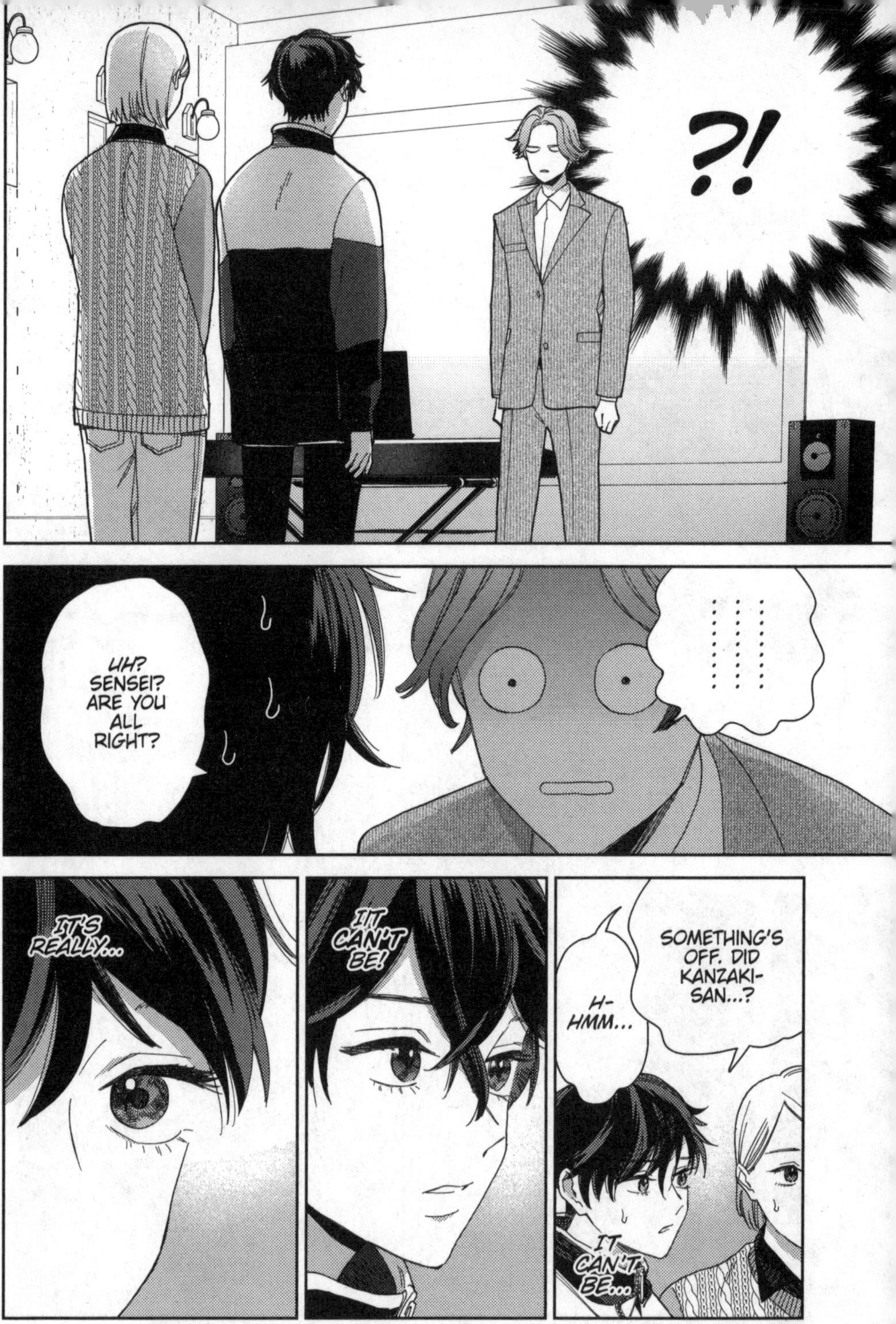
?!
......
UH? SENSEI? ARE YOU ALL RIGHT?
SOMETHING'S OFF. DID KANZAKI-SAN...?
H-HMM...
IT CAN'T BE...
IT CAN'T BE!
IT'S REALLY...

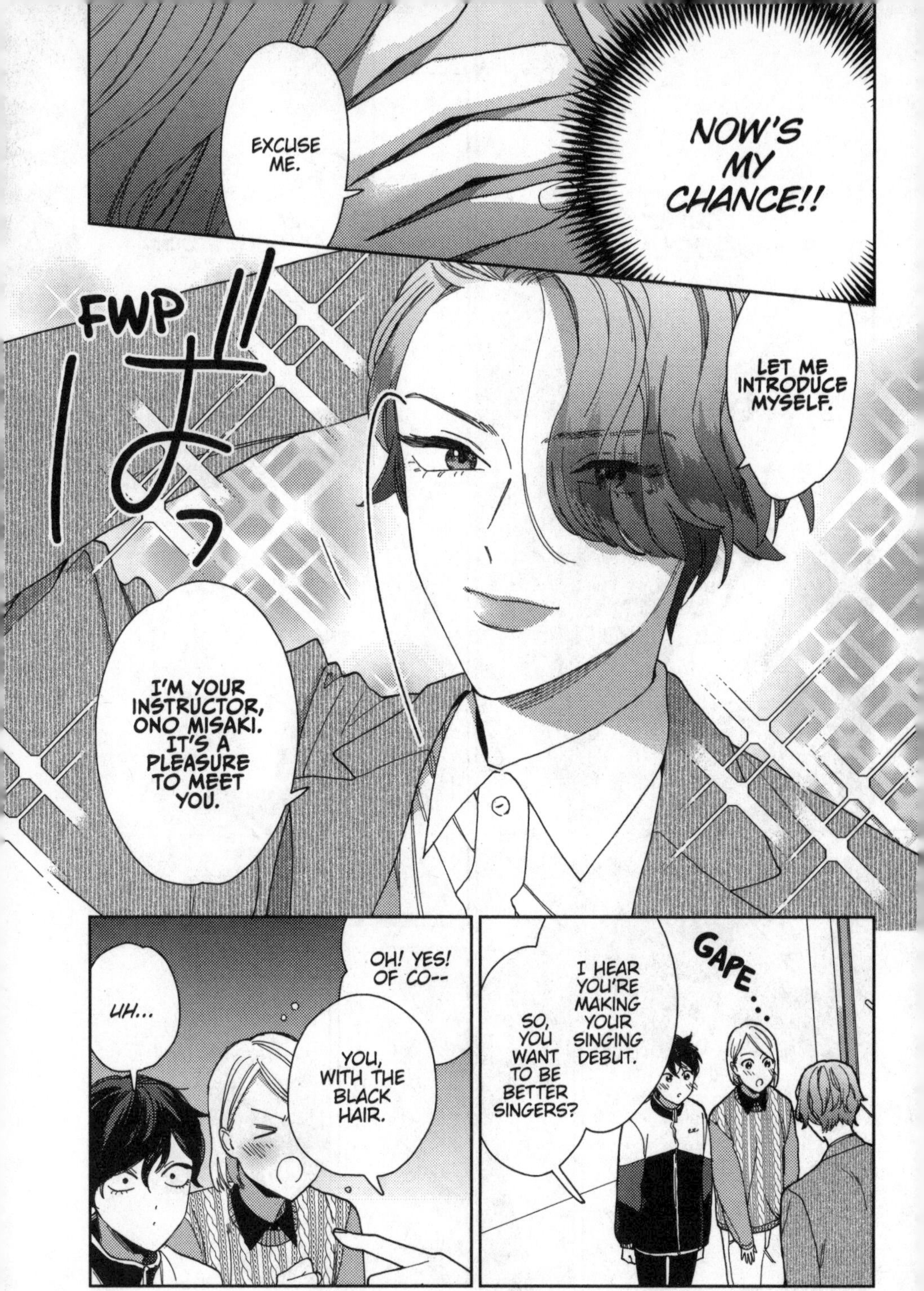
NOW'S MY CHANCE!!
EXCUSE ME.
LET ME INTRODUCE MYSELF.
FWP
I'M YOUR INSTRUCTOR, ONO MISAKI. IT'S A PLEASURE TO MEET YOU.
GAPE...
I HEAR YOU'RE MAKING YOUR SINGING DEBUT.
SO, YOU WANT TO BE BETTER SINGERS?
OH! YES! OF CO--
UH...
YOU, WITH THE BLACK HAIR.

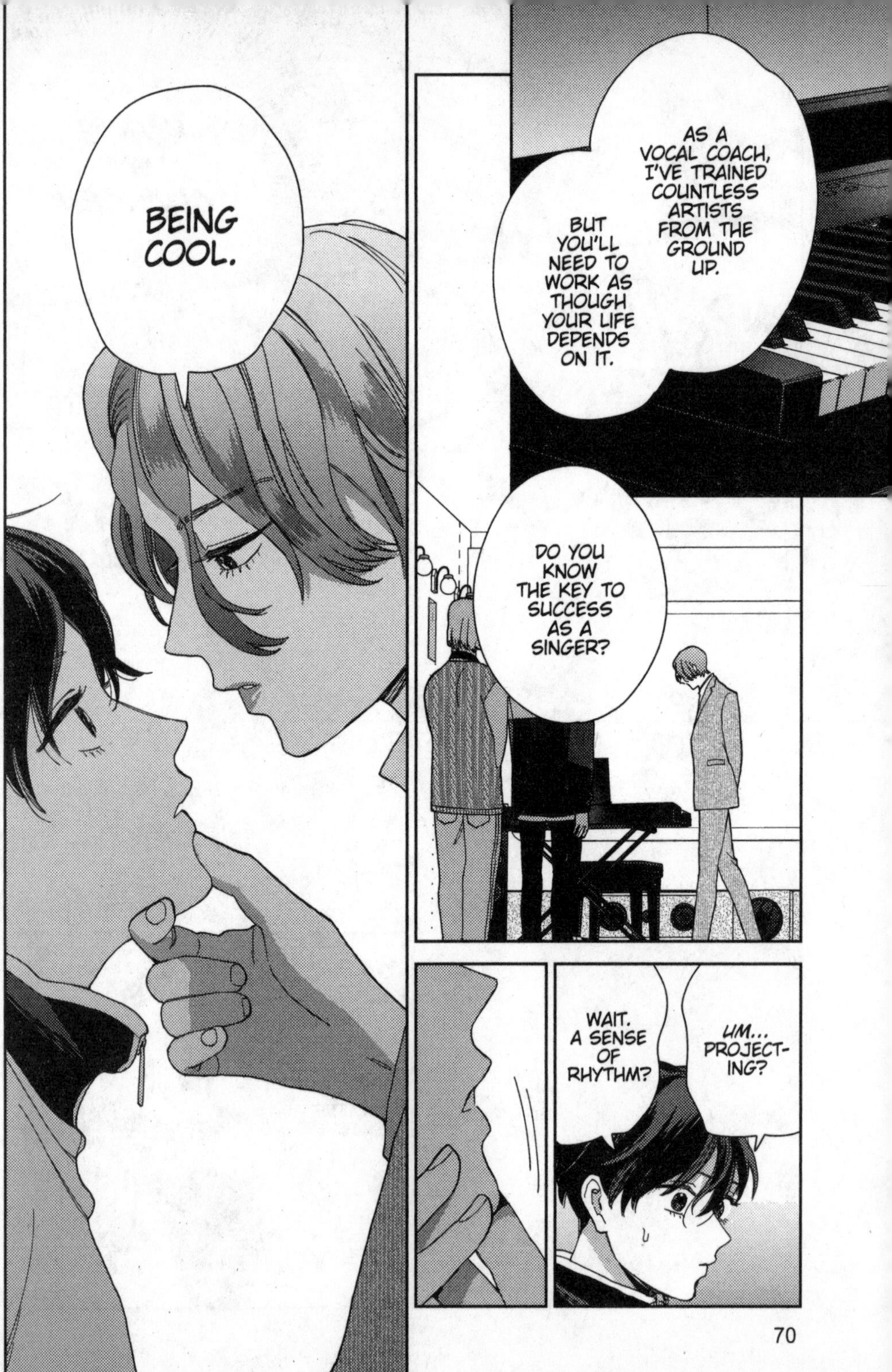
AS A VOCAL COACH, I'VE TRAINED COUNTLESS ARTISTS FROM THE GROUND UP.
BUT YOU'LL NEED TO WORK AS THOUGH YOUR LIFE DEPENDS ON IT.
DO YOU KNOW THE KEY TO SUCCESS AS A SINGER?
UM... PROJECTING?
WAIT. A SENSE OF RHYTHM?
BEING COOL.

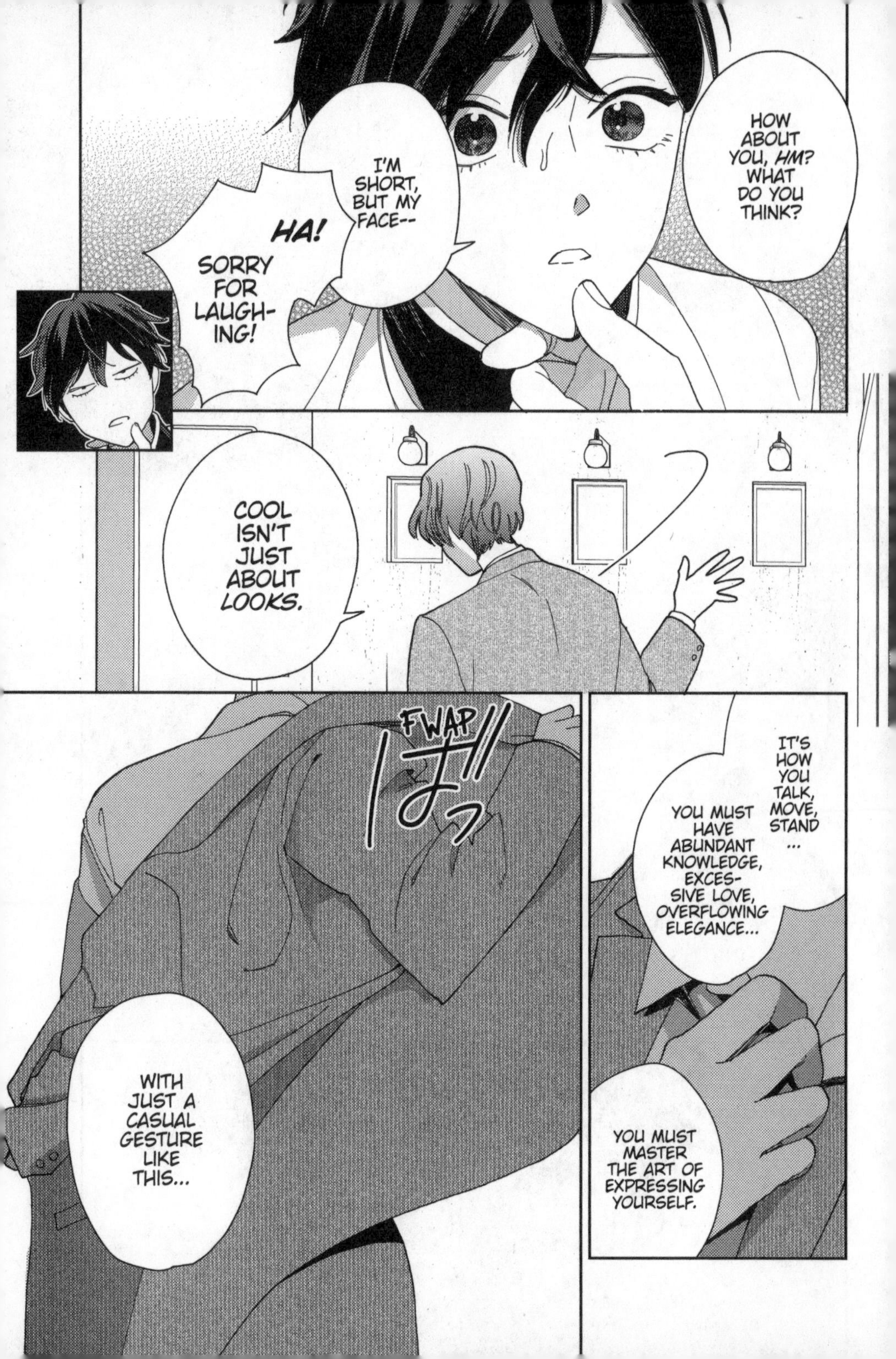
HOW ABOUT YOU, *HM*? WHAT DO YOU THINK?
I'M SHORT, BUT MY FACE--
HA!
SORRY FOR LAUGHING!
COOL ISN'T JUST ABOUT *LOOKS.*
IT'S HOW YOU TALK, MOVE, STAND ...
YOU MUST HAVE ABUNDANT KNOWLEDGE, EXCES-SIVE LOVE, OVERFLOWING ELEGANCE...
YOU MUST MASTER THE ART OF EXPRESSING YOURSELF.
FWAP
WITH JUST A CASUAL GESTURE LIKE THIS...

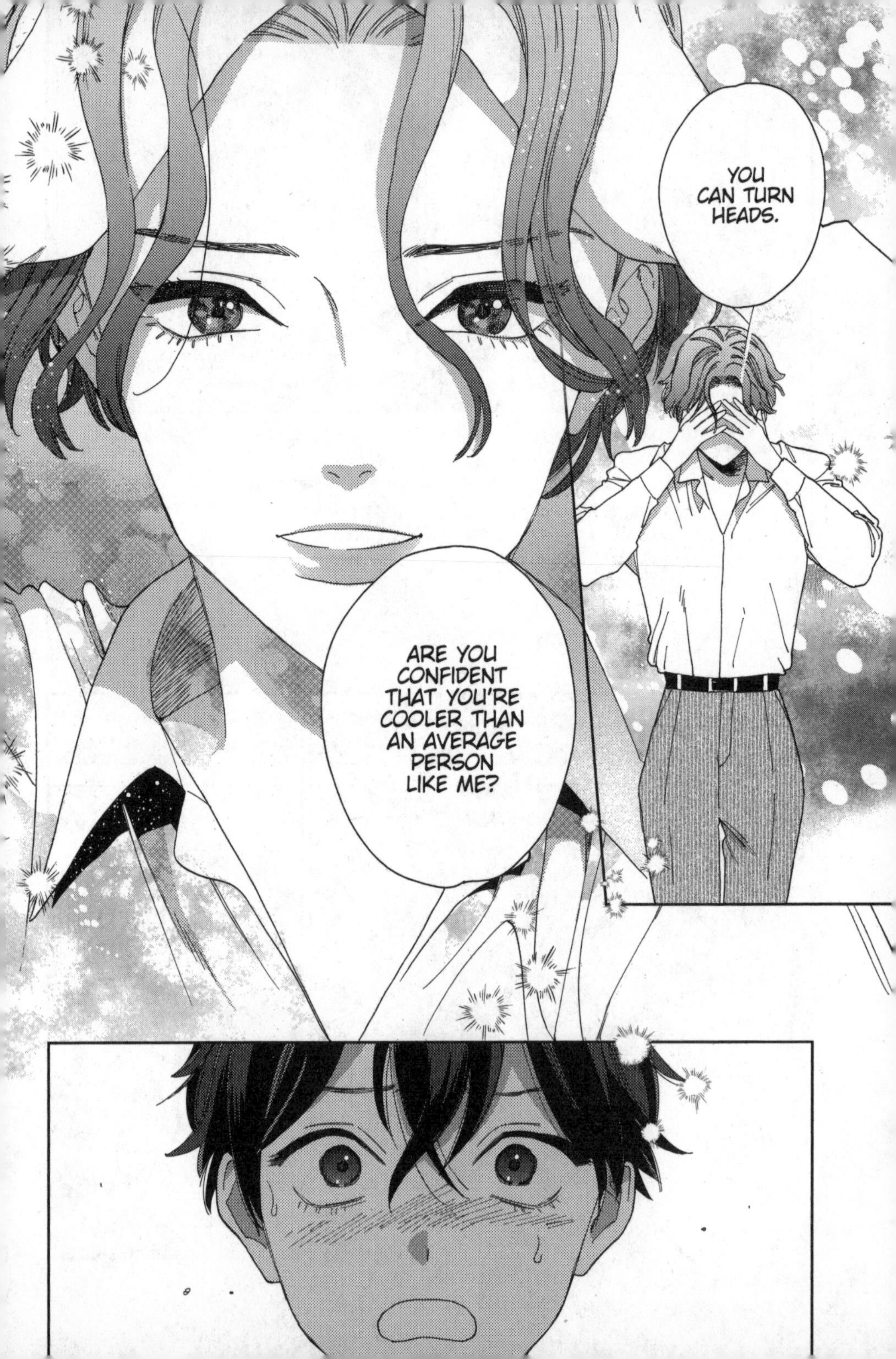
YOU CAN TURN HEADS.
ARE YOU CONFIDENT THAT YOU'RE COOLER THAN AN AVERAGE PERSON LIKE ME?

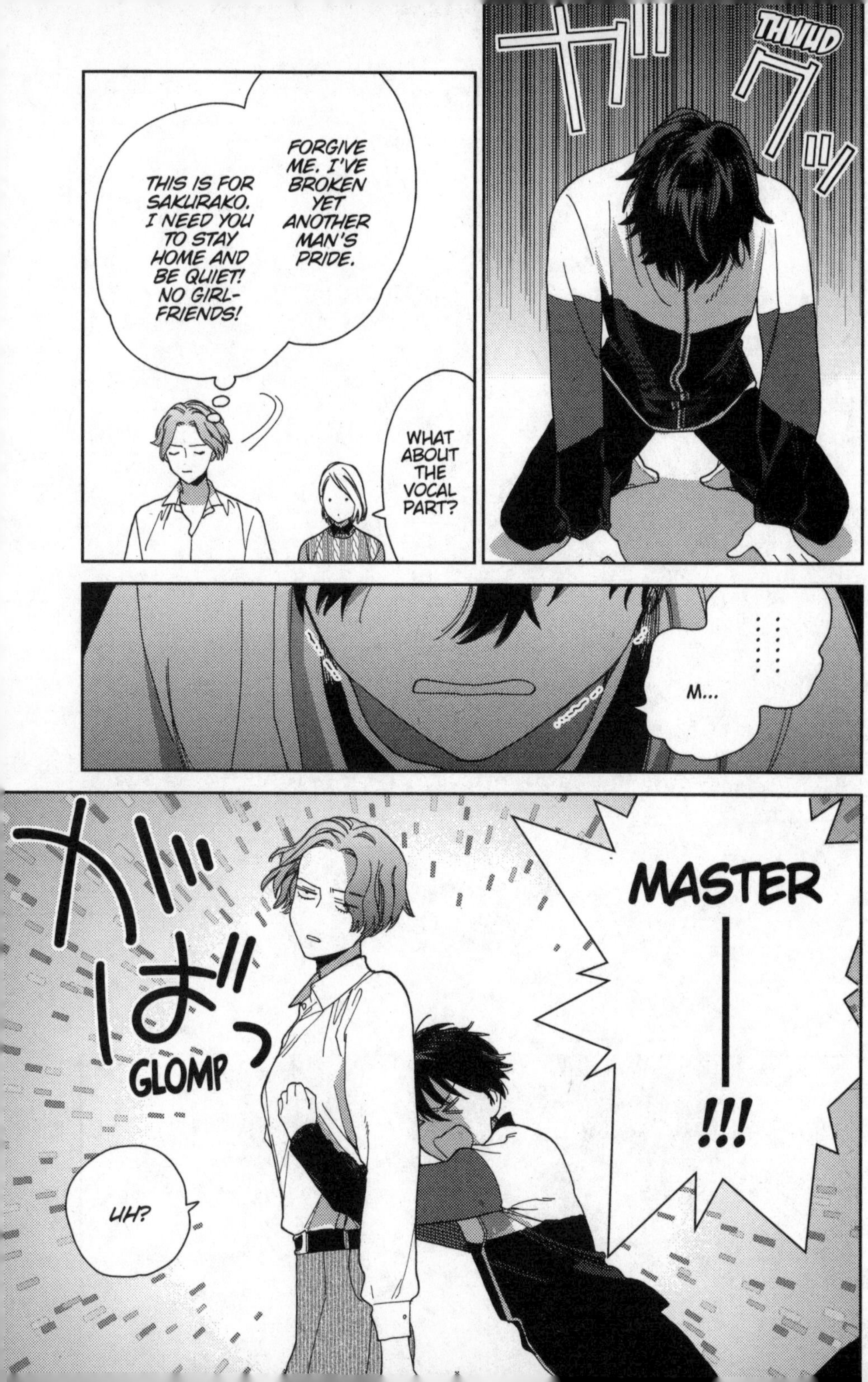
THWUD
FORGIVE ME. I'VE BROKEN YET ANOTHER MAN'S PRIDE.
THIS IS FOR SAKURAKO. I NEED YOU TO STAY HOME AND BE QUIET! NO GIRL-FRIENDS!
WHAT ABOUT THE VOCAL PART?
......
M...
MASTER—!!!
GLOMP
UH?

The Twenty-Fifth One

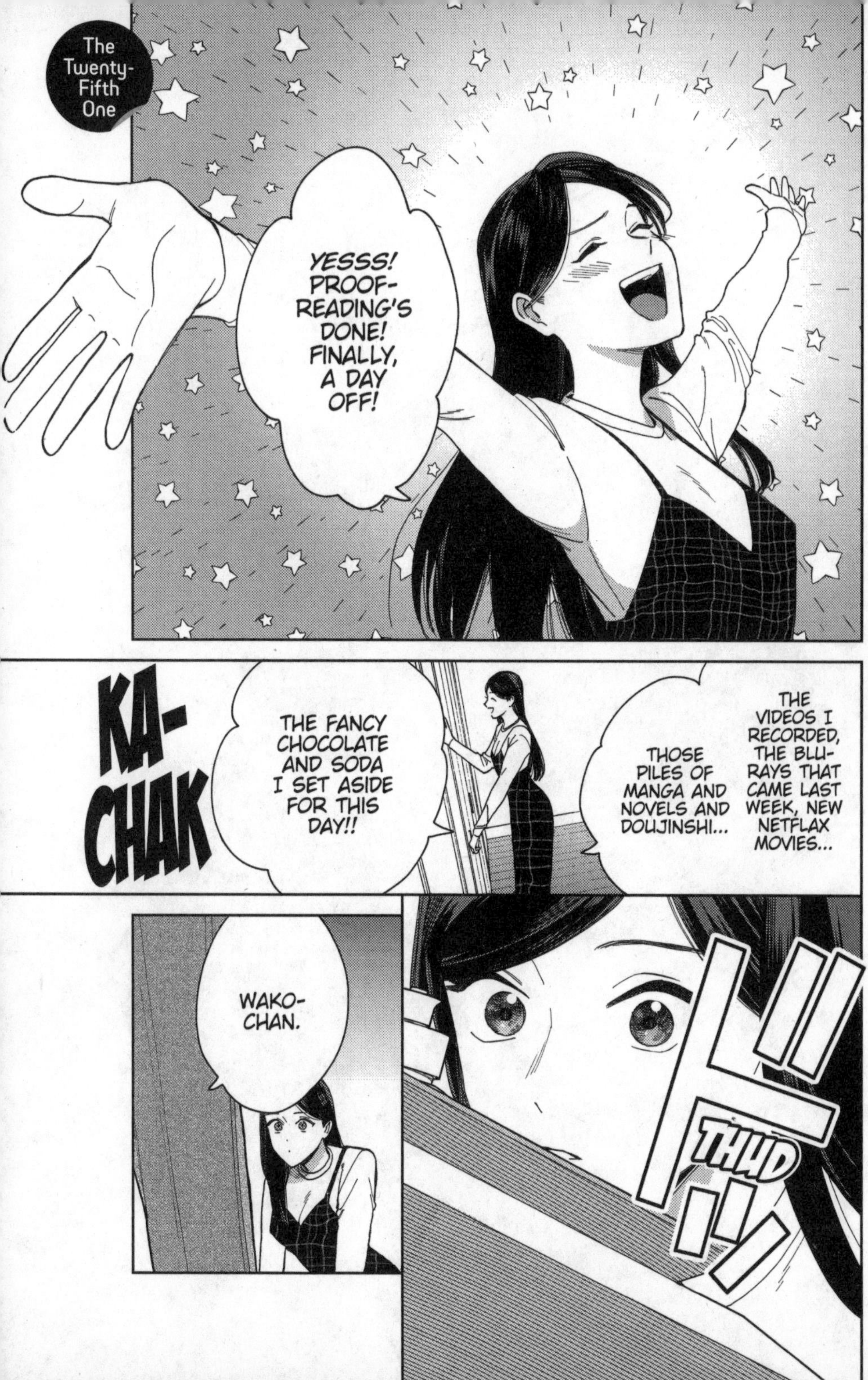
YESSS! PROOF-READING'S DONE! FINALLY, A DAY OFF!
THE VIDEOS I RECORDED, THE BLU-RAYS THAT CAME LAST WEEK, NEW NETFLAX MOVIES...
THOSE PILES OF MANGA AND NOVELS AND DOUJINSHI...
THE FANCY CHOCOLATE AND SODA I SET ASIDE FOR THIS DAY!!
KA-CHAK
THUD
!!
WAKO-CHAN.

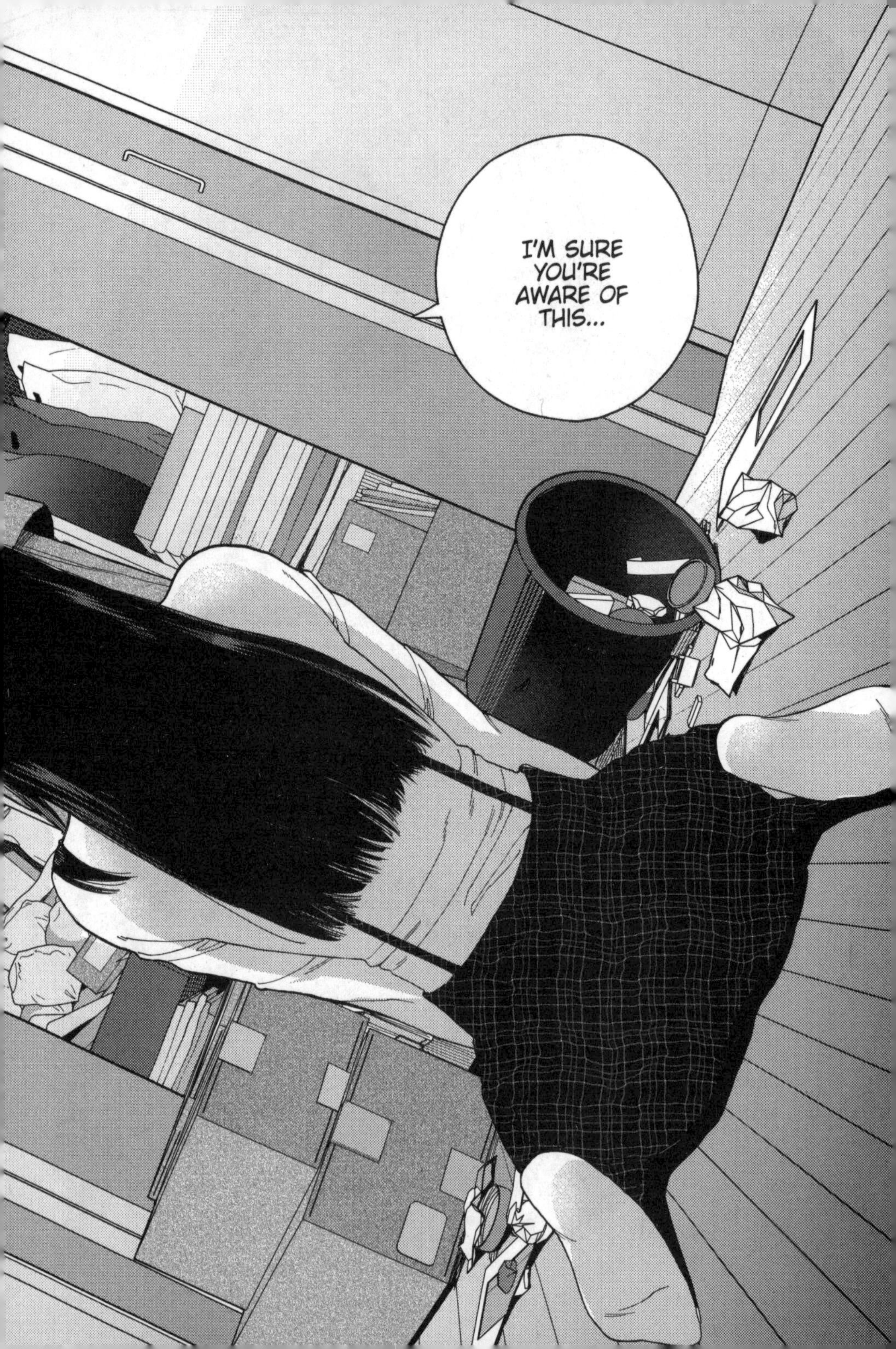
I'M SURE YOU'RE AWARE OF THIS...

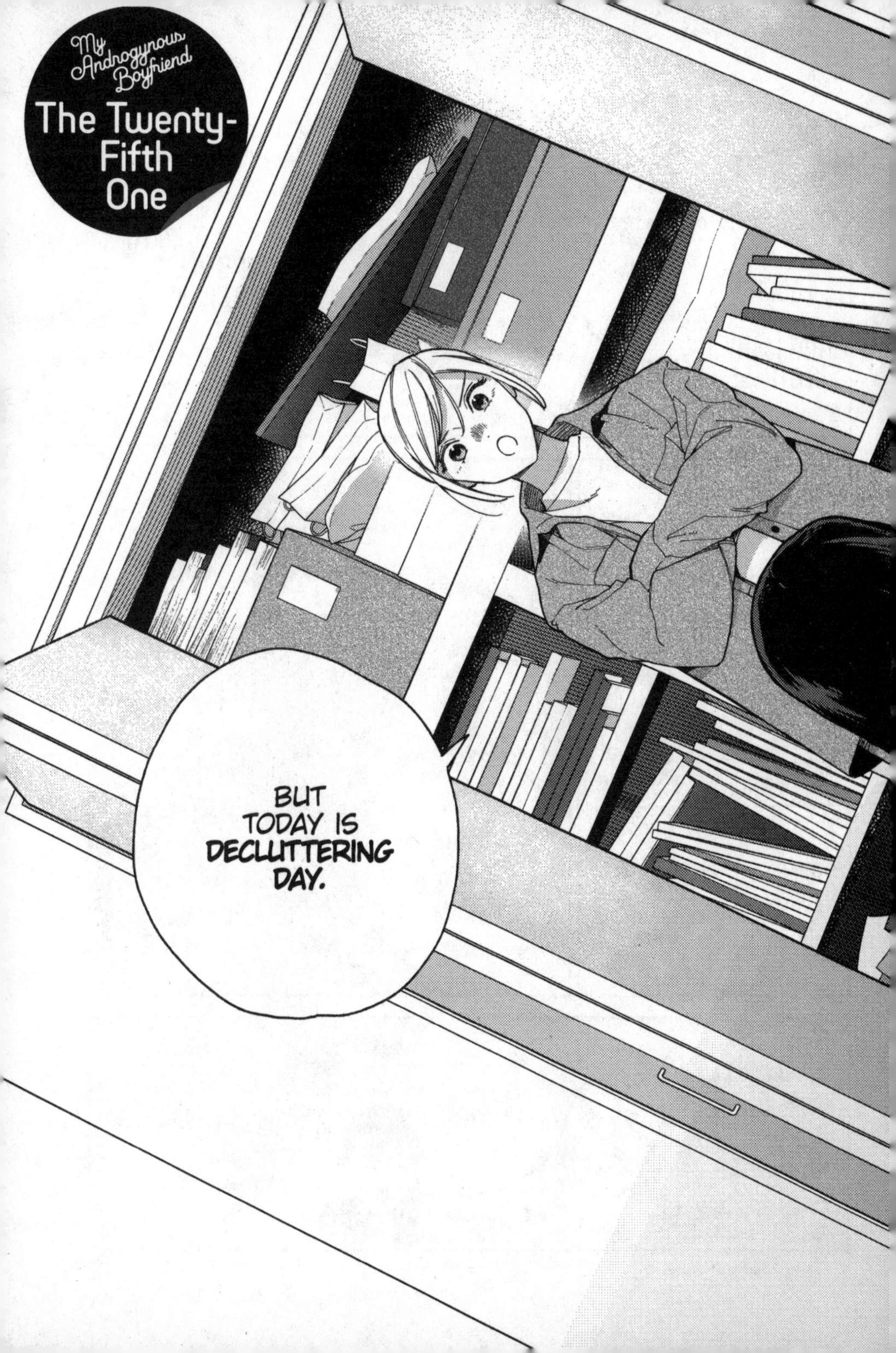
My Androgynous Boyfriend
The Twenty-Fifth One
BUT TODAY IS DECLUTTERING DAY.

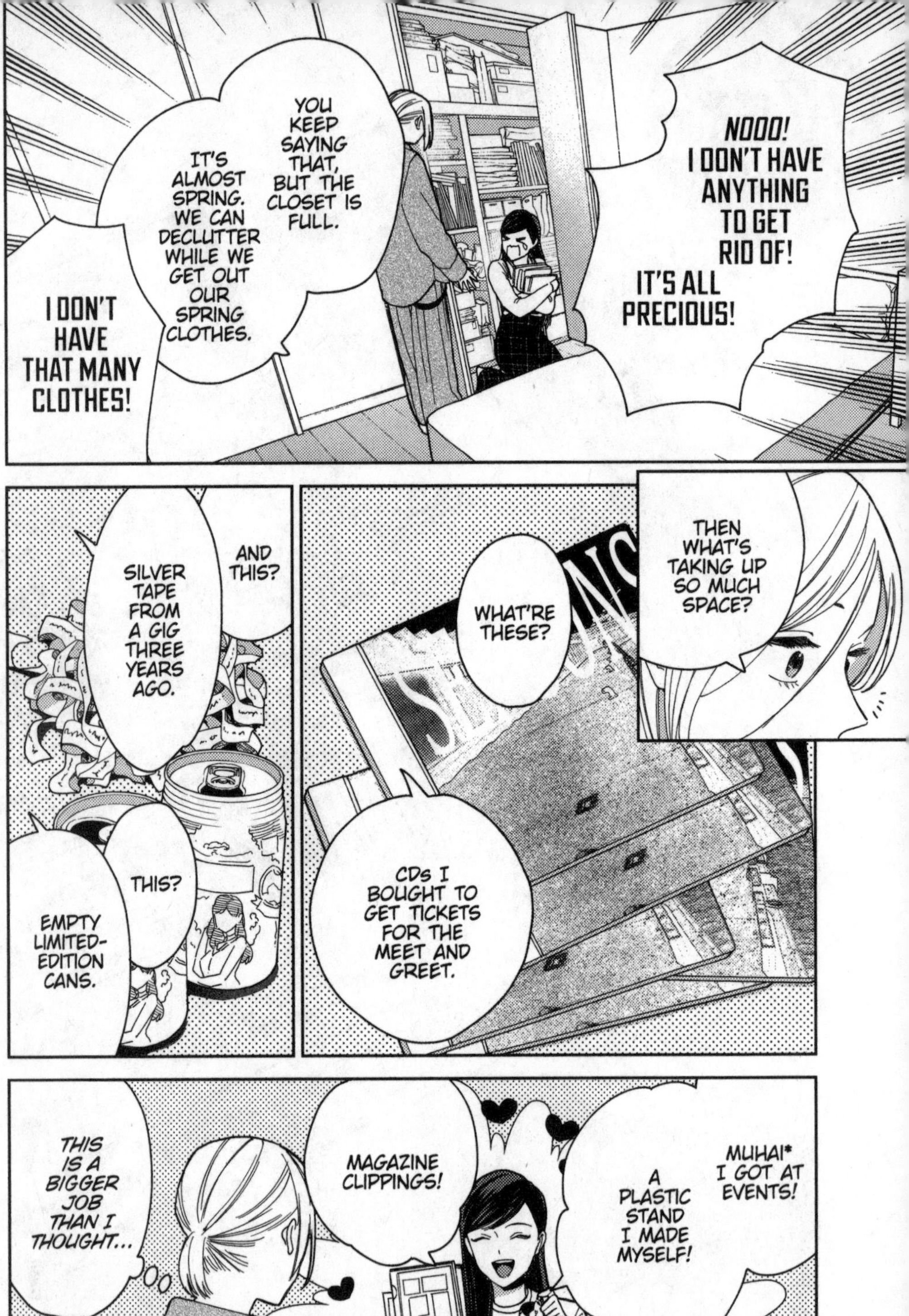
NOOO! I DON'T HAVE ANYTHING TO GET RID OF!
IT'S ALL PRECIOUS!
YOU KEEP SAYING THAT, BUT THE CLOSET IS FULL.
IT'S ALMOST SPRING. WE CAN DECLUTTER WHILE WE GET OUT OUR SPRING CLOTHES.
I DON'T HAVE THAT MANY CLOTHES!
THEN WHAT'S TAKING UP SO MUCH SPACE?
WHAT'RE THESE?
CDs I BOUGHT TO GET TICKETS FOR THE MEET AND GREET.
AND THIS?
SILVER TAPE FROM A GIG THREE YEARS AGO.
THIS?
EMPTY LIMITED-EDITION CANS.
MUHAI* I GOT AT EVENTS!
A PLASTIC STAND I MADE MYSELF!
MAGAZINE CLIPPINGS!
THIS IS A BIGGER JOB THAN I THOUGHT...

*Free merchandise and pamphlets.

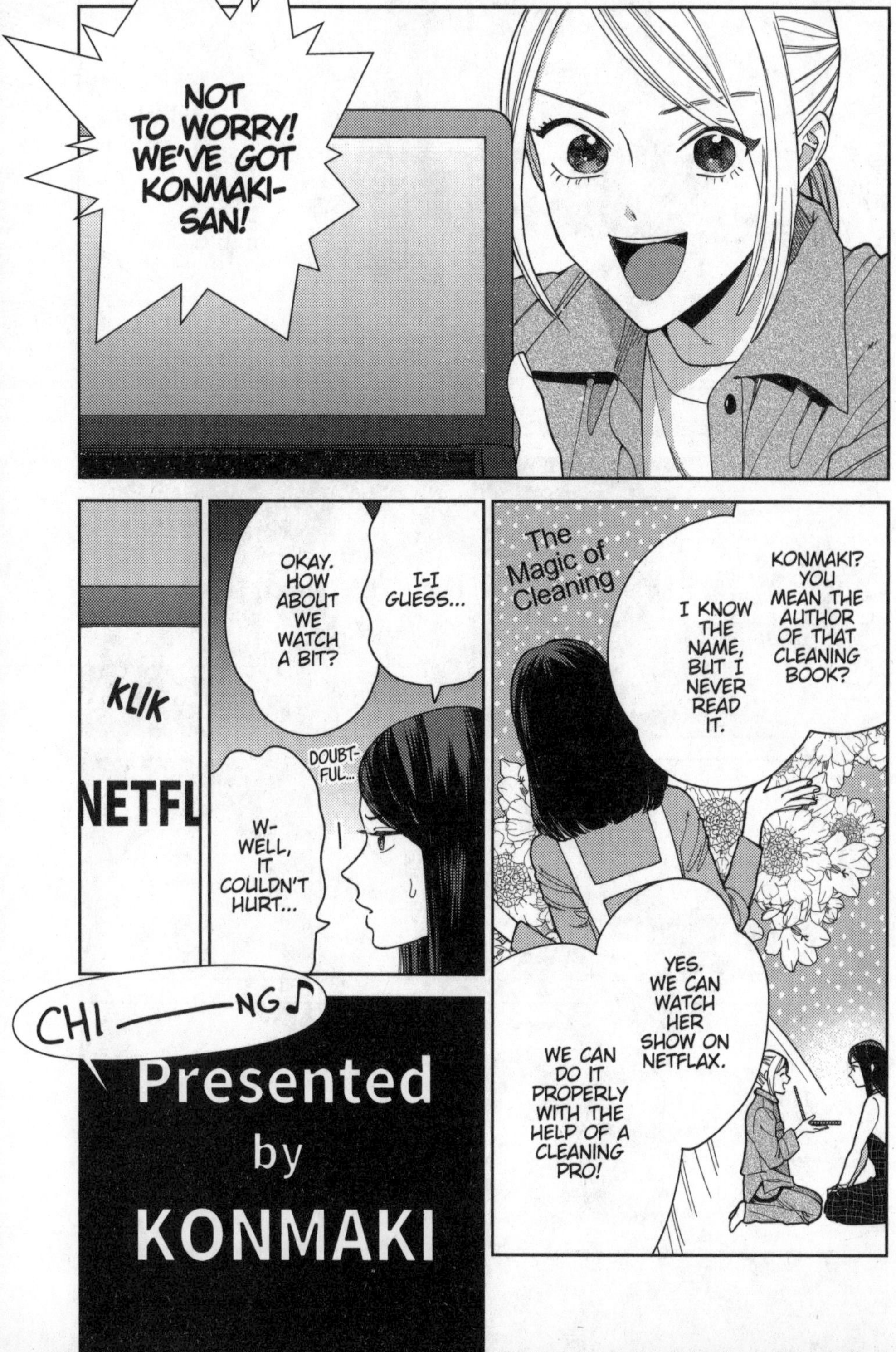
NOT TO WORRY! WE'VE GOT KONMAKI-SAN!
The Magic of Cleaning
KONMAKI? YOU MEAN THE AUTHOR OF THAT CLEANING BOOK?
I KNOW THE NAME, BUT I NEVER READ IT.
YES. WE CAN WATCH HER SHOW ON NETFLAX.
WE CAN DO IT PROPERLY WITH THE HELP OF A CLEANING PRO!
I-I GUESS...
OKAY. HOW ABOUT WE WATCH A BIT?
DOUBTFUL...
W-WELL, IT COULDN'T HURT...
KLIK
NETFL
CHI——NG♪
Presented by KONMAKI

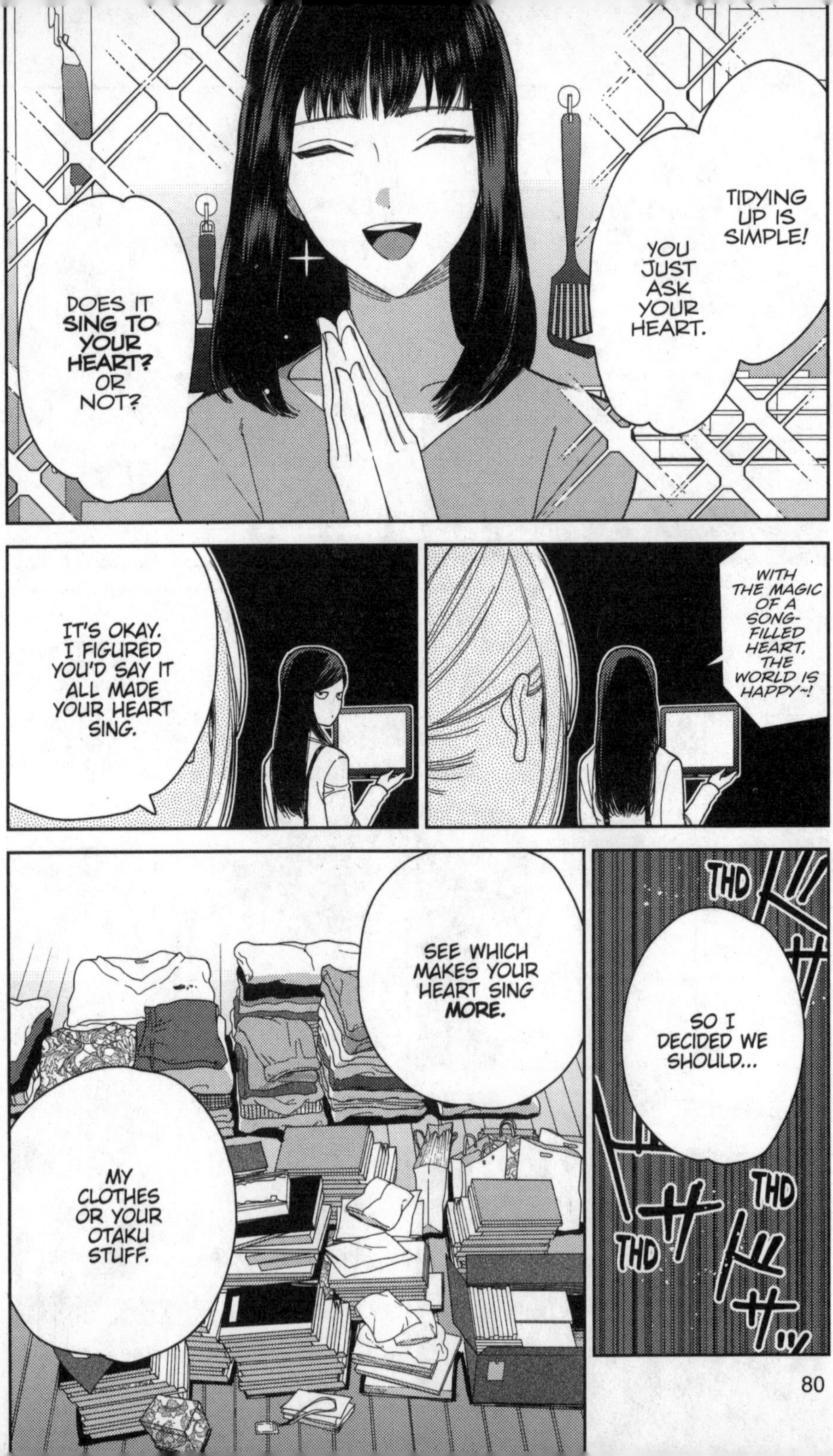
TIDYING UP IS SIMPLE!
YOU JUST ASK YOUR HEART.
DOES IT SING TO YOUR HEART? OR NOT?
WITH THE MAGIC OF A SONG-FILLED HEART, THE WORLD IS HAPPY~!
IT'S OKAY. I FIGURED YOU'D SAY IT ALL MADE YOUR HEART SING.
THD
SO I DECIDED WE SHOULD...
THD
THD
SEE WHICH MAKES YOUR HEART SING MORE.
MY CLOTHES OR YOUR OTAKU STUFF.

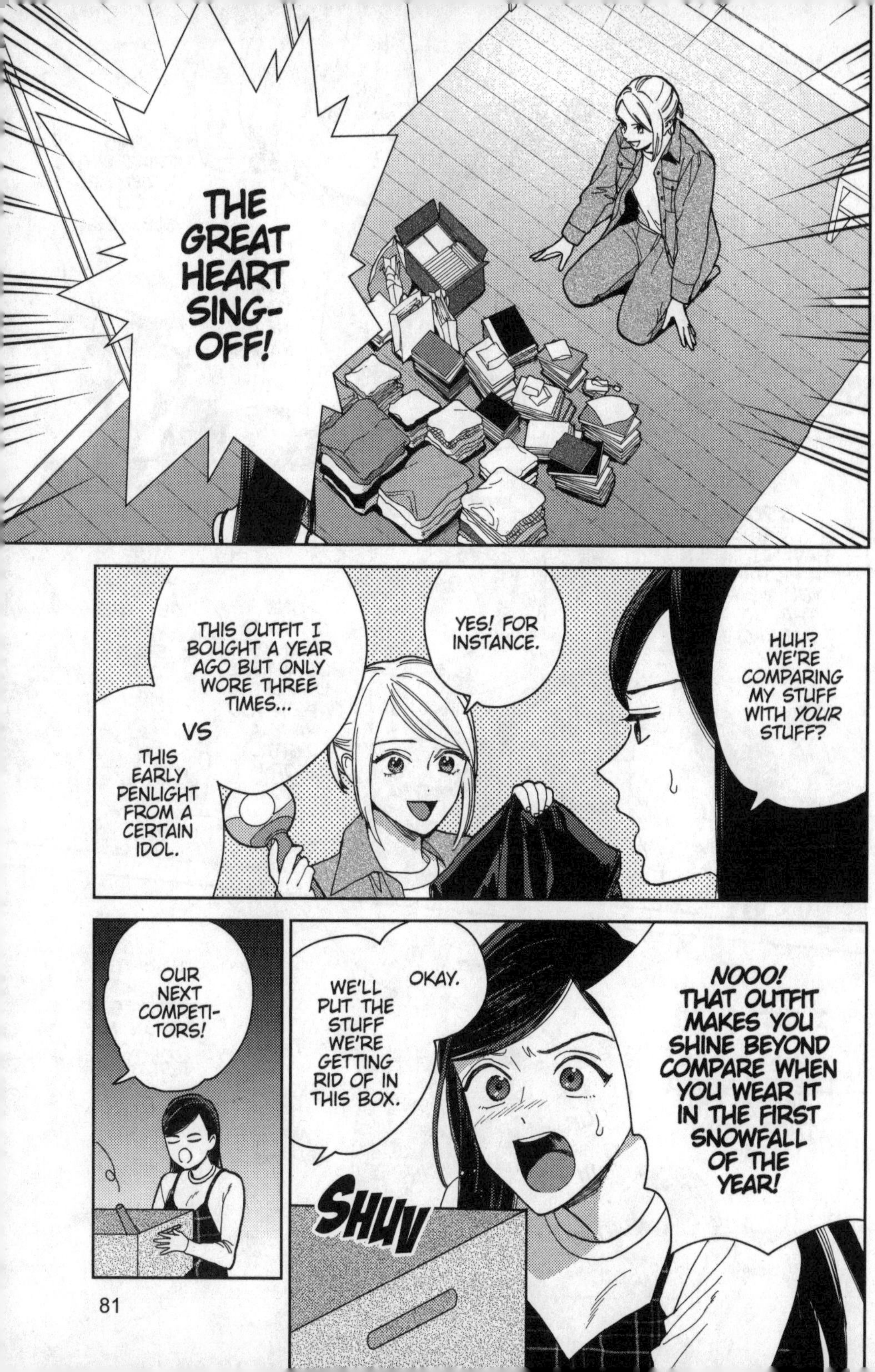
THE GREAT HEART SING-OFF!
HUH? WE'RE COMPARING MY STUFF WITH *YOUR* STUFF?
YES! FOR INSTANCE.
THIS OUTFIT I BOUGHT A YEAR AGO BUT ONLY WORE THREE TIMES...
VS
THIS EARLY PENLIGHT FROM A CERTAIN IDOL.
NOOO! THAT OUTFIT MAKES YOU SHINE BEYOND COMPARE WHEN YOU WEAR IT IN THE FIRST SNOWFALL OF THE YEAR!
OKAY.
WE'LL PUT THE STUFF WE'RE GETTING RID OF IN THIS BOX.
SHUV
OUR NEXT COMPETI-TORS!

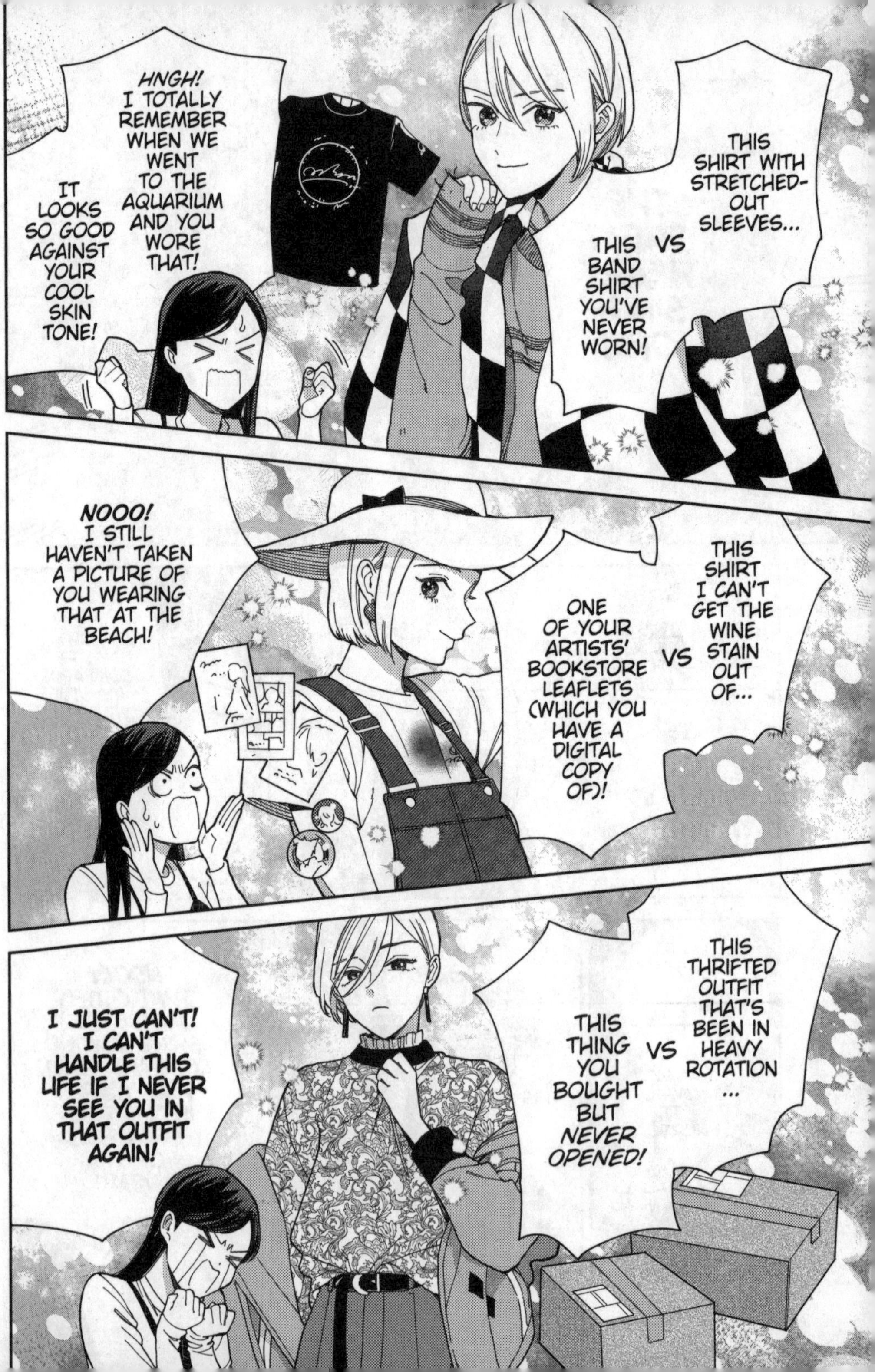
THIS SHIRT WITH STRETCHED-OUT SLEEVES... VS THIS BAND SHIRT YOU'VE NEVER WORN!
HNGH! I TOTALLY REMEMBER WHEN WE WENT TO THE AQUARIUM AND YOU WORE THAT!
IT LOOKS SO GOOD AGAINST YOUR COOL SKIN TONE!
THIS SHIRT I CAN'T GET THE WINE STAIN OUT OF... VS ONE OF YOUR ARTISTS' BOOKSTORE LEAFLETS (WHICH YOU HAVE A DIGITAL COPY OF)!
NOOO! I STILL HAVEN'T TAKEN A PICTURE OF YOU WEARING THAT AT THE BEACH!
THIS THRIFTED OUTFIT THAT'S BEEN IN HEAVY ROTATION... VS THIS THING YOU BOUGHT BUT NEVER OPENED!
I JUST CAN'T! I CAN'T HANDLE THIS LIFE IF I NEVER SEE YOU IN THAT OUTFIT AGAIN!

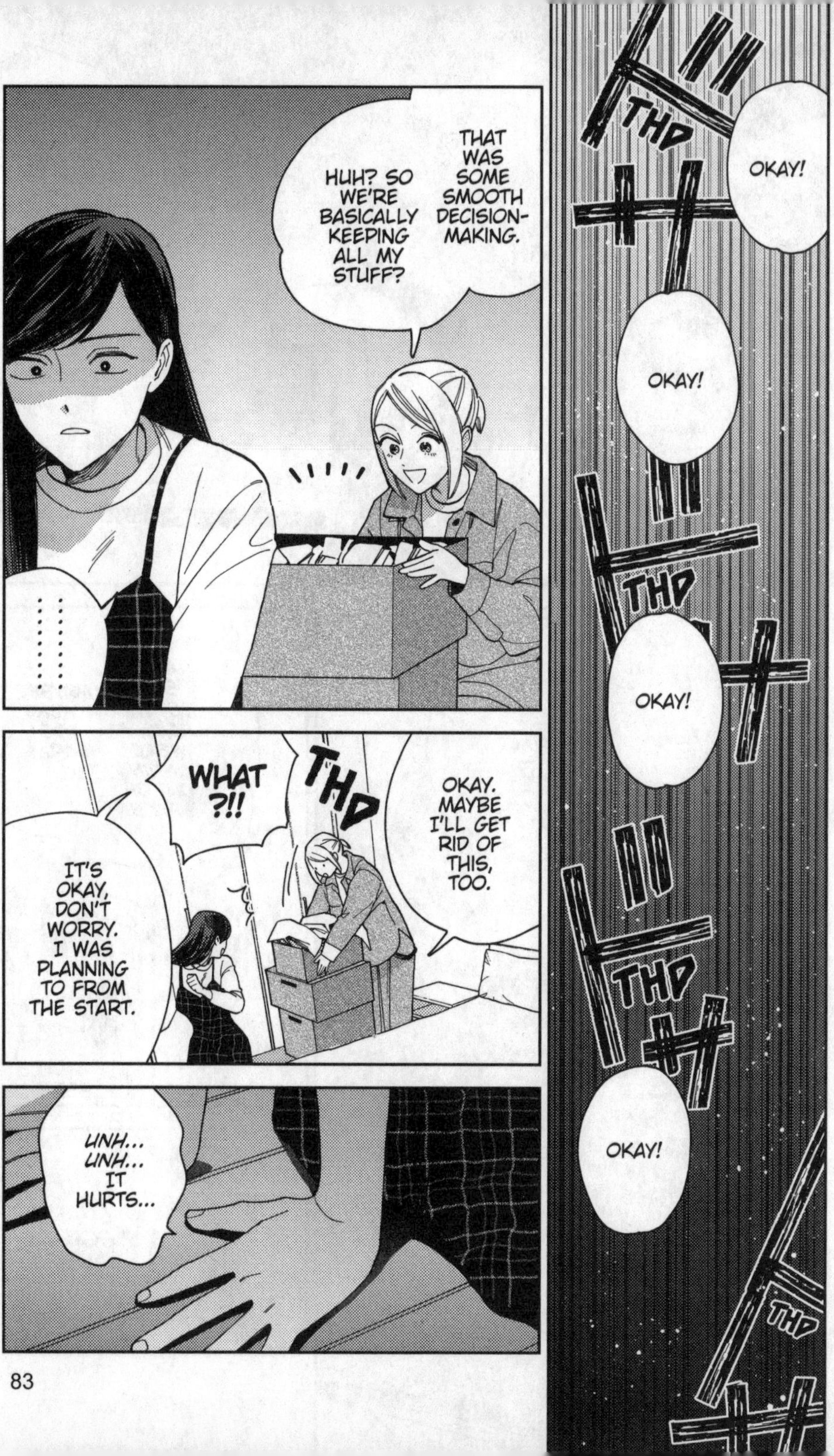
THD
OKAY!
OKAY!
THD
OKAY!
THD
OKAY!
THD
THAT WAS SOME SMOOTH DECISION-MAKING.
HUH? SO WE'RE BASICALLY KEEPING ALL MY STUFF?
......
OKAY. MAYBE I'LL GET RID OF THIS, TOO.
THD
WHAT?!!
IT'S OKAY, DON'T WORRY. I WAS PLANNING TO FROM THE START.
UNH... UNH... IT HURTS...

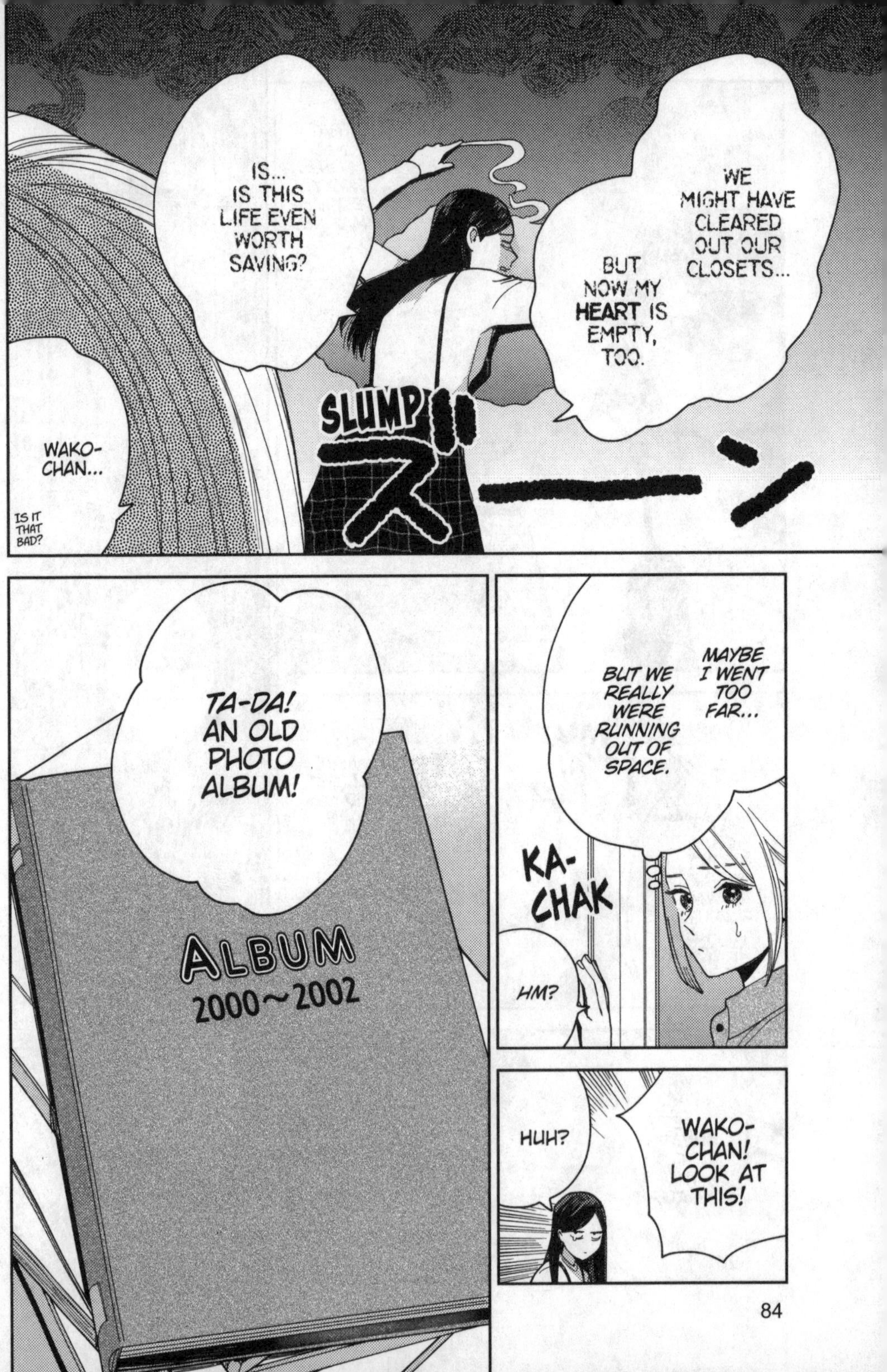
WE MIGHT HAVE CLEARED OUT OUR CLOSETS...
BUT NOW MY HEART IS EMPTY, TOO.
IS... IS THIS LIFE EVEN WORTH SAVING?
SLUMP
WAKO-CHAN...
IS IT THAT BAD?
MAYBE I WENT TOO FAR...
BUT WE REALLY WERE RUNNING OUT OF SPACE.
KA-CHAK
HM?
WAKO-CHAN! LOOK AT THIS!
HUH?
TA-DA! AN OLD PHOTO ALBUM!
ALBUM
2000~2002

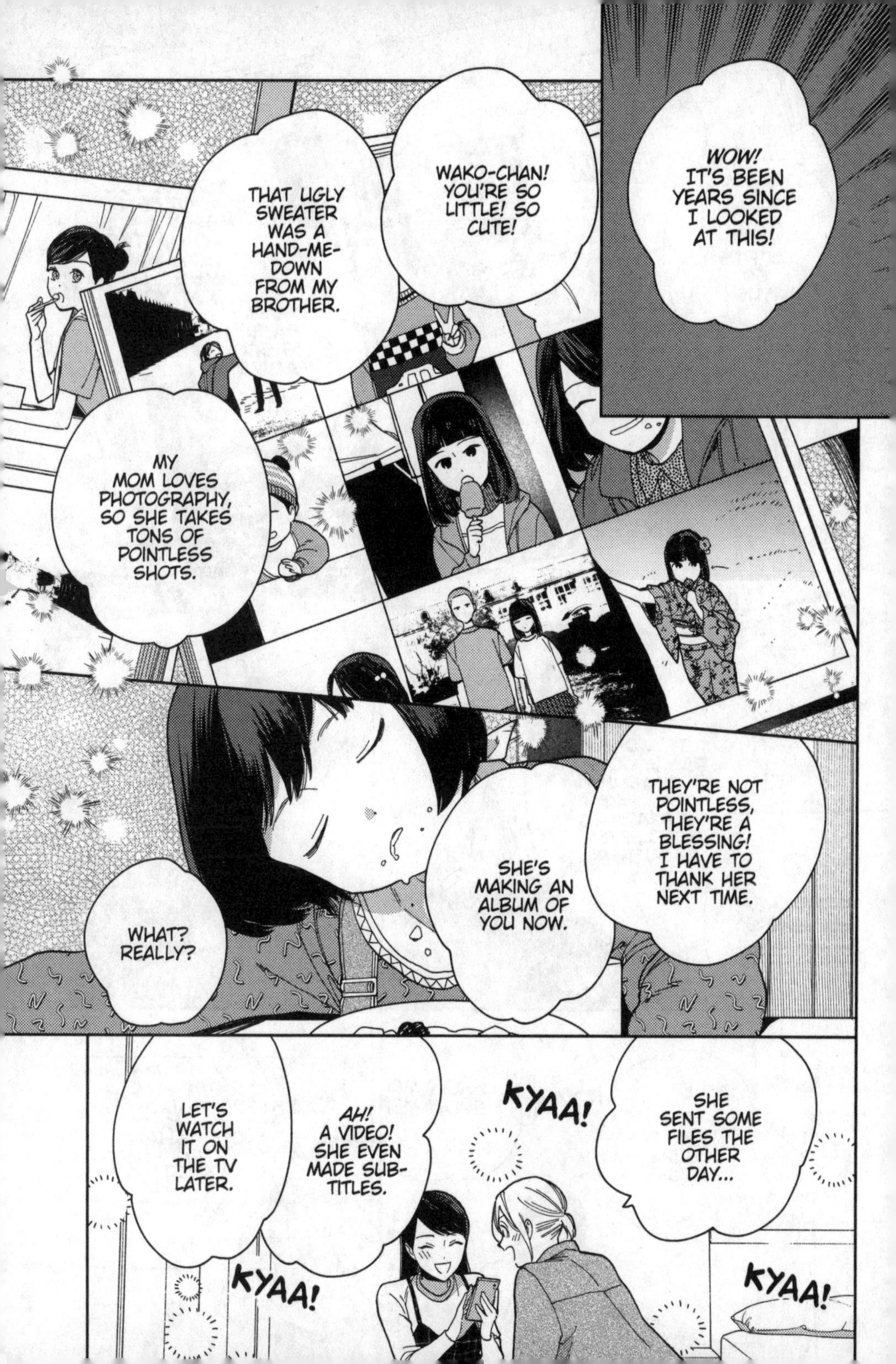
WOW! IT'S BEEN YEARS SINCE I LOOKED AT THIS!
WAKO-CHAN! YOU'RE SO LITTLE! SO CUTE!
THAT UGLY SWEATER WAS A HAND-ME-DOWN FROM MY BROTHER.
MY MOM LOVES PHOTOGRAPHY, SO SHE TAKES TONS OF POINTLESS SHOTS.
THEY'RE NOT POINTLESS, THEY'RE A BLESSING! I HAVE TO THANK HER NEXT TIME.
SHE'S MAKING AN ALBUM OF YOU NOW.
WHAT? REALLY?
SHE SENT SOME FILES THE OTHER DAY...
KYAA!
KYAA!
AH! A VIDEO! SHE EVEN MADE SUB-TITLES.
KYAA!
LET'S WATCH IT ON THE TV LATER.

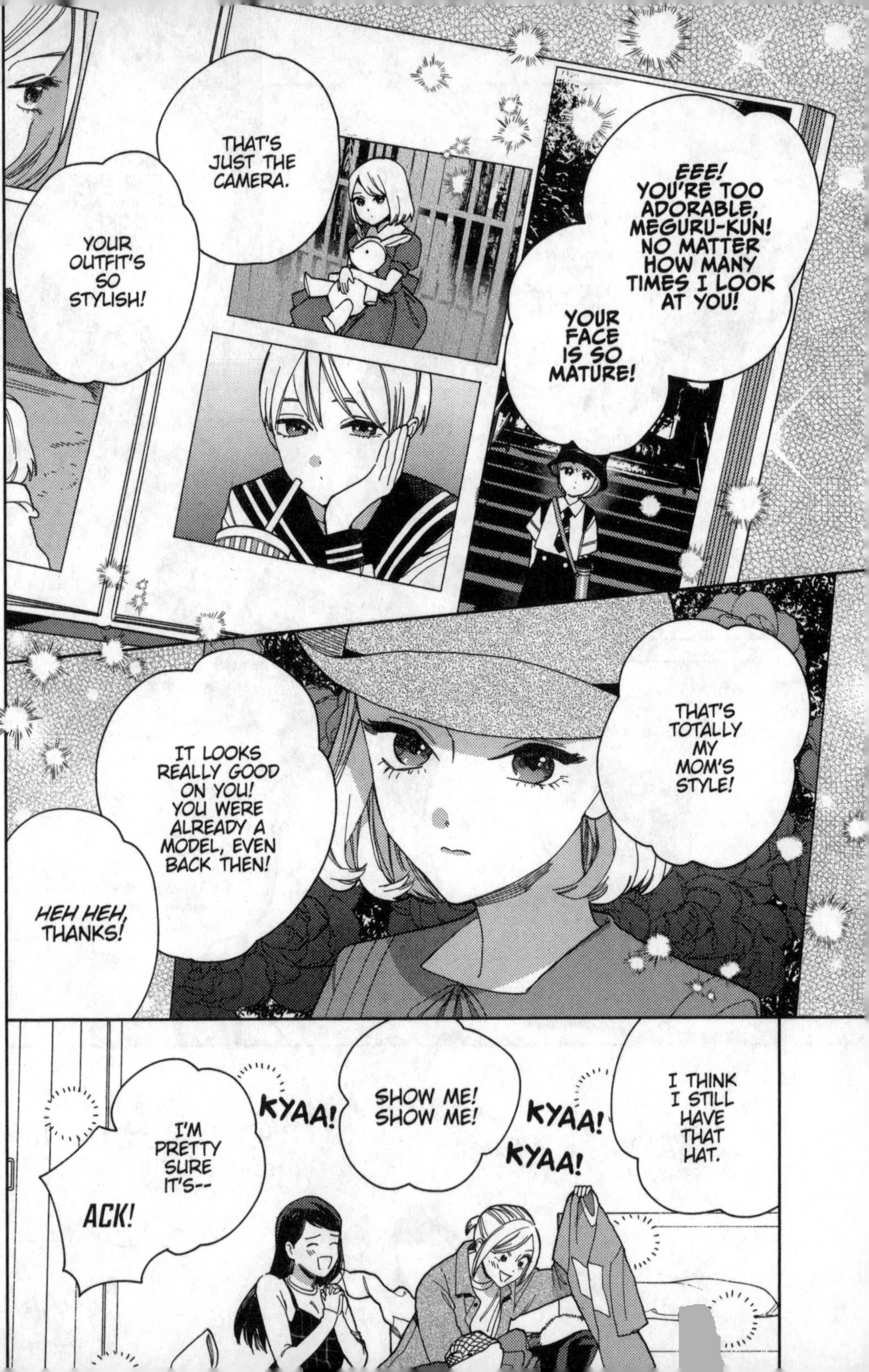
EEE! YOU'RE TOO ADORABLE, MEGURU-KUN! NO MATTER HOW MANY TIMES I LOOK AT YOU!
YOUR FACE IS SO MATURE!
THAT'S JUST THE CAMERA.
YOUR OUTFIT'S SO STYLISH!
THAT'S TOTALLY MY MOM'S STYLE!
IT LOOKS REALLY GOOD ON YOU! YOU WERE ALREADY A MODEL, EVEN BACK THEN!
HEH HEH, THANKS!
I THINK I STILL HAVE THAT HAT.
KYAA!
KYAA!
SHOW ME! SHOW ME!
KYAA!
I'M PRETTY SURE IT'S--
ACK!

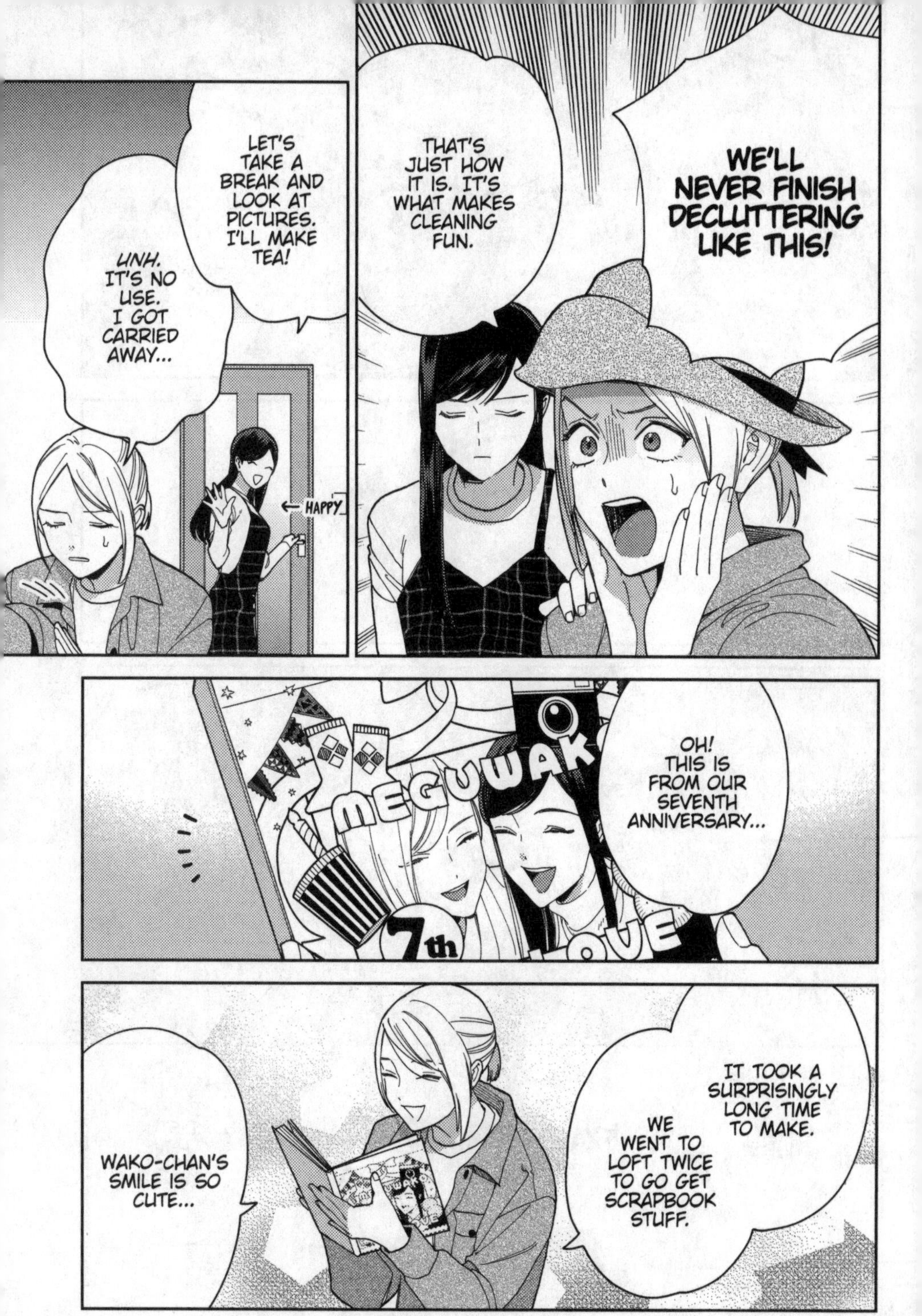
WE'LL NEVER FINISH DECLUTTERING LIKE THIS!
THAT'S JUST HOW IT IS. IT'S WHAT MAKES CLEANING FUN.
LET'S TAKE A BREAK AND LOOK AT PICTURES. I'LL MAKE TEA!
UNH. IT'S NO USE. I GOT CARRIED AWAY...
← HAPPY
OH! THIS IS FROM OUR SEVENTH ANNIVERSARY...
7th
IT TOOK A SURPRISINGLY LONG TIME TO MAKE.
WE WENT TO LOFT TWICE TO GO GET SCRAPBOOK STUFF.
WAKO-CHAN'S SMILE IS SO CUTE...

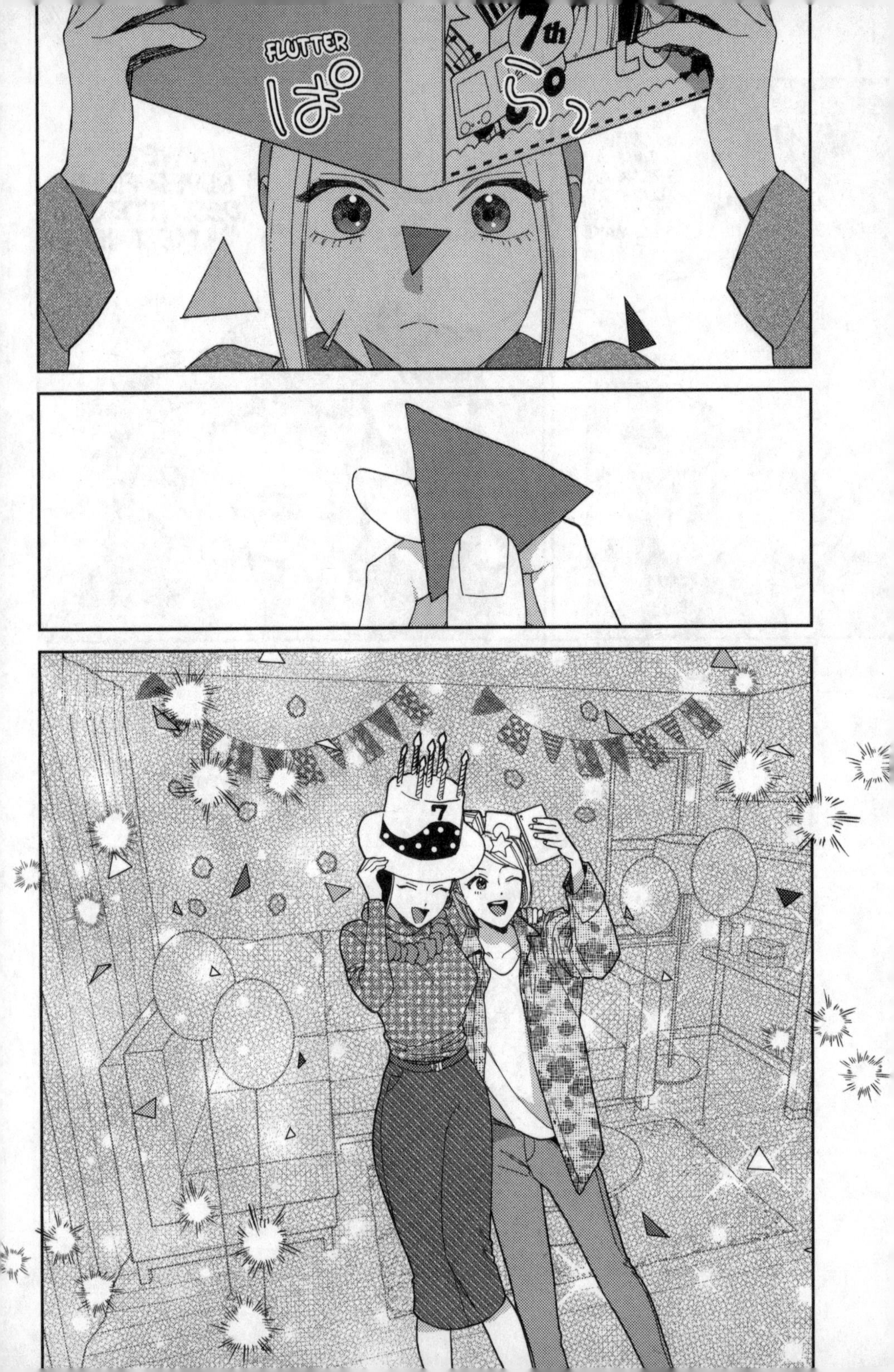
FLUTTER
ぱらっ

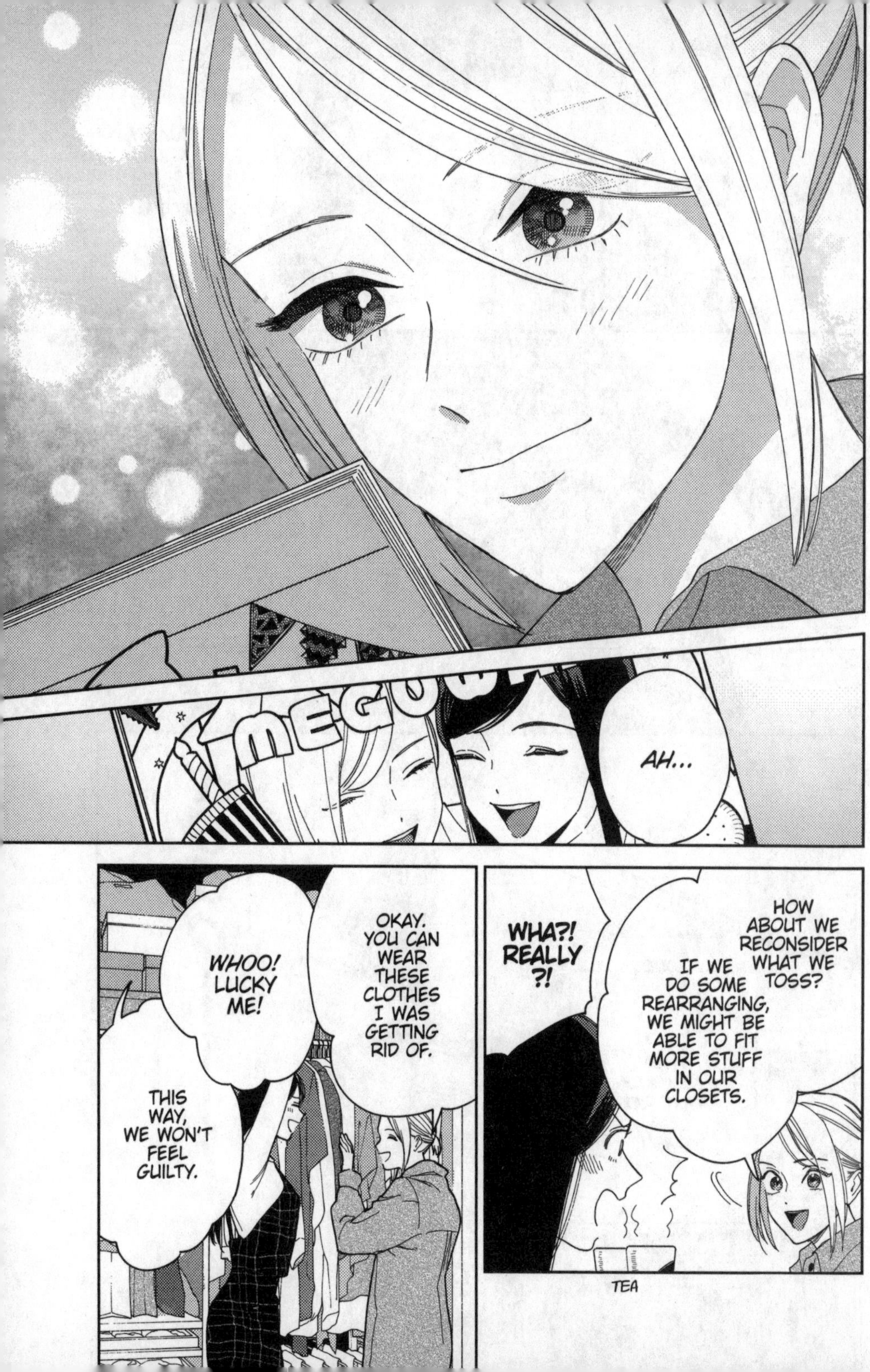
AH...
HOW ABOUT WE RECONSIDER WHAT WE TOSS?
IF WE DO SOME REARRANGING, WE MIGHT BE ABLE TO FIT MORE STUFF IN OUR CLOSETS.
WHA?! REALLY?!
TEA
OKAY. YOU CAN WEAR THESE CLOTHES I WAS GETTING RID OF.
WHOO! LUCKY ME!
THIS WAY, WE WON'T FEEL GUILTY.

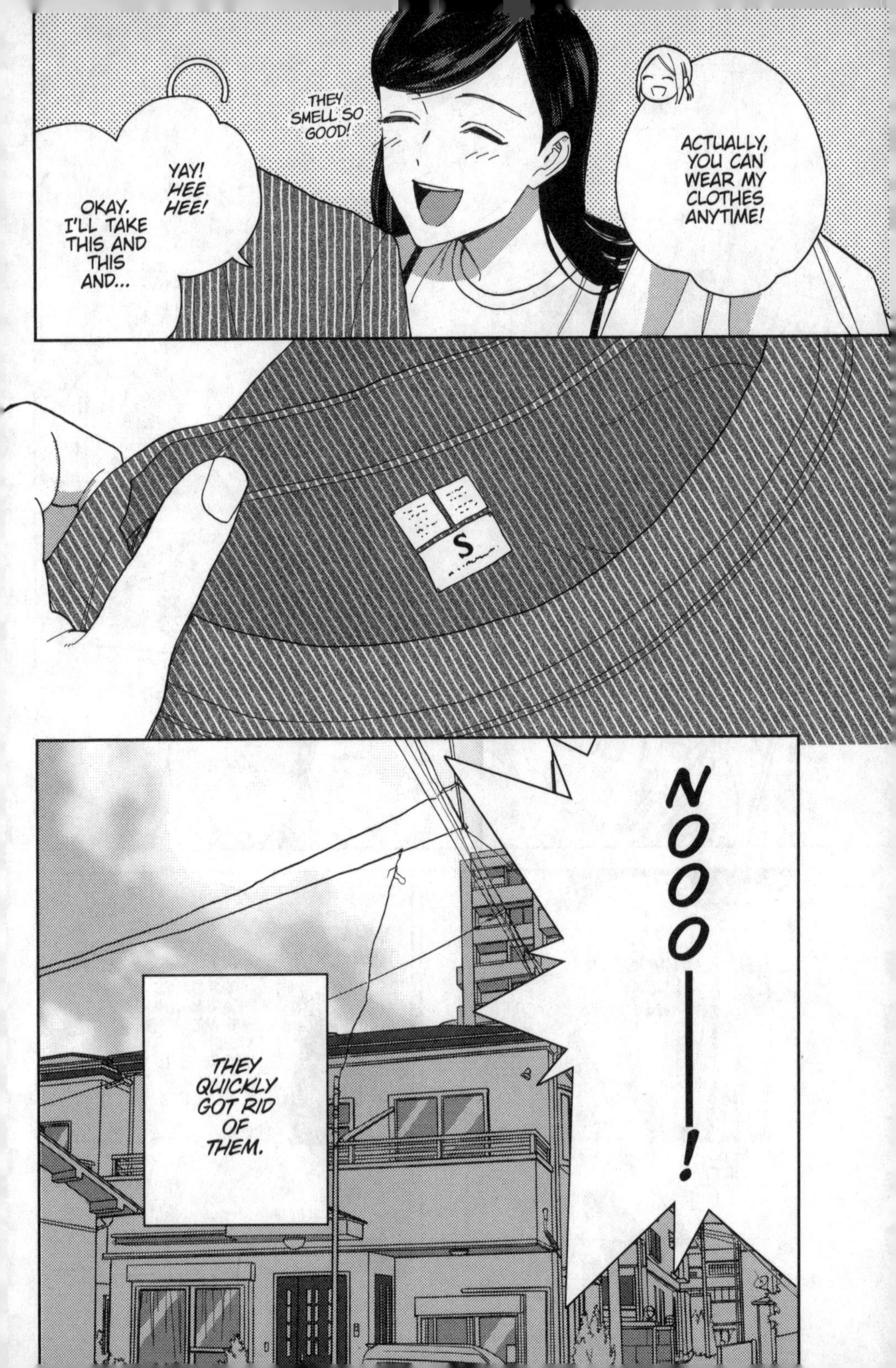
ACTUALLY, YOU CAN WEAR MY CLOTHES ANYTIME!
THEY SMELL SO GOOD!
YAY! HEE HEE!
OKAY. I'LL TAKE THIS AND THIS AND...
S
NOOO——!
THEY QUICKLY GOT RID OF THEM.

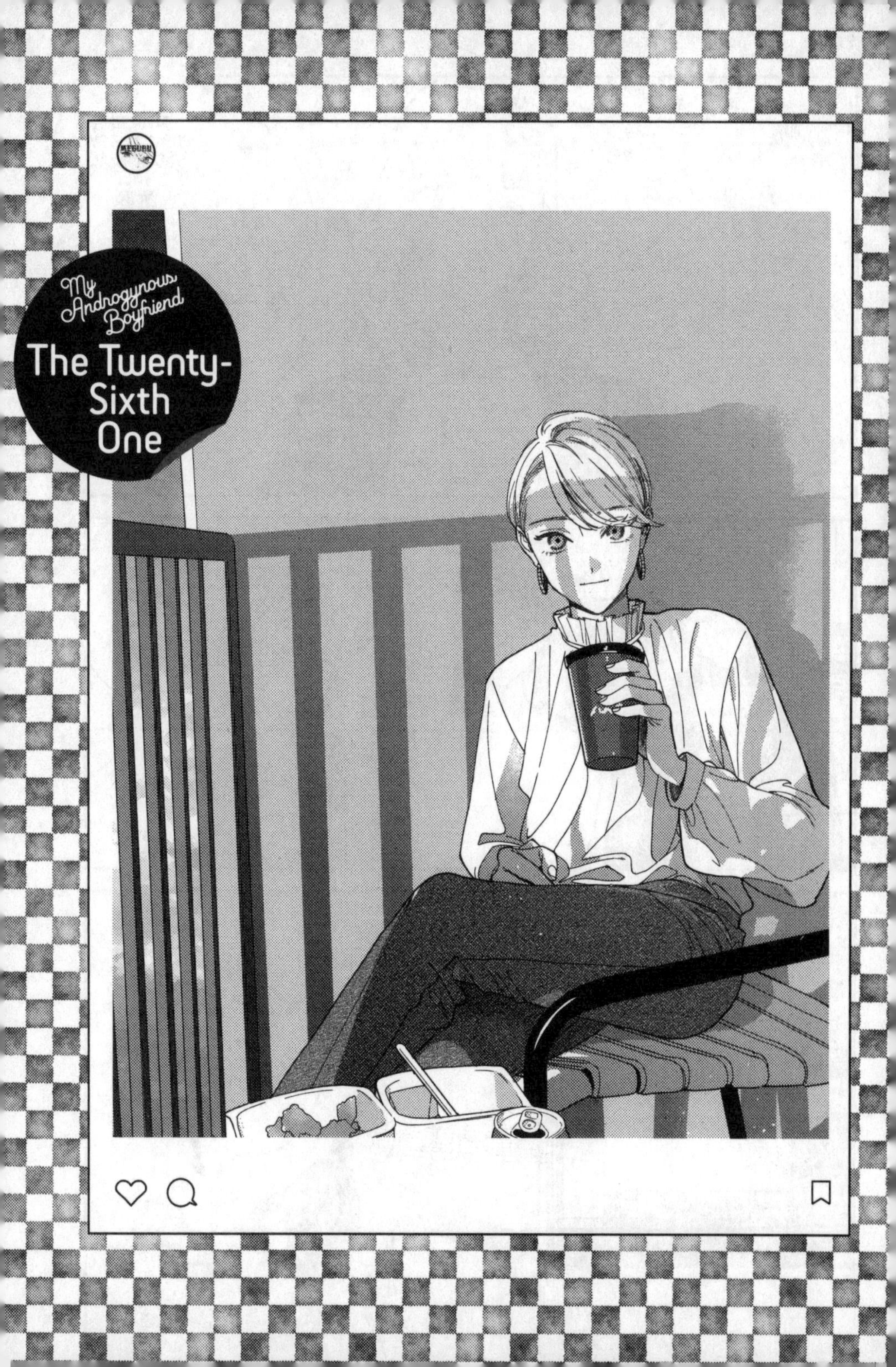
My Androgynous Boyfriend
The Twenty-Sixth One

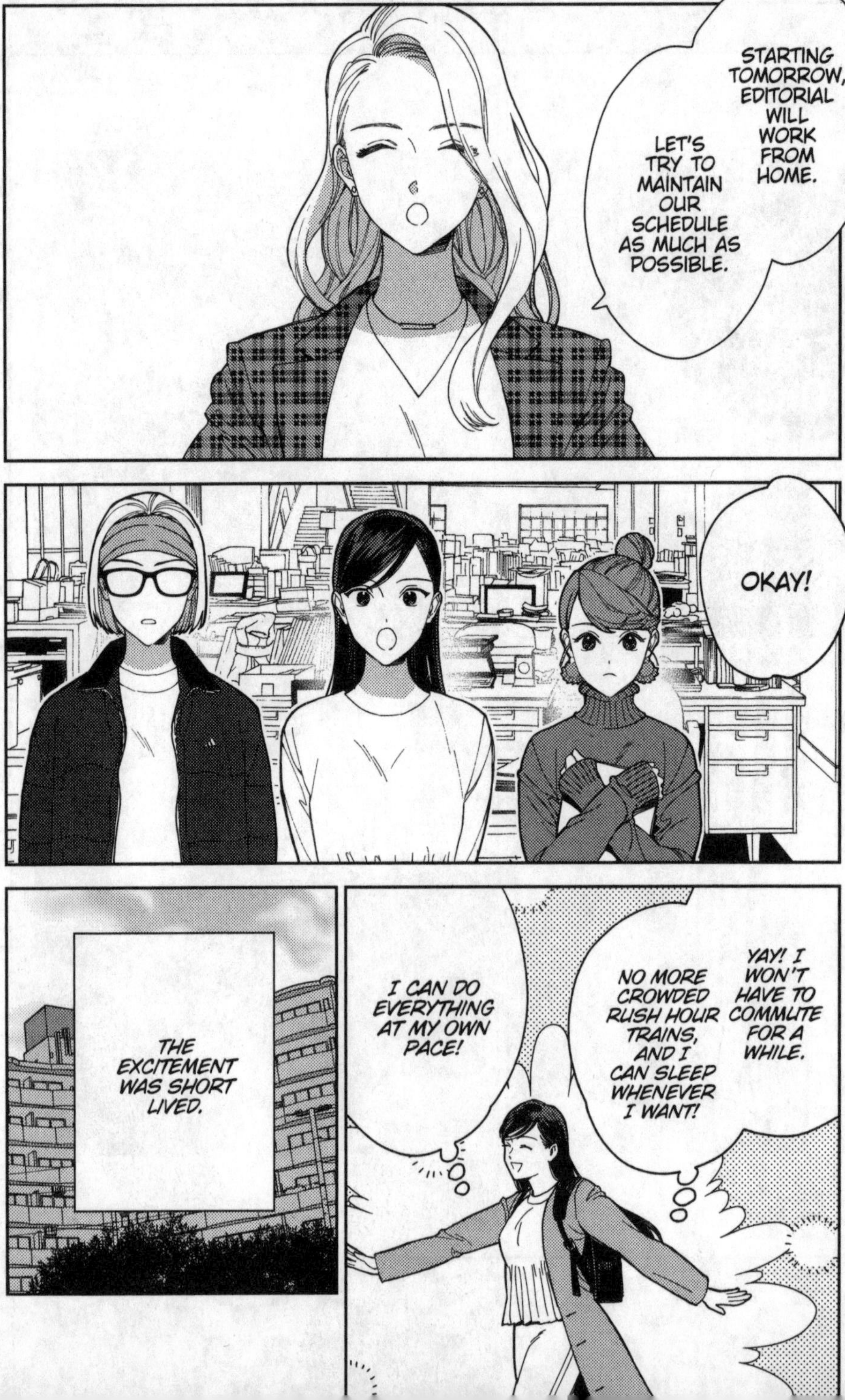
STARTING TOMORROW, EDITORIAL WILL WORK FROM HOME.
LET'S TRY TO MAINTAIN OUR SCHEDULE AS MUCH AS POSSIBLE.
OKAY!
YAY! I WON'T HAVE TO COMMUTE FOR A WHILE.
NO MORE CROWDED RUSH HOUR TRAINS, AND I CAN SLEEP WHENEVER I WANT!
I CAN DO EVERYTHING AT MY OWN PACE!
THE EXCITEMENT WAS SHORT LIVED.

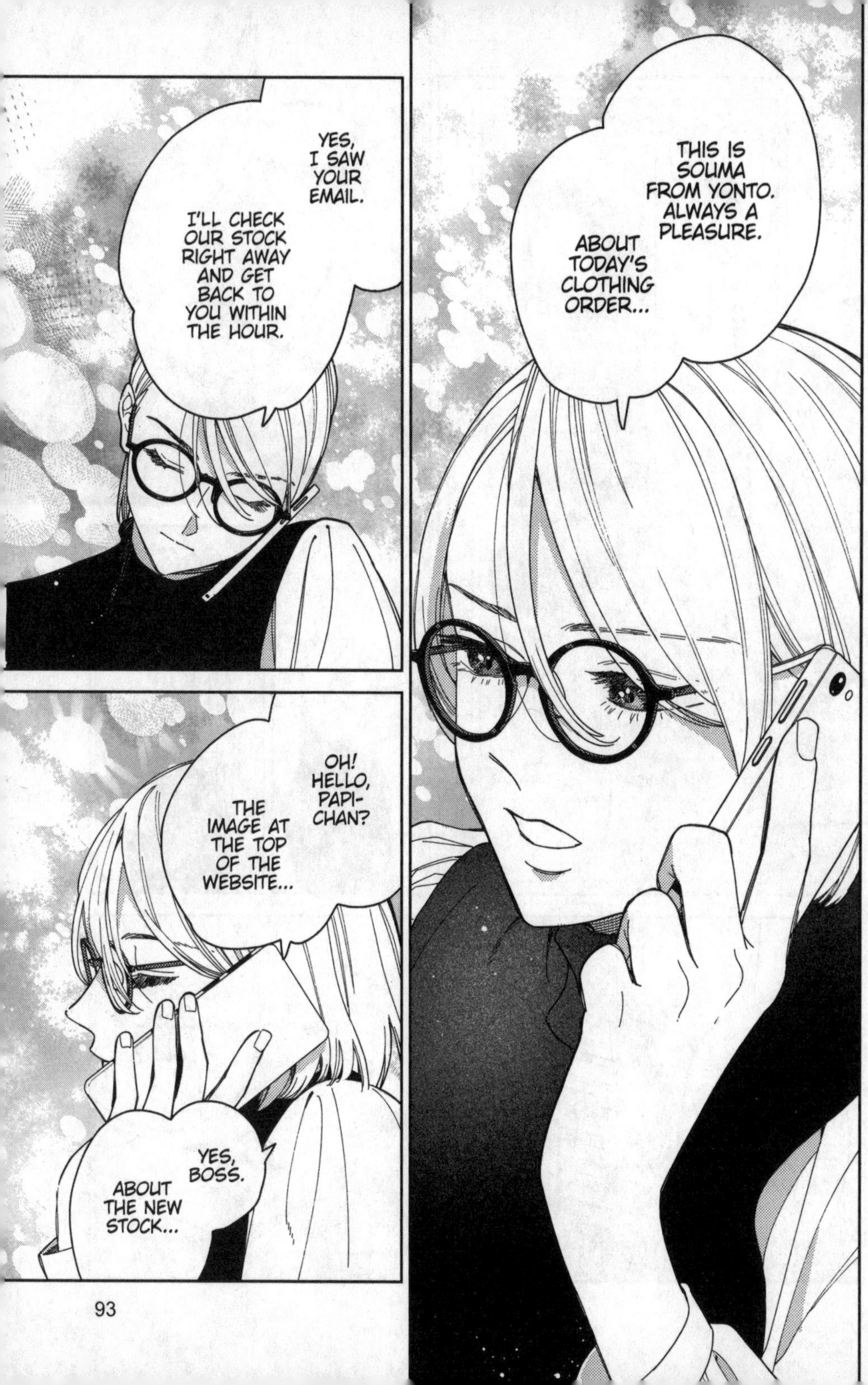
THIS IS SOUMA FROM YONTO. ALWAYS A PLEASURE.
ABOUT TODAY'S CLOTHING ORDER...
YES, I SAW YOUR EMAIL.
I'LL CHECK OUR STOCK RIGHT AWAY AND GET BACK TO YOU WITHIN THE HOUR.
OH! HELLO, PAPI-CHAN?
THE IMAGE AT THE TOP OF THE WEBSITE...
YES, BOSS.
ABOUT THE NEW STOCK...

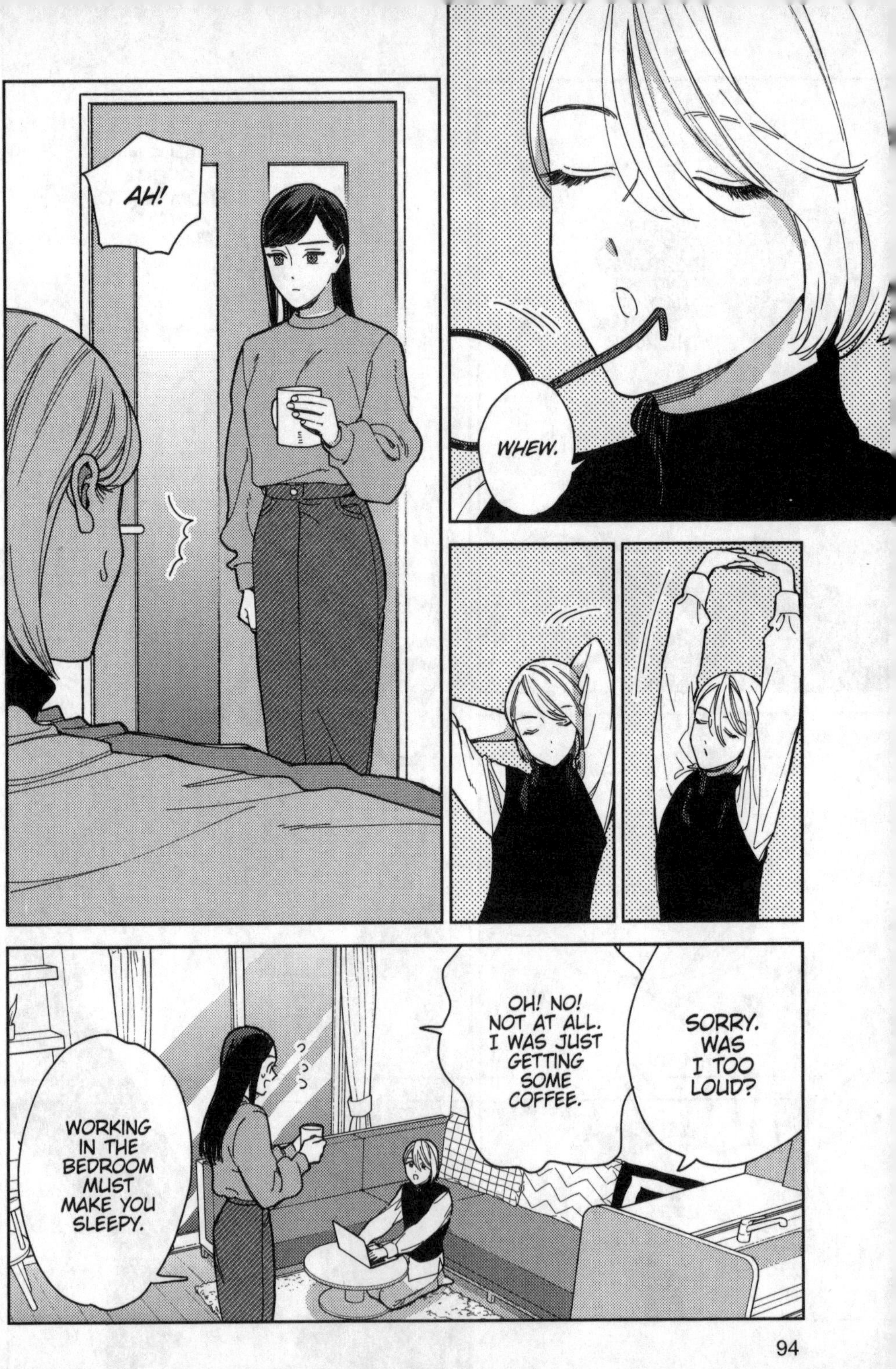
WHEW.
AH!
SORRY. WAS I TOO LOUD?
OH! NO! NOT AT ALL. I WAS JUST GETTING SOME COFFEE.
WORKING IN THE BEDROOM MUST MAKE YOU SLEEPY.

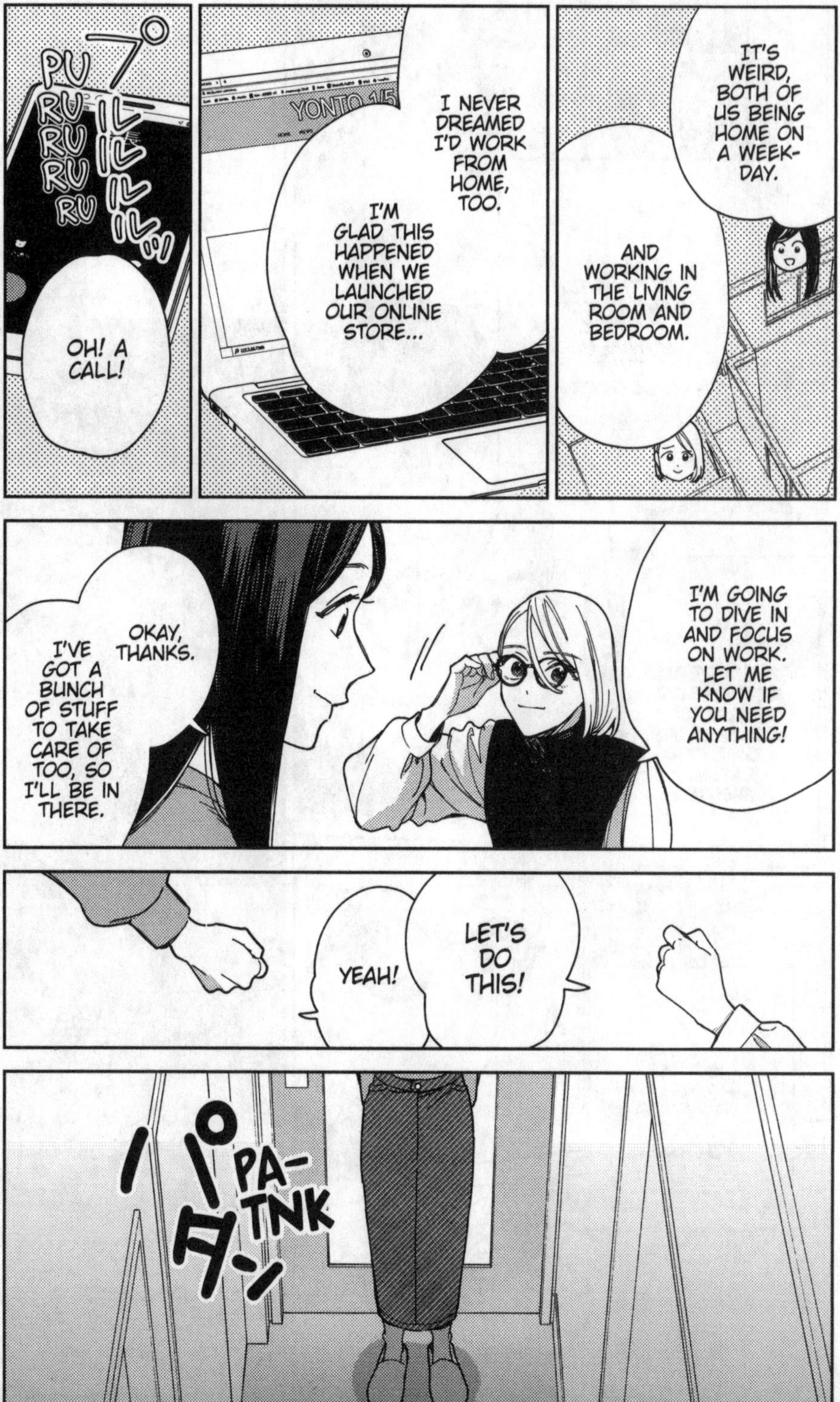
IT'S WEIRD, BOTH OF US BEING HOME ON A WEEK-DAY.
AND WORKING IN THE LIVING ROOM AND BEDROOM.
I NEVER DREAMED I'D WORK FROM HOME, TOO.
I'M GLAD THIS HAPPENED WHEN WE LAUNCHED OUR ONLINE STORE...
PU RU RU RU RU
OH! A CALL!
I'M GOING TO DIVE IN AND FOCUS ON WORK. LET ME KNOW IF YOU NEED ANYTHING!
OKAY, THANKS.
I'VE GOT A BUNCH OF STUFF TO TAKE CARE OF TOO, SO I'LL BE IN THERE.
LET'S DO THIS!
YEAH!
PA-TNK

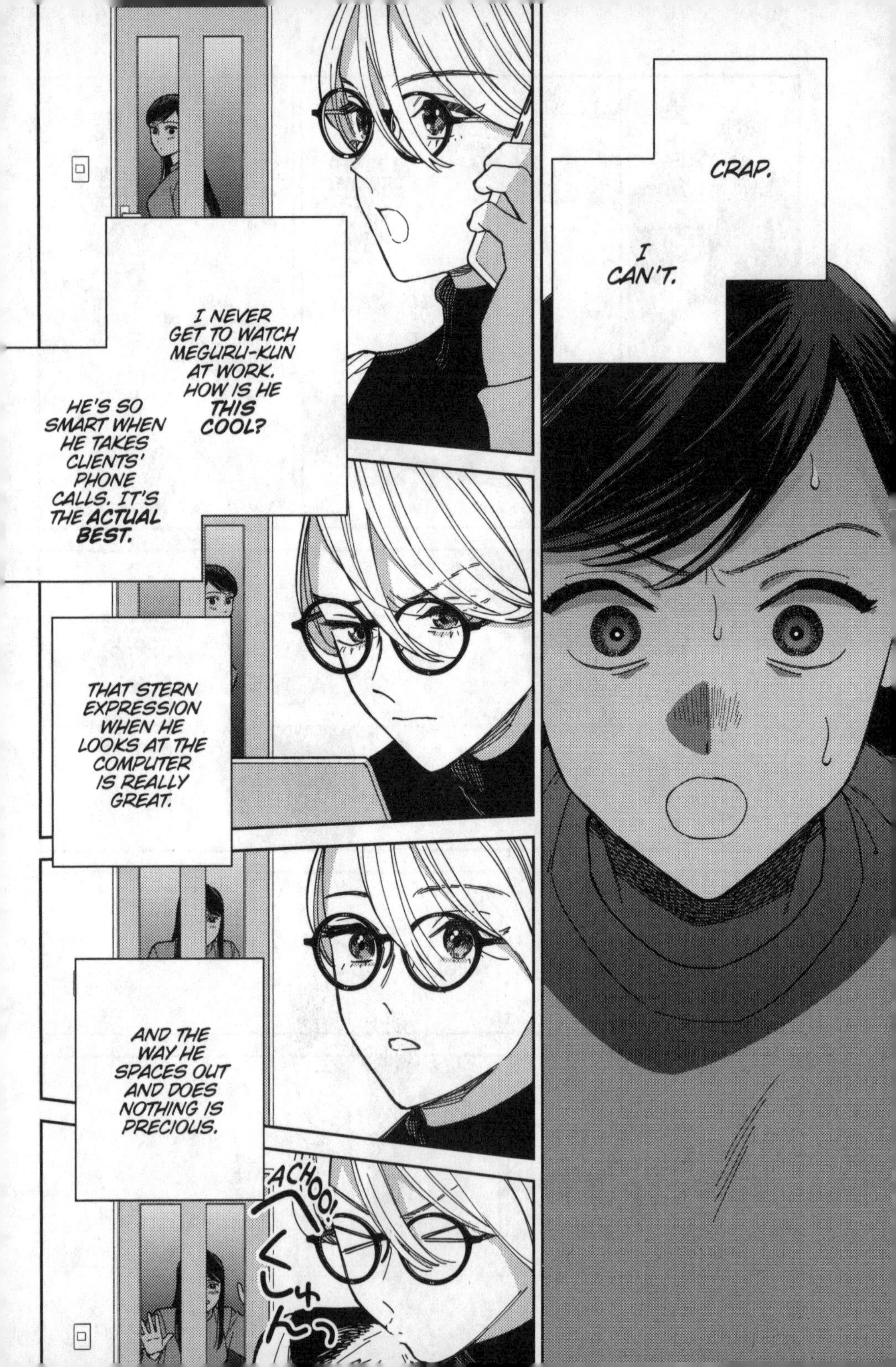
I NEVER GET TO WATCH MEGURU-KUN AT WORK. HOW IS HE THIS COOL?
HE'S SO SMART WHEN HE TAKES CLIENTS' PHONE CALLS. IT'S THE ACTUAL BEST.
THAT STERN EXPRESSION WHEN HE LOOKS AT THE COMPUTER IS REALLY GREAT.
AND THE WAY HE SPACES OUT AND DOES NOTHING IS PRECIOUS.
ACHOO!
くしゅん
CRAP.
I CAN'T.

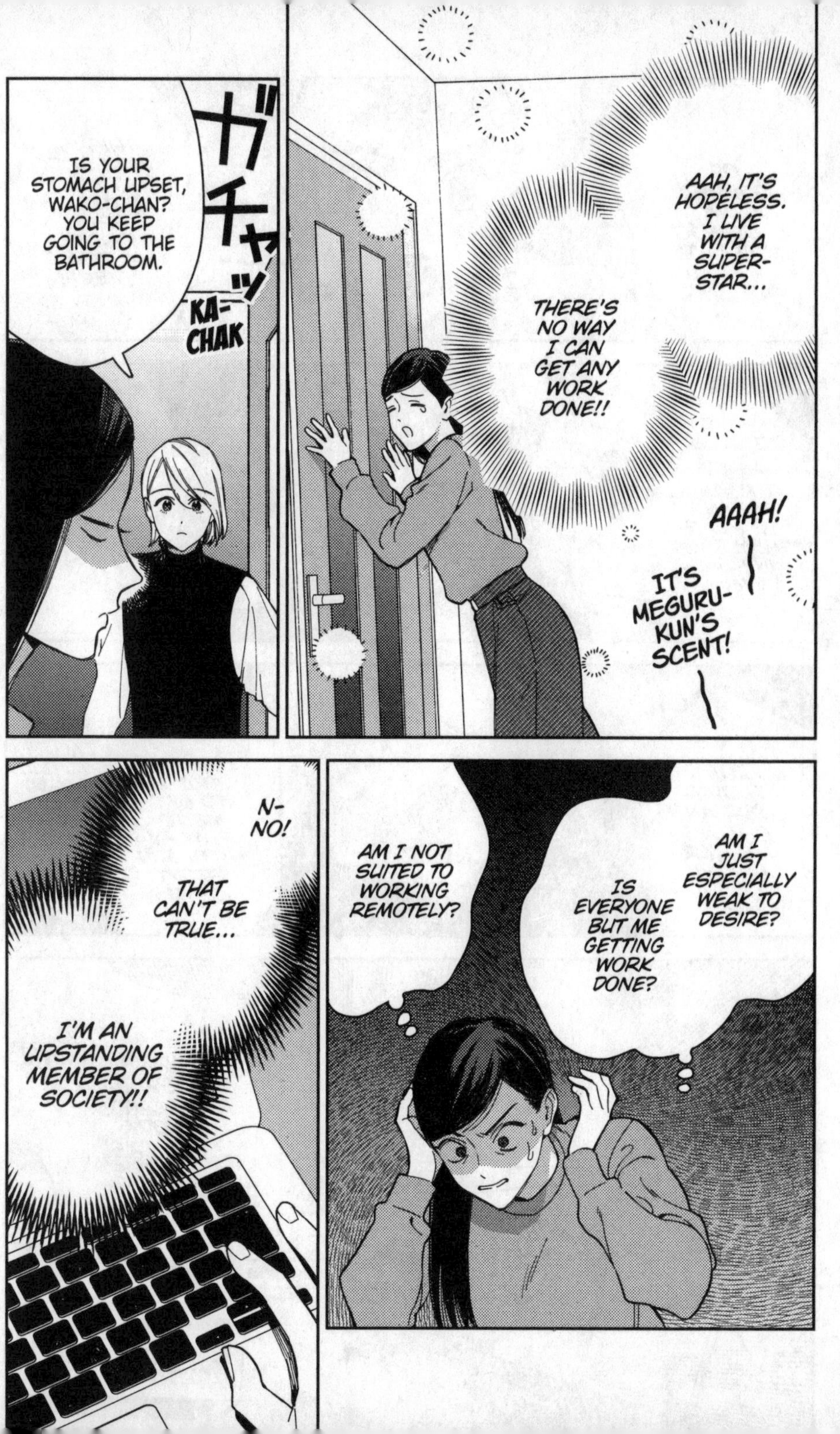
AAH, IT'S HOPELESS. I LIVE WITH A SUPER-STAR...
THERE'S NO WAY I CAN GET ANY WORK DONE!!
AAAH! IT'S MEGURU-KUN'S SCENT!
ガチャッ
KA-CHAK
IS YOUR STOMACH UPSET, WAKO-CHAN? YOU KEEP GOING TO THE BATHROOM.
AM I JUST ESPECIALLY WEAK TO DESIRE?
IS EVERYONE BUT ME GETTING WORK DONE?
AM I NOT SUITED TO WORKING REMOTELY?
N-NO!
THAT CAN'T BE TRUE...
I'M AN UPSTANDING MEMBER OF SOCIETY!!

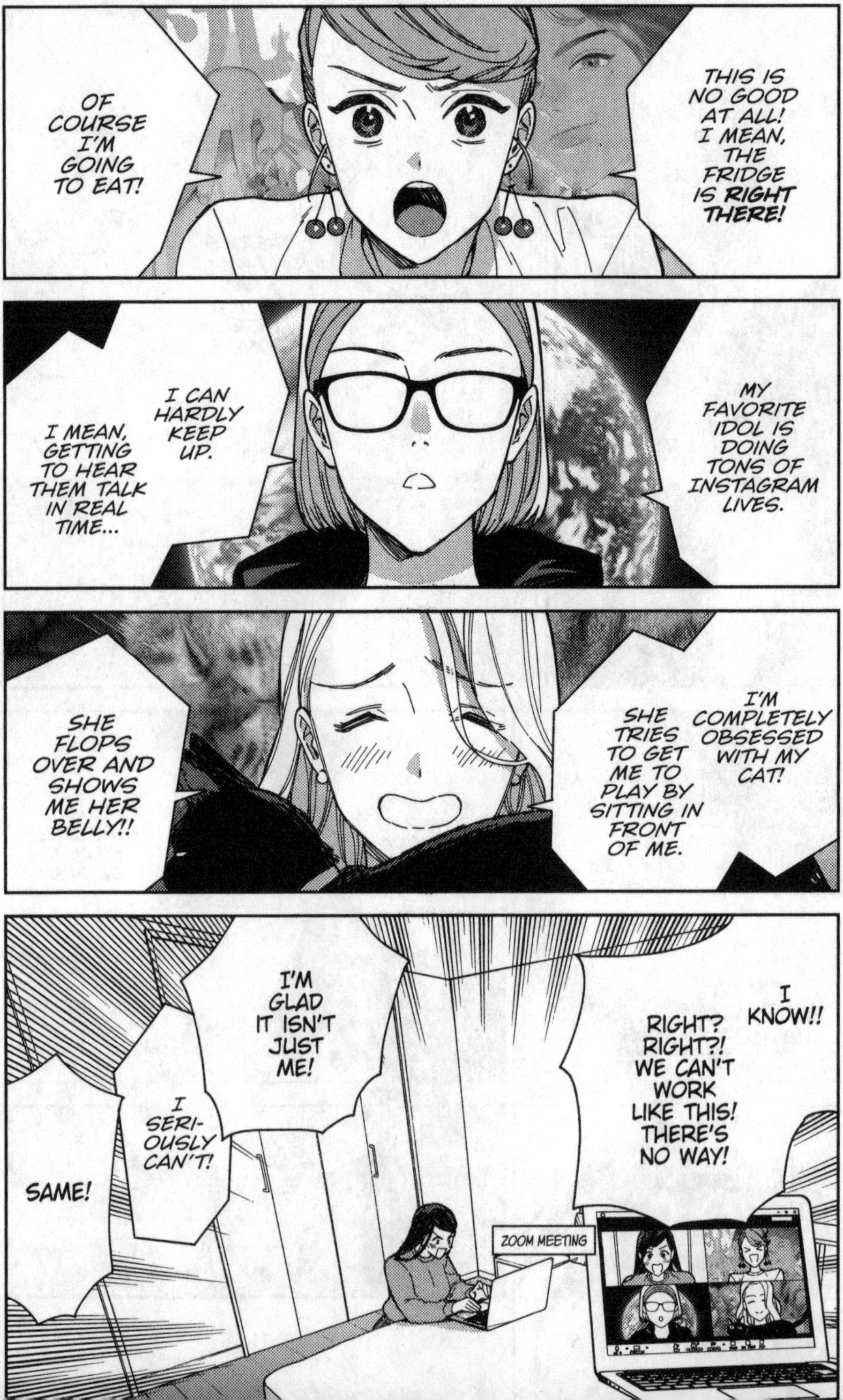
THIS IS NO GOOD AT ALL! I MEAN, THE FRIDGE IS **RIGHT THERE!**
OF COURSE I'M GOING TO EAT!
MY FAVORITE IDOL IS DOING TONS OF INSTAGRAM LIVES.
I CAN HARDLY KEEP UP.
I MEAN, GETTING TO HEAR THEM TALK IN REAL TIME...
I'M COMPLETELY OBSESSED WITH MY CAT!
SHE TRIES TO GET ME TO PLAY BY SITTING IN FRONT OF ME.
SHE FLOPS OVER AND SHOWS ME HER BELLY!!
I KNOW!!
RIGHT? RIGHT?! WE CAN'T WORK LIKE THIS! THERE'S NO WAY!
I'M GLAD IT ISN'T JUST ME!
I SERI-OUSLY CAN'T!
SAME!
ZOOM MEETING

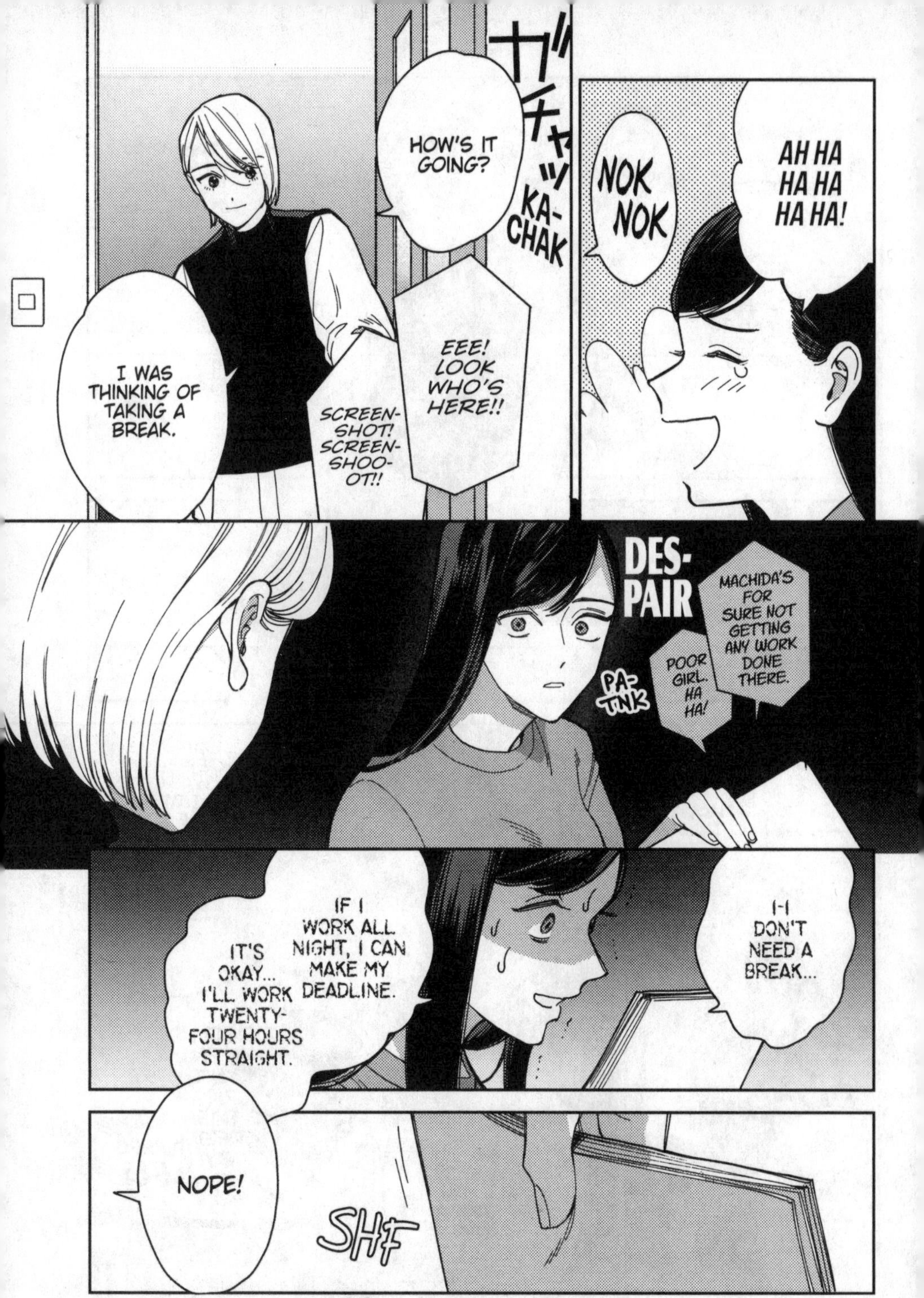
AH HA HA HA HA HA!
NOK NOK
KA-CHAK
HOW'S IT GOING?
EEE! LOOK WHO'S HERE!!
SCREEN-SHOT! SCREEN-SHOOO-OT!!
I WAS THINKING OF TAKING A BREAK.
DES-PAIR
MACHIDA'S FOR SURE NOT GETTING ANY WORK DONE THERE.
POOR GIRL. HA HA!
PA-TNK
I-I DON'T NEED A BREAK...
IF I WORK ALL NIGHT, I CAN MAKE MY DEADLINE.
IT'S OKAY... I'LL WORK TWENTY-FOUR HOURS STRAIGHT.
SHF
NOPE!

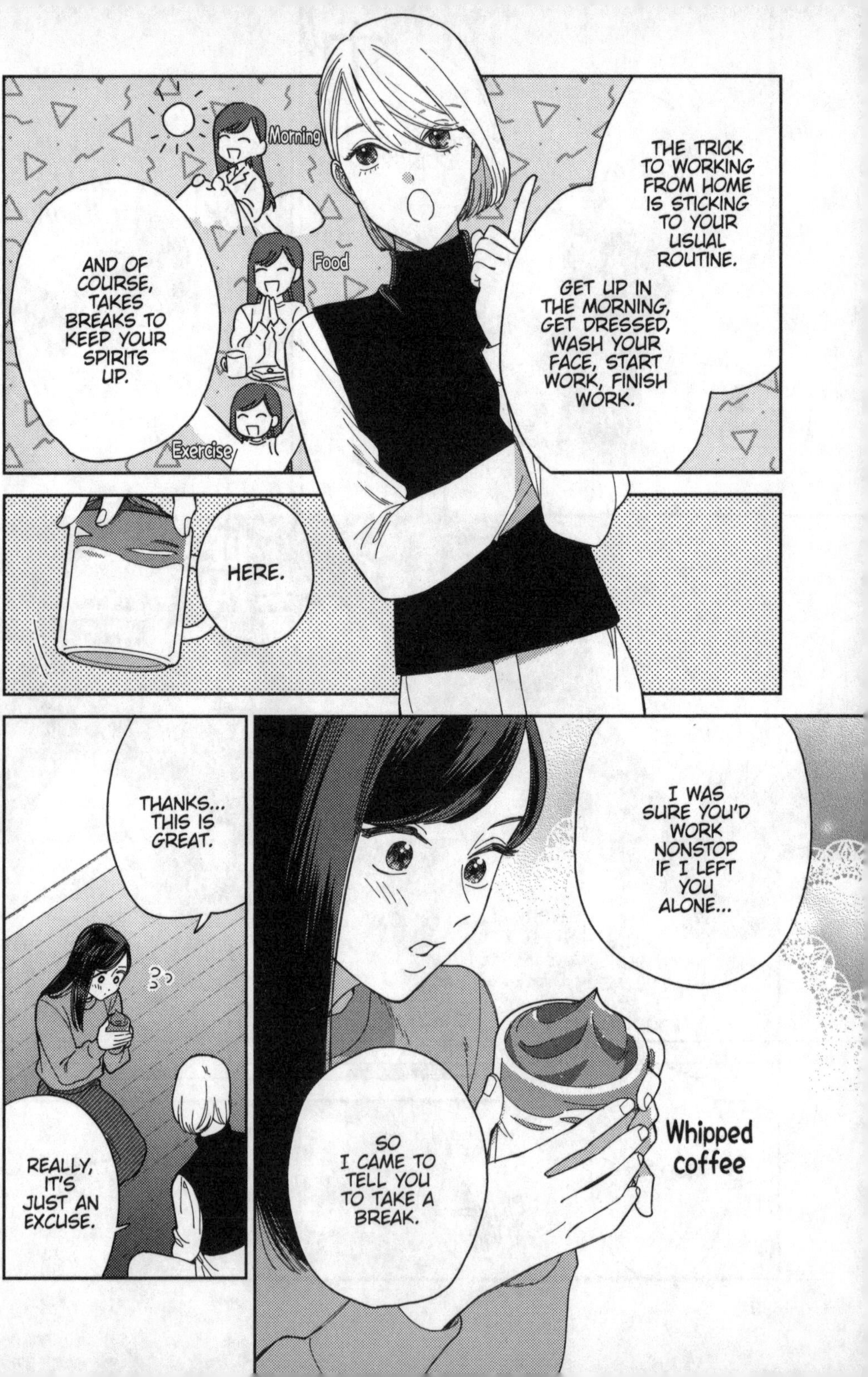
THE TRICK TO WORKING FROM HOME IS STICKING TO YOUR USUAL ROUTINE.
GET UP IN THE MORNING, GET DRESSED, WASH YOUR FACE, START WORK, FINISH WORK.
Morning
Food
Exercise
AND OF COURSE, TAKES BREAKS TO KEEP YOUR SPIRITS UP.
HERE.
I WAS SURE YOU'D WORK NONSTOP IF I LEFT YOU ALONE...
Whipped coffee
SO I CAME TO TELL YOU TO TAKE A BREAK.
THANKS... THIS IS GREAT.
REALLY, IT'S JUST AN EXCUSE.

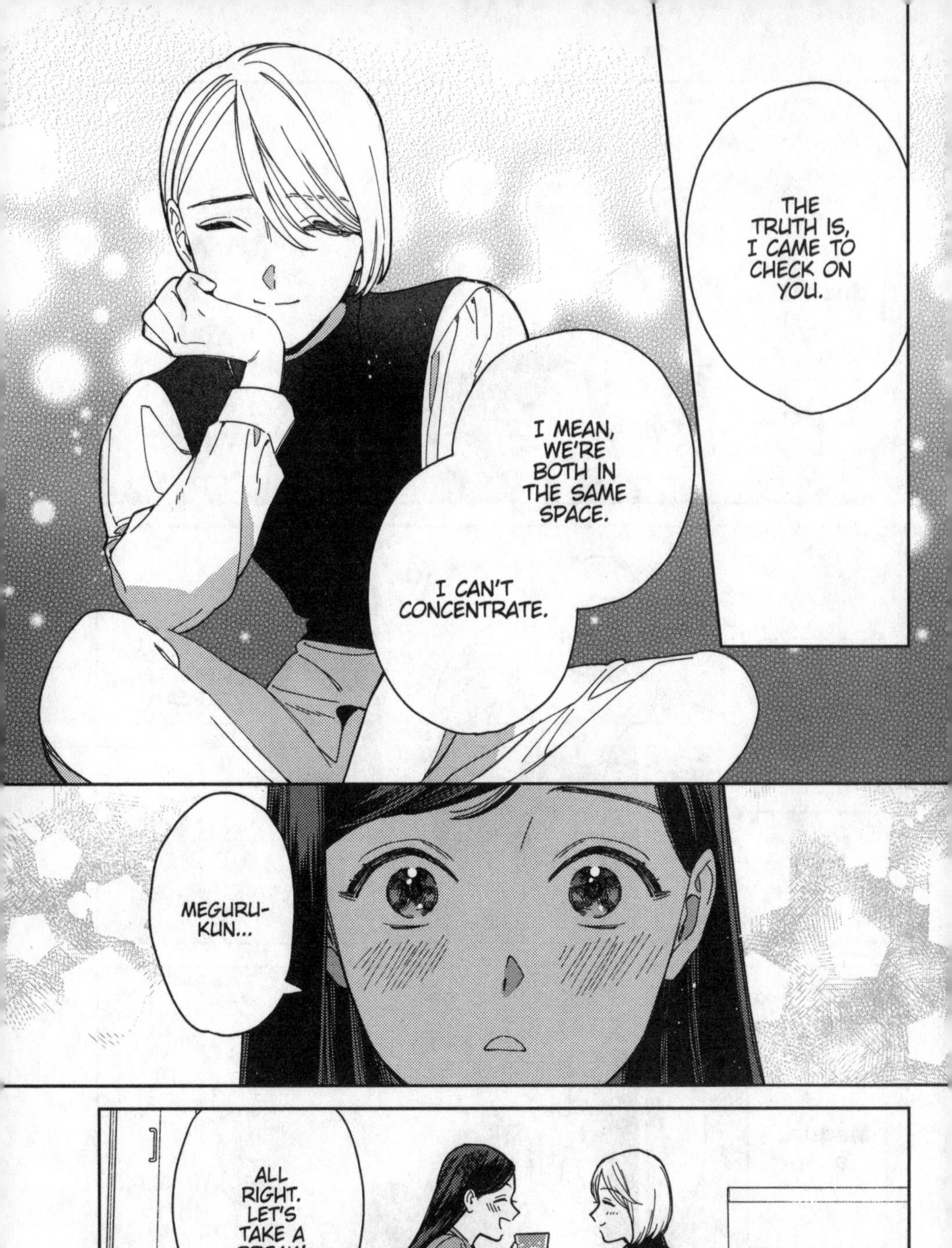
THE TRUTH IS, I CAME TO CHECK ON YOU.
I MEAN, WE'RE BOTH IN THE SAME SPACE.
I CAN'T CONCENTRATE.
MEGURU-KUN...
ALL RIGHT. LET'S TAKE A BREAK!

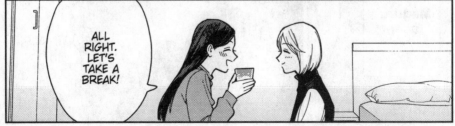

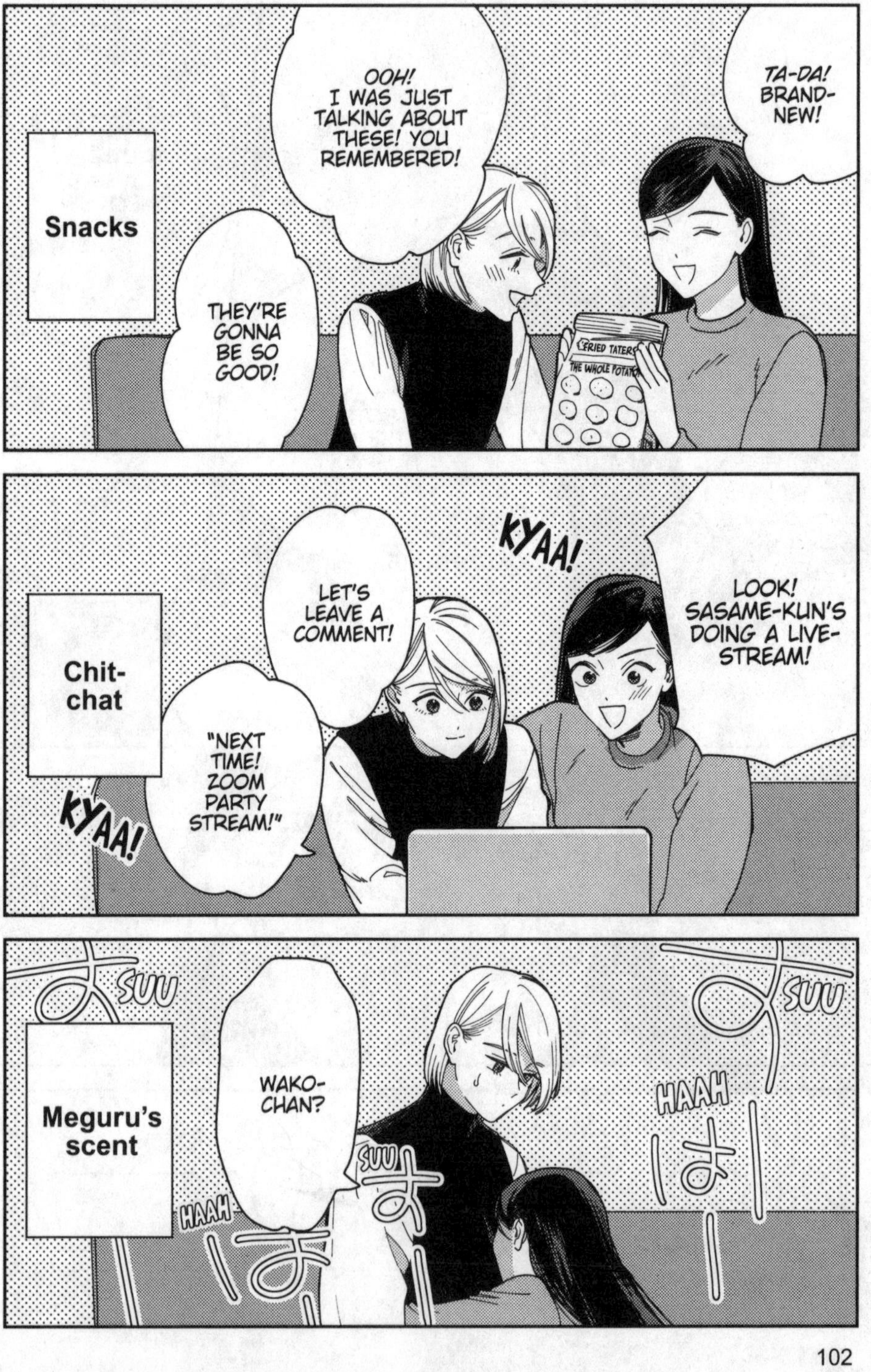
TA-DA! BRAND-NEW!
OOH! I WAS JUST TALKING ABOUT THESE! YOU REMEMBERED!
FRIED TATERS
THE WHOLE POTATO
THEY'RE GONNA BE SO GOOD!
Snacks
LOOK! SASAME-KUN'S DOING A LIVE-STREAM!
KYAA!
LET'S LEAVE A COMMENT!
"NEXT TIME! ZOOM PARTY STREAM!"
KYAA!
Chit-chat
SUU
HAAH
WAKO-CHAN?
SUU
SUU
HAAH
Meguru's scent

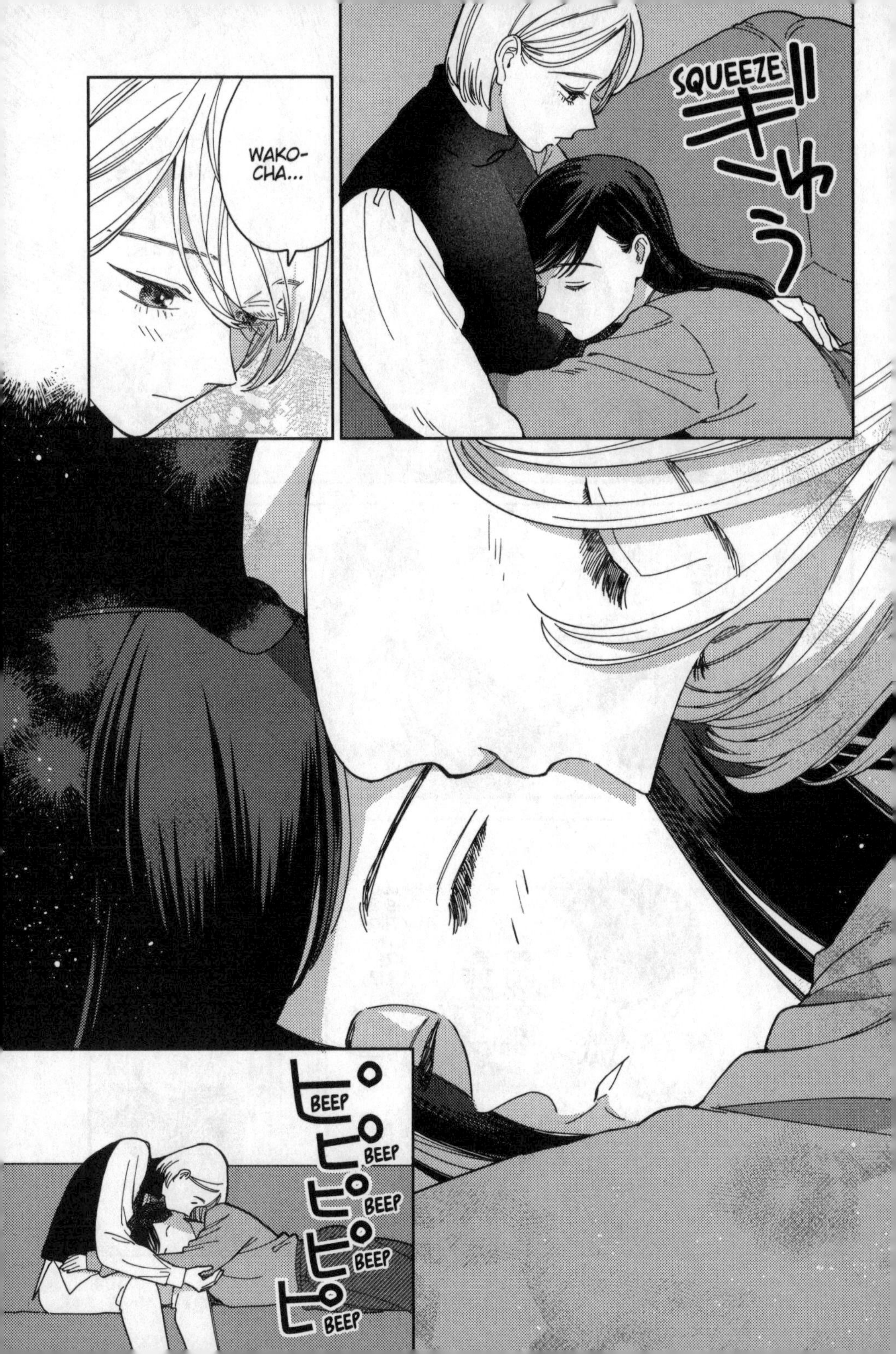
SQUEEZE
ぎゅう
WAKO-CHA...
ピピピピピ
BEEP
BEEP
BEEP
BEEP
BEEP

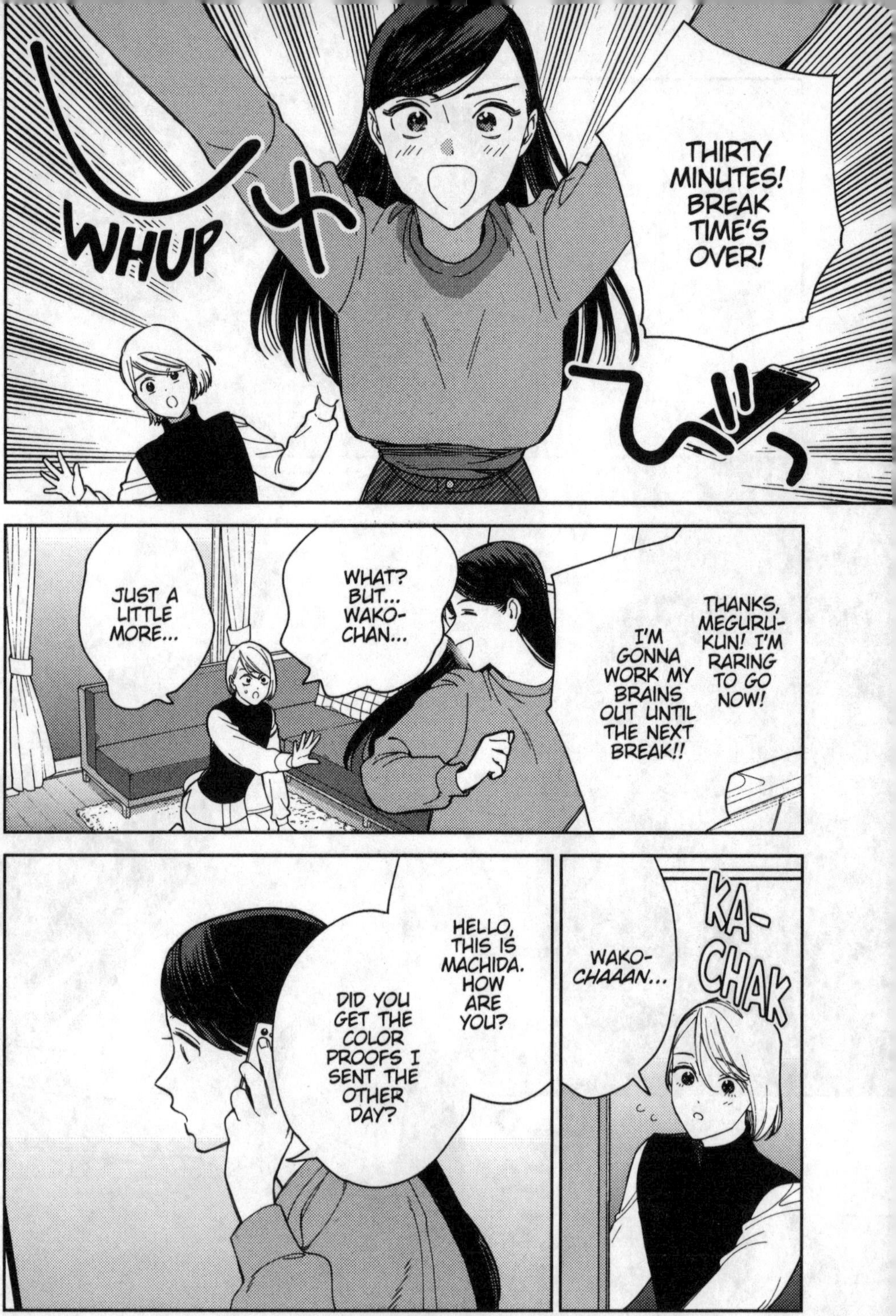
THIRTY MINUTES! BREAK TIME'S OVER!
WHUP
THANKS, MEGURU-KUN! I'M RARING TO GO NOW!
I'M GONNA WORK MY BRAINS OUT UNTIL THE NEXT BREAK!!
WHAT? BUT... WAKO-CHAN...
JUST A LITTLE MORE...
KA-CHAK
WAKO-CHAAAN...
HELLO, THIS IS MACHIDA. HOW ARE YOU?
DID YOU GET THE COLOR PROOFS I SENT THE OTHER DAY?

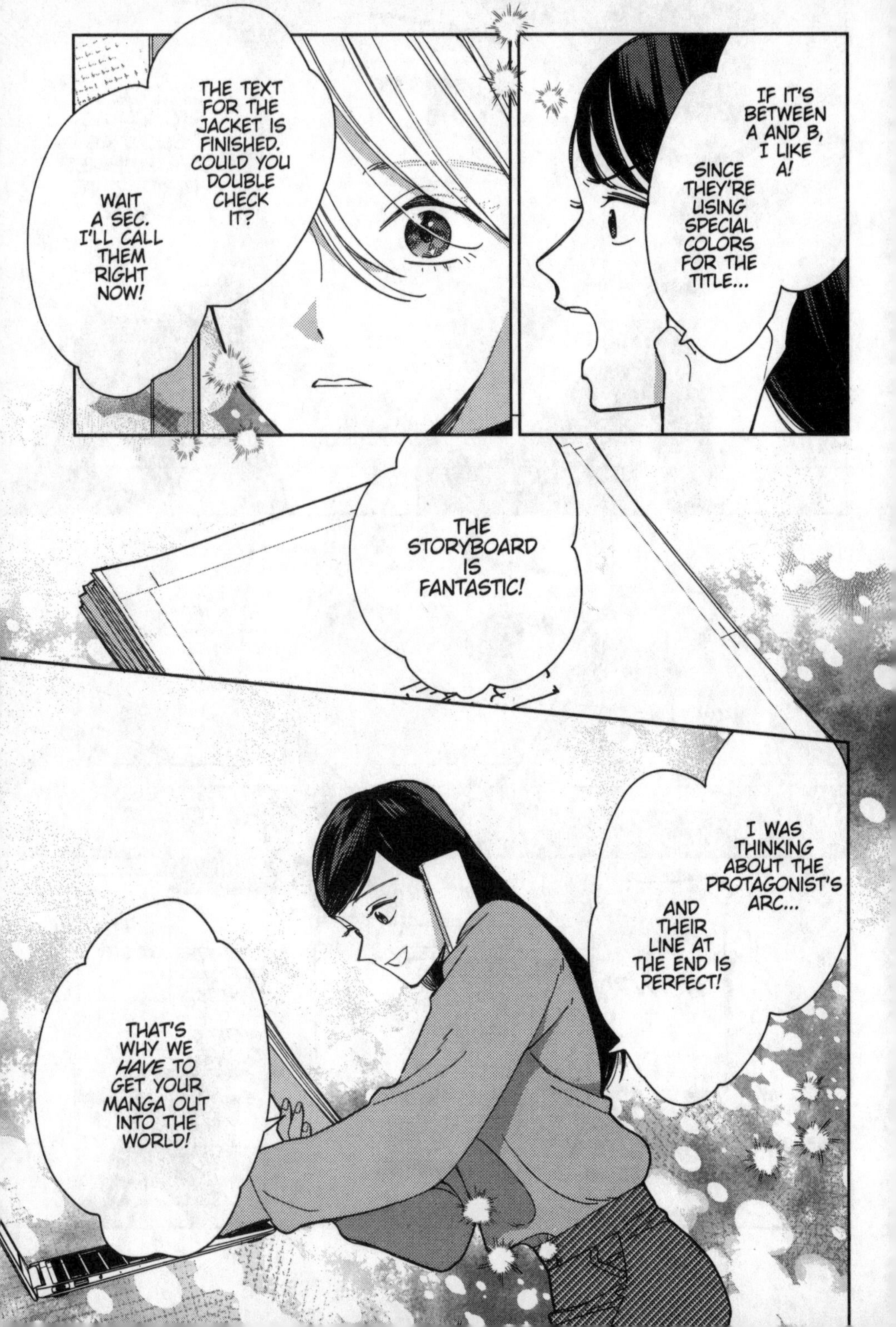
IF IT'S BETWEEN A AND B, I LIKE A!
SINCE THEY'RE USING SPECIAL COLORS FOR THE TITLE...
THE TEXT FOR THE JACKET IS FINISHED. COULD YOU DOUBLE CHECK IT?
WAIT A SEC. I'LL CALL THEM RIGHT NOW!
THE STORYBOARD IS FANTASTIC!
I WAS THINKING ABOUT THE PROTAGONIST'S ARC...
AND THEIR LINE AT THE END IS PERFECT!
THAT'S WHY WE *HAVE* TO GET YOUR MANGA OUT INTO THE WORLD!

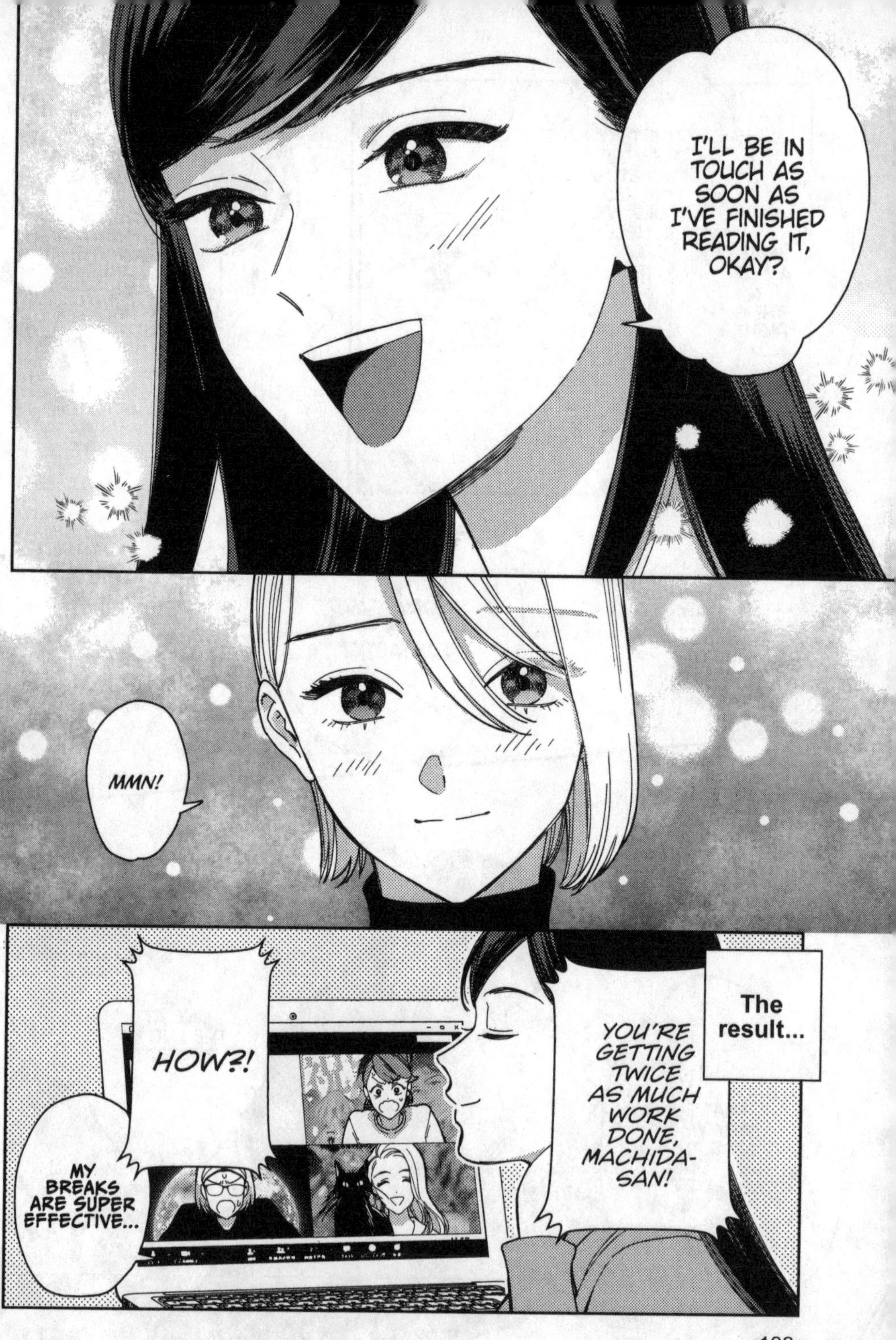
I'LL BE IN TOUCH AS SOON AS I'VE FINISHED READING IT, OKAY?
MMN!
The result...
YOU'RE GETTING TWICE AS MUCH WORK DONE, MACHIDA-SAN!
HOW?!
MY BREAKS ARE SUPER EFFECTIVE...

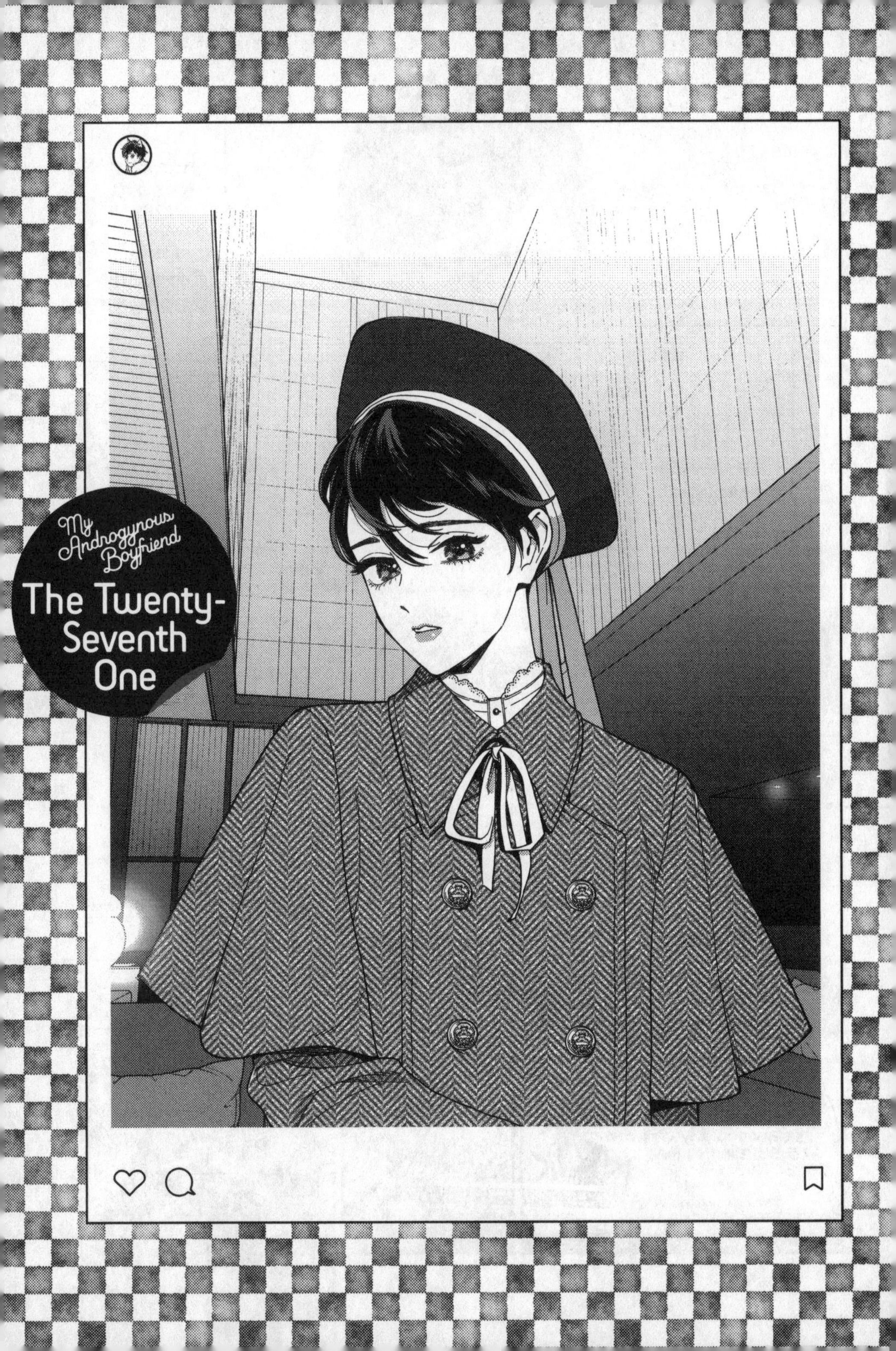
My Androgynous Boyfriend
The Twenty-Seventh One

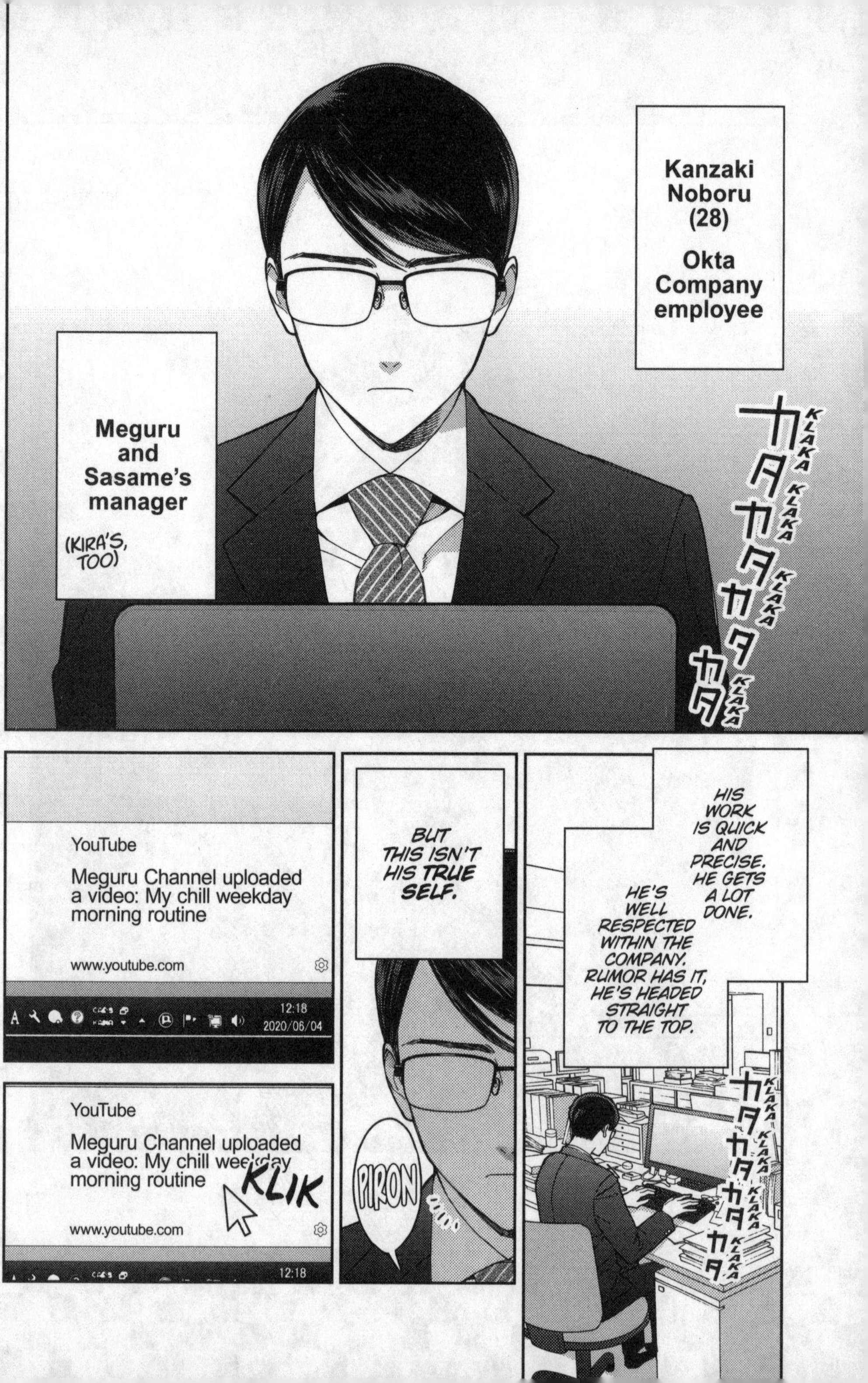

Kanzaki Noboru (28)
Okta Company employee
カタカタカタカタ
KLAKA KLAKA KLAKA KLAKA
Meguru and Sasame's manager
(KIRA'S, TOO)
HIS WORK IS QUICK AND PRECISE. HE GETS A LOT DONE.
HE'S WELL RESPECTED WITHIN THE COMPANY. RUMOR HAS IT, HE'S HEADED STRAIGHT TO THE TOP.
カタカタカタカタ
KLAKA KLAKA KLAKA KLAKA
BUT THIS ISN'T HIS TRUE SELF.
PIRON
YouTube
Meguru Channel uploaded a video: My chill weekday morning routine
www.youtube.com
12:18
2020/06/04
YouTube
Meguru Channel uploaded a video: My chill weekday morning routine
KLIK
www.youtube.com
12:18

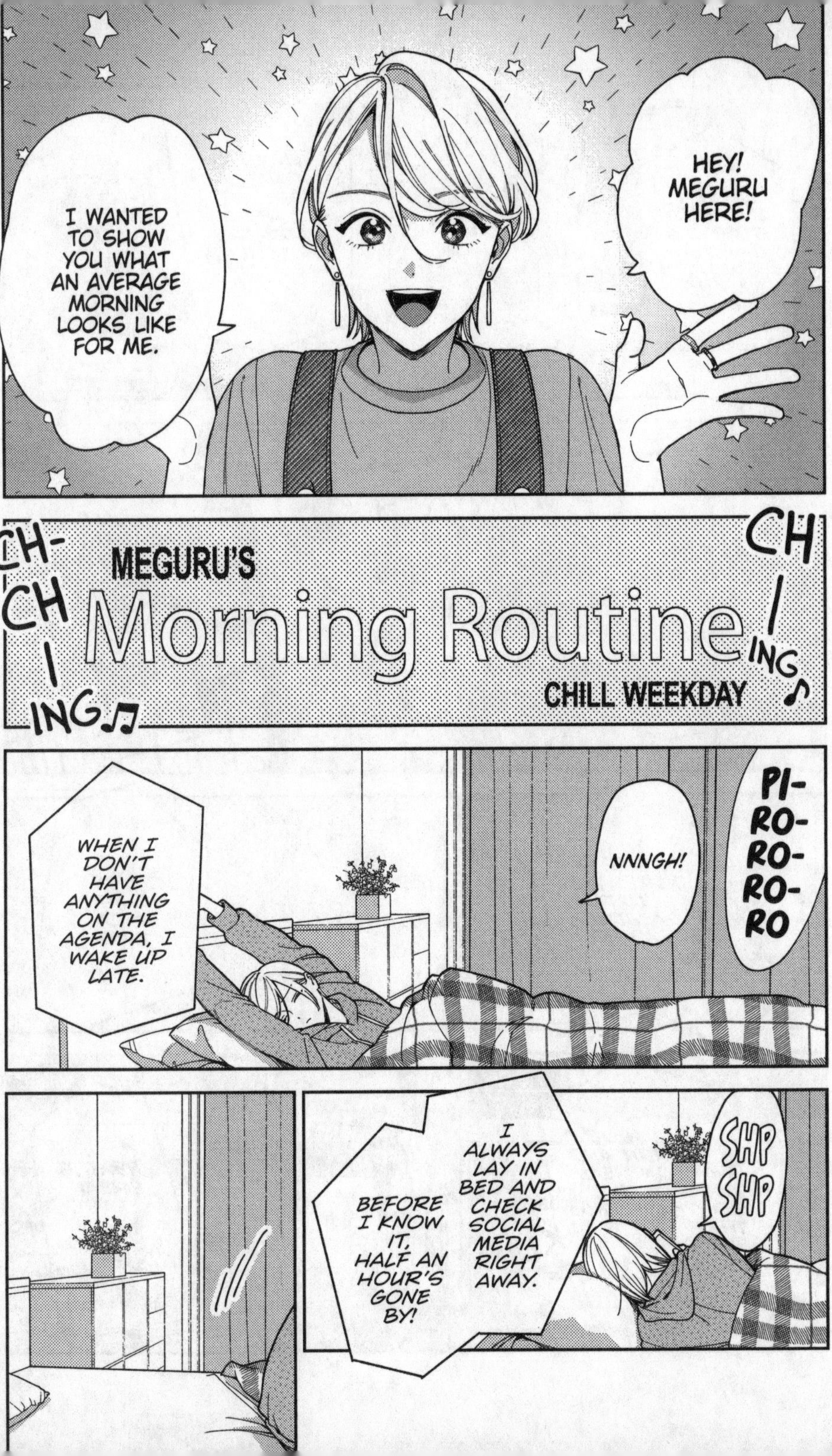
HEY! MEGURU HERE!
I WANTED TO SHOW YOU WHAT AN AVERAGE MORNING LOOKS LIKE FOR ME.
CH-ING♪
MEGURU'S
Morning Routine
CHILL WEEKDAY
CH-CH-ING♫
PI-RO-RO-RO-RO
NNNGH!
WHEN I DON'T HAVE ANYTHING ON THE AGENDA, I WAKE UP LATE.
SHP SHP
I ALWAYS LAY IN BED AND CHECK SOCIAL MEDIA RIGHT AWAY.
BEFORE I KNOW IT, HALF AN HOUR'S GONE BY!

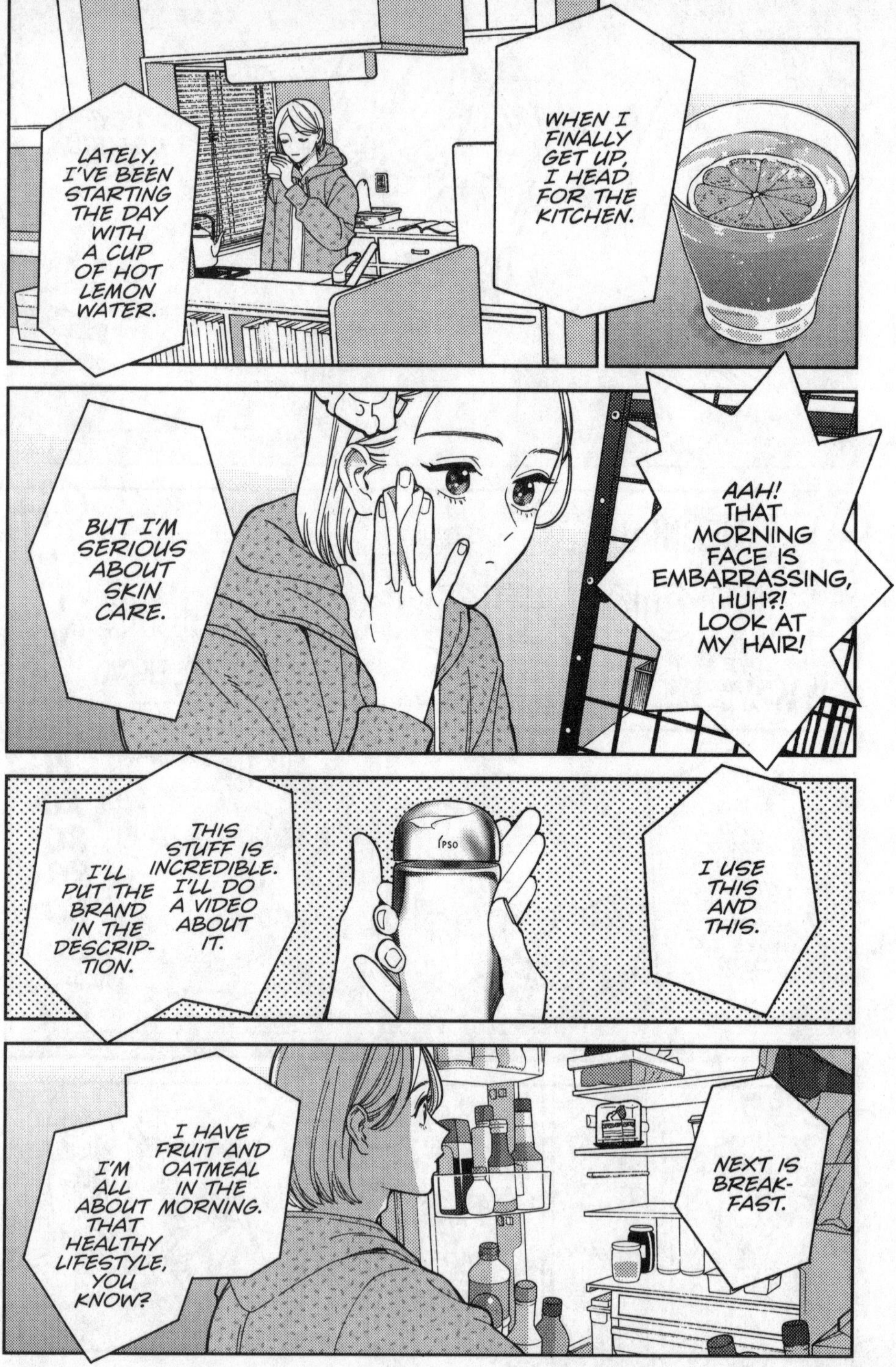
WHEN I FINALLY GET UP, I HEAD FOR THE KITCHEN.
LATELY, I'VE BEEN STARTING THE DAY WITH A CUP OF HOT LEMON WATER.
AAH! THAT MORNING FACE IS EMBARRASSING, HUH?! LOOK AT MY HAIR!
BUT I'M SERIOUS ABOUT SKIN CARE.
I USE THIS AND THIS.
THIS STUFF IS INCREDIBLE. I'LL DO A VIDEO ABOUT IT.
I'LL PUT THE BRAND IN THE DESCRIPTION.
NEXT IS BREAKFAST.
I HAVE FRUIT AND OATMEAL IN THE MORNING.
I'M ALL ABOUT THAT HEALTHY LIFESTYLE, YOU KNOW?

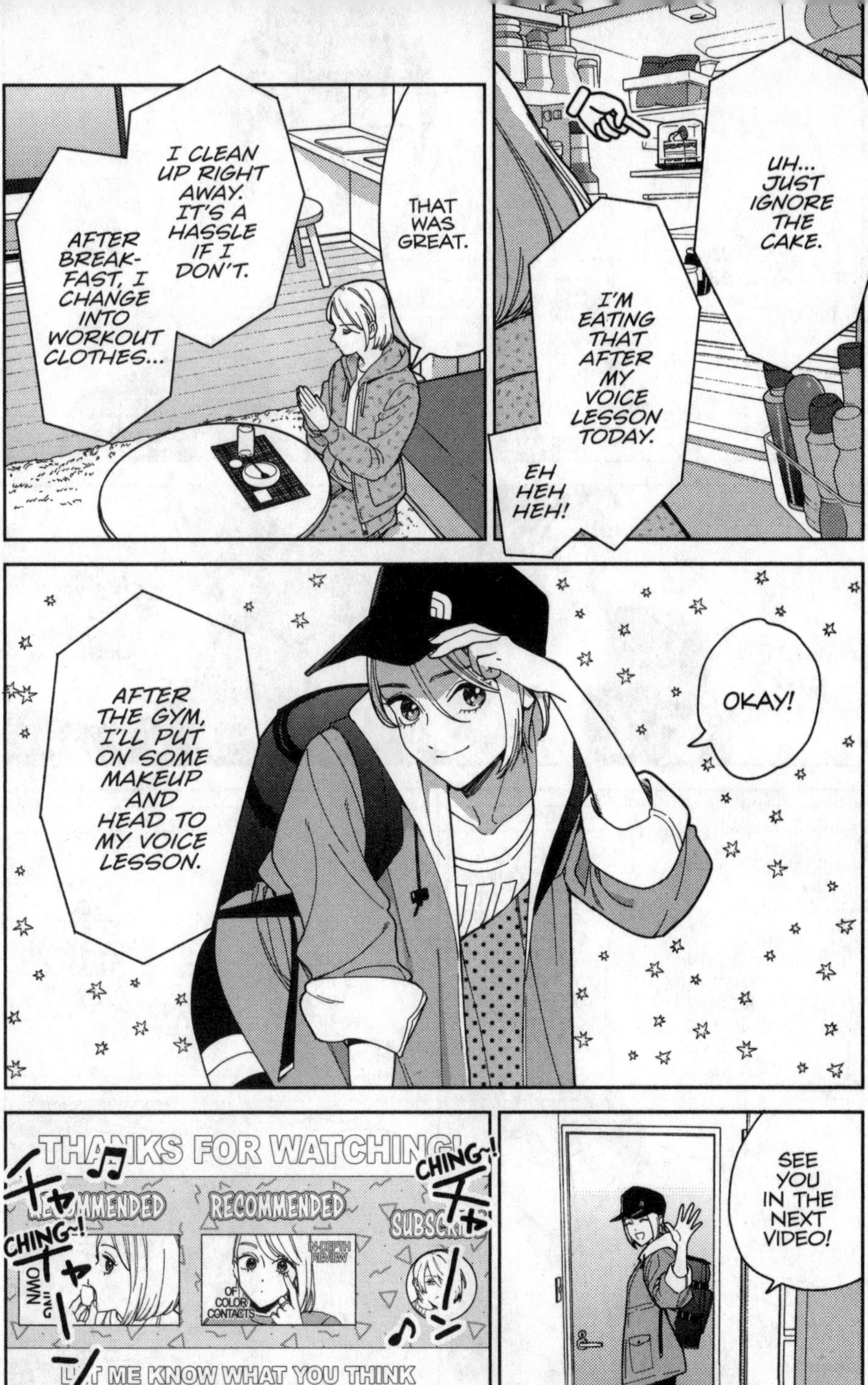

UH... JUST IGNORE THE CAKE.
I'M EATING THAT AFTER MY VOICE LESSON TODAY.
EH HEH HEH!
THAT WAS GREAT.
I CLEAN UP RIGHT AWAY. IT'S A HASSLE IF I DON'T.
AFTER BREAK-FAST, I CHANGE INTO WORKOUT CLOTHES...
OKAY!
AFTER THE GYM, I'LL PUT ON SOME MAKEUP AND HEAD TO MY VOICE LESSON.
SEE YOU IN THE NEXT VIDEO!
THANKS FOR WATCHING!
CHING~!
RECOMMENDED
IN-DEPTH REVIEW OF COLOR CONTACTS
CHING~!
LET ME KNOW WHAT YOU THINK IN THE COMMENTS!

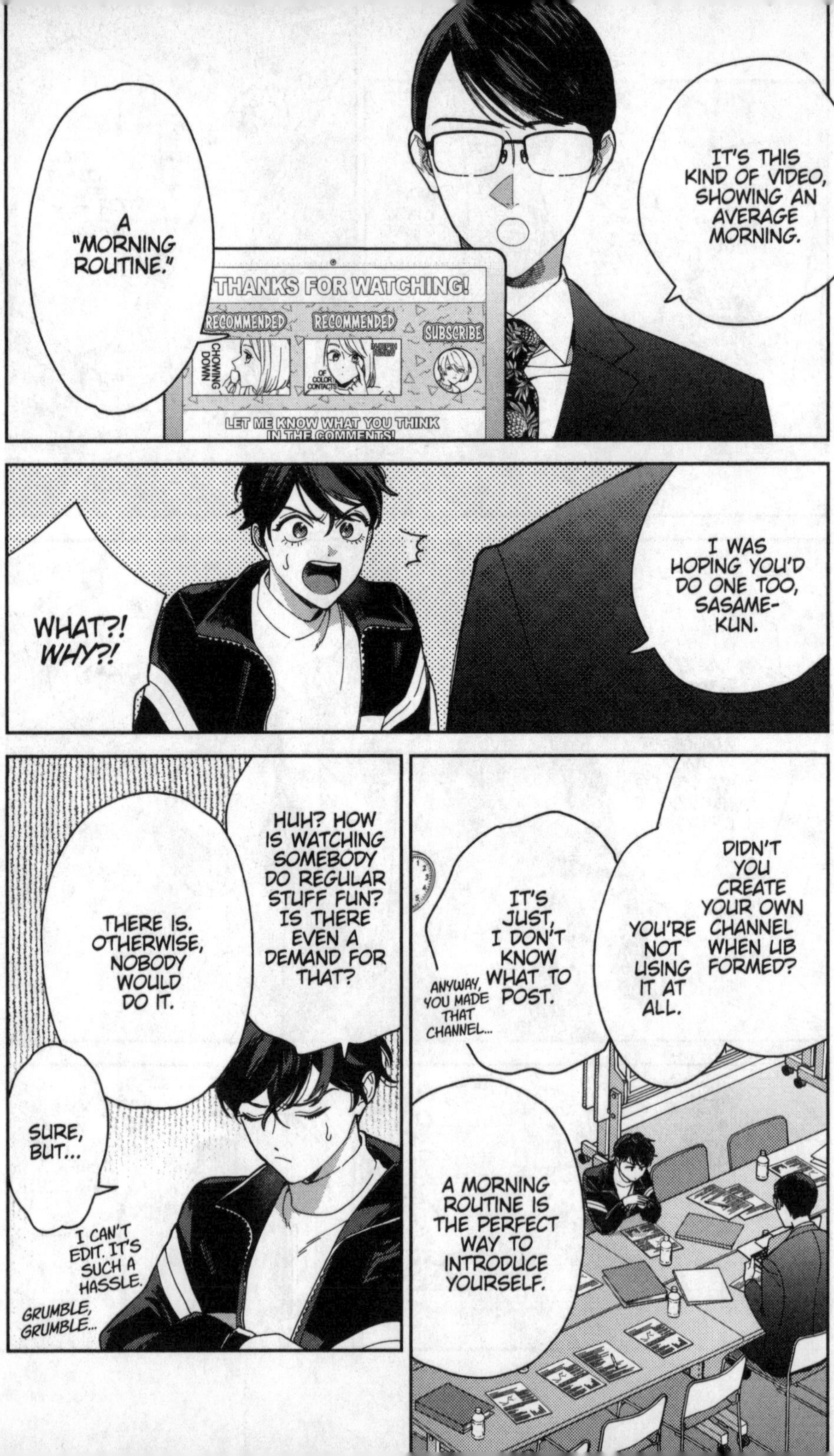
IT'S THIS KIND OF VIDEO, SHOWING AN AVERAGE MORNING.
A "MORNING ROUTINE."
THANKS FOR WATCHING!
RECOMMENDED
RECOMMENDED
SUBSCRIBE
CHOWING DOWN
OF COLOR CONTACTS
LET ME KNOW WHAT YOU THINK IN THE COMMENTS!
I WAS HOPING YOU'D DO ONE TOO, SASAME-KUN.
WHAT?! WHY?!
DIDN'T YOU CREATE YOUR OWN CHANNEL WHEN UB FORMED?
YOU'RE NOT USING IT AT ALL.
IT'S JUST, I DON'T KNOW WHAT TO POST.
ANYWAY, YOU MADE THAT CHANNEL...
A MORNING ROUTINE IS THE PERFECT WAY TO INTRODUCE YOURSELF.
HUH? HOW IS WATCHING SOMEBODY DO REGULAR STUFF FUN? IS THERE EVEN A DEMAND FOR THAT?
THERE IS. OTHERWISE, NOBODY WOULD DO IT.
SURE, BUT...
I CAN'T EDIT. IT'S SUCH A HASSLE.
GRUMBLE, GRUMBLE...

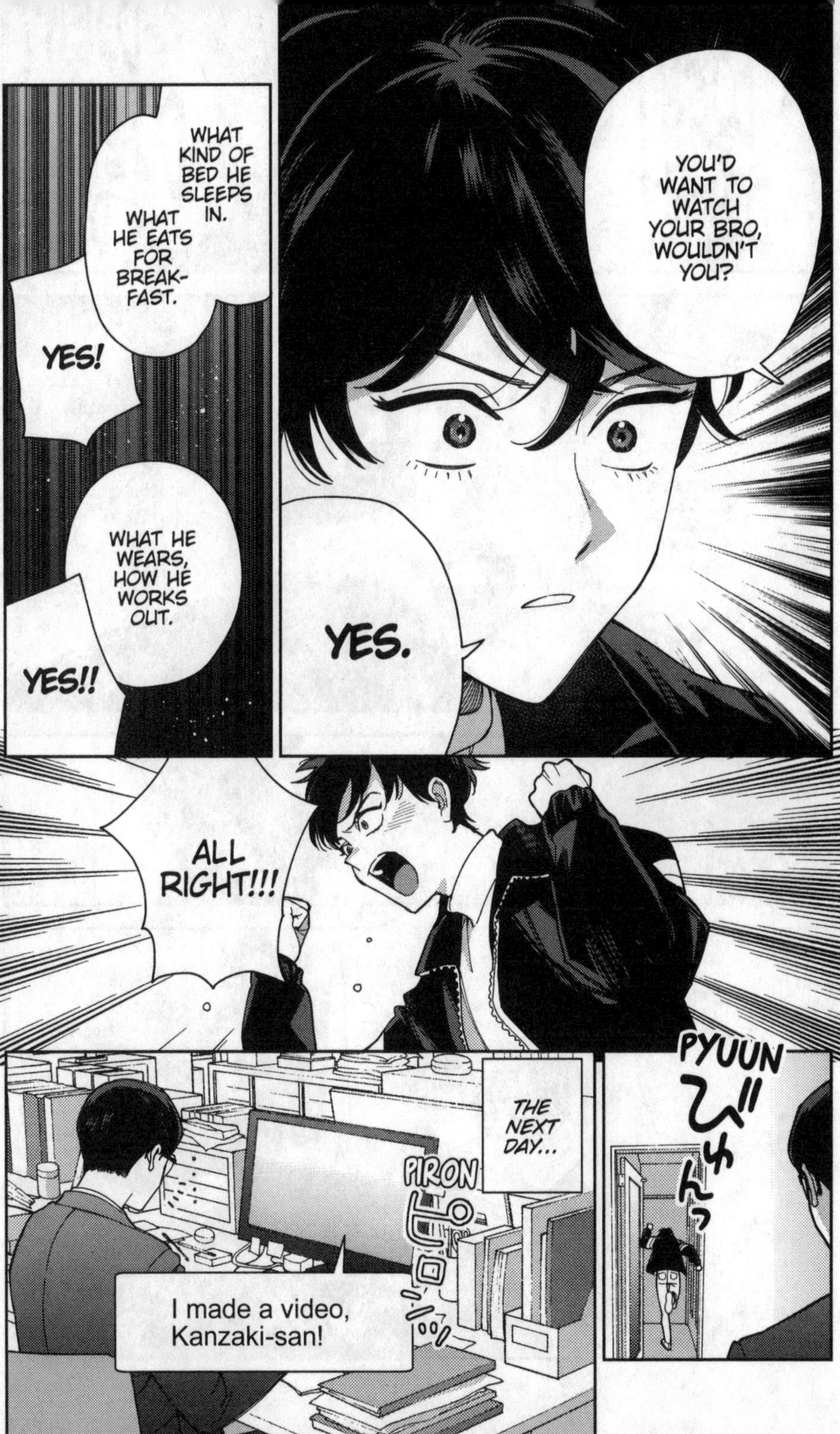
YOU'D WANT TO WATCH YOUR BRO, WOULDN'T YOU?
YES.
WHAT KIND OF BED HE SLEEPS IN.
WHAT HE EATS FOR BREAK-FAST.
YES!
WHAT HE WEARS, HOW HE WORKS OUT.
YES!!
ALL RIGHT!!!
PYUUN
びゅんっ
THE NEXT DAY...
PIRON
I made a video, Kanzaki-san!

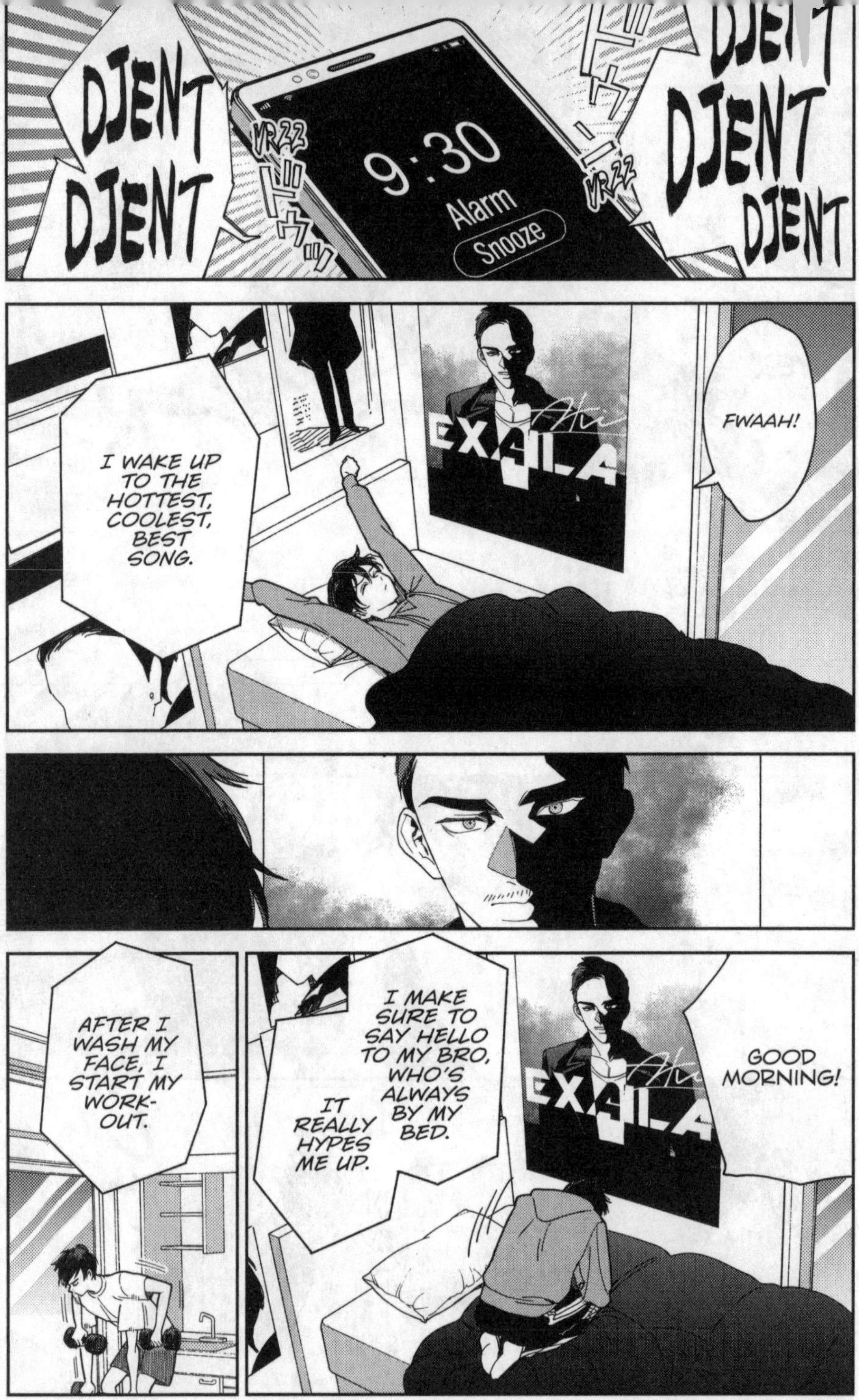
DJENT DJENT DJENT
9:30
Alarm
Snooze
DJENT DJENT
FWAAH!
I WAKE UP TO THE HOTTEST, COOLEST, BEST SONG.
GOOD MORNING!
I MAKE SURE TO SAY HELLO TO MY BRO, WHO'S ALWAYS BY MY BED.
IT REALLY HYPES ME UP.
AFTER I WASH MY FACE, I START MY WORK-OUT.

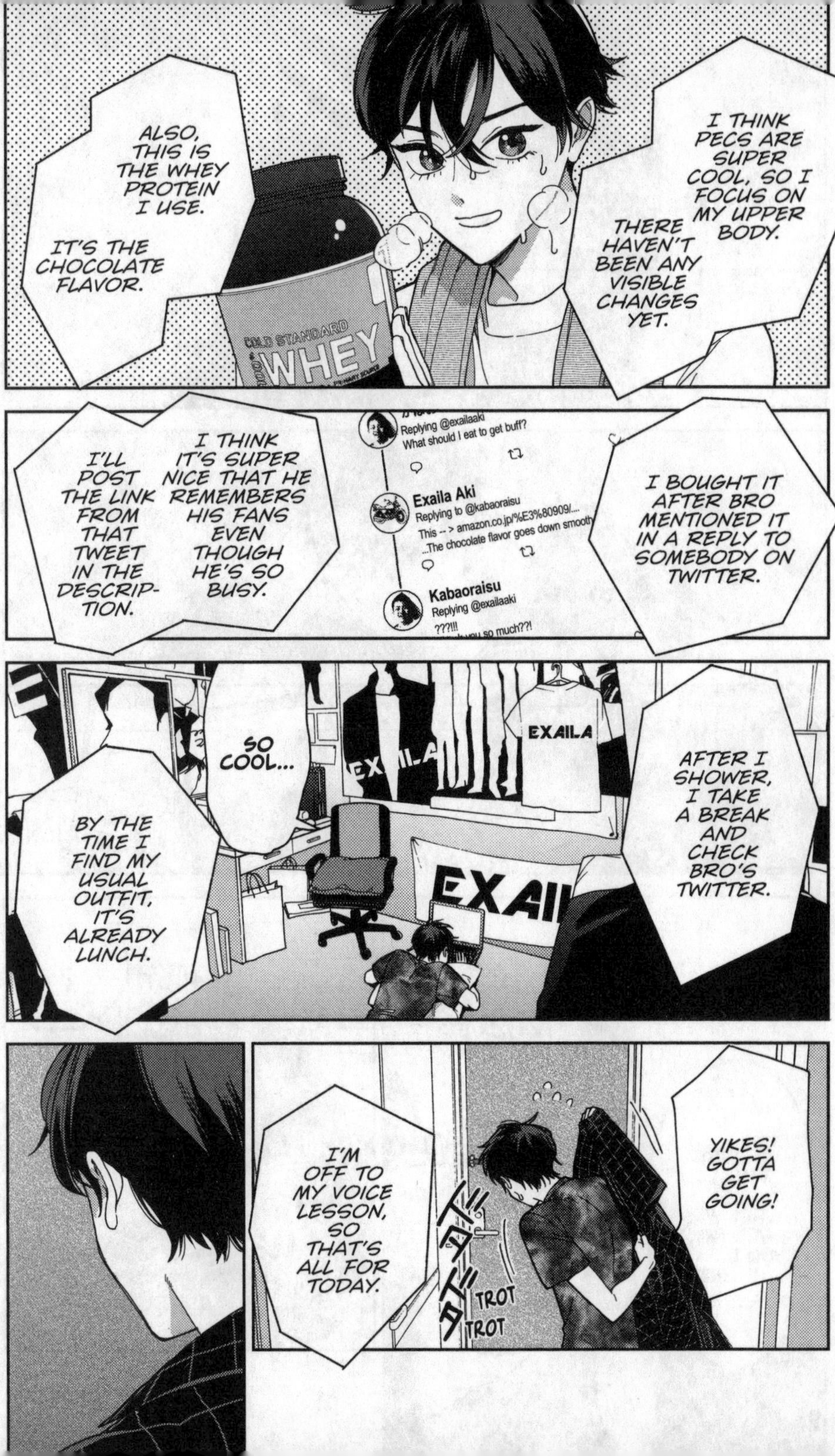
I THINK PECS ARE SUPER COOL, SO I FOCUS ON MY UPPER BODY.
THERE HAVEN'T BEEN ANY VISIBLE CHANGES YET.
WHEY
ALSO, THIS IS THE WHEY PROTEIN I USE.
IT'S THE CHOCOLATE FLAVOR.
I BOUGHT IT AFTER BRO MENTIONED IT IN A REPLY TO SOMEBODY ON TWITTER.
Replying @exailaaki
What should I eat to get buff?
Exaila Aki
Replying to @kabaoraisu
This --> amazon.co.jp/%E3%80909/....
...The chocolate flavor goes down smooth
Kabaoraisu
Replying @exailaaki
???!!!
I THINK IT'S SUPER NICE THAT HE REMEMBERS HIS FANS EVEN THOUGH HE'S SO BUSY.
I'LL POST THE LINK FROM THAT TWEET IN THE DESCRIPTION.
AFTER I SHOWER, I TAKE A BREAK AND CHECK BRO'S TWITTER.
EXAILA
EXAILA
EXAIL
SO COOL...
BY THE TIME I FIND MY USUAL OUTFIT, IT'S ALREADY LUNCH.
YIKES! GOTTA GET GOING!
TROT TROT
I'M OFF TO MY VOICE LESSON, SO THAT'S ALL FOR TODAY.

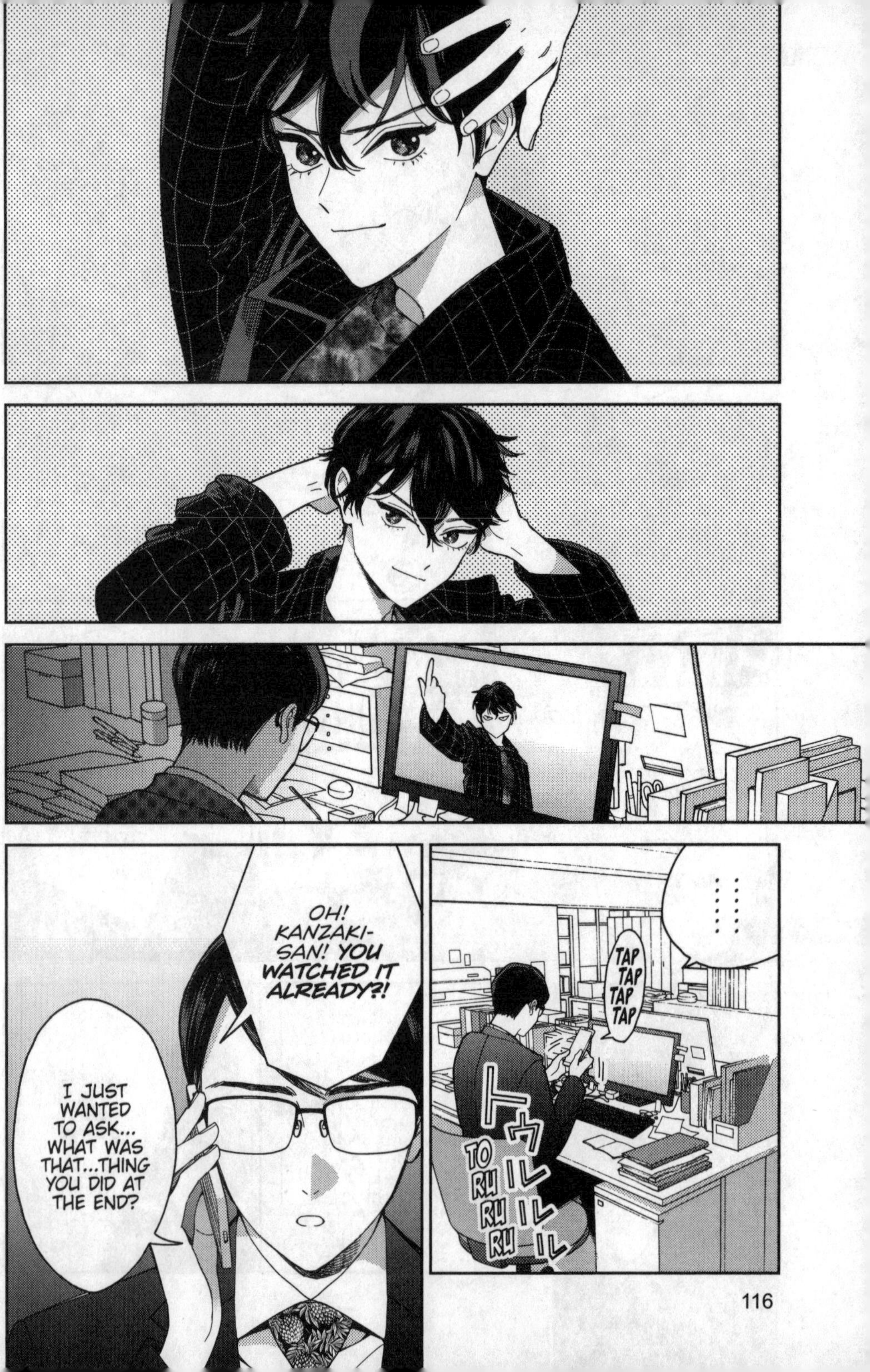
......
TAP TAP TAP TAP
トゥルルル
TORURURU
OH! KANZAKI-SAN! YOU WATCHED IT ALREADY?!
I JUST WANTED TO ASK... WHAT WAS THAT...THING YOU DID AT THE END?

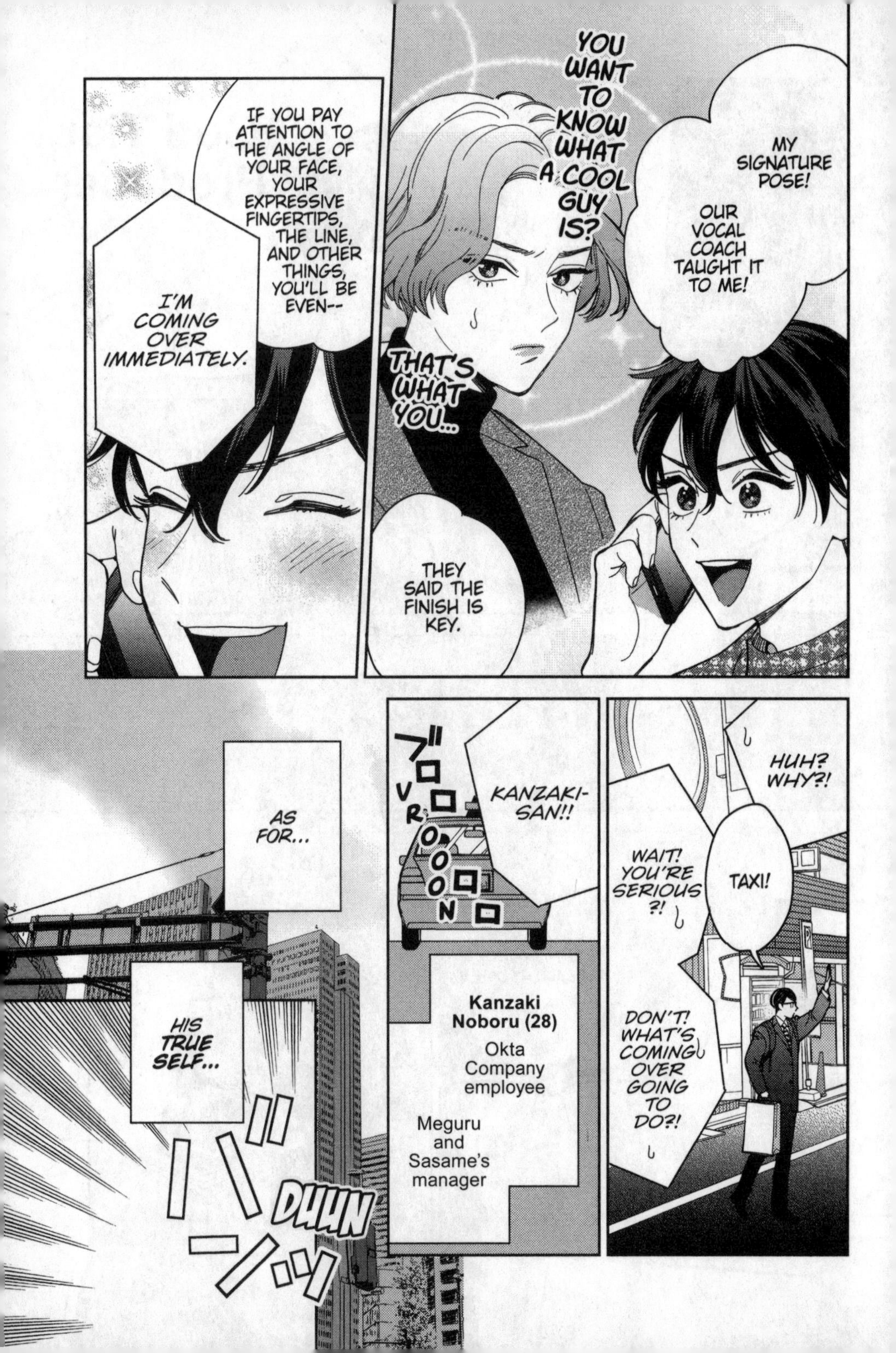
YOU WANT TO KNOW WHAT A COOL GUY IS?
MY SIGNATURE POSE!
OUR VOCAL COACH TAUGHT IT TO ME!
THAT'S WHAT YOU...
THEY SAID THE FINISH IS KEY.
IF YOU PAY ATTENTION TO THE ANGLE OF YOUR FACE, YOUR EXPRESSIVE FINGERTIPS, THE LINE, AND OTHER THINGS, YOU'LL BE EVEN--
I'M COMING OVER IMMEDIATELY.
HUH? WHY?!
TAXI!
WAIT! YOU'RE SERIOUS?!
DON'T! WHAT'S COMING OVER GOING TO DO?!
KANZAKI-SAN!!
VROOOON
Kanzaki Noboru (28)
Okta Company employee
Meguru and Sasame's manager
AS FOR...
HIS TRUE SELF...
DUUN

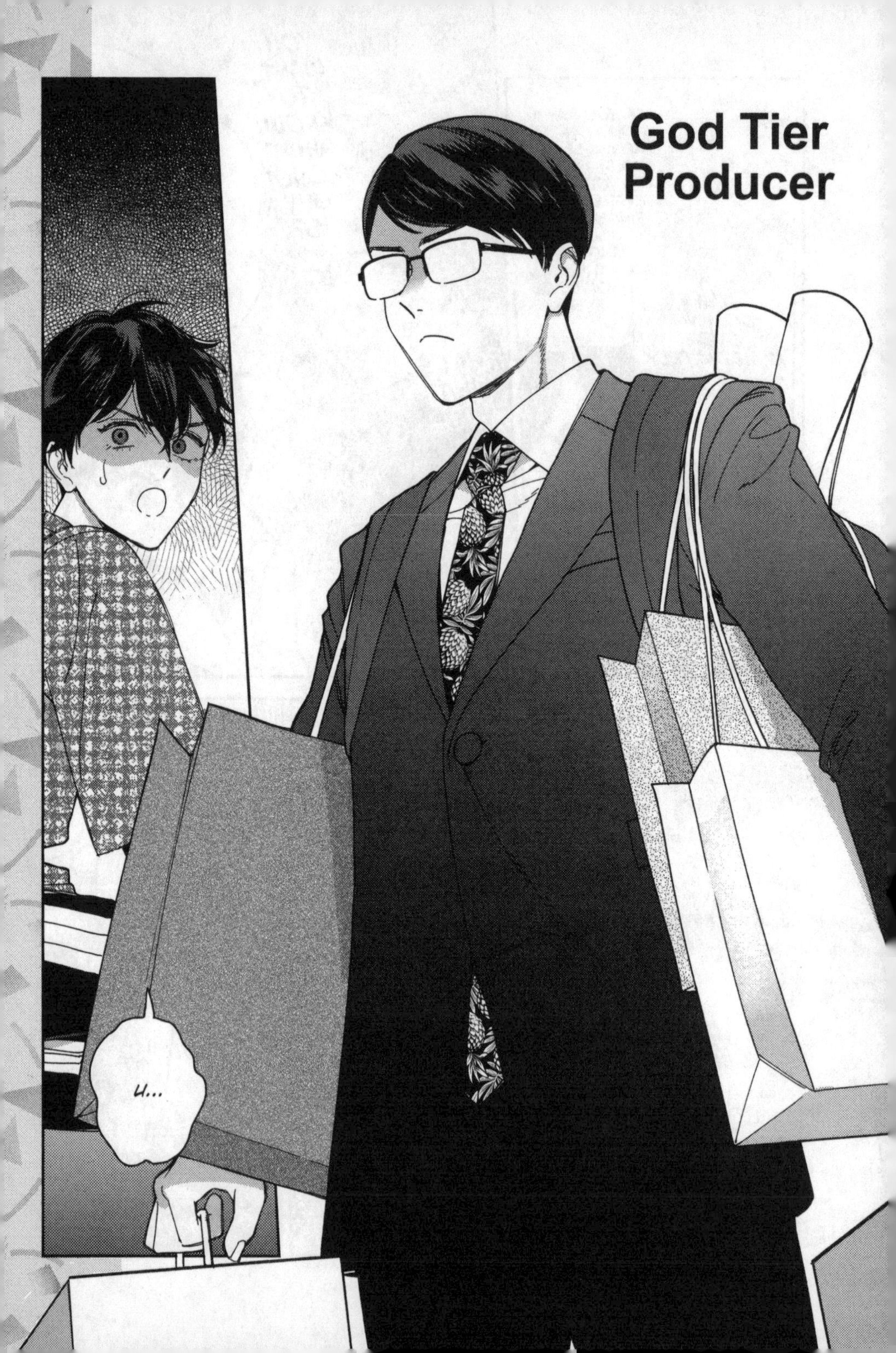
God Tier Producer
U...

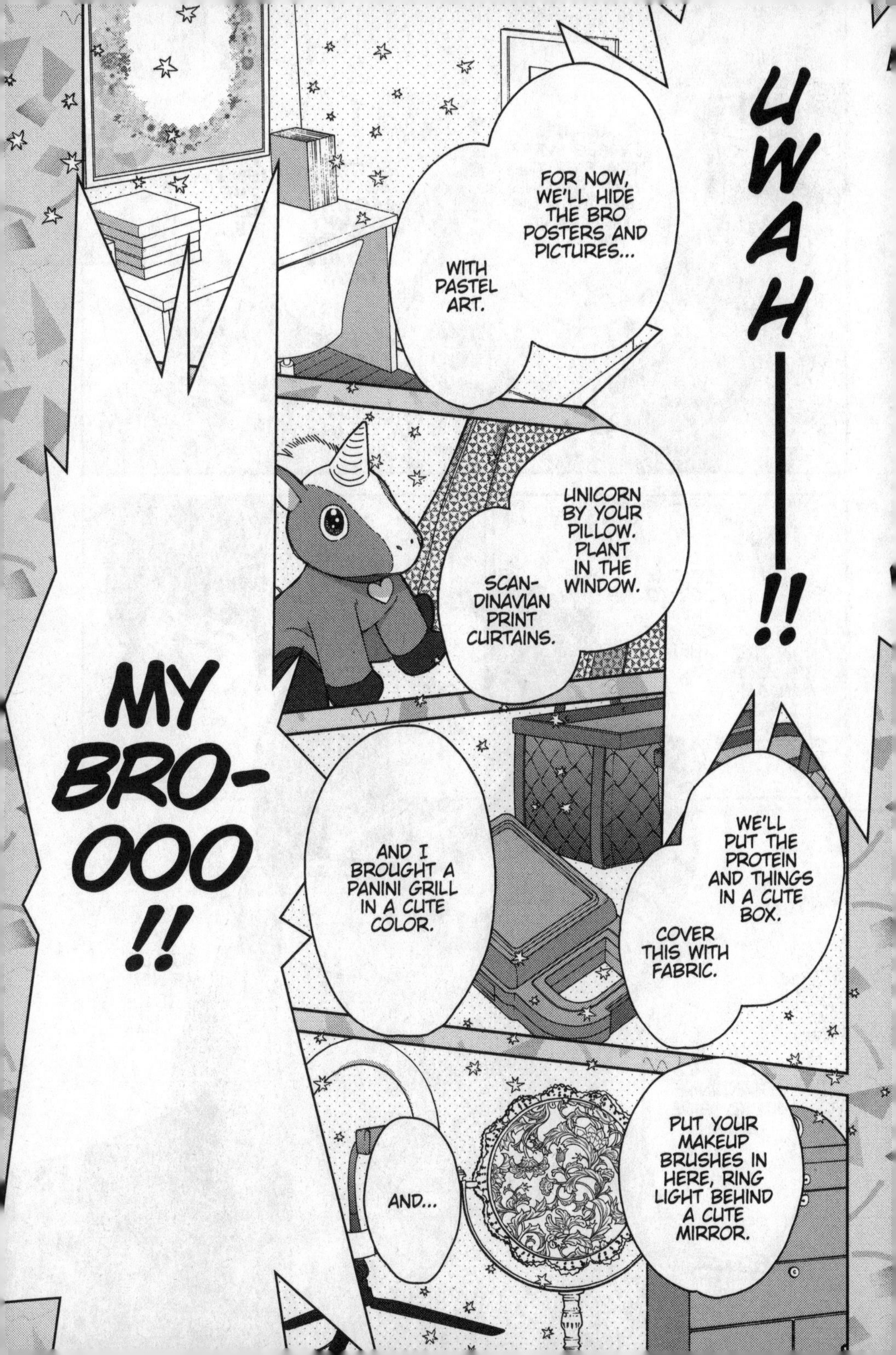
UWAH——!!
FOR NOW, WE'LL HIDE THE BRO POSTERS AND PICTURES...
WITH PASTEL ART.
UNICORN BY YOUR PILLOW. PLANT IN THE WINDOW.
SCAN-DINAVIAN PRINT CURTAINS.
WE'LL PUT THE PROTEIN AND THINGS IN A CUTE BOX.
COVER THIS WITH FABRIC.
AND I BROUGHT A PANINI GRILL IN A CUTE COLOR.
PUT YOUR MAKEUP BRUSHES IN HERE, RING LIGHT BEHIND A CUTE MIRROR.
AND...
MY BRO-OOO!!

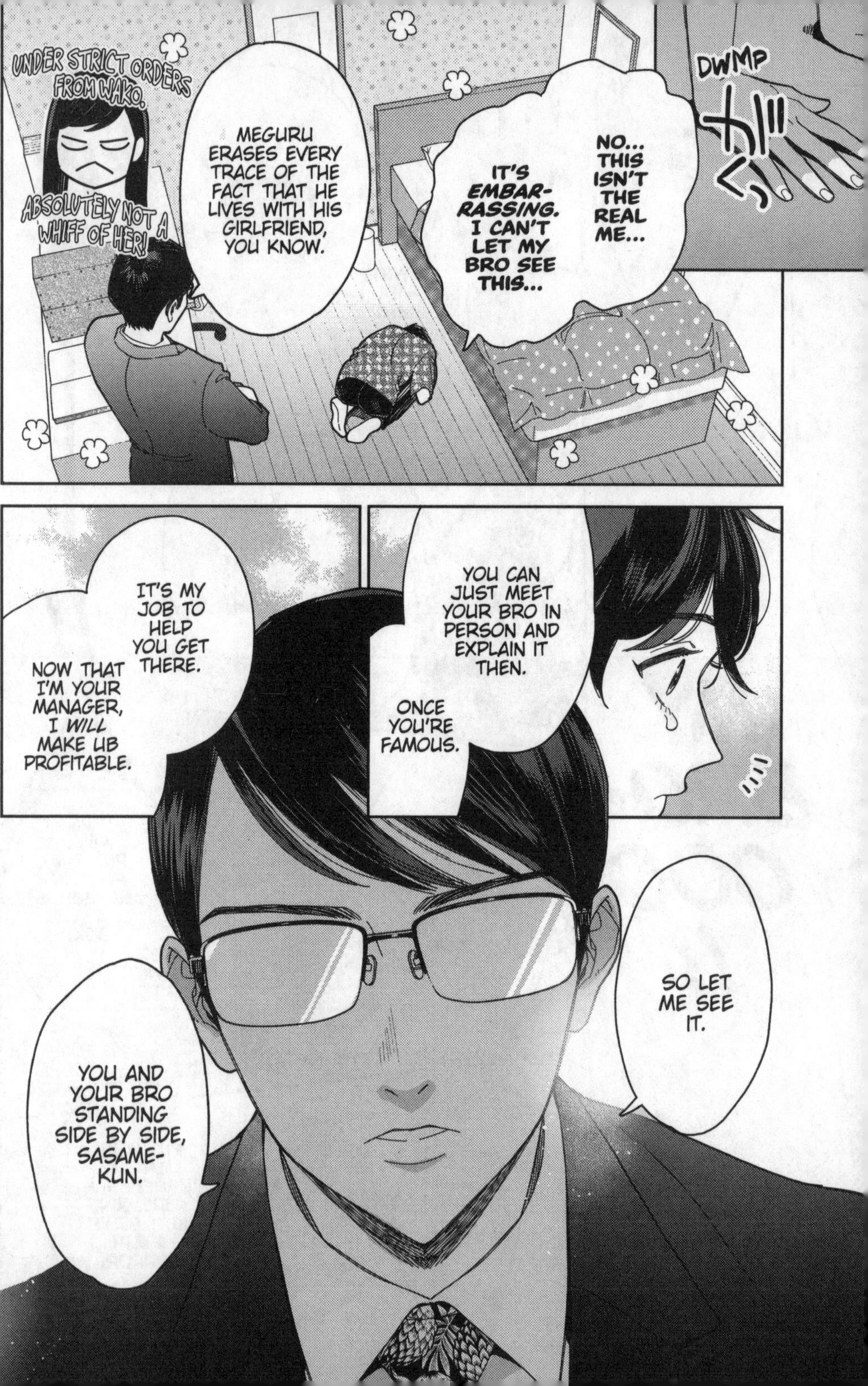
DWMP
NO... THIS ISN'T THE REAL ME...
IT'S EMBARRASSING. I CAN'T LET MY BRO SEE THIS...
MEGURU ERASES EVERY TRACE OF THE FACT THAT HE LIVES WITH HIS GIRLFRIEND, YOU KNOW.
UNDER STRICT ORDERS FROM WAKO.
ABSOLUTELY NOT A WHIFF OF HER!
YOU CAN JUST MEET YOUR BRO IN PERSON AND EXPLAIN IT THEN.
ONCE YOU'RE FAMOUS.
IT'S MY JOB TO HELP YOU GET THERE.
NOW THAT I'M YOUR MANAGER, I WILL MAKE UB PROFITABLE.
SO LET ME SEE IT.
YOU AND YOUR BRO STANDING SIDE BY SIDE, SASAME-KUN.

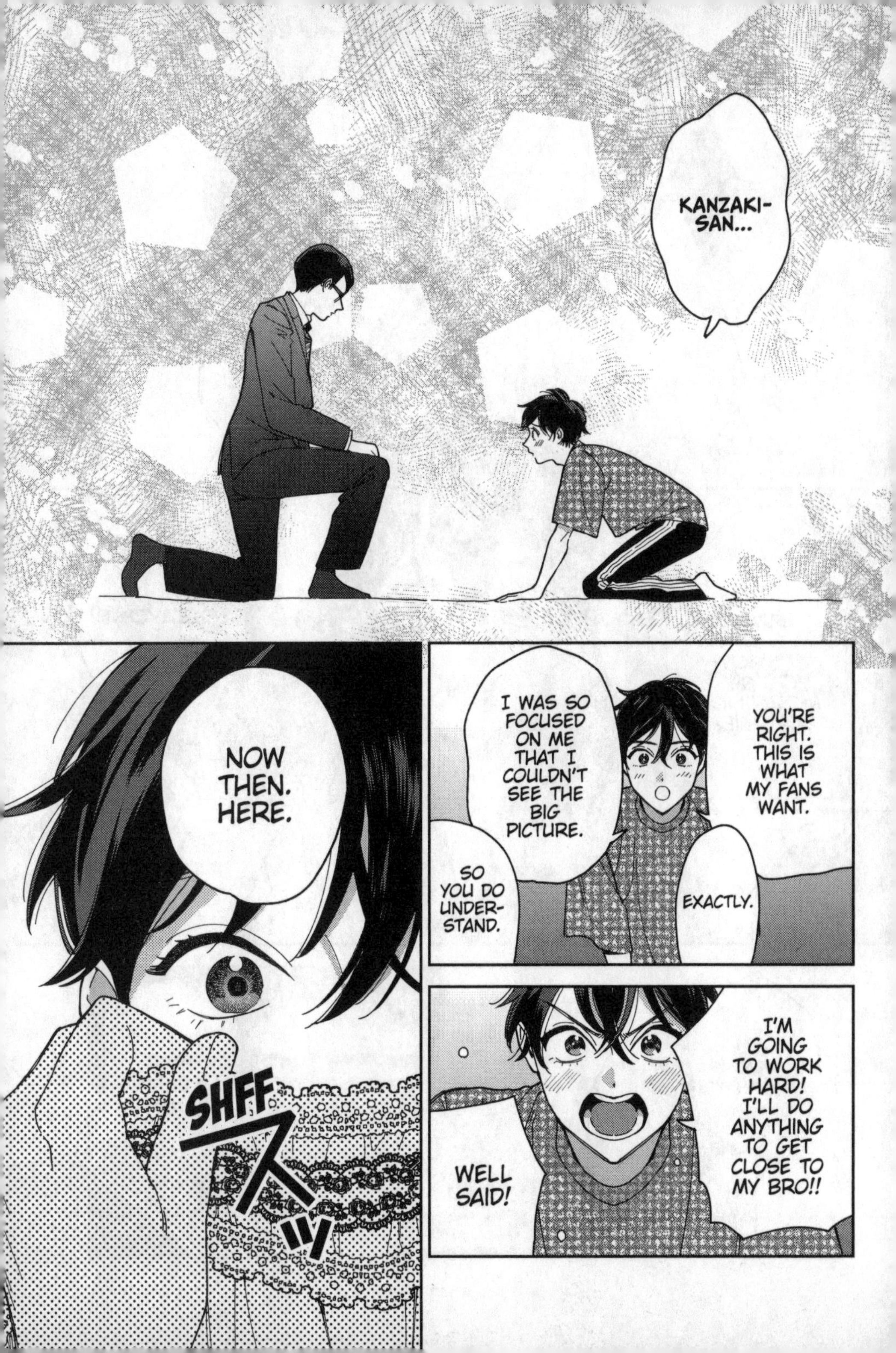

KANZAKI-SAN...
YOU'RE RIGHT. THIS IS WHAT MY FANS WANT.
I WAS SO FOCUSED ON ME THAT I COULDN'T SEE THE BIG PICTURE.
EXACTLY.
SO YOU DO UNDER-STAND.
I'M GOING TO WORK HARD! I'LL DO ANYTHING TO GET CLOSE TO MY BRO!!
WELL SAID!
NOW THEN. HERE.
SHFF

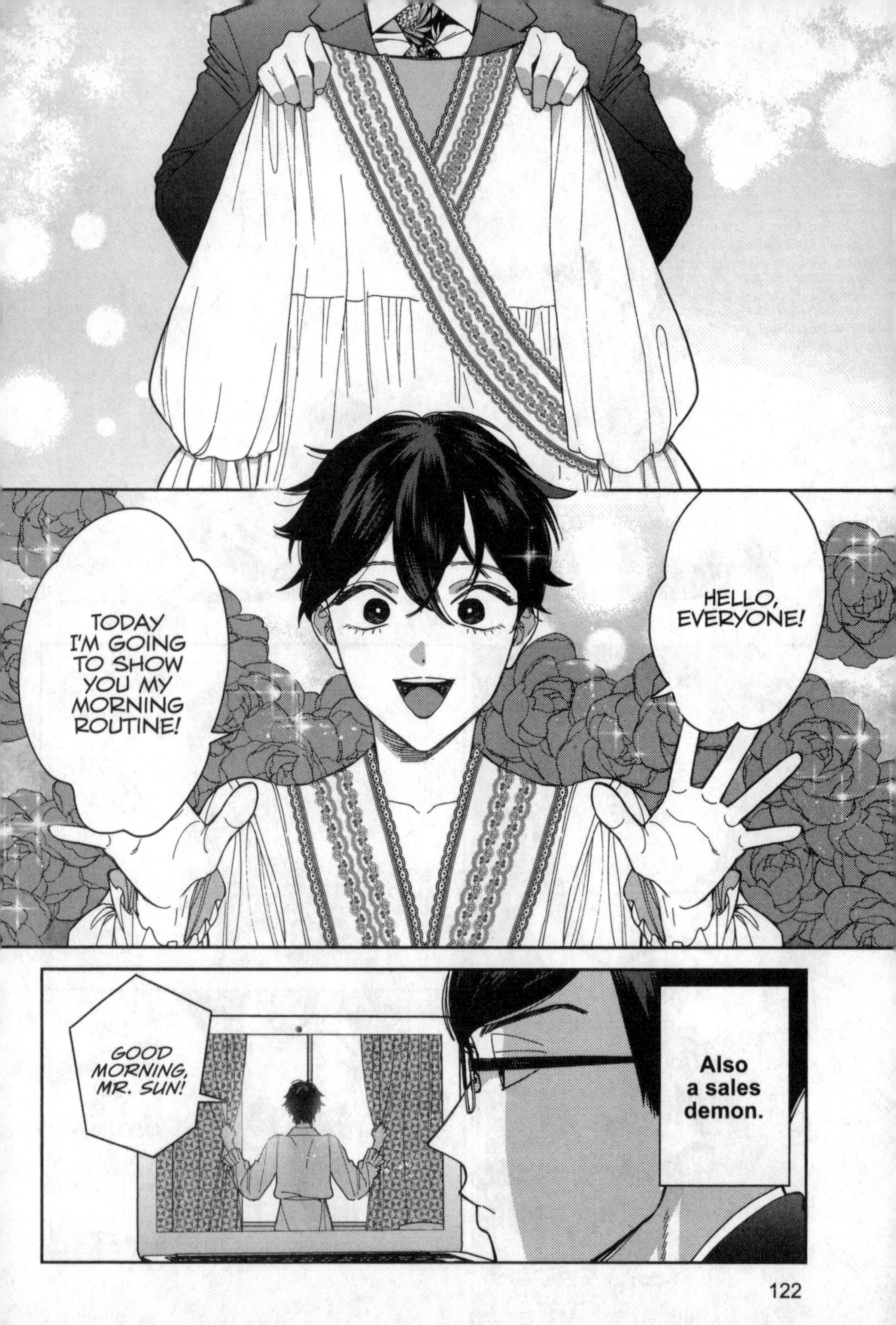
HELLO, EVERYONE!
TODAY I'M GOING TO SHOW YOU MY MORNING ROUTINE!
Also a sales demon.
GOOD MORNING, MR. SUN!

The Twenty-Eighth One

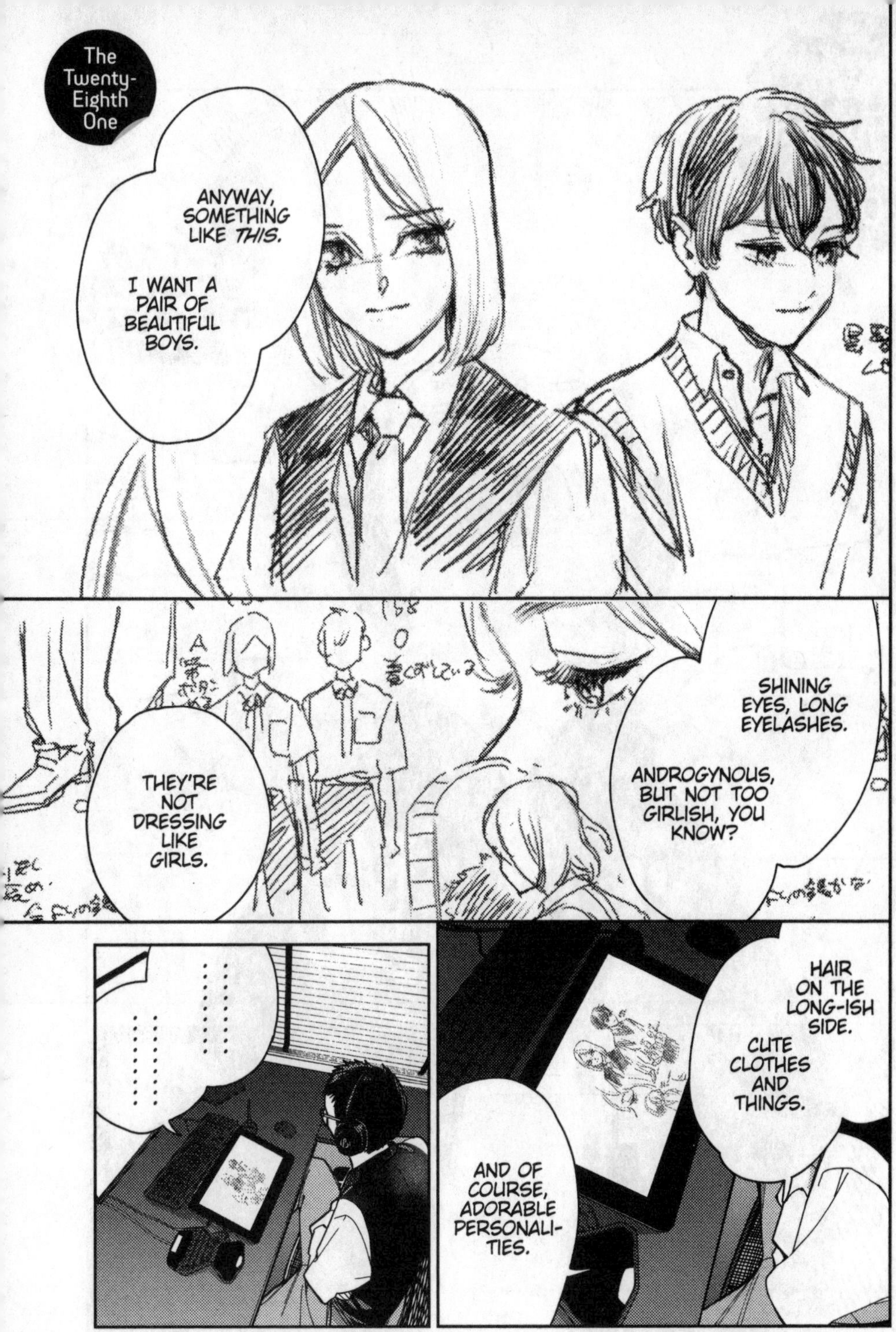
ANYWAY, SOMETHING LIKE *THIS.*
I WANT A PAIR OF BEAUTIFUL BOYS.
SHINING EYES, LONG EYELASHES.
ANDROGYNOUS, BUT NOT TOO GIRLISH, YOU KNOW?
THEY'RE NOT DRESSING LIKE GIRLS.
HAIR ON THE LONG-ISH SIDE.
CUTE CLOTHES AND THINGS.
AND OF COURSE, ADORABLE PERSONALITIES.
......
......

My Androgynous Boyfriend

The Twenty-Eighth One

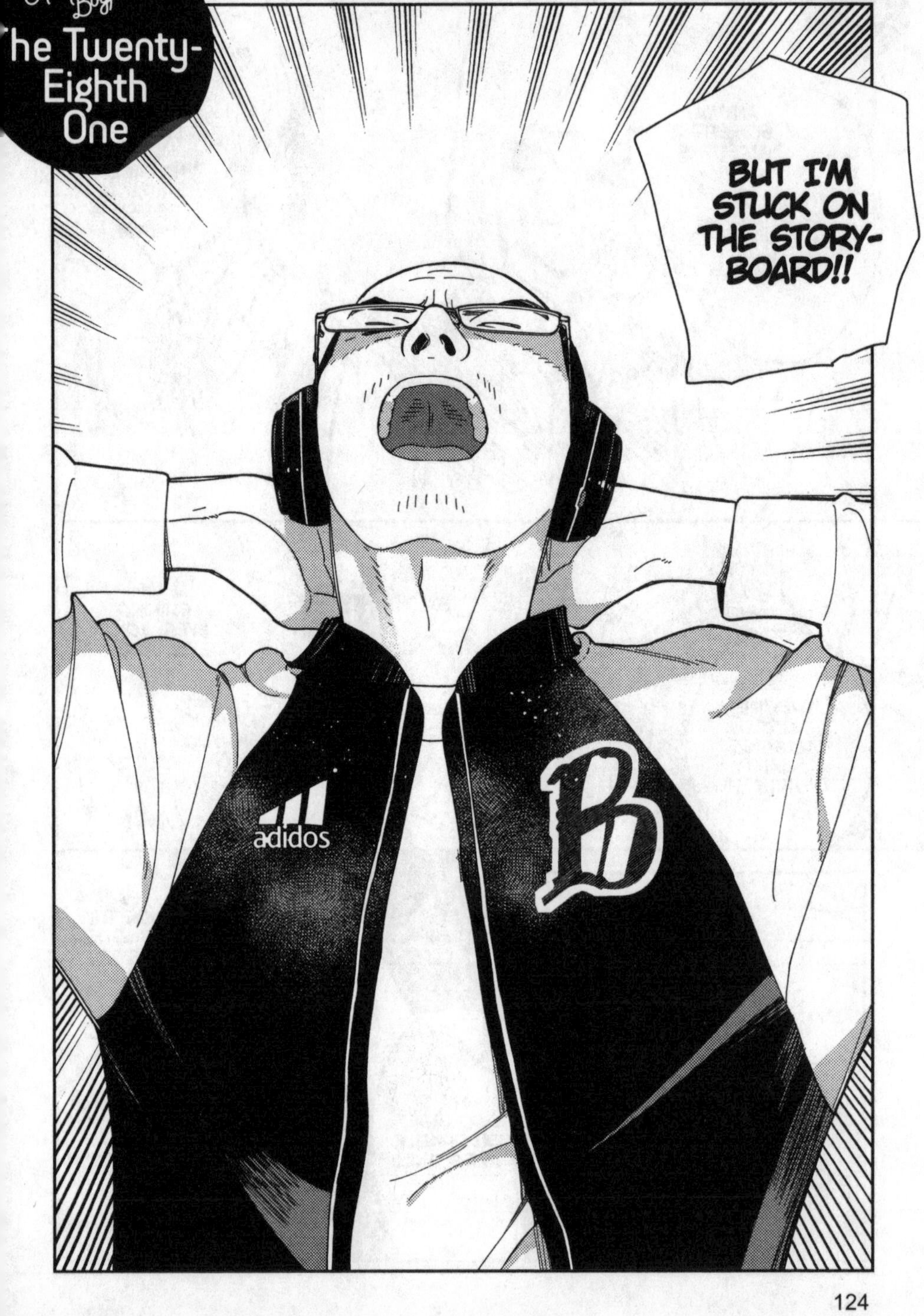
BUT I'M STUCK ON THE STORY-BOARD!!
adidos

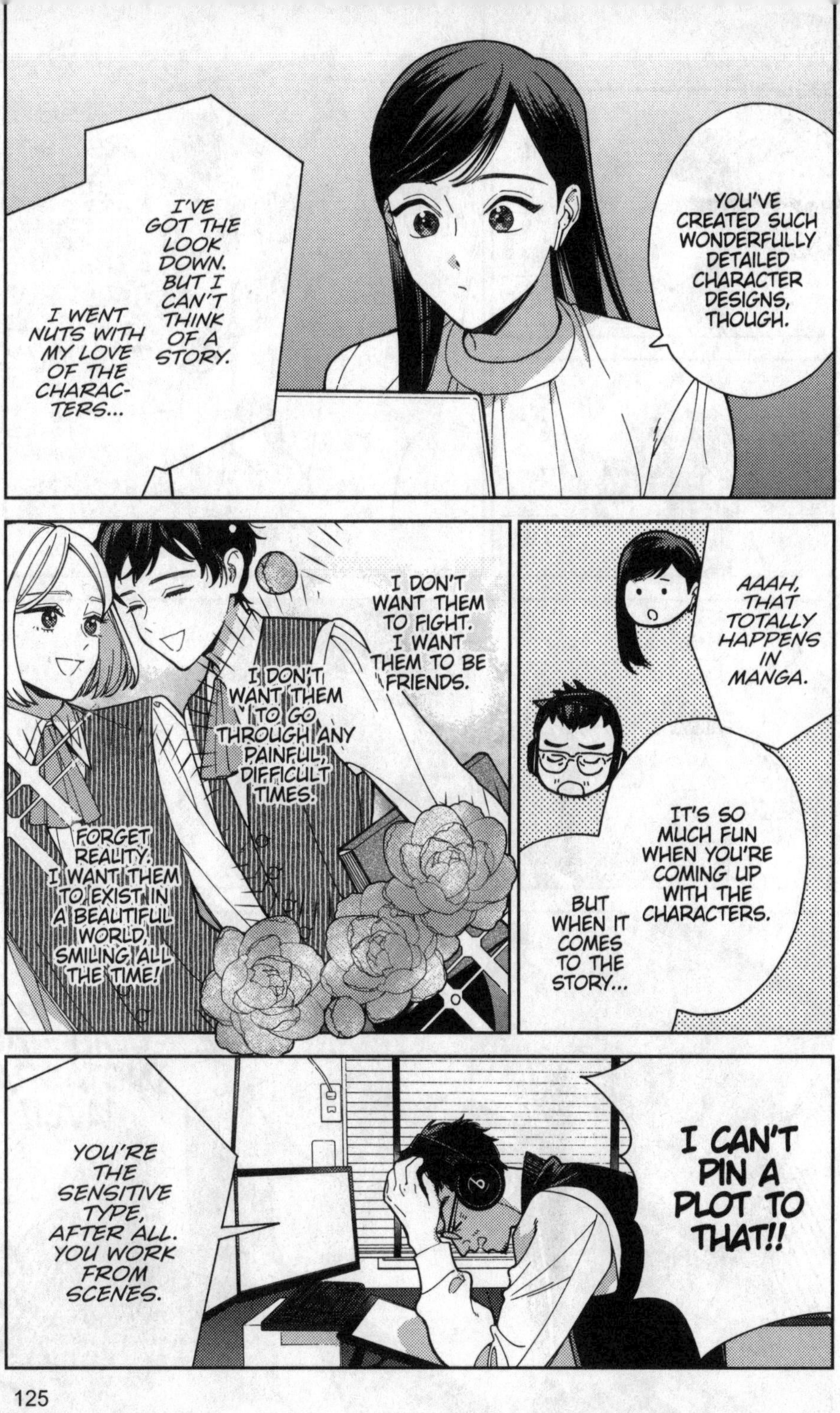
YOU'VE CREATED SUCH WONDERFULLY DETAILED CHARACTER DESIGNS, THOUGH.
I'VE GOT THE LOOK DOWN. BUT I CAN'T THINK OF A STORY.
I WENT NUTS WITH MY LOVE OF THE CHARAC-TERS...
AAAH, THAT TOTALLY HAPPENS IN MANGA.
IT'S SO MUCH FUN WHEN YOU'RE COMING UP WITH THE CHARACTERS.
BUT WHEN IT COMES TO THE STORY...
I DON'T WANT THEM TO FIGHT. I WANT THEM TO BE FRIENDS.
I DON'T WANT THEM TO GO THROUGH ANY PAINFUL, DIFFICULT TIMES.
FORGET REALITY. I WANT THEM TO EXIST IN A BEAUTIFUL WORLD, SMILING ALL THE TIME!
I CAN'T PIN A PLOT TO THAT!!
YOU'RE THE SENSITIVE TYPE, AFTER ALL. YOU WORK FROM SCENES.

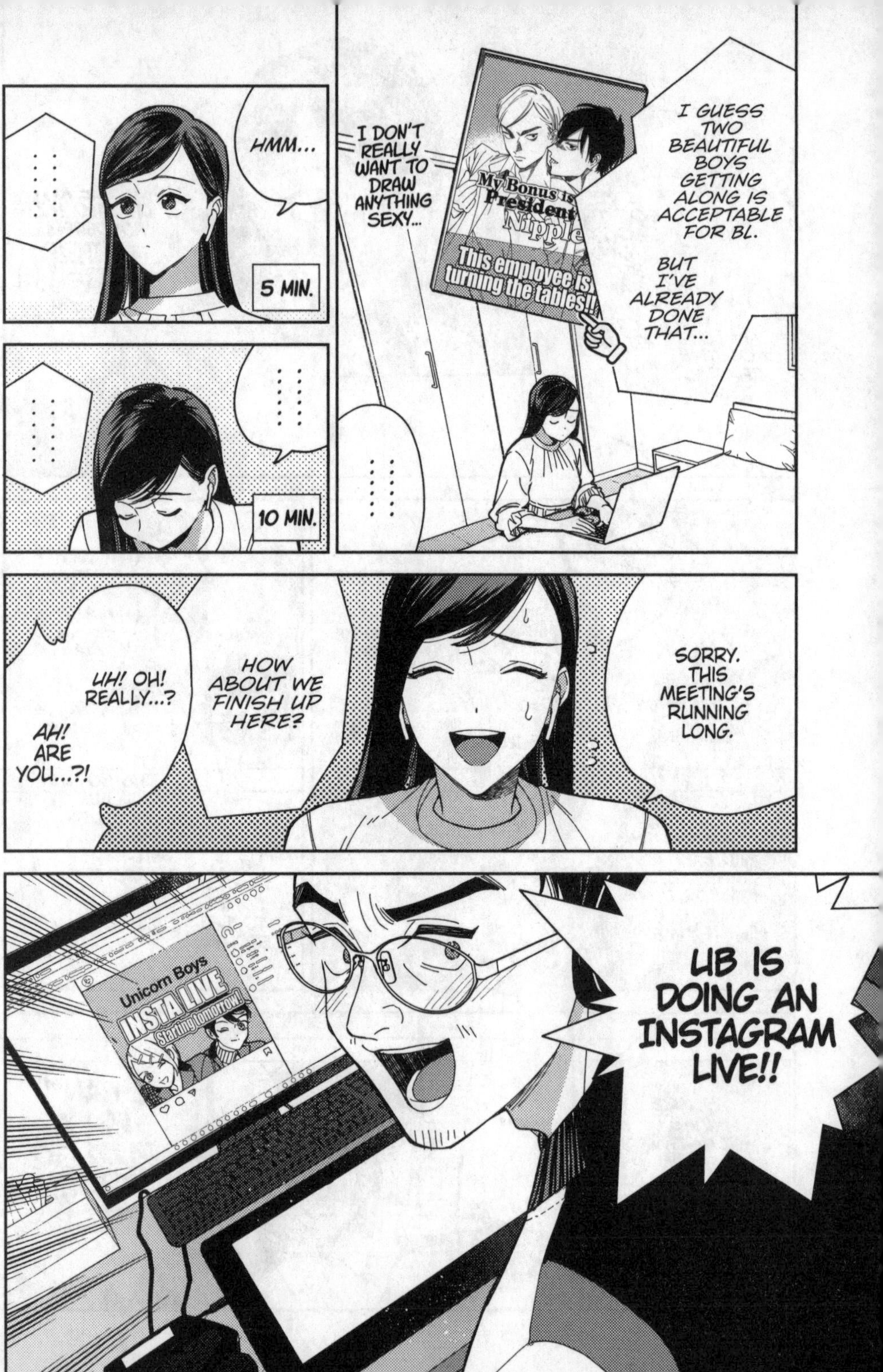
I GUESS TWO BEAUTIFUL BOYS GETTING ALONG IS ACCEPTABLE FOR BL.
BUT I'VE ALREADY DONE THAT...
My Bonus is President Nipple
This employee is turning the tables!!
I DON'T REALLY WANT TO DRAW ANYTHING SEXY...
......
HMM...
......
5 MIN.
......
......
10 MIN.
SORRY. THIS MEETING'S RUNNING LONG.
HOW ABOUT WE FINISH UP HERE?
UH! OH! REALLY...?
AH! ARE YOU...?!
UB IS DOING AN INSTAGRAM LIVE!!
Unicorn Boys
INSTA LIVE
Starting tomorrow!

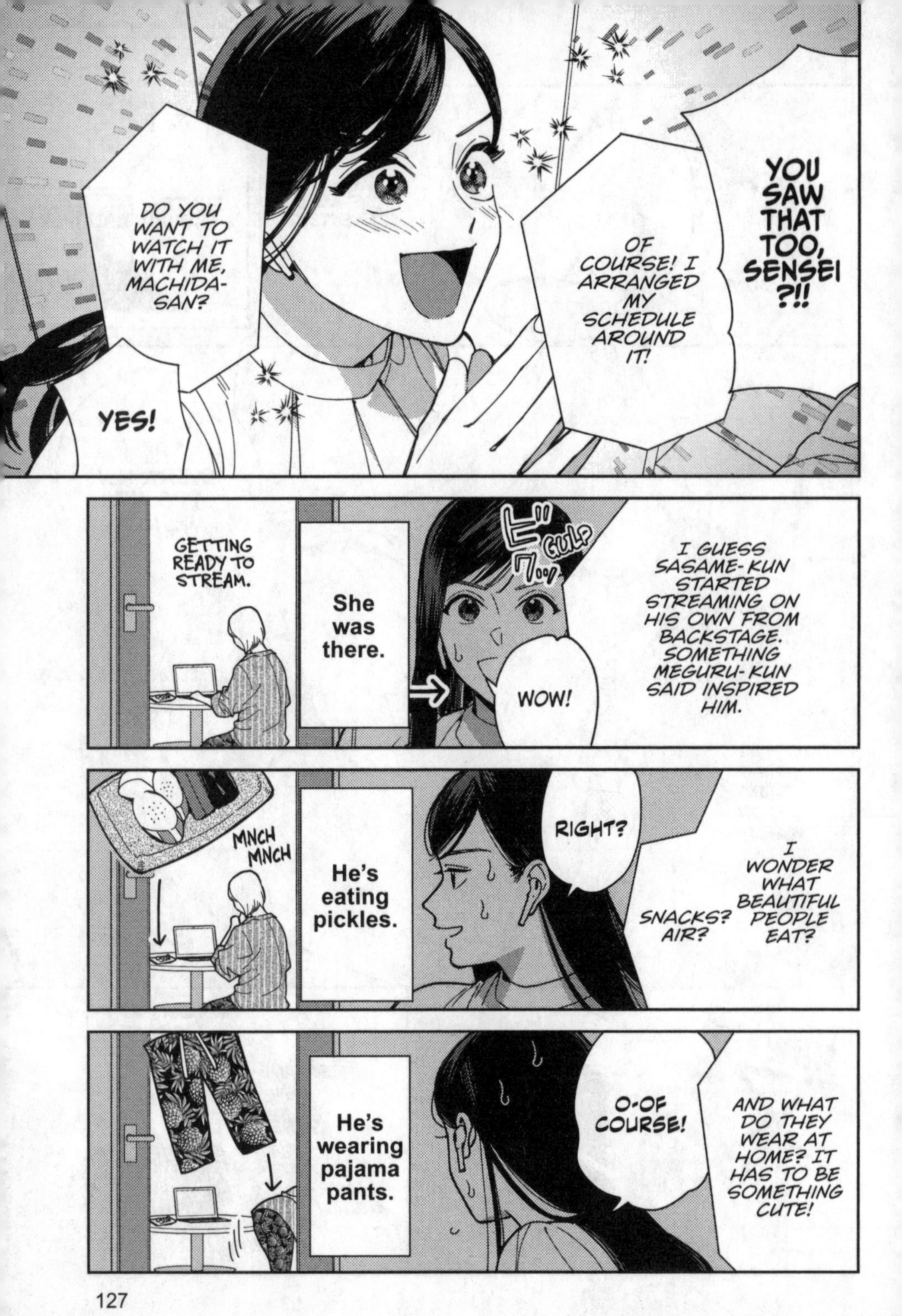
YOU SAW THAT TOO, SENSEI?!!
OF COURSE! I ARRANGED MY SCHEDULE AROUND IT!
DO YOU WANT TO WATCH IT WITH ME, MACHIDA-SAN?
YES!
I GUESS SASAME-KUN STARTED STREAMING ON HIS OWN FROM BACKSTAGE. SOMETHING MEGURU-KUN SAID INSPIRED HIM.
GULP
WOW!
She was there.
GETTING READY TO STREAM.
I WONDER WHAT BEAUTIFUL PEOPLE EAT?
SNACKS? AIR?
RIGHT?
He's eating pickles.
MNCH MNCH
AND WHAT DO THEY WEAR AT HOME? IT HAS TO BE SOMETHING CUTE!
O-OF COURSE!
He's wearing pajama pants.

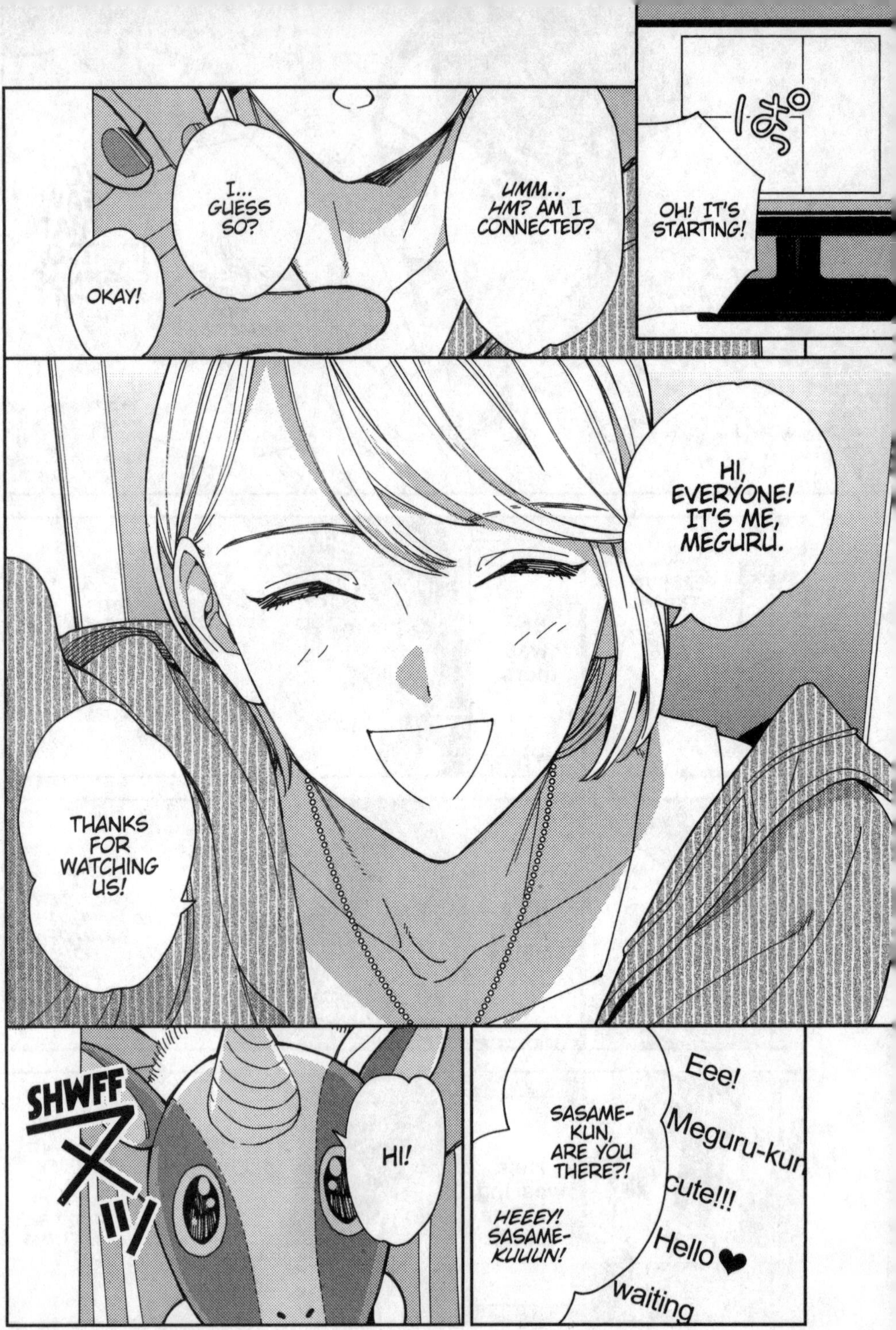

ぽっ
OH! IT'S STARTING!
UMM... HM? AM I CONNECTED?
I... GUESS SO?
OKAY!
HI, EVERYONE! IT'S ME, MEGURU.
THANKS FOR WATCHING US!
Eee!
Meguru-kun
cute!!!
Hello
waiting
SASAME-KUN, ARE YOU THERE?!
HEEEY! SASAME-KUUUN!
HI!
SHWFF
スッ

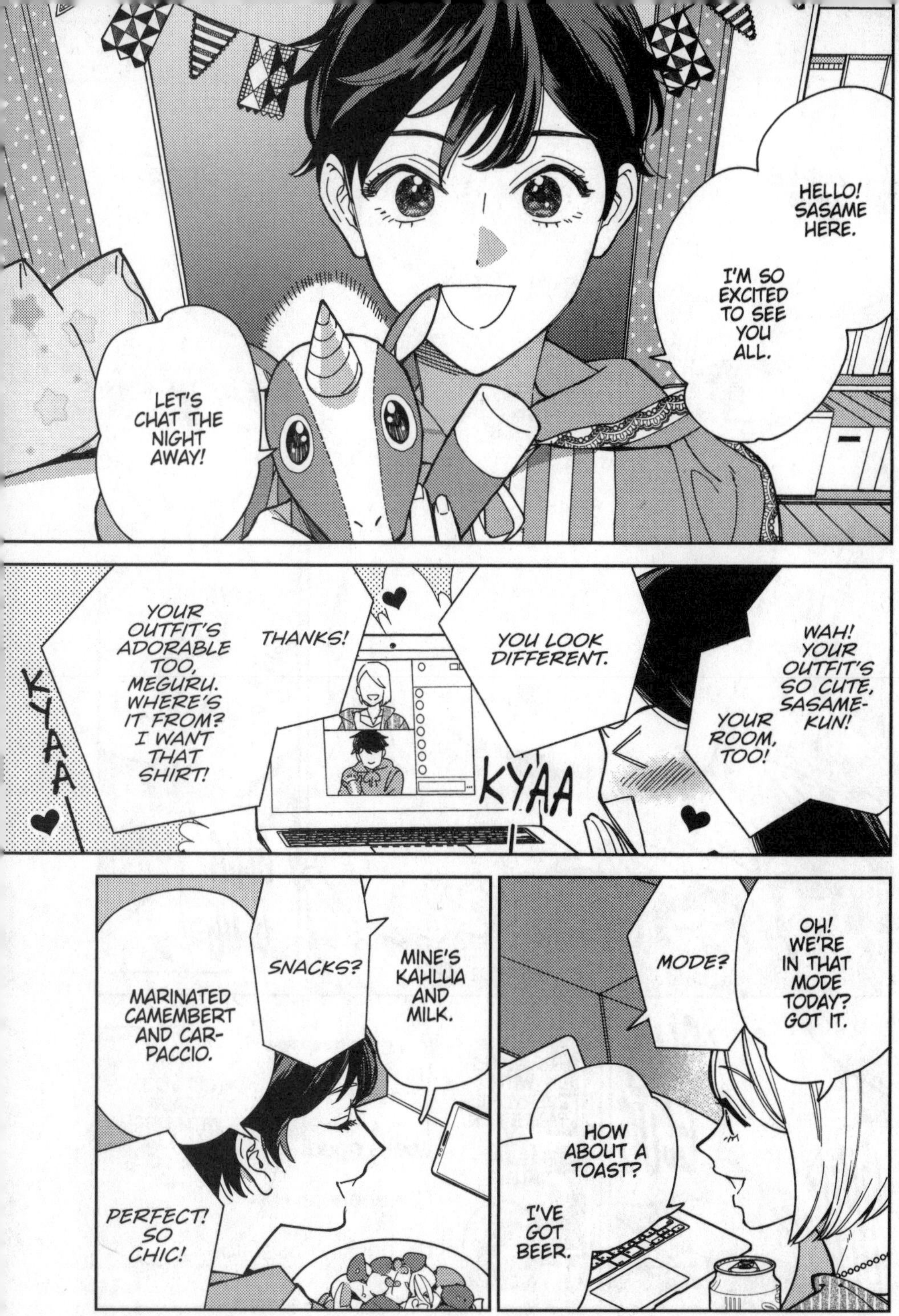
HELLO! SASAME HERE.
I'M SO EXCITED TO SEE YOU ALL.
LET'S CHAT THE NIGHT AWAY!
WAH! YOUR OUTFIT'S SO CUTE, SASAME-KUN!
YOUR ROOM, TOO!
KYAA
YOU LOOK DIFFERENT.
THANKS!
YOUR OUTFIT'S ADORABLE TOO, MEGURU. WHERE'S IT FROM? I WANT THAT SHIRT!
KYAA
OH! WE'RE IN THAT MODE TODAY? GOT IT.
MODE?
HOW ABOUT A TOAST?
I'VE GOT BEER.
MINE'S KAHLUA AND MILK.
SNACKS?
MARINATED CAMEMBERT AND CAR-PACCIO.
PERFECT! SO CHIC!

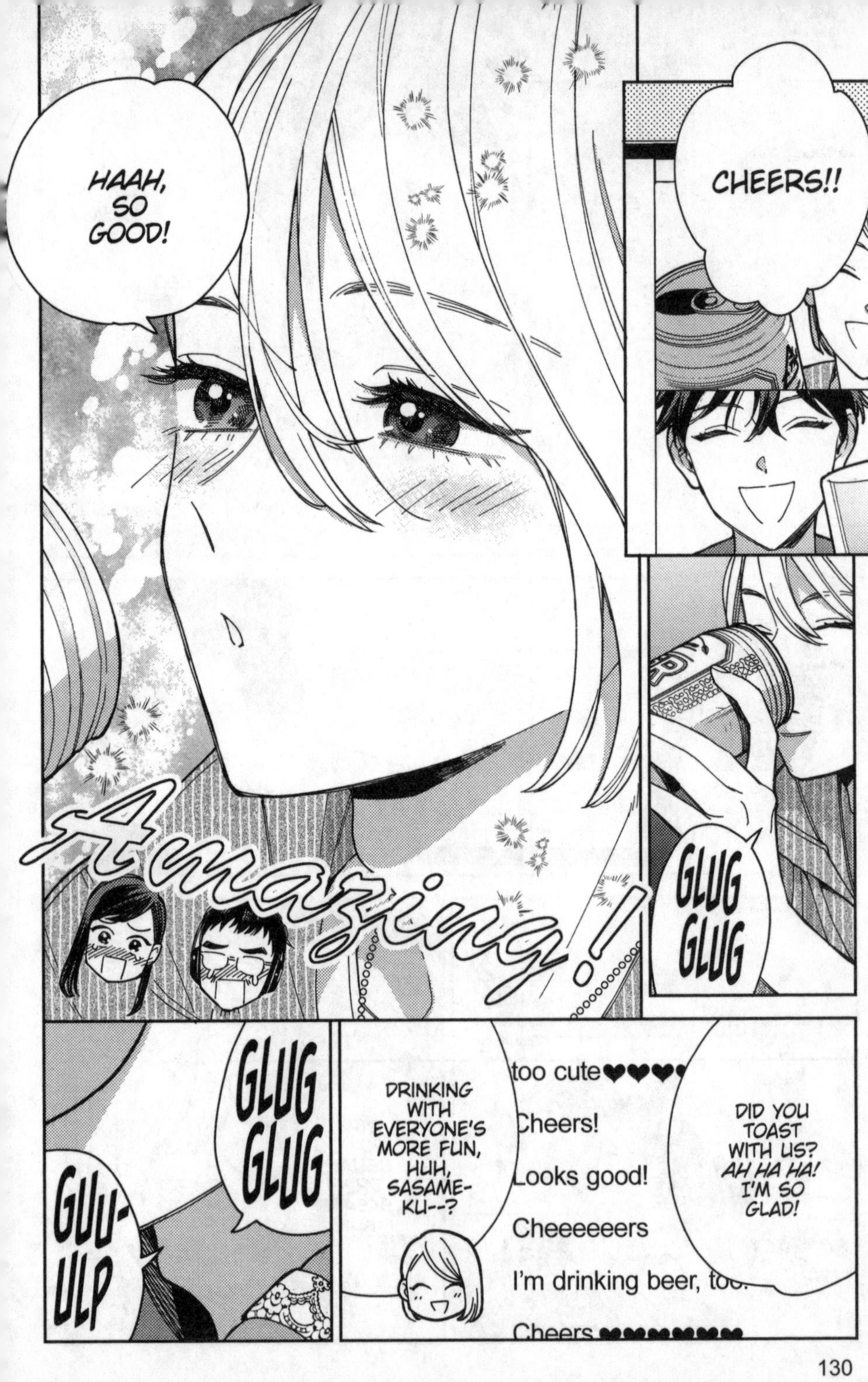
CHEERS!!
GLUG GLUG
HAAH, SO GOOD!
Amazing!
DID YOU TOAST WITH US? AH HA HA! I'M SO GLAD!
too cute❤❤❤
Cheers!
Looks good!
Cheeeeeers
I'm drinking beer, too.
DRINKING WITH EVERYONE'S MORE FUN, HUH, SASAME-KU--?
GLUG GLUG
GUU-ULP

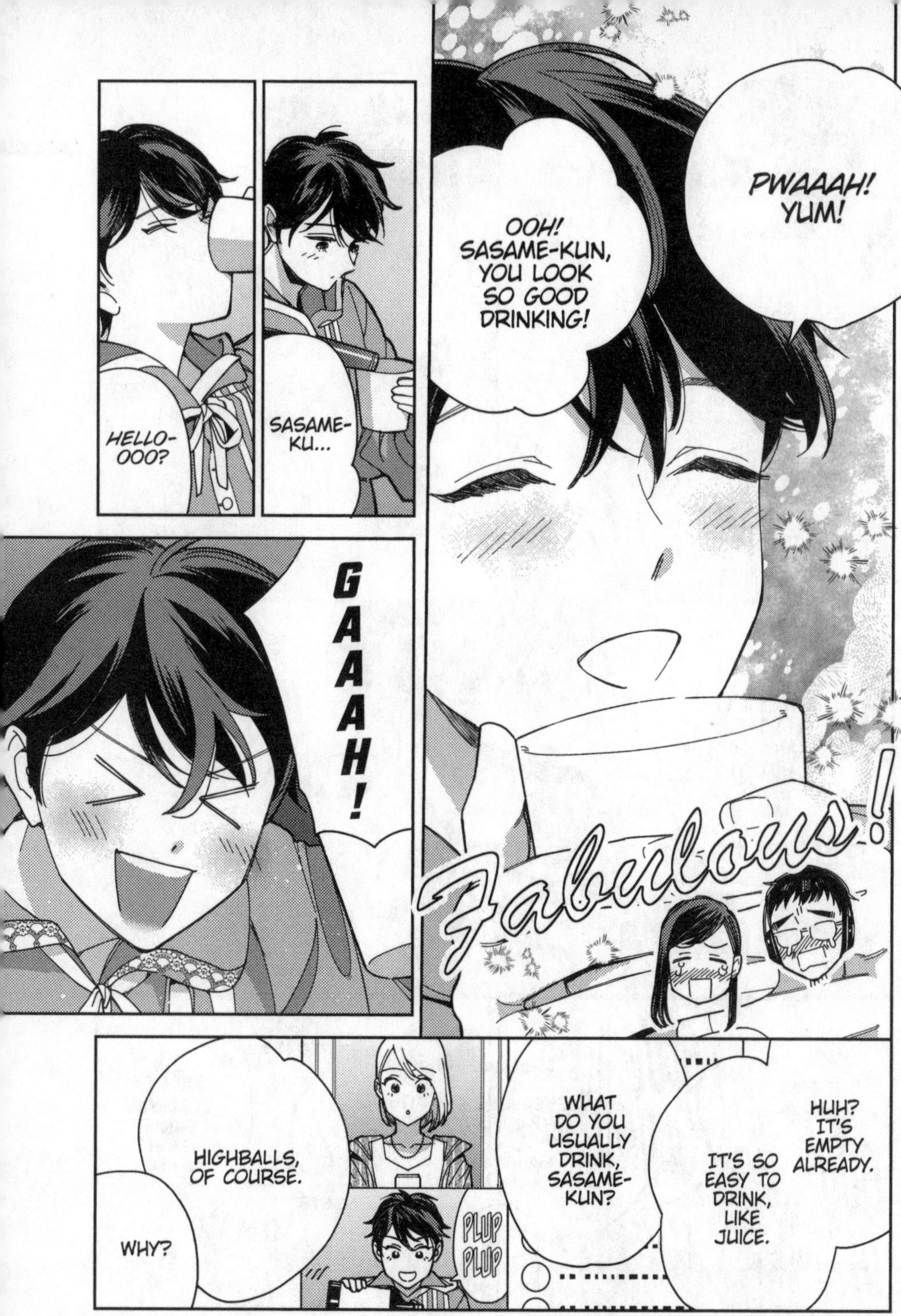
PWAAAH! YUM!
OOH! SASAME-KUN, YOU LOOK SO GOOD DRINKING!
Fabulous!
SASAME-KU...
HELLO-OOO?
GAAAAH!
HUH? IT'S EMPTY ALREADY.
IT'S SO EASY TO DRINK, LIKE JUICE.
WHAT DO YOU USUALLY DRINK, SASAME-KUN?
PLUP PLUP
HIGHBALLS, OF COURSE.
WHY?

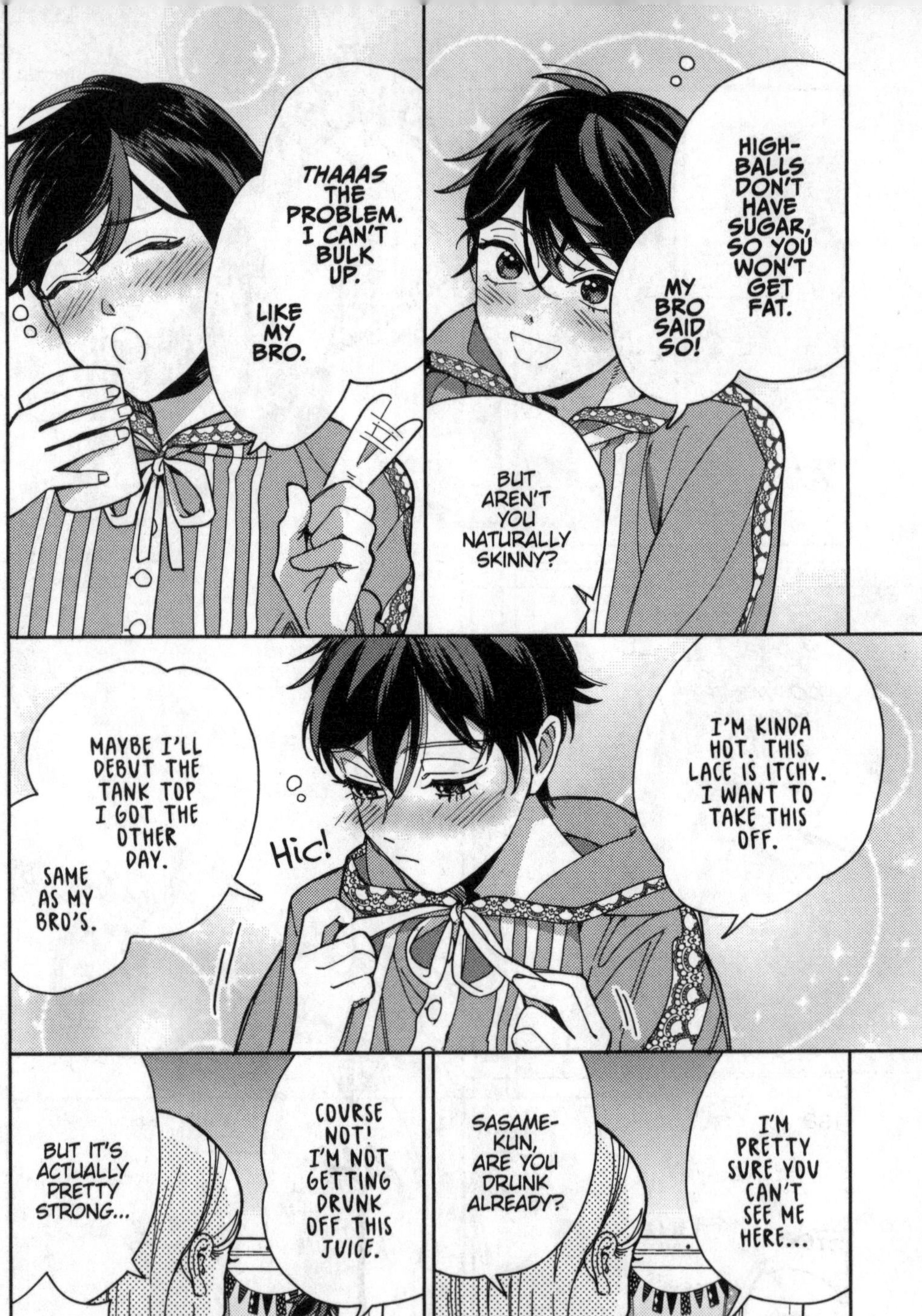
HIGH-BALLS DON'T HAVE SUGAR, SO YOU WON'T GET FAT.
MY BRO SAID SO!
BUT AREN'T YOU NATURALLY SKINNY?
THAAAS THE PROBLEM. I CAN'T BULK UP.
LIKE MY BRO.
I'M KINDA HOT. THIS LACE IS ITCHY. I WANT TO TAKE THIS OFF.
Hic!
MAYBE I'LL DEBUT THE TANK TOP I GOT THE OTHER DAY.
SAME AS MY BRO'S.
I'M PRETTY SURE YOU CAN'T SEE ME HERE...
SASAME-KUN, ARE YOU DRUNK ALREADY?
RSTL RSTL
COURSE NOT! I'M NOT GETTING DRUNK OFF THIS JUICE.
BUT IT'S ACTUALLY PRETTY STRONG...
PFT!

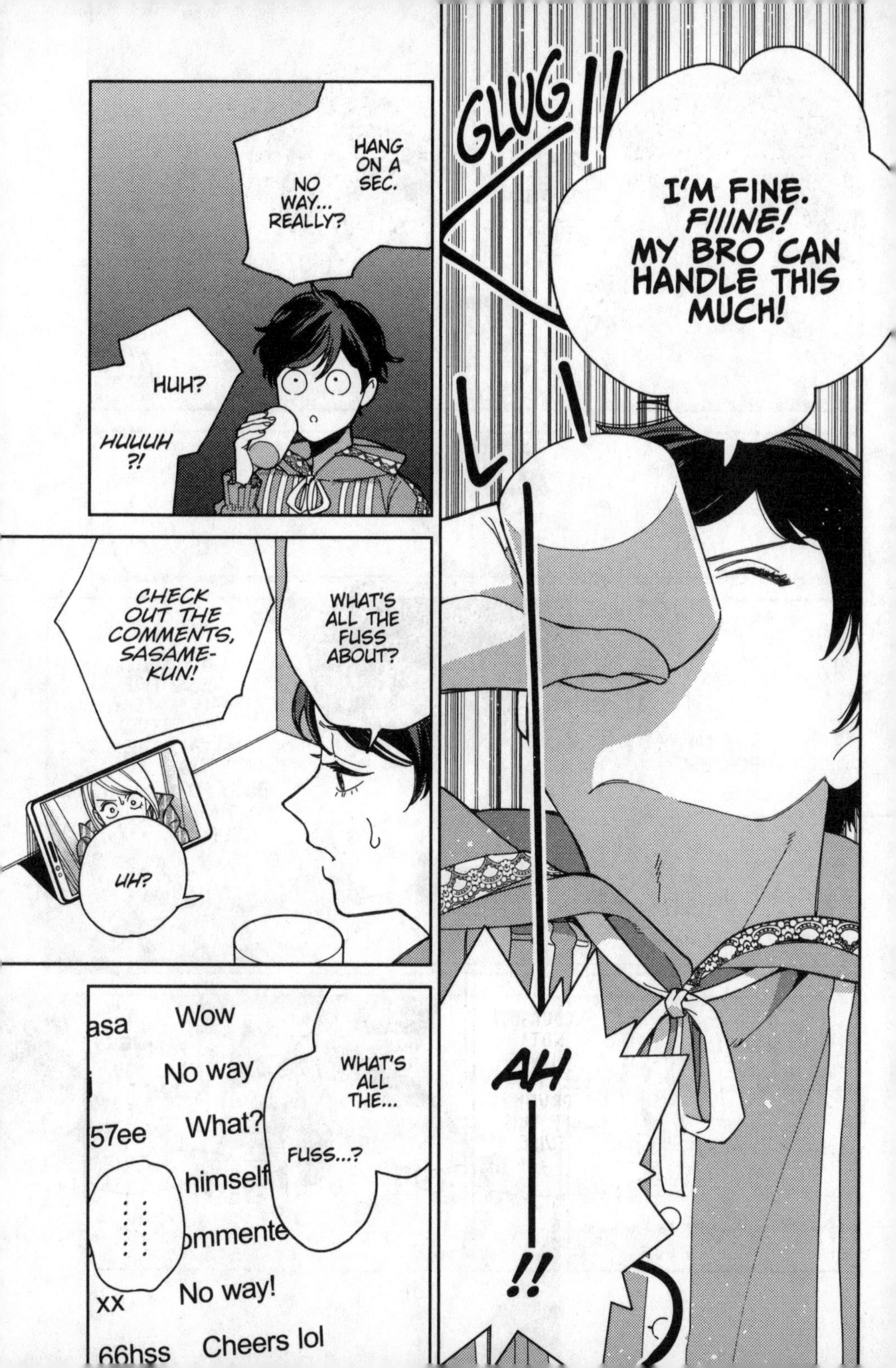
GLUG
I'M FINE. FIIINE! MY BRO CAN HANDLE THIS MUCH!
AH——!!
HANG ON A SEC.
NO WAY... REALLY?
HUH?
HUUUH?!
WHAT'S ALL THE FUSS ABOUT?
CHECK OUT THE COMMENTS, SASAME-KUN!
UH?
WHAT'S ALL THE...
FUSS...?
asa Wow
No way
57ee What?
himself
xx No way!
66hss Cheers lol

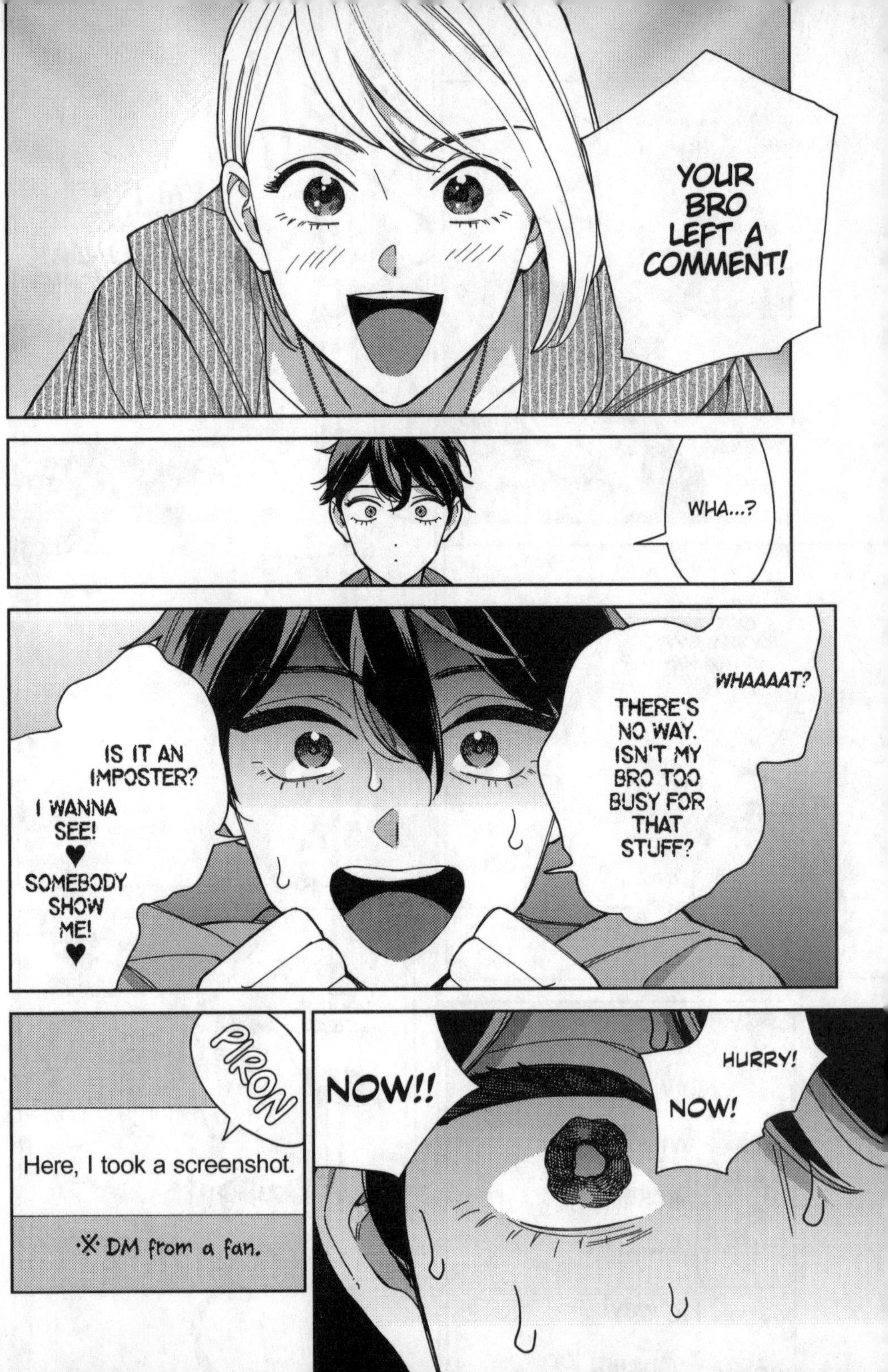
YOUR BRO LEFT A COMMENT!
WHA...?
WHAAAAT?
THERE'S NO WAY. ISN'T MY BRO TOO BUSY FOR THAT STUFF?
IS IT AN IMPOSTER?
I WANNA SEE! ♥ SOMEBODY SHOW ME! ♥
HURRY!
NOW!
NOW!!
PIRON
Here, I took a screenshot.
※ DM from a fan.

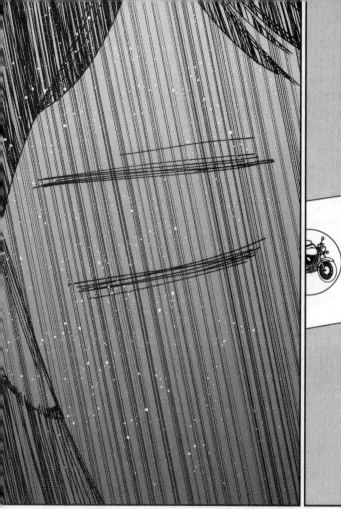

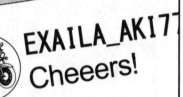

EXAILA_AKI77
Cheeers!
ISN'T THAT GREAT, SASAME-KUN?!
I CAN'T BELIEVE HE'S DRINKING WITH US!
GOOD THING WE DID THIS STREAM!
AKI-SAAAN! ARE YOU WATCHING?
FEEL FREE TO COMMENT AGAIN IF YOU WANT...
THWUD
バタン

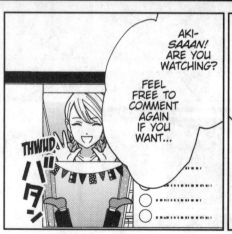

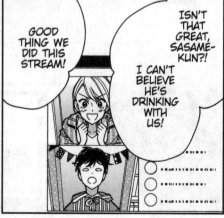

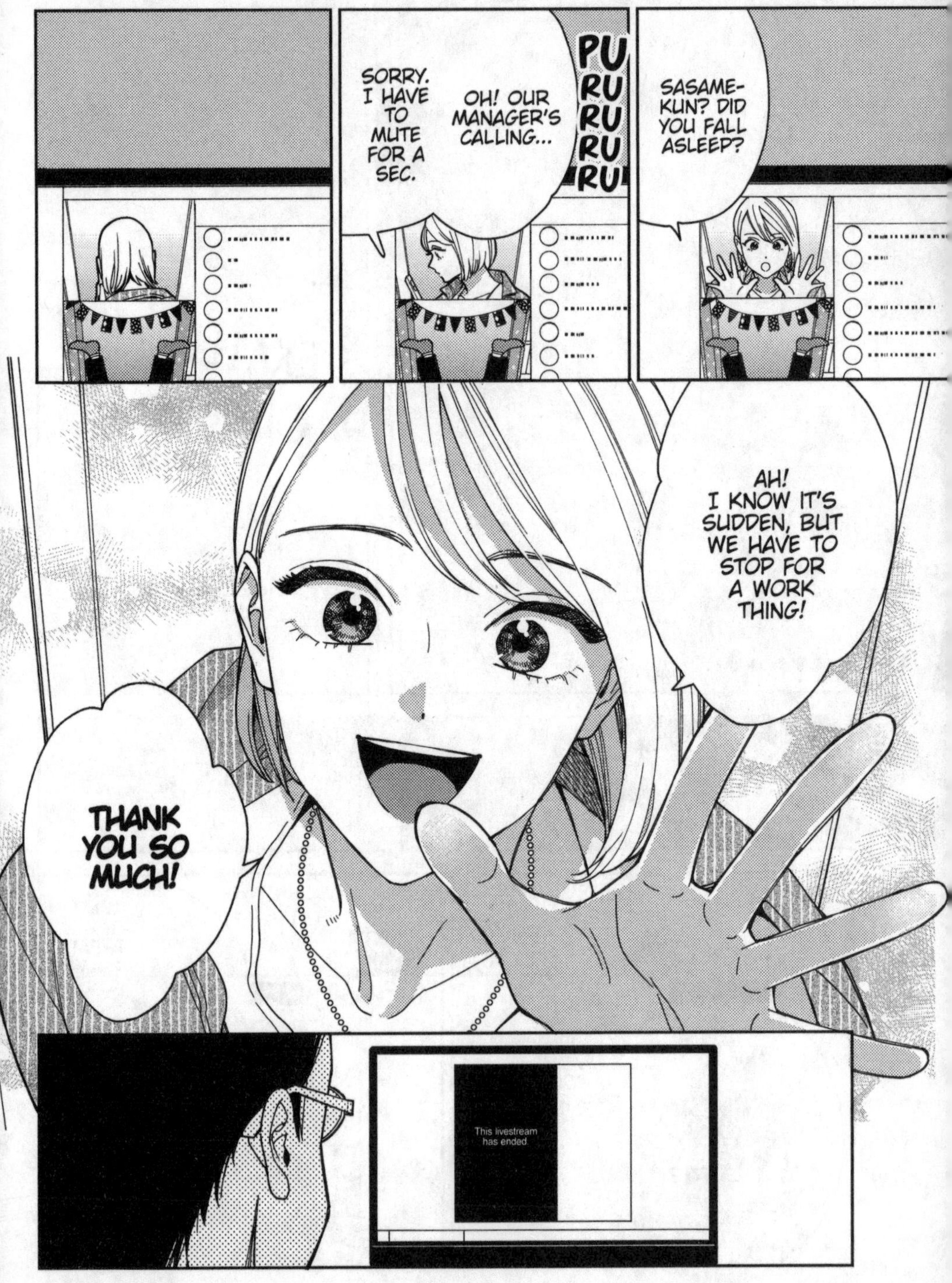
SASAME-KUN? DID YOU FALL ASLEEP?
PURURURURU
OH! OUR MANAGER'S CALLING...
SORRY. I HAVE TO MUTE FOR A SEC.
AH! I KNOW IT'S SUDDEN, BUT WE HAVE TO STOP FOR A WORK THING!
THANK YOU SO MUCH!
This livestream has ended.

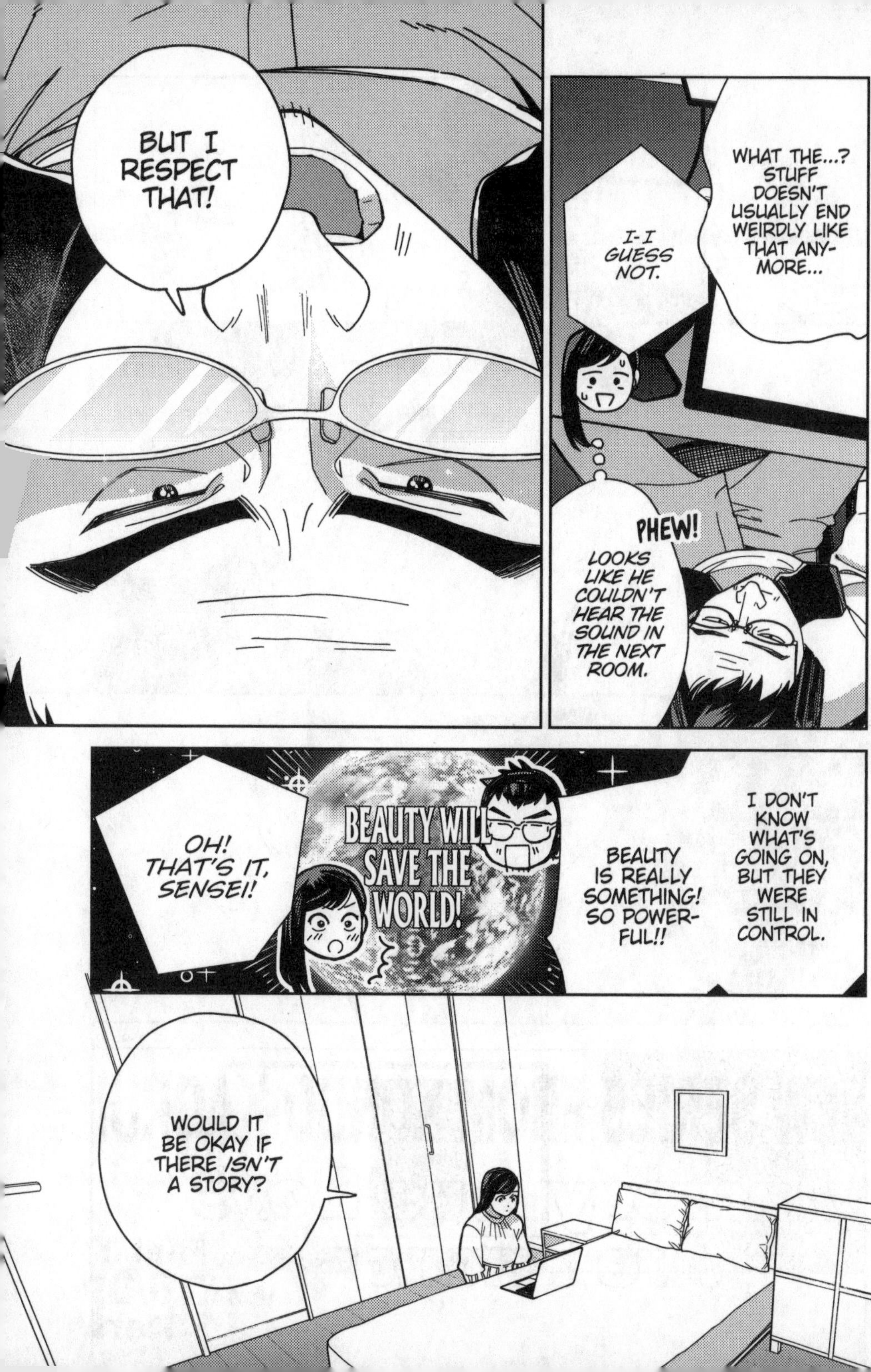
WHAT THE...? STUFF DOESN'T USUALLY END WEIRDLY LIKE THAT ANYMORE...
I-I GUESS NOT.
PHEW!
LOOKS LIKE HE COULDN'T HEAR THE SOUND IN THE NEXT ROOM.
BUT I RESPECT THAT!
I DON'T KNOW WHAT'S GOING ON, BUT THEY WERE STILL IN CONTROL.
BEAUTY IS REALLY SOMETHING! SO POWERFUL!!
BEAUTY WILL SAVE THE WORLD!
OH! THAT'S IT, SENSEI!
WOULD IT BE OKAY IF THERE *ISN'T* A STORY?

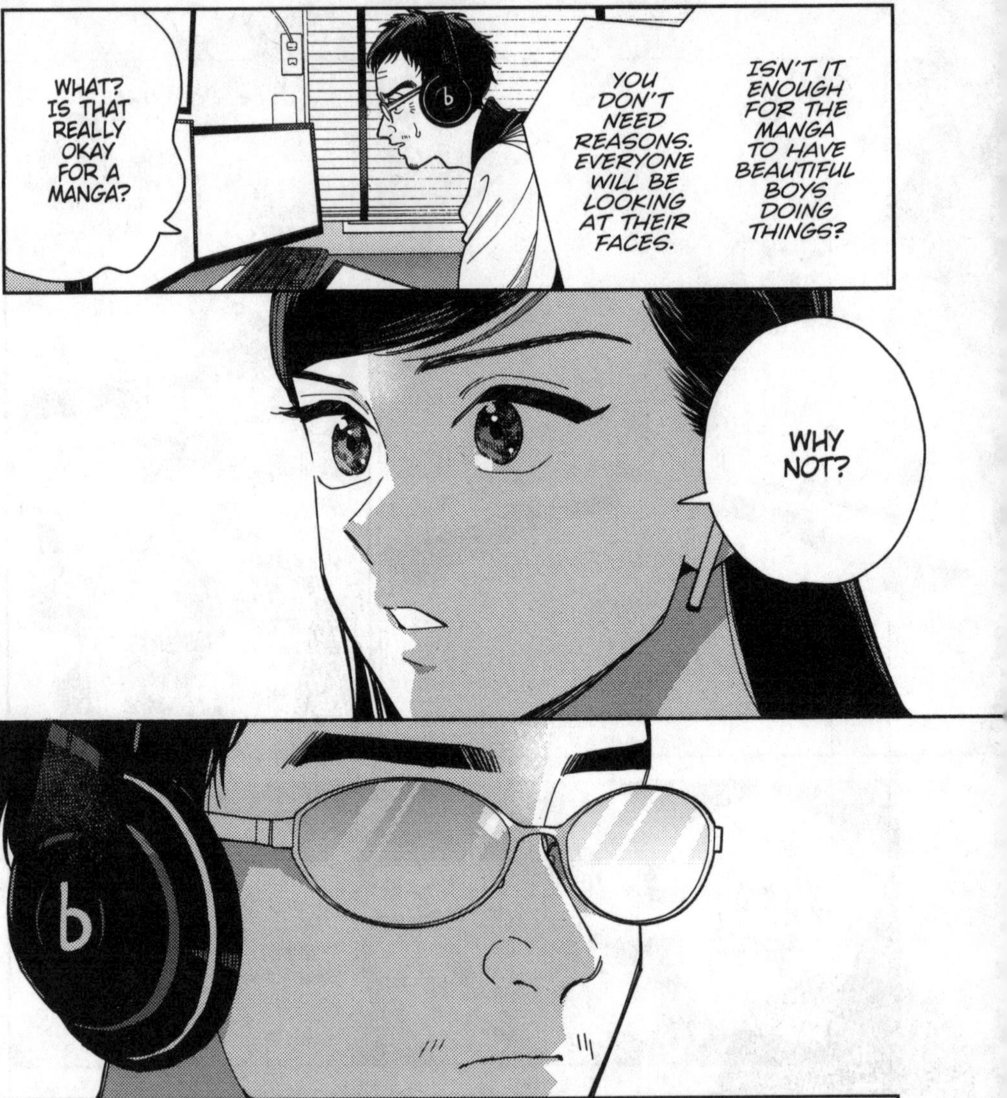
ISN'T IT ENOUGH FOR THE MANGA TO HAVE BEAUTIFUL BOYS DOING THINGS?
YOU DON'T NEED REASONS. EVERYONE WILL BE LOOKING AT THEIR FACES.
WHAT? IS THAT REALLY OKAY FOR A MANGA?
WHY NOT?

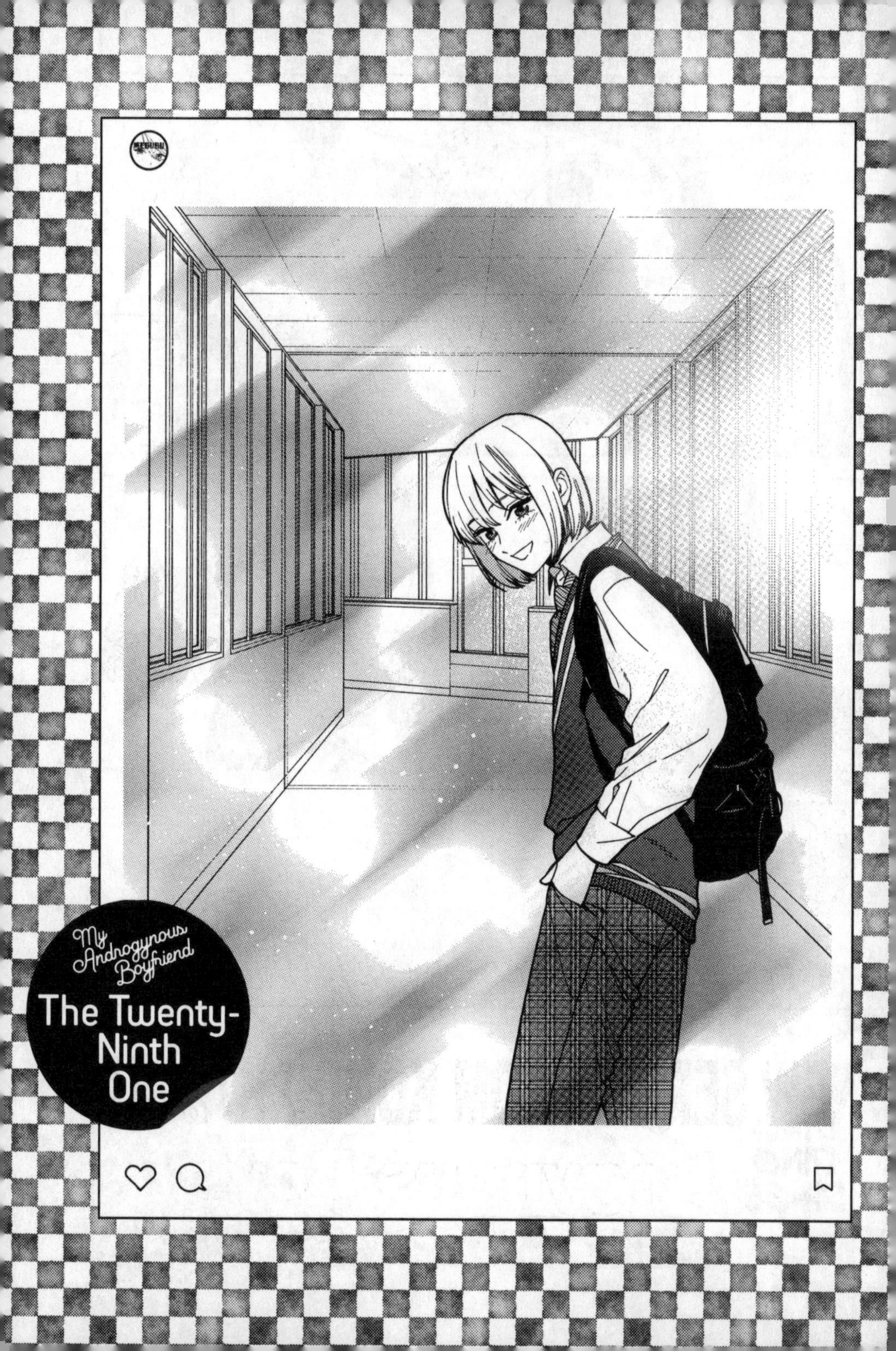
My Androgynous Boyfriend
The Twenty-Ninth One

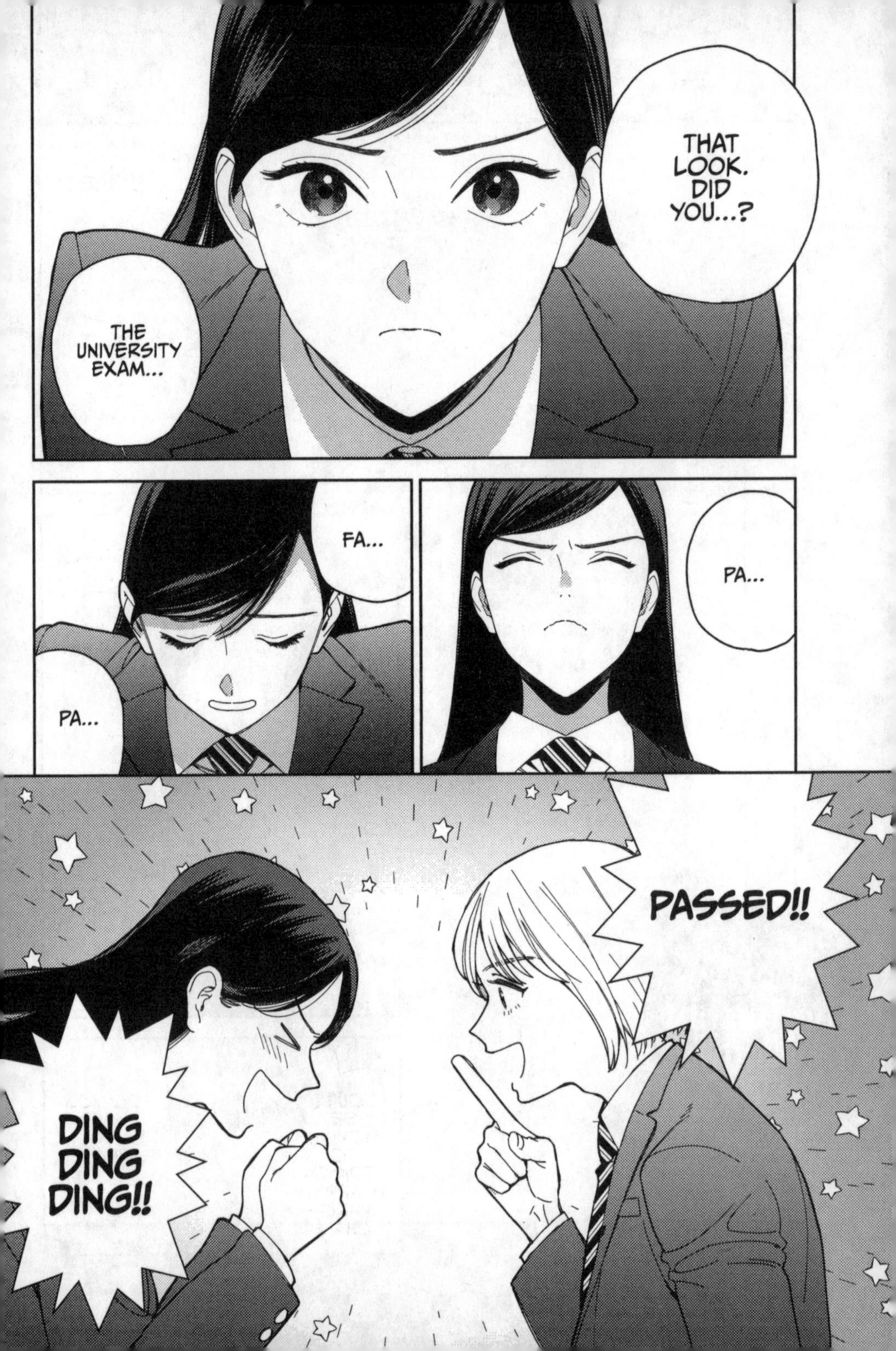
THAT LOOK. DID YOU...?
THE UNIVERSITY EXAM...
PA...
FA...
PA...
PASSED!!
DING DING DING!!

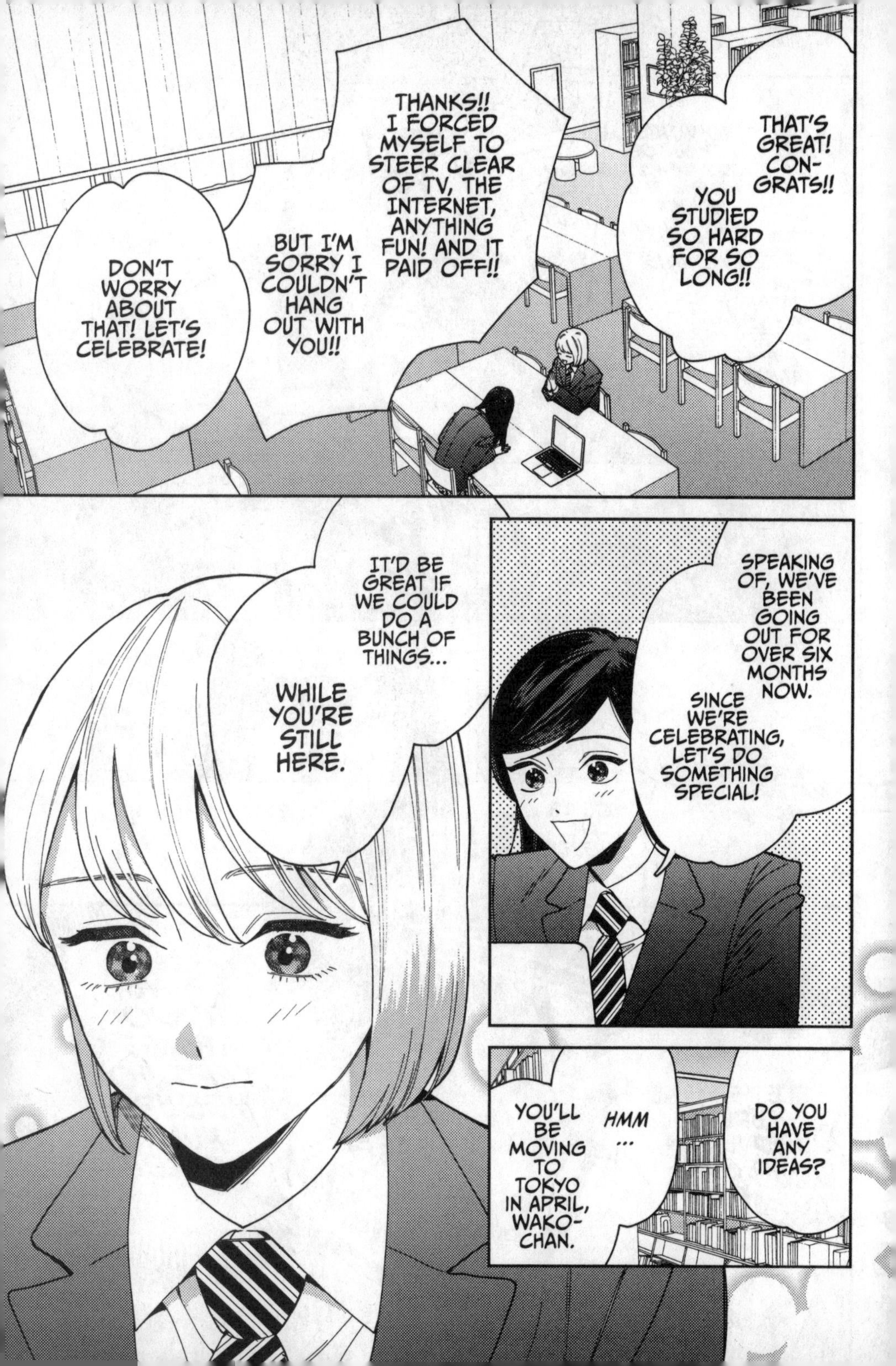
THAT'S GREAT! CON-GRATS!!
YOU STUDIED SO HARD FOR SO LONG!!
THANKS!! I FORCED MYSELF TO STEER CLEAR OF TV, THE INTERNET, ANYTHING FUN! AND IT PAID OFF!!
BUT I'M SORRY I COULDN'T HANG OUT WITH YOU!!
DON'T WORRY ABOUT THAT! LET'S CELEBRATE!
SPEAKING OF, WE'VE BEEN GOING OUT FOR OVER SIX MONTHS NOW.
SINCE WE'RE CELEBRATING, LET'S DO SOMETHING SPECIAL!
DO YOU HAVE ANY IDEAS?
HMM ...
YOU'LL BE MOVING TO TOKYO IN APRIL, WAKO-CHAN.
IT'D BE GREAT IF WE COULD DO A BUNCH OF THINGS...
WHILE YOU'RE STILL HERE.

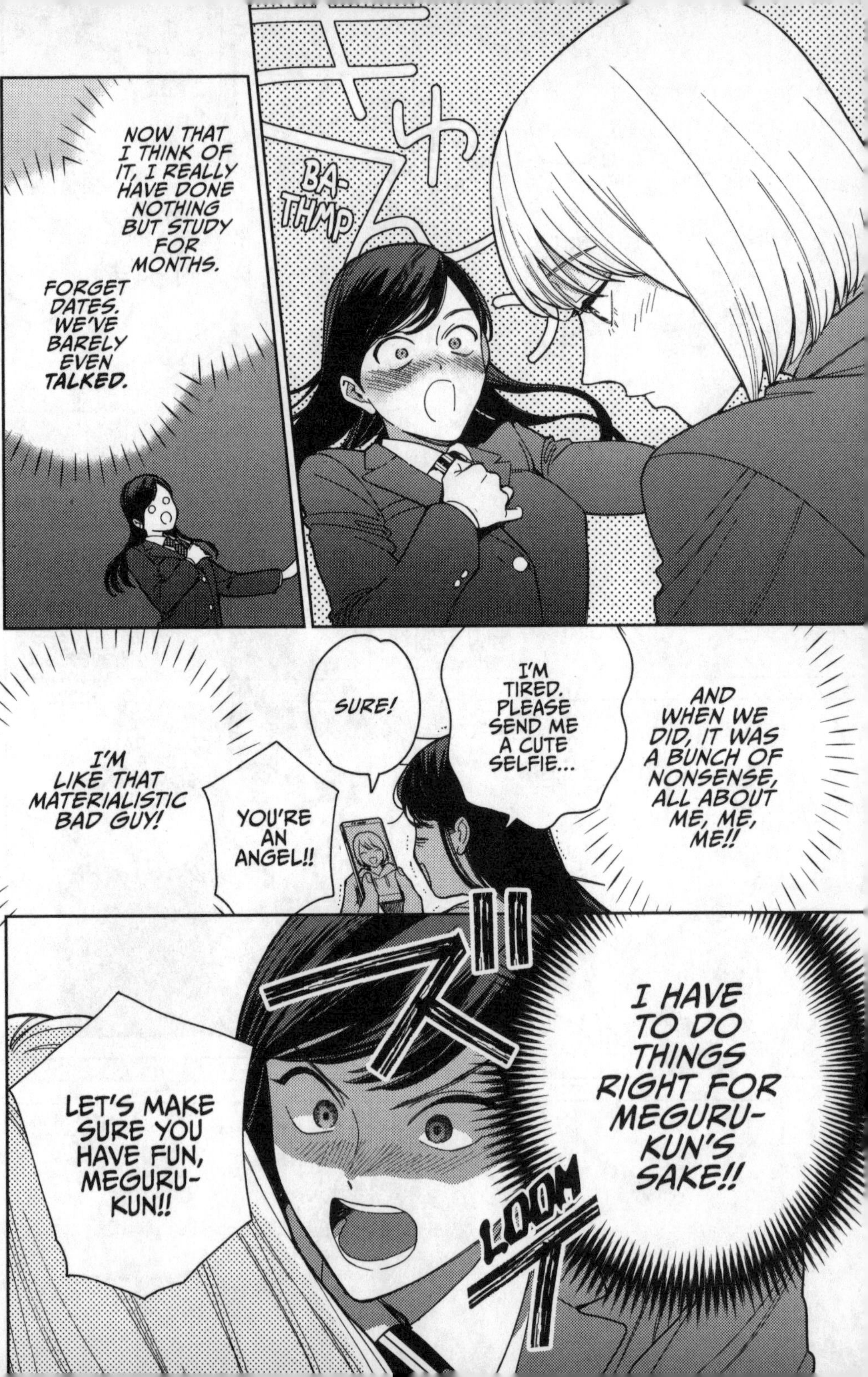
BA-THMP
NOW THAT I THINK OF IT, I REALLY HAVE DONE NOTHING BUT STUDY FOR MONTHS.
FORGET DATES. WE'VE BARELY EVEN TALKED.
AND WHEN WE DID, IT WAS A BUNCH OF NONSENSE, ALL ABOUT ME, ME, ME!!
I'M TIRED. PLEASE SEND ME A CUTE SELFIE...
SURE!
YOU'RE AN ANGEL!!
I'M LIKE THAT MATERIALISTIC BAD GUY!
I HAVE TO DO THINGS RIGHT FOR MEGURU-KUN'S SAKE!!
LOOM
LET'S MAKE SURE YOU HAVE FUN, MEGURU-KUN!!

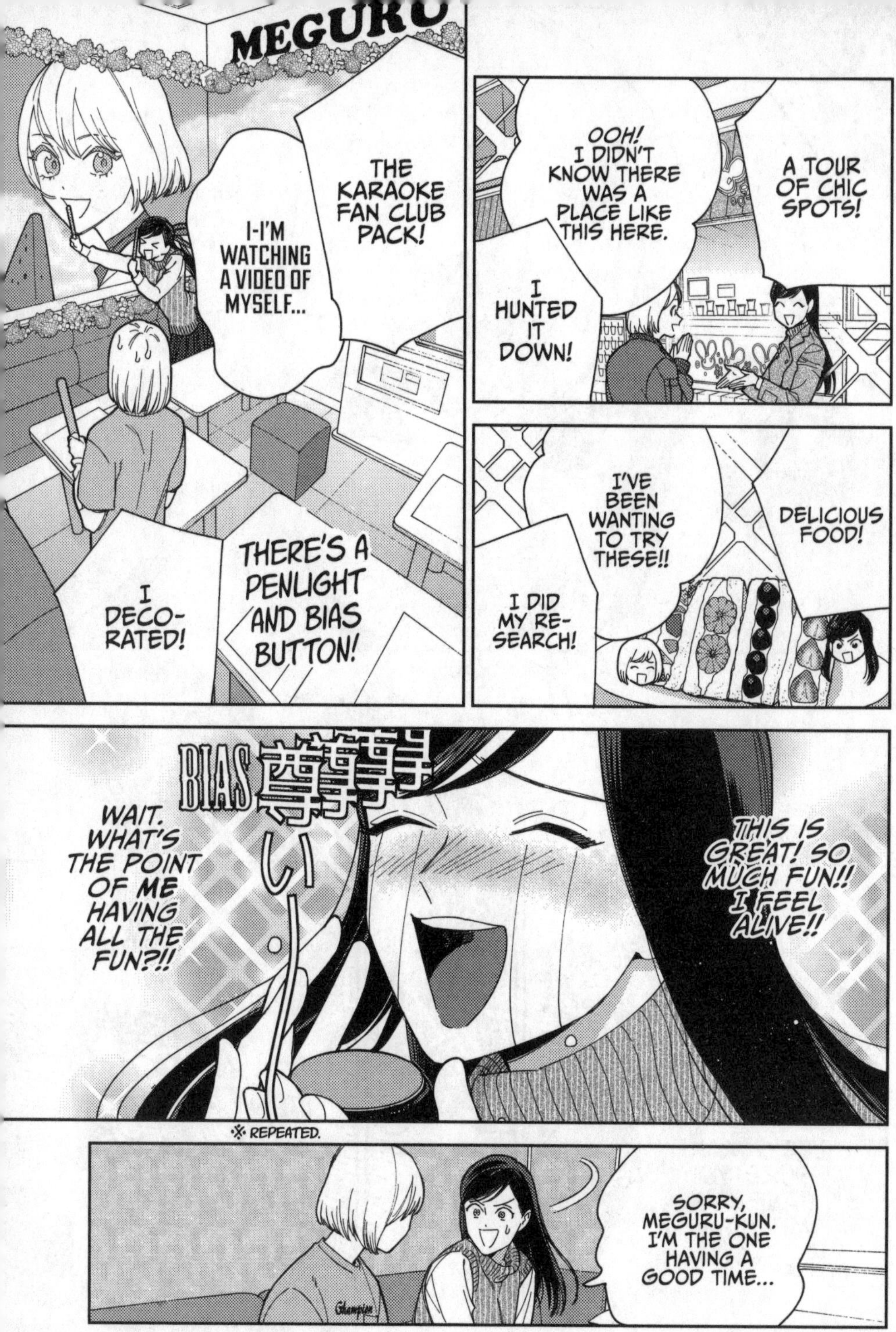
A TOUR OF CHIC SPOTS!
OOH! I DIDN'T KNOW THERE WAS A PLACE LIKE THIS HERE.
I HUNTED IT DOWN!
DELICIOUS FOOD!
I'VE BEEN WANTING TO TRY THESE!!
I DID MY RE-SEARCH!
MEGURU
THE KARAOKE FAN CLUB PACK!
I-I'M WATCHING A VIDEO OF MYSELF...
THERE'S A PENLIGHT AND BIAS BUTTON!
I DECO-RATED!
THIS IS GREAT! SO MUCH FUN!! I FEEL ALIVE!!
BIAS 尊尊尊尊い
WAIT. WHAT'S THE POINT OF ME HAVING ALL THE FUN?!!
※REPEATED.
SORRY, MEGURU-KUN. I'M THE ONE HAVING A GOOD TIME...
Champion

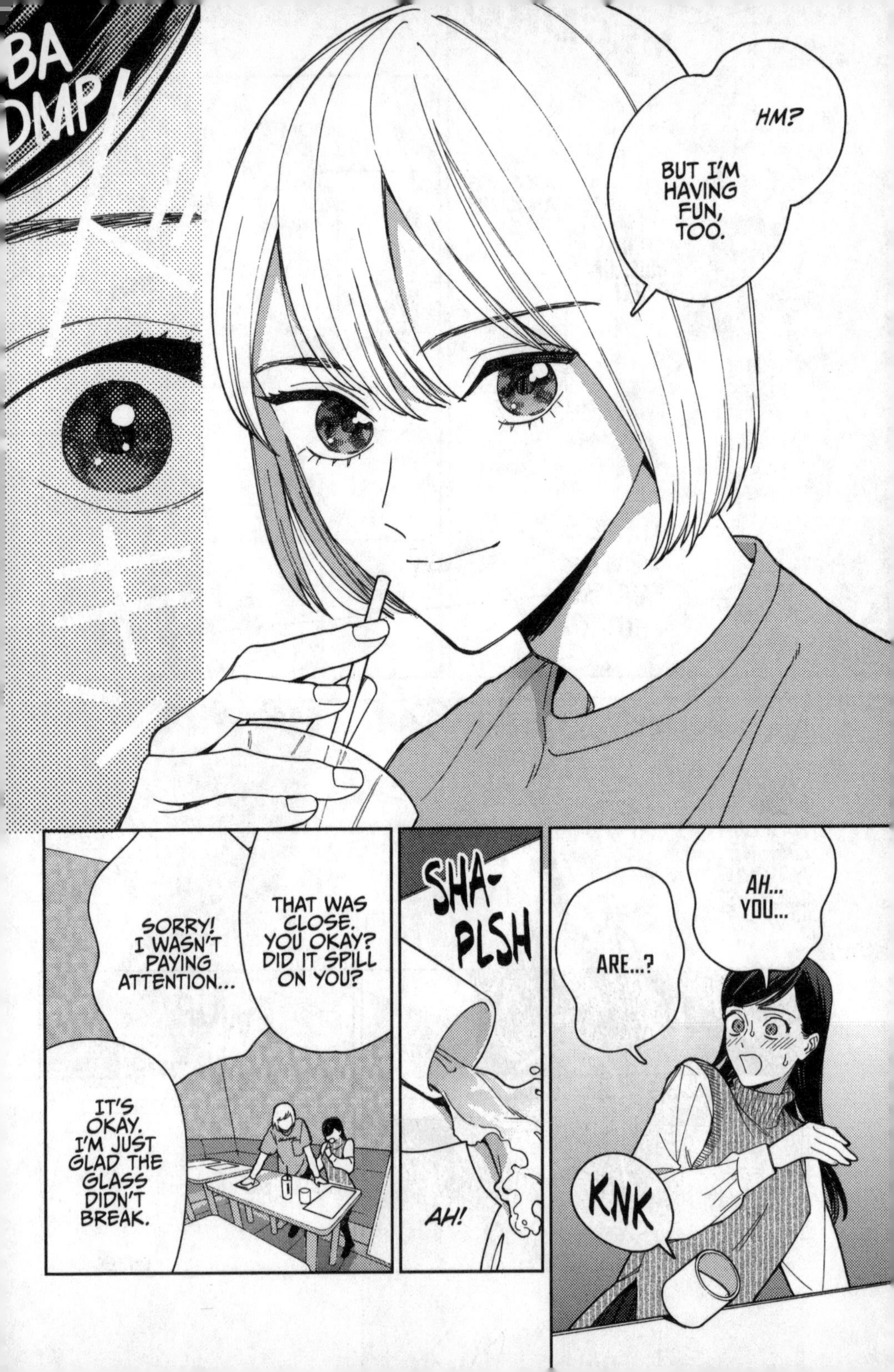
HM?
BUT I'M HAVING FUN, TOO.
BA DMP
AH... YOU...
ARE...?
KNK
SHA-PLSH
AH!
THAT WAS CLOSE. YOU OKAY? DID IT SPILL ON YOU?
SORRY! I WASN'T PAYING ATTENTION...
IT'S OKAY. I'M JUST GLAD THE GLASS DIDN'T BREAK.

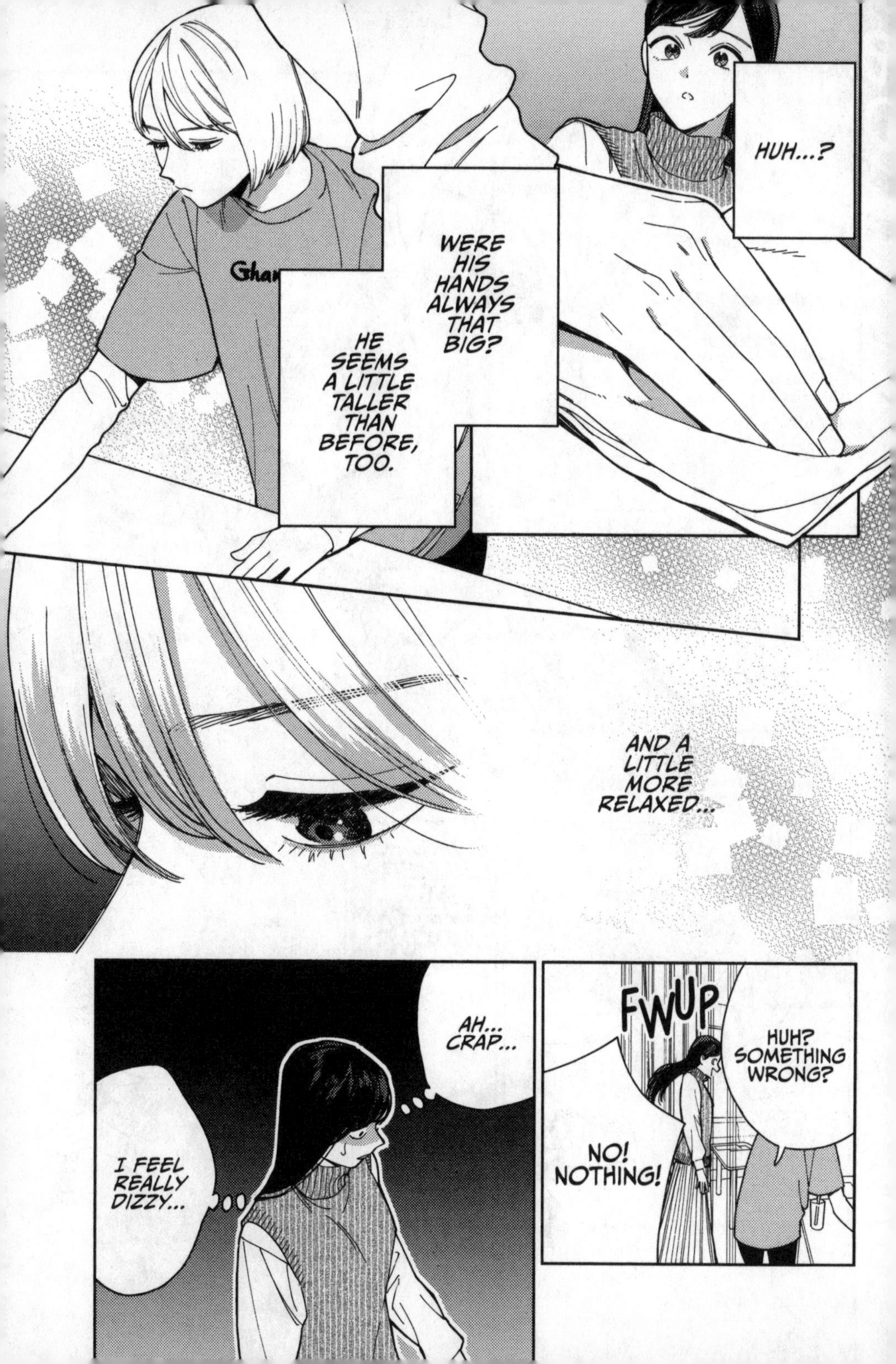
HUH...?
WERE HIS HANDS ALWAYS THAT BIG?
HE SEEMS A LITTLE TALLER THAN BEFORE, TOO.
AND A LITTLE MORE RELAXED...
HUH? SOMETHING WRONG?
FWUP
NO! NOTHING!
AH... CRAP...
I FEEL REALLY DIZZY...

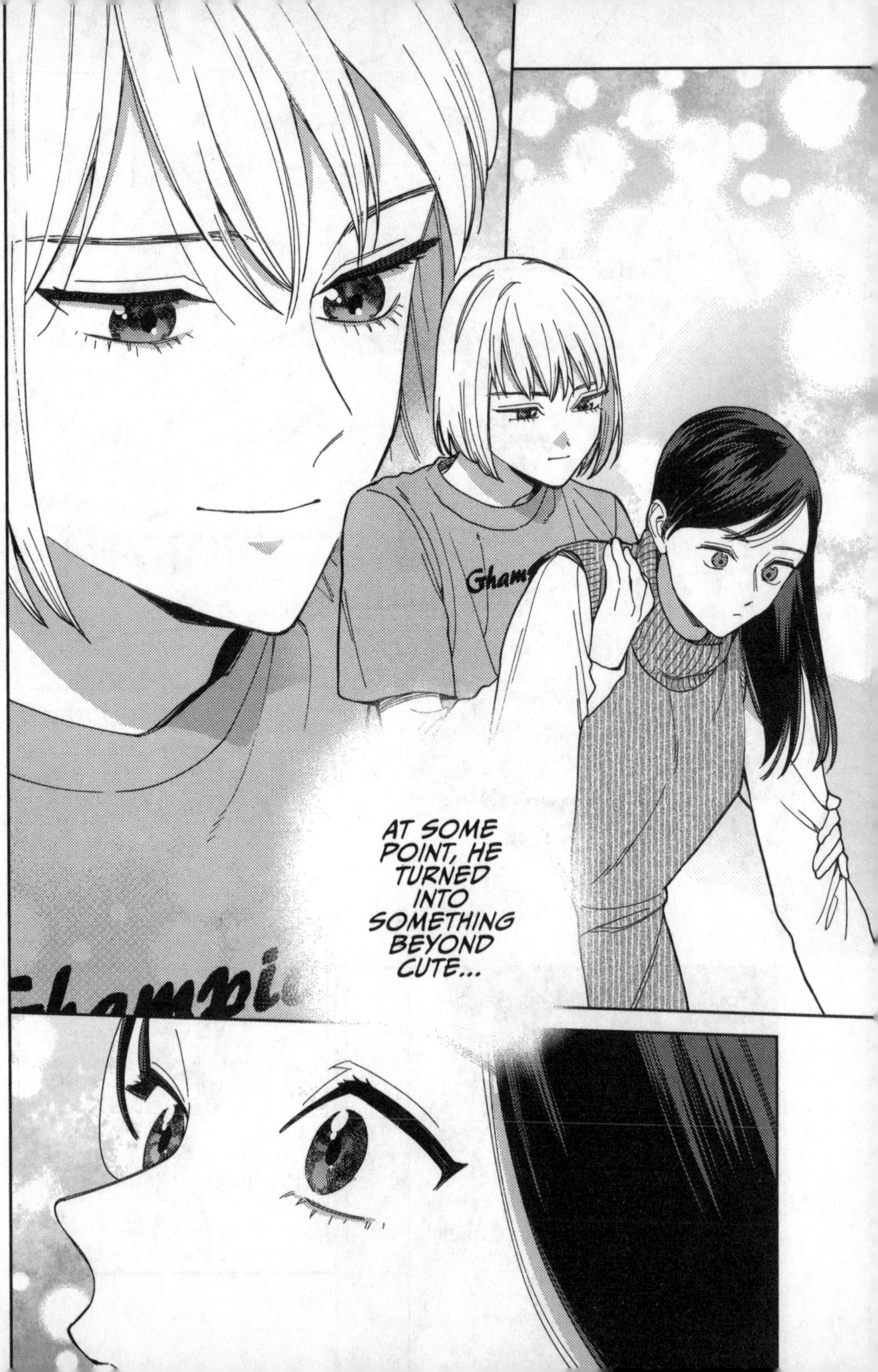
AT SOME POINT, HE TURNED INTO SOMETHING BEYOND CUTE...

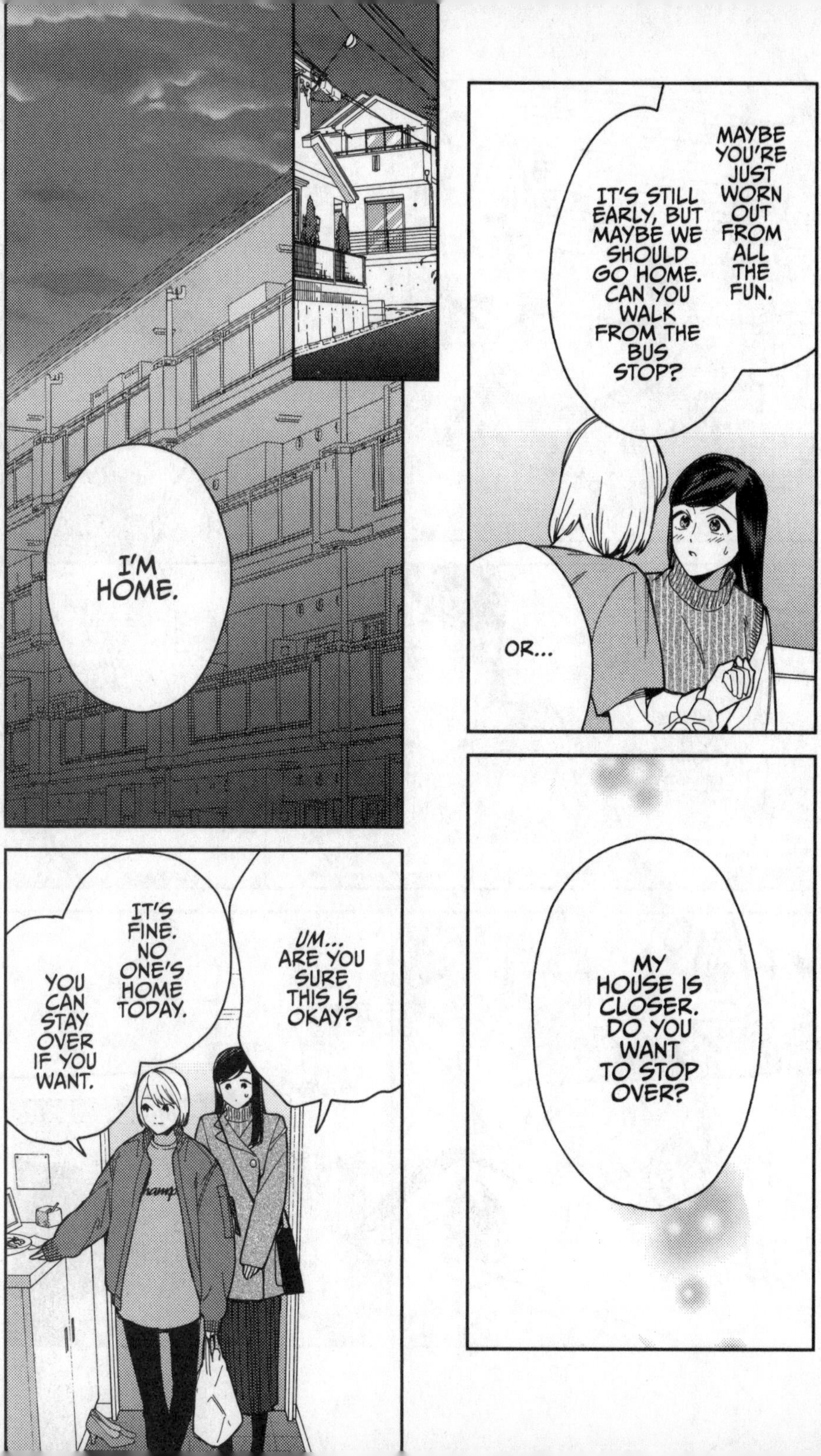
MAYBE YOU'RE JUST WORN OUT FROM ALL THE FUN.
IT'S STILL EARLY, BUT MAYBE WE SHOULD GO HOME. CAN YOU WALK FROM THE BUS STOP?
OR...
MY HOUSE IS CLOSER. DO YOU WANT TO STOP OVER?
I'M HOME.
UM... ARE YOU SURE THIS IS OKAY?
IT'S FINE. NO ONE'S HOME TODAY.
YOU CAN STAY OVER IF YOU WANT.

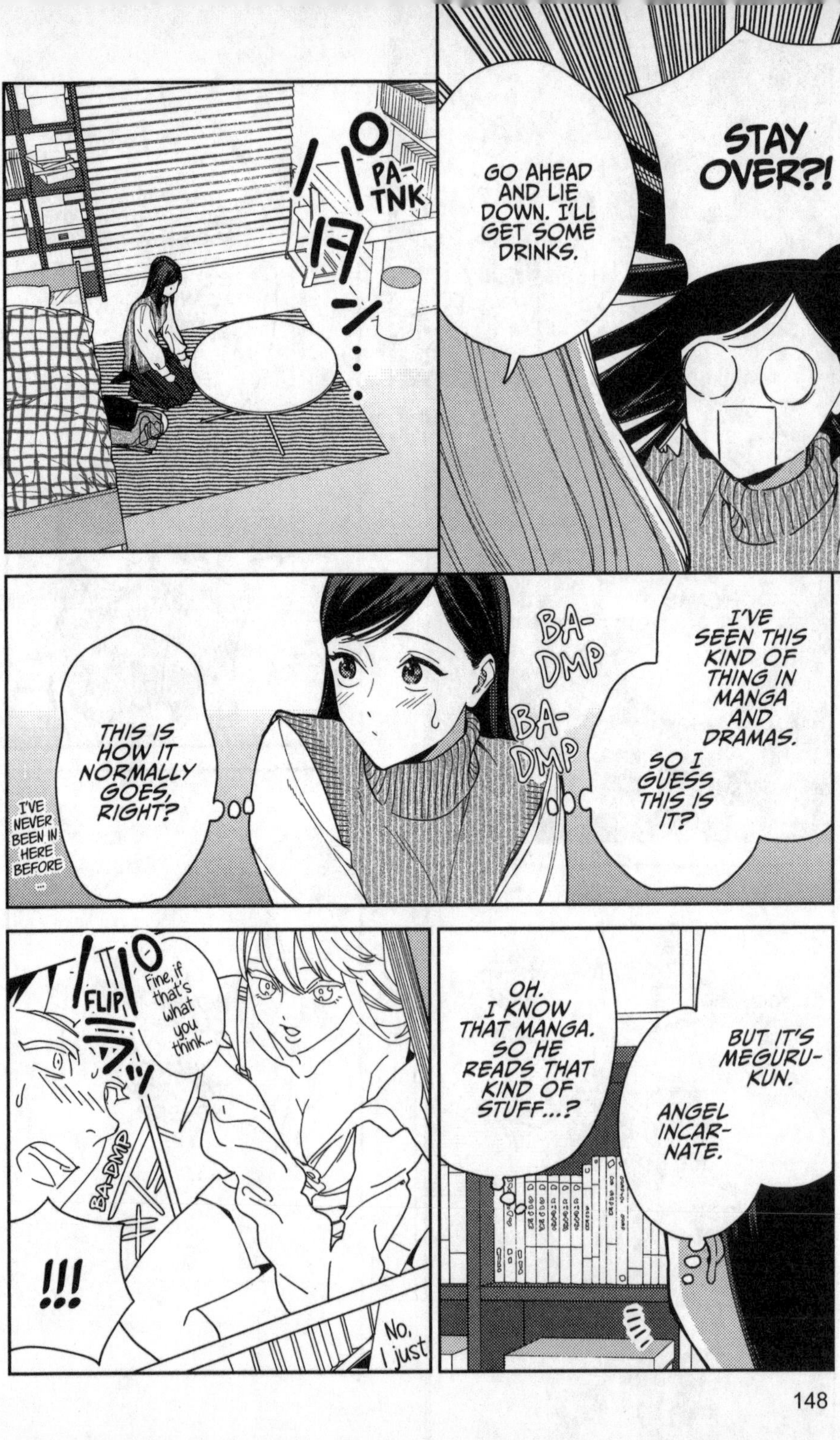
STAY OVER?!
GO AHEAD AND LIE DOWN. I'LL GET SOME DRINKS.
PA-TNK
...
I'VE SEEN THIS KIND OF THING IN MANGA AND DRAMAS.
SO I GUESS THIS IS IT?
BA-DMP BA-DMP
THIS IS HOW IT NORMALLY GOES, RIGHT?
I'VE NEVER BEEN IN HERE BEFORE...
BUT IT'S MEGURU-KUN.
ANGEL INCARNATE.
OH. I KNOW THAT MANGA. SO HE READS THAT KIND OF STUFF...?
FLIP
Fine, if that's what you think...
BA-DMP
!!!
No, I just

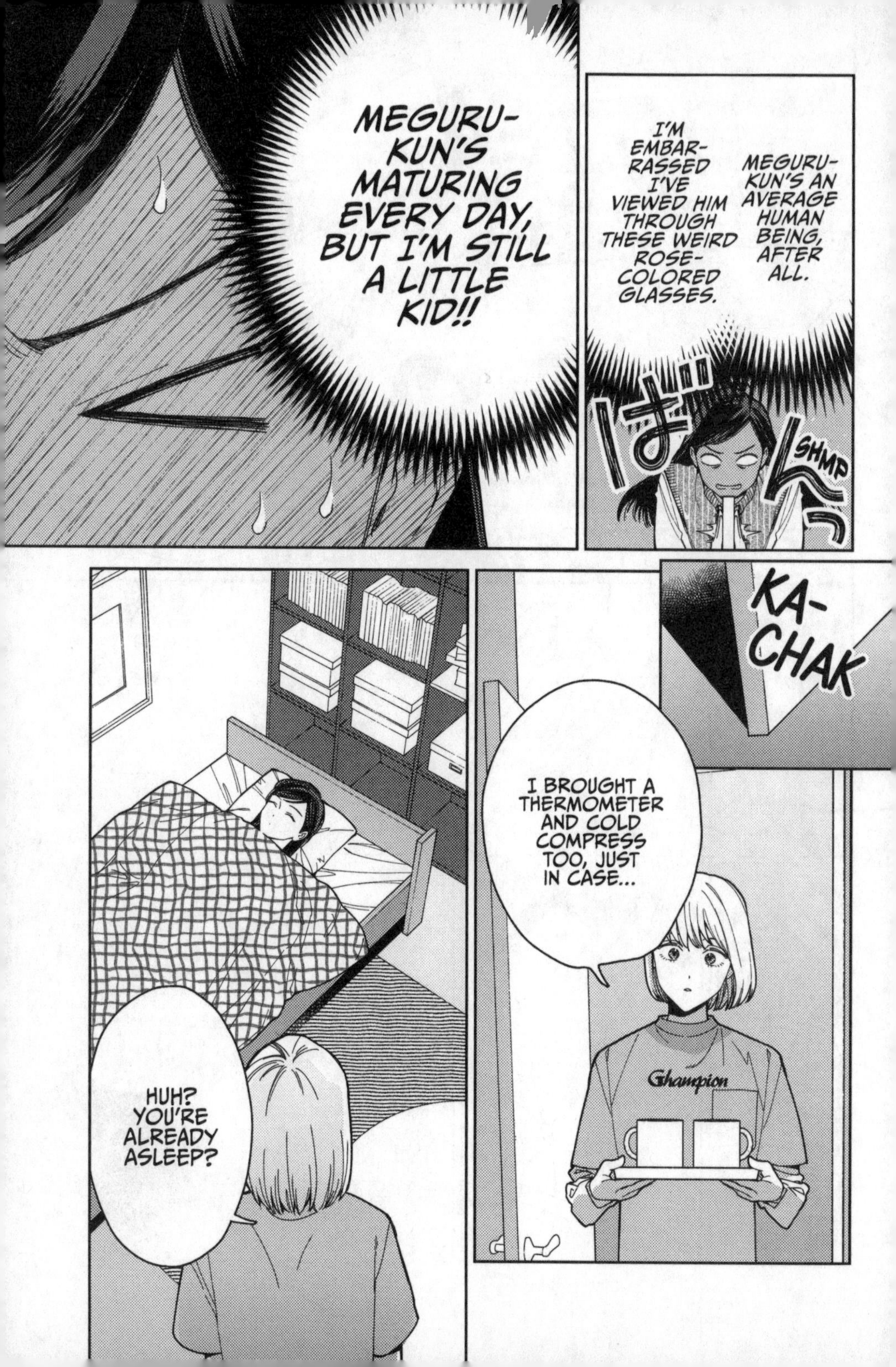
MEGURU-KUN'S AN AVERAGE HUMAN BEING, AFTER ALL.
I'M EMBARRASSED I'VE VIEWED HIM THROUGH THESE WEIRD ROSE-COLORED GLASSES.
SHMP
MEGURU-KUN'S MATURING EVERY DAY, BUT I'M STILL A LITTLE KID!!
KA-CHAK
I BROUGHT A THERMOMETER AND COLD COMPRESS TOO, JUST IN CASE...
HUH? YOU'RE ALREADY ASLEEP?

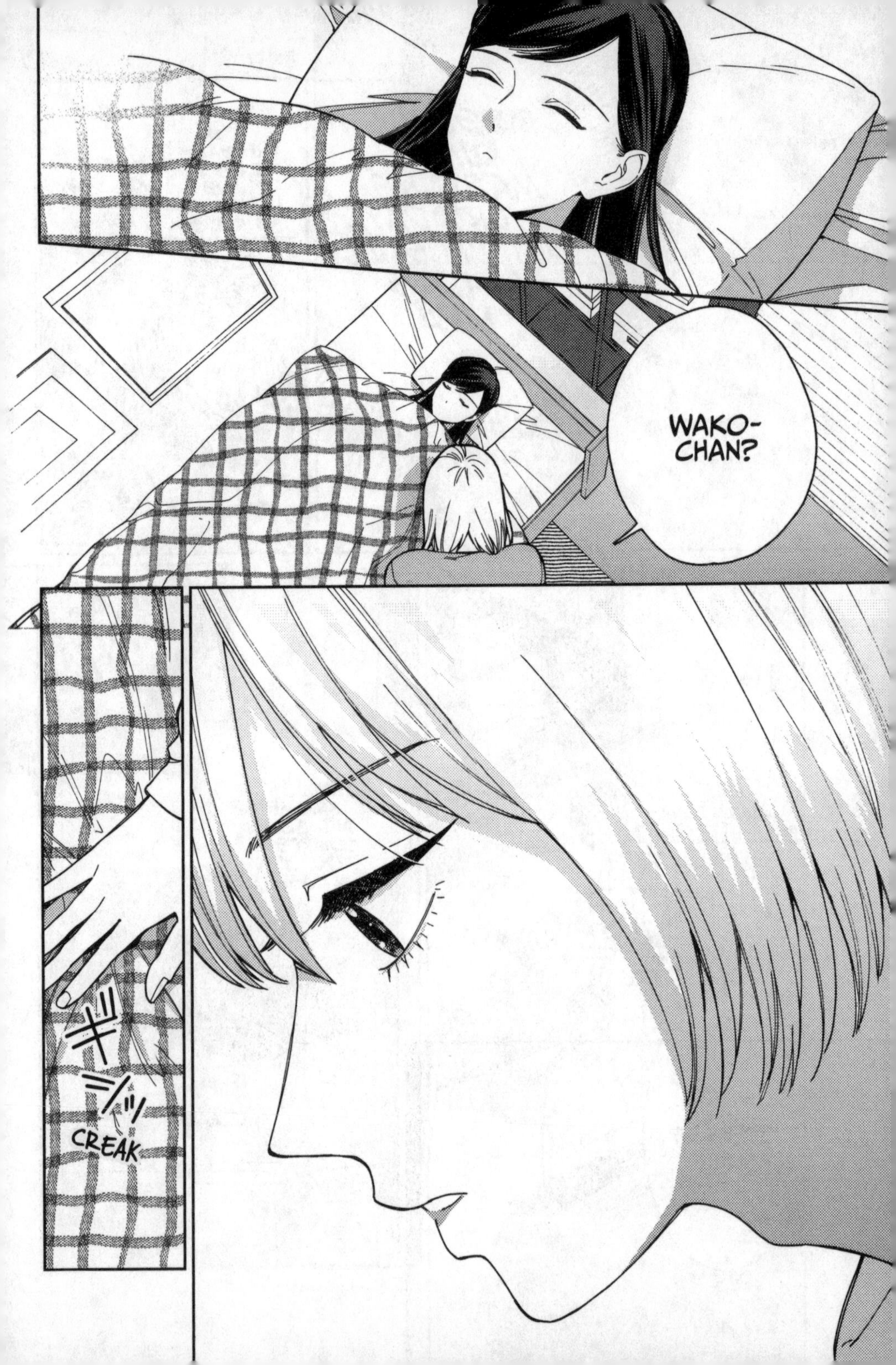
WAKO-
CHAN?
CREAK

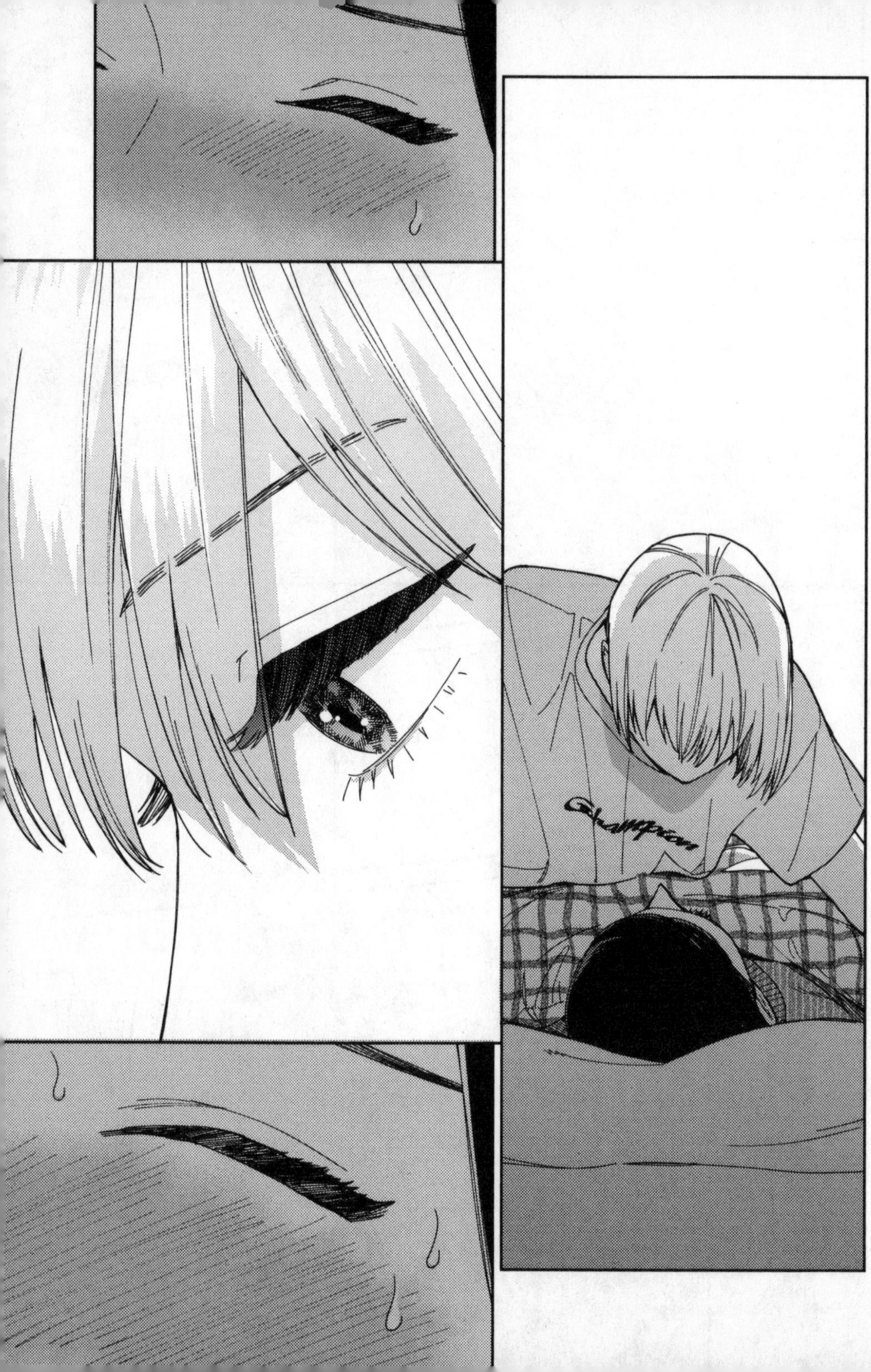

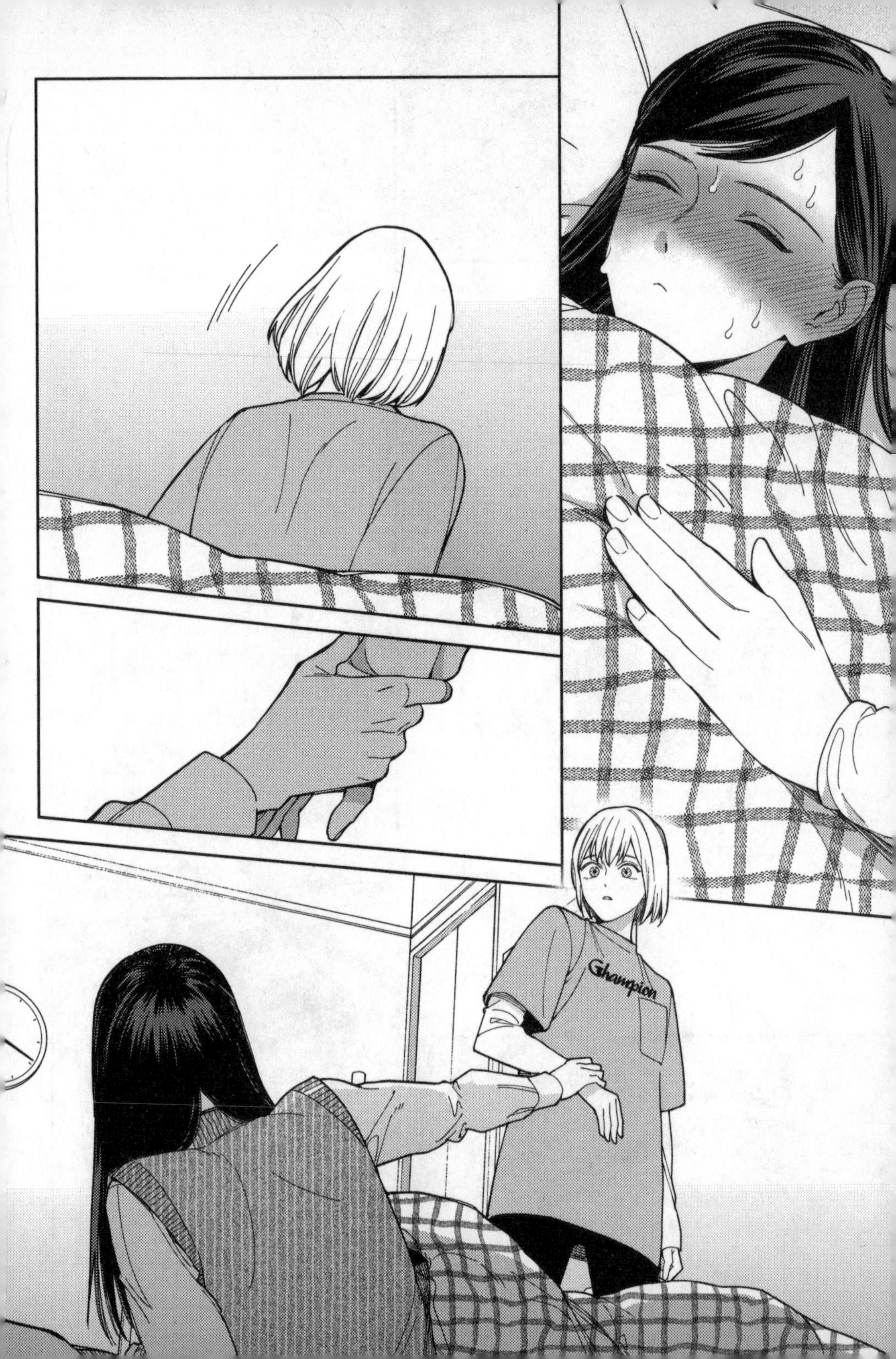
Champion

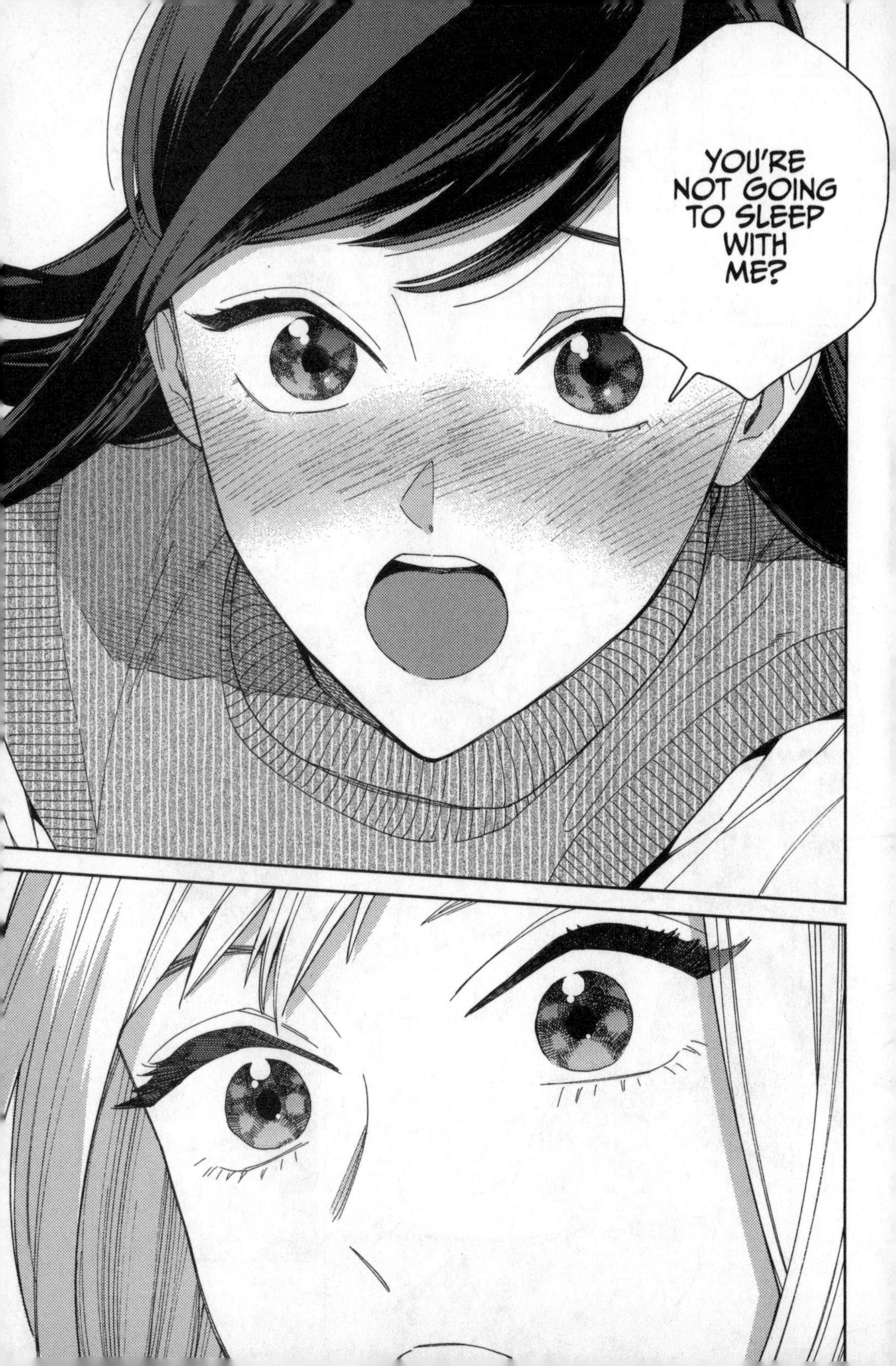
YOU'RE NOT GOING TO SLEEP WITH ME?

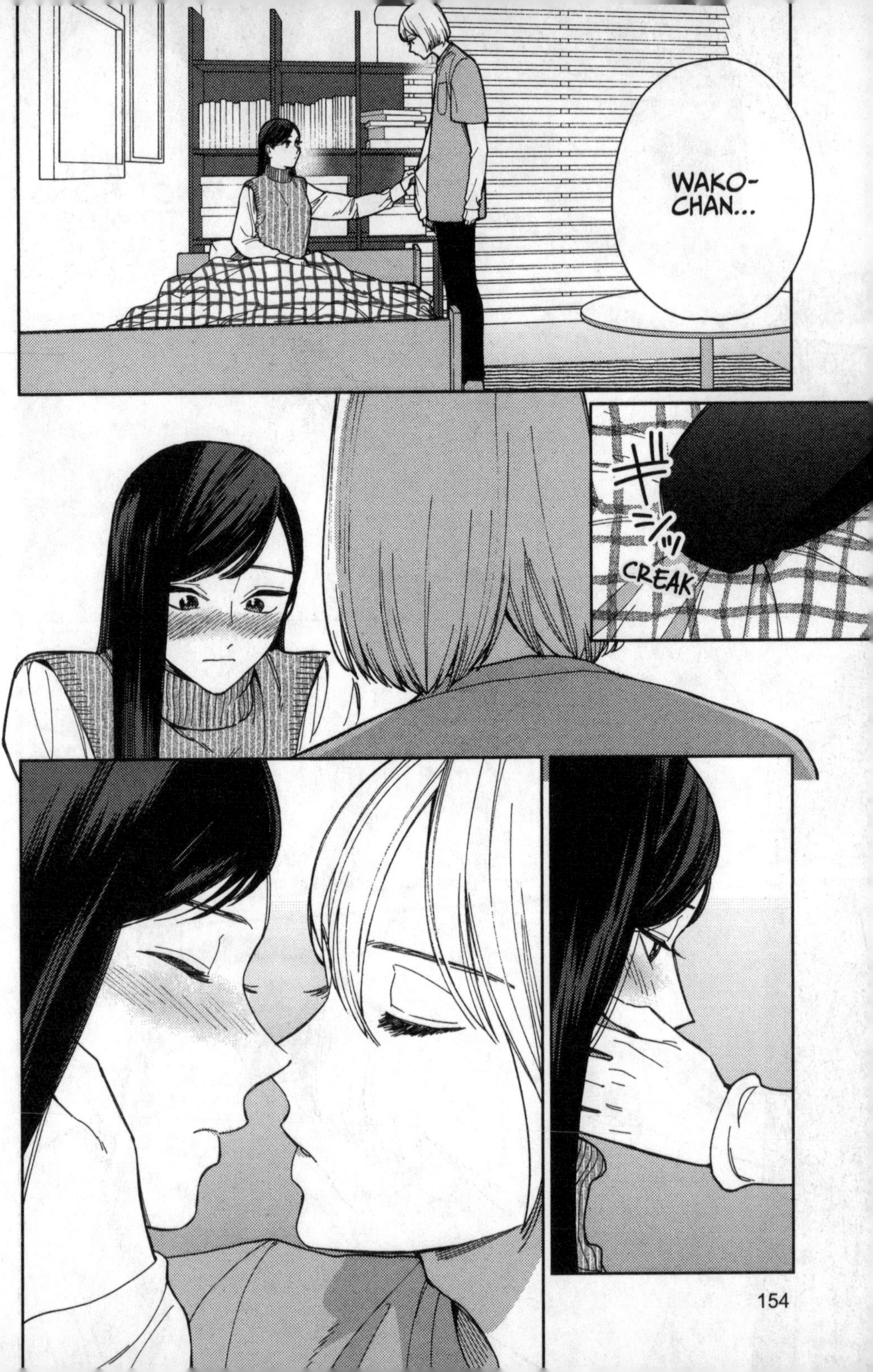
WAKO-CHAN...
ギシッ
CREAK

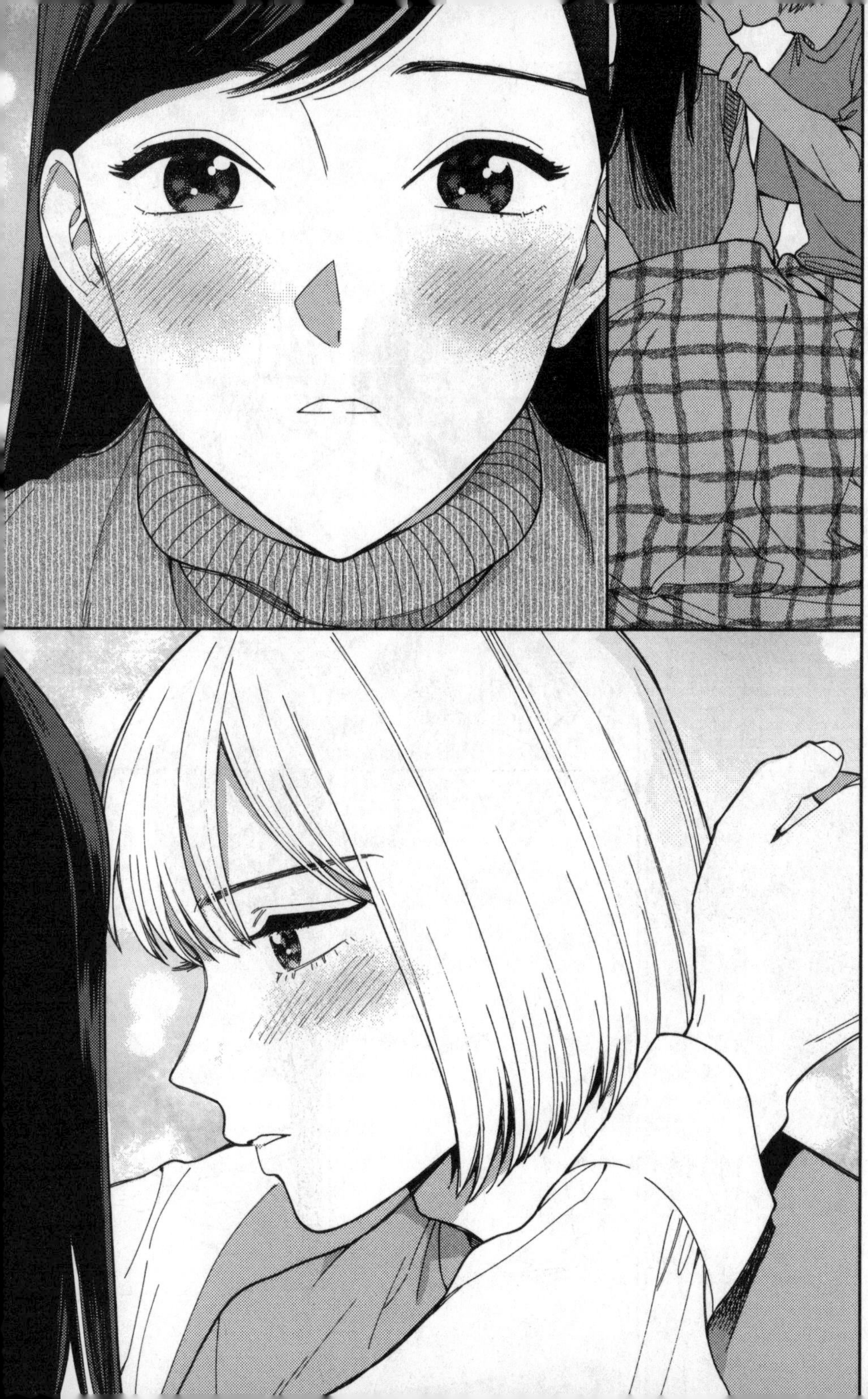

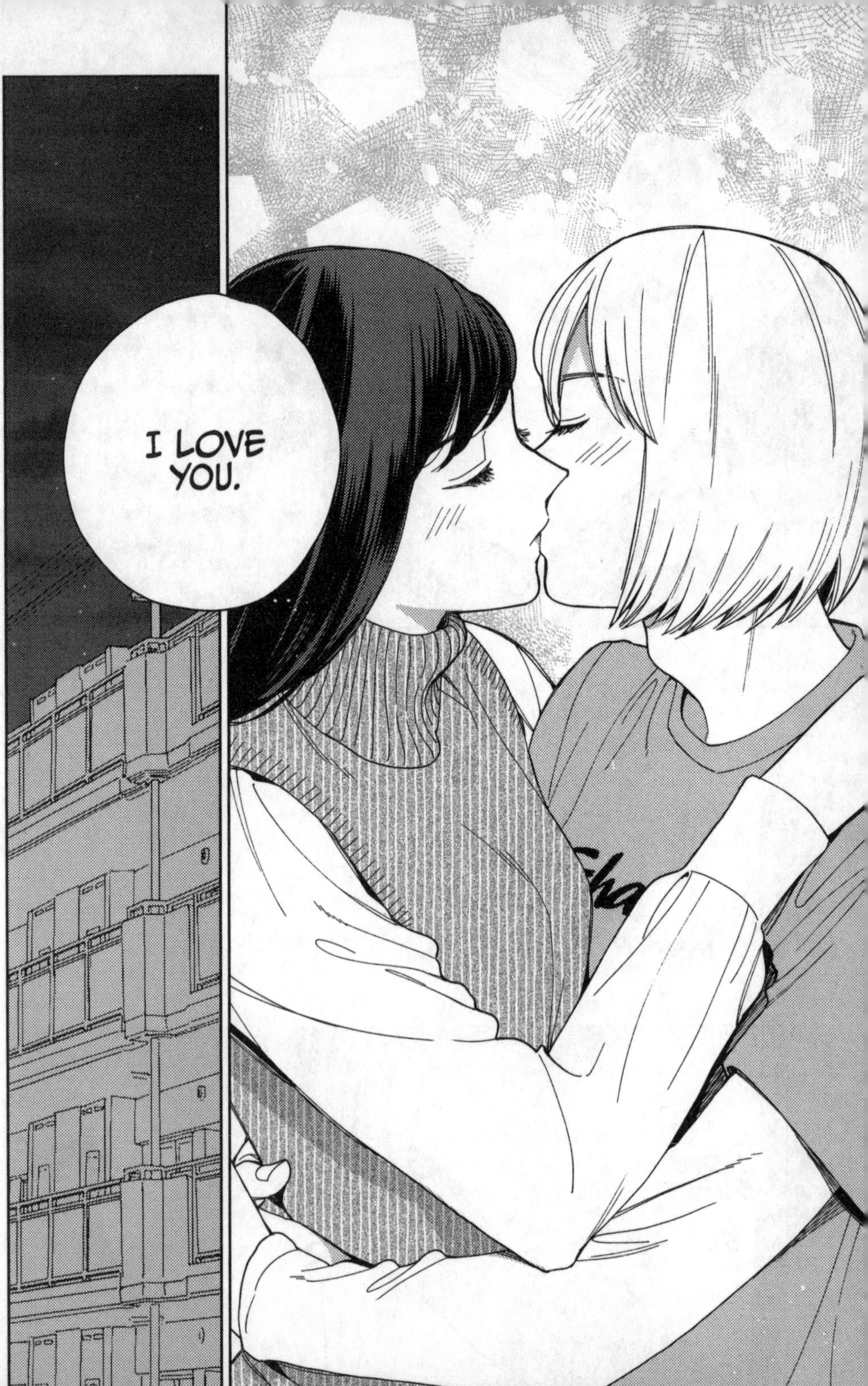
I LOVE YOU.

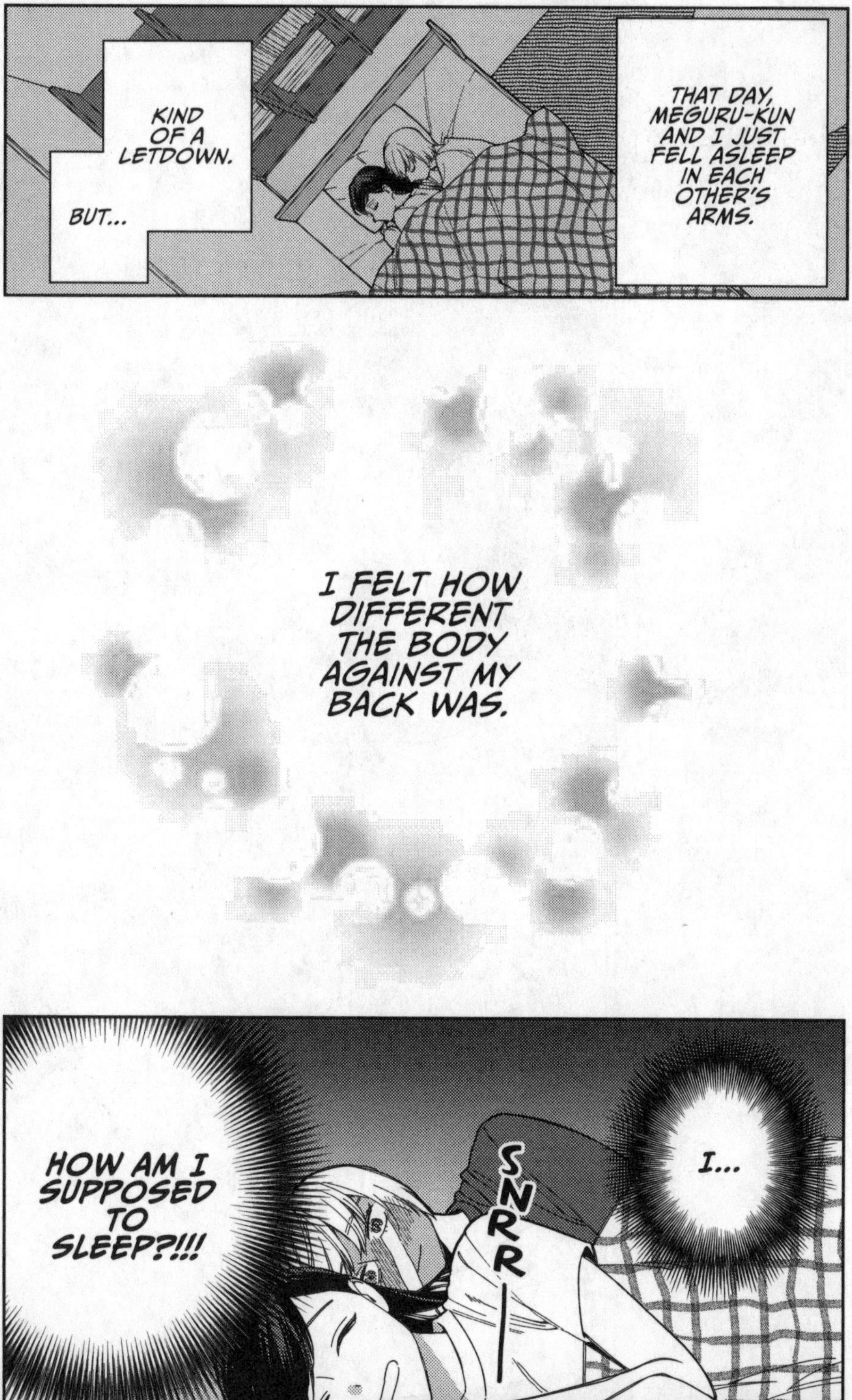
THAT DAY, MEGURU-KUN AND I JUST FELL ASLEEP IN EACH OTHER'S ARMS.
KIND OF A LETDOWN.
BUT...
I FELT HOW DIFFERENT THE BODY AGAINST MY BACK WAS.
I...
SNRR
HOW AM I SUPPOSED TO SLEEP?!!!

My Androgynous Boyfriend

My Androgynous Boyfriend

The Thirtieth One

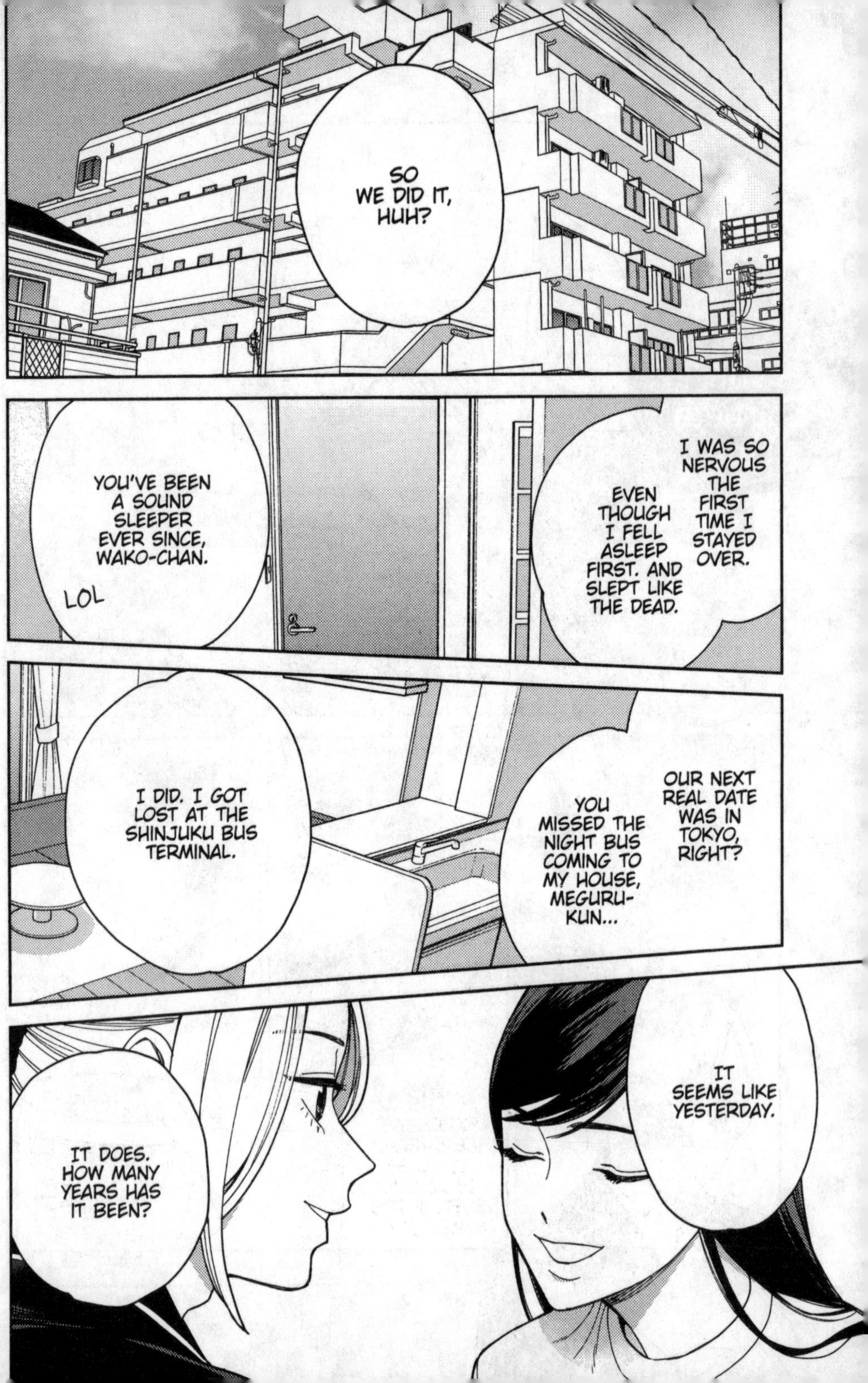
SO WE DID IT, HUH?
I WAS SO NERVOUS THE FIRST TIME I STAYED OVER.
EVEN THOUGH I FELL ASLEEP FIRST. AND SLEPT LIKE THE DEAD.
YOU'VE BEEN A SOUND SLEEPER EVER SINCE, WAKO-CHAN.
LOL
OUR NEXT REAL DATE WAS IN TOKYO, RIGHT?
YOU MISSED THE NIGHT BUS COMING TO MY HOUSE, MEGURU-KUN...
I DID. I GOT LOST AT THE SHINJUKU BUS TERMINAL.
IT SEEMS LIKE YESTERDAY.
IT DOES. HOW MANY YEARS HAS IT BEEN?

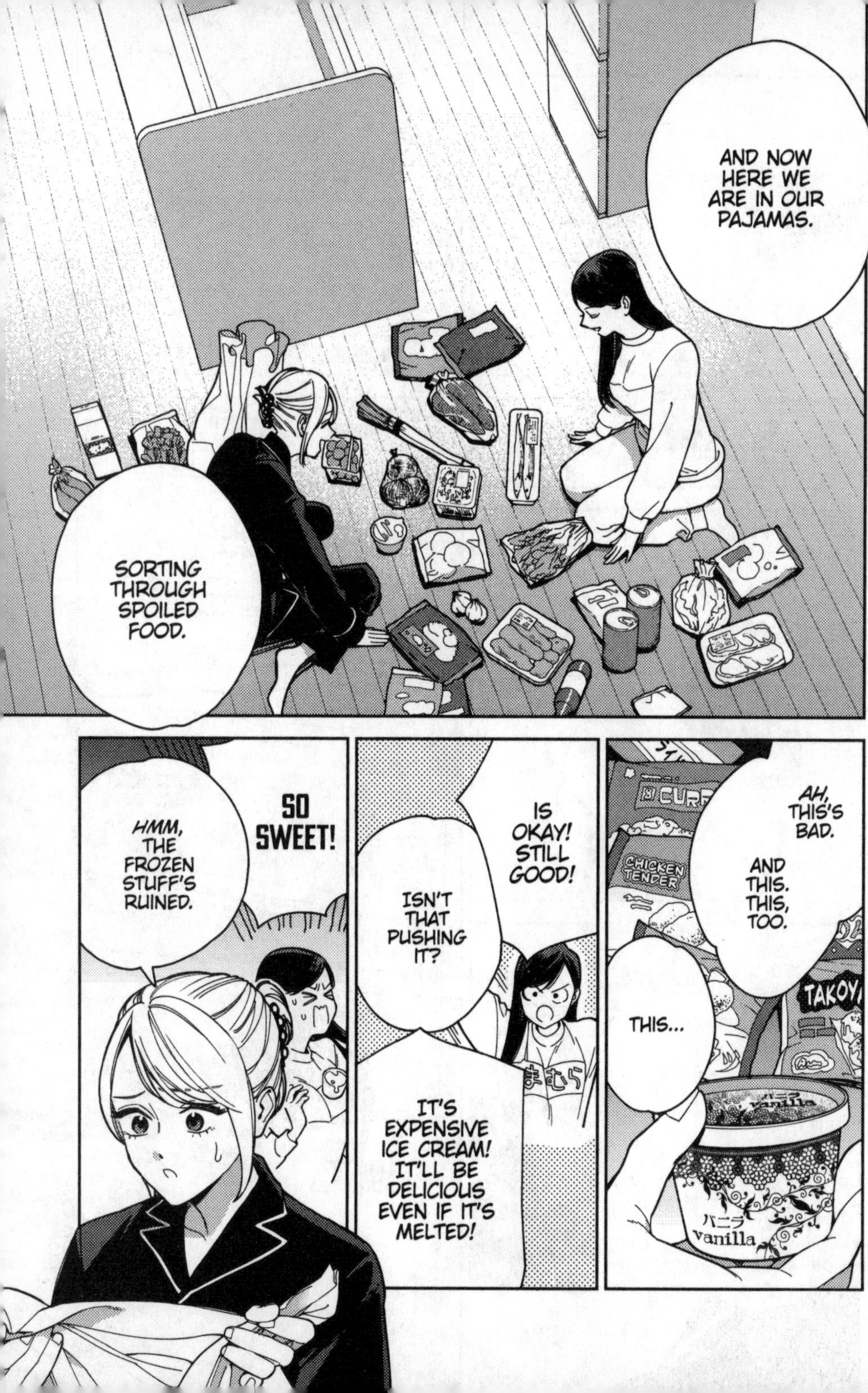
AND NOW HERE WE ARE IN OUR PAJAMAS.
SORTING THROUGH SPOILED FOOD.
AH, THIS'S BAD.
AND THIS. THIS, TOO.
CHICKEN TENDER
THIS...
バニラ vanilla
IS OKAY! STILL GOOD!
ISN'T THAT PUSHING IT?
IT'S EXPENSIVE ICE CREAM! IT'LL BE DELICIOUS EVEN IF IT'S MELTED!
SO SWEET!
HMM, THE FROZEN STUFF'S RUINED.

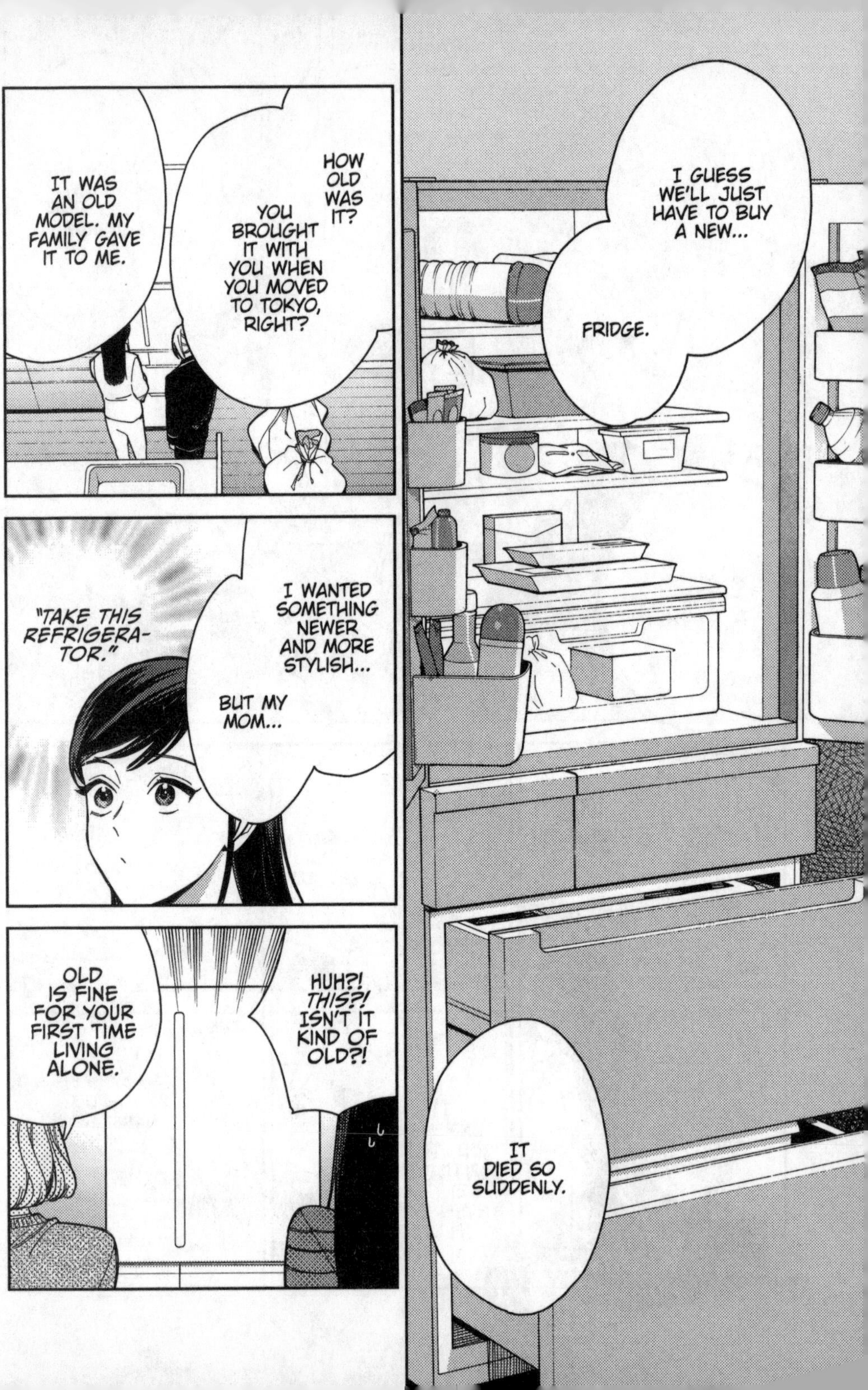
I GUESS WE'LL JUST HAVE TO BUY A NEW... FRIDGE.
IT DIED SO SUDDENLY.
HOW OLD WAS IT?
YOU BROUGHT IT WITH YOU WHEN YOU MOVED TO TOKYO, RIGHT?
IT WAS AN OLD MODEL. MY FAMILY GAVE IT TO ME.
I WANTED SOMETHING NEWER AND MORE STYLISH...
BUT MY MOM...
"TAKE THIS REFRIGERATOR."
HUH?! *THIS?!* ISN'T IT KIND OF OLD?!
OLD IS FINE FOR YOUR FIRST TIME LIVING ALONE.

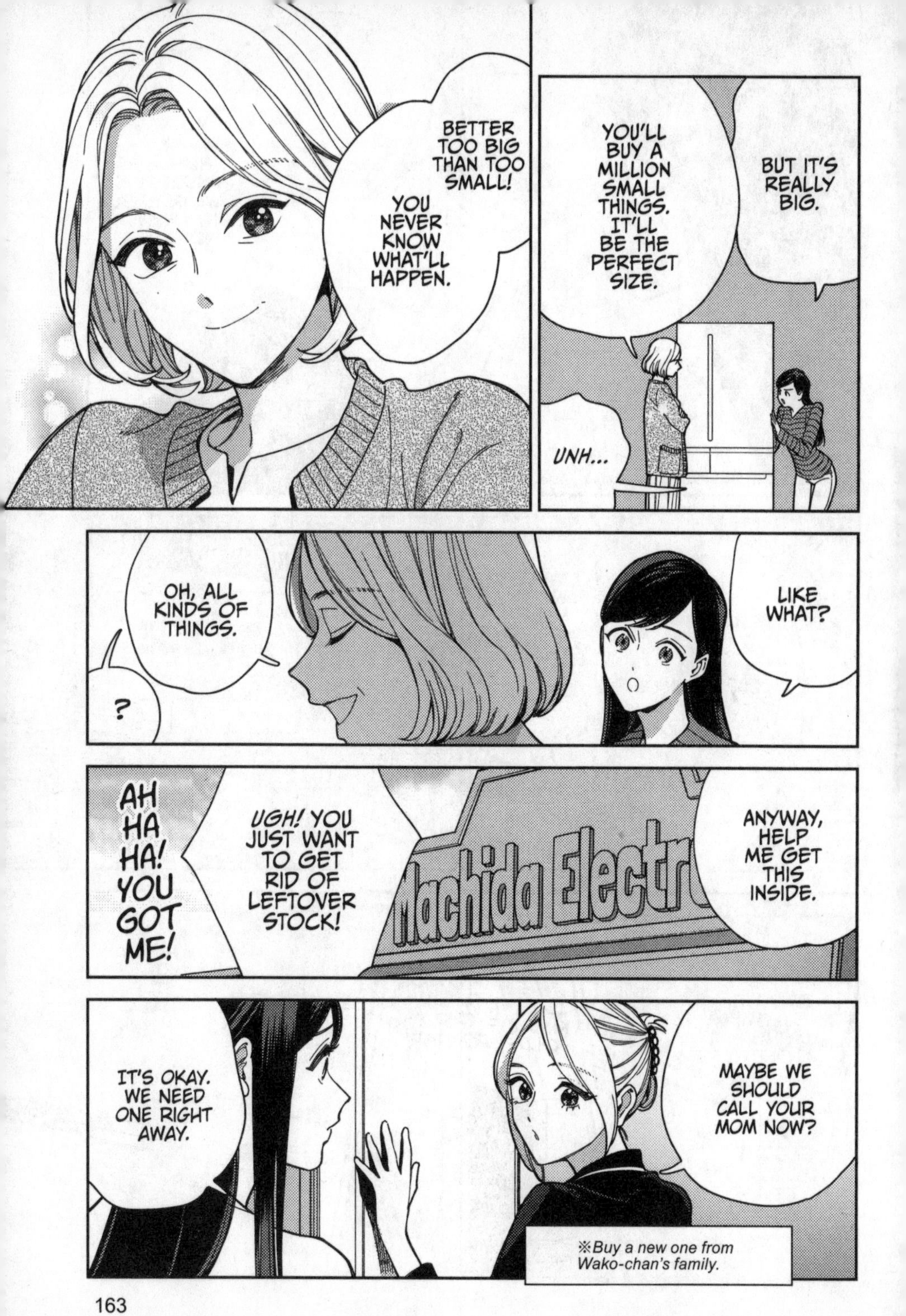
BUT IT'S REALLY BIG.
YOU'LL BUY A MILLION SMALL THINGS. IT'LL BE THE PERFECT SIZE.
UNH...
BETTER TOO BIG THAN TOO SMALL!
YOU NEVER KNOW WHAT'LL HAPPEN.
LIKE WHAT?
OH, ALL KINDS OF THINGS.
?
ANYWAY, HELP ME GET THIS INSIDE.
Machida Electr
UGH! YOU JUST WANT TO GET RID OF LEFTOVER STOCK!
AH HA HA! YOU GOT ME!
MAYBE WE SHOULD CALL YOUR MOM NOW?
IT'S OKAY. WE NEED ONE RIGHT AWAY.
※Buy a new one from Wako-chan's family.

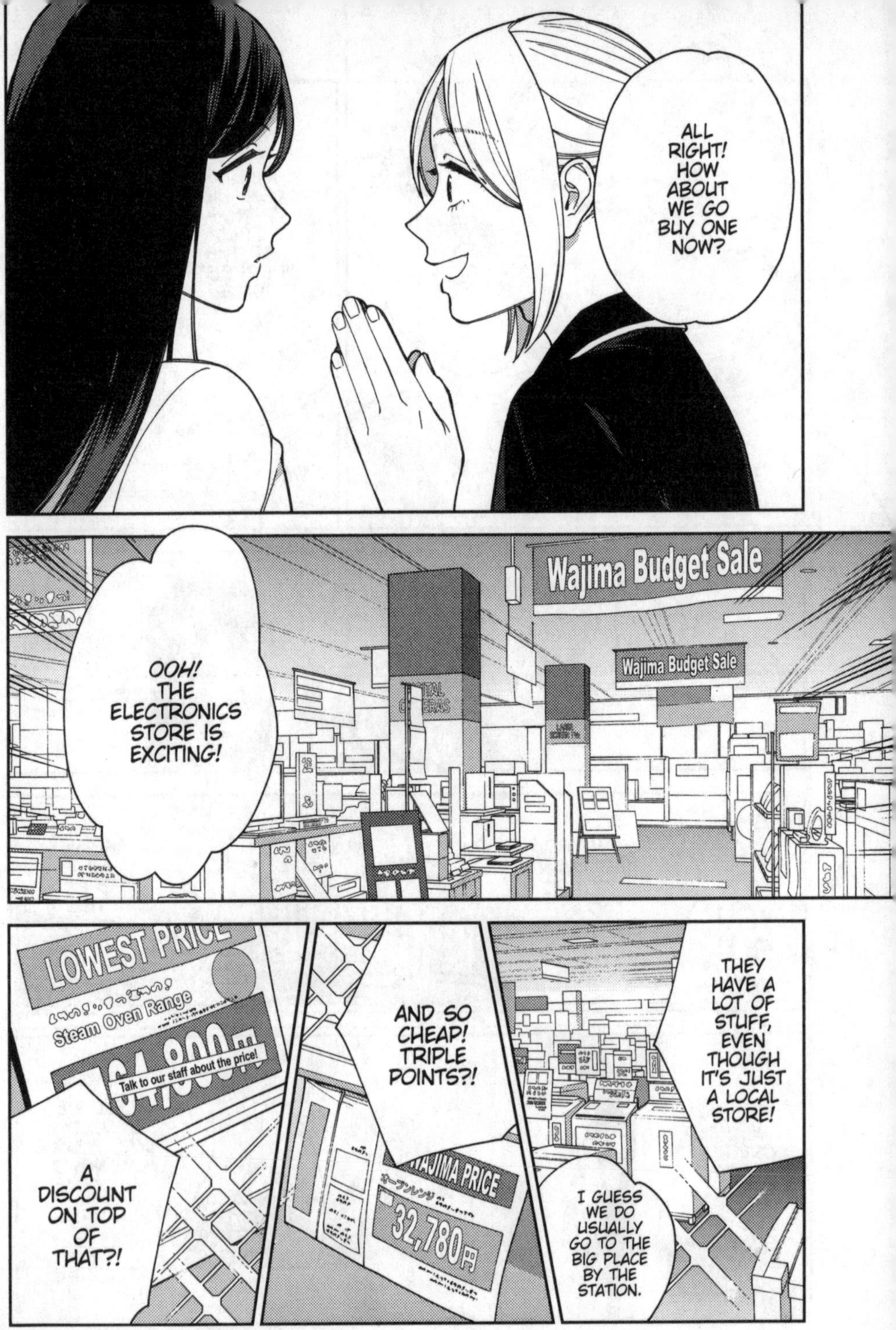
ALL RIGHT! HOW ABOUT WE GO BUY ONE NOW?
Wajima Budget Sale
OOH! THE ELECTRONICS STORE IS EXCITING!
Wajima Budget Sale
THEY HAVE A LOT OF STUFF, EVEN THOUGH IT'S JUST A LOCAL STORE!
I GUESS WE DO USUALLY GO TO THE BIG PLACE BY THE STATION.
AND SO CHEAP! TRIPLE POINTS?!
WAJIMA PRICE
32,780円
LOWEST PRICE
Steam Oven Range
Talk to our staff about the price!
A DISCOUNT ON TOP OF THAT?!

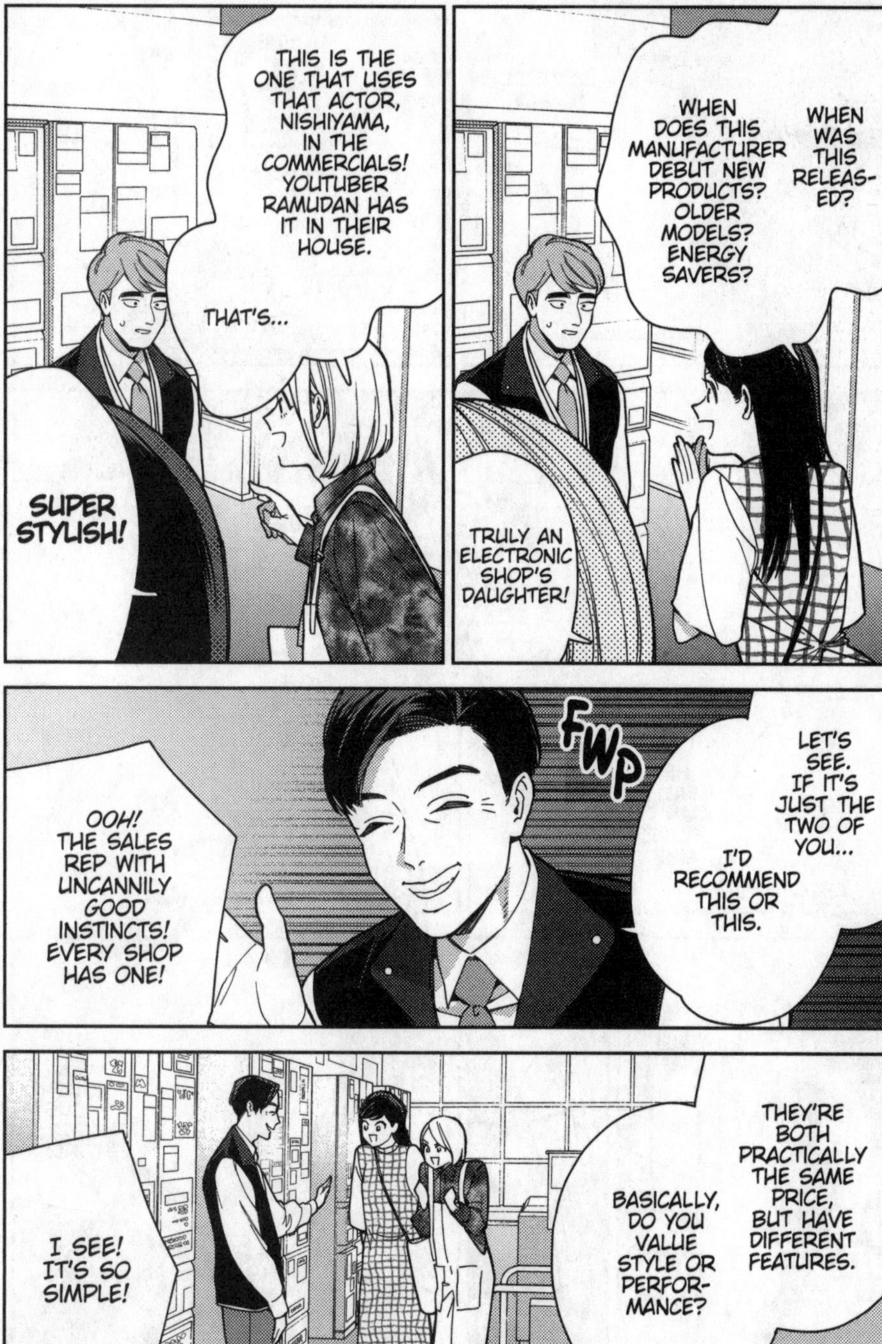
WHEN WAS THIS RELEAS-ED?
WHEN DOES THIS MANUFACTURER DEBUT NEW PRODUCTS? OLDER MODELS? ENERGY SAVERS?
TRULY AN ELECTRONIC SHOP'S DAUGHTER!
THIS IS THE ONE THAT USES THAT ACTOR, NISHIYAMA, IN THE COMMERCIALS! YOUTUBER RAMUDAN HAS IT IN THEIR HOUSE.
THAT'S...
SUPER STYLISH!
FWP
LET'S SEE. IF IT'S JUST THE TWO OF YOU...
I'D RECOMMEND THIS OR THIS.
OOH! THE SALES REP WITH UNCANNILY GOOD INSTINCTS! EVERY SHOP HAS ONE!
THEY'RE BOTH PRACTICALLY THE SAME PRICE, BUT HAVE DIFFERENT FEATURES.
BASICALLY, DO YOU VALUE STYLE OR PERFOR-MANCE?
I SEE! IT'S SO SIMPLE!

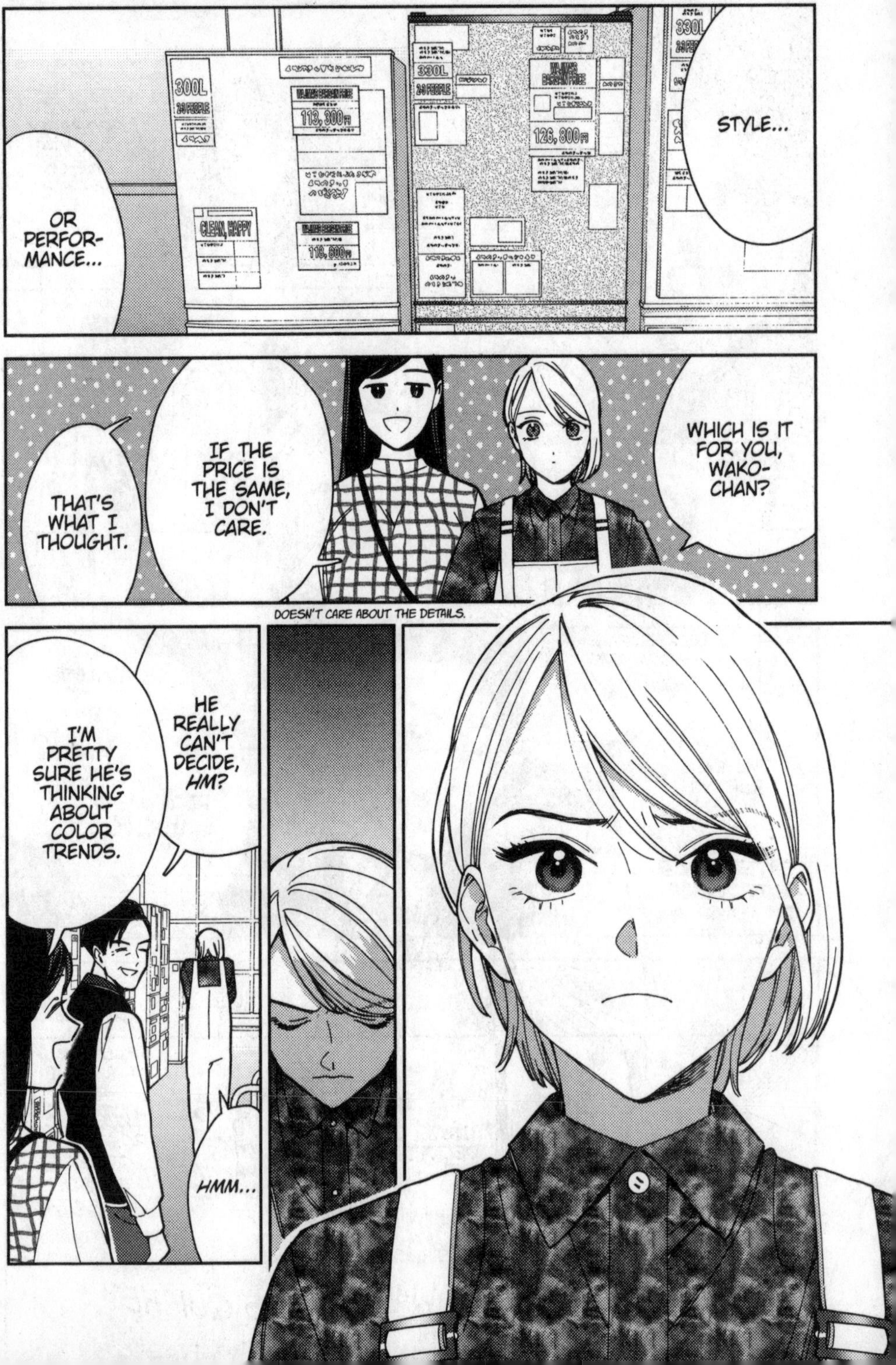
STYLE...
OR PERFORMANCE...
WHICH IS IT FOR YOU, WAKO-CHAN?
IF THE PRICE IS THE SAME, I DON'T CARE.
THAT'S WHAT I THOUGHT.
DOESN'T CARE ABOUT THE DETAILS.
HE REALLY CAN'T DECIDE, HM?
I'M PRETTY SURE HE'S THINKING ABOUT COLOR TRENDS.
HMM...

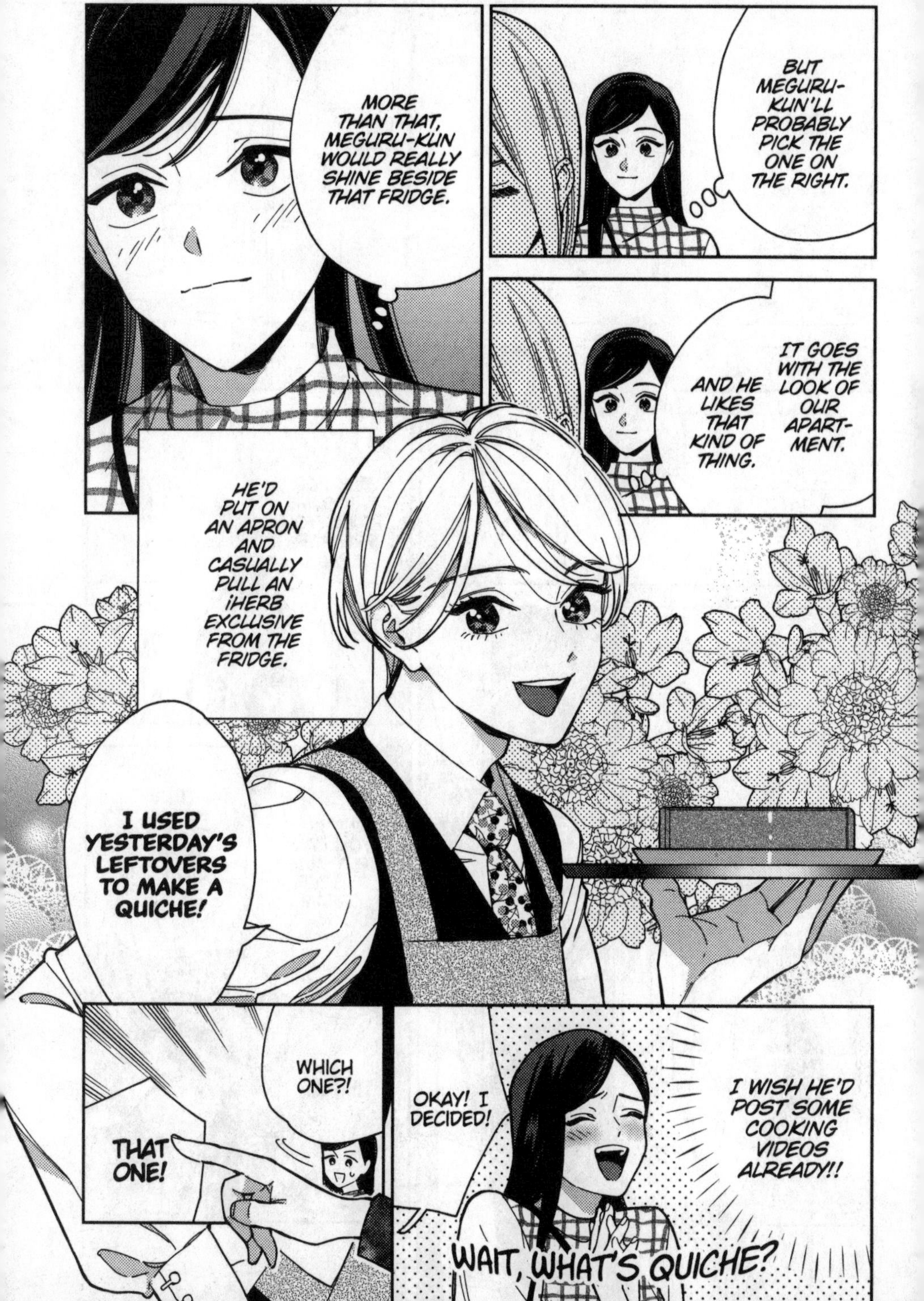

BUT MEGURU-KUN'LL PROBABLY PICK THE ONE ON THE RIGHT.
IT GOES WITH THE LOOK OF OUR APART-MENT.
AND HE LIKES THAT KIND OF THING.
MORE THAN THAT, MEGURU-KUN WOULD REALLY SHINE BESIDE THAT FRIDGE.
HE'D PUT ON AN APRON AND CASUALLY PULL AN iHERB EXCLUSIVE FROM THE FRIDGE.
I USED YESTERDAY'S LEFTOVERS TO MAKE A QUICHE!
I WISH HE'D POST SOME COOKING VIDEOS ALREADY!!
WAIT, WHAT'S QUICHE?
OKAY! I DECIDED!
WHICH ONE?!
THAT ONE!

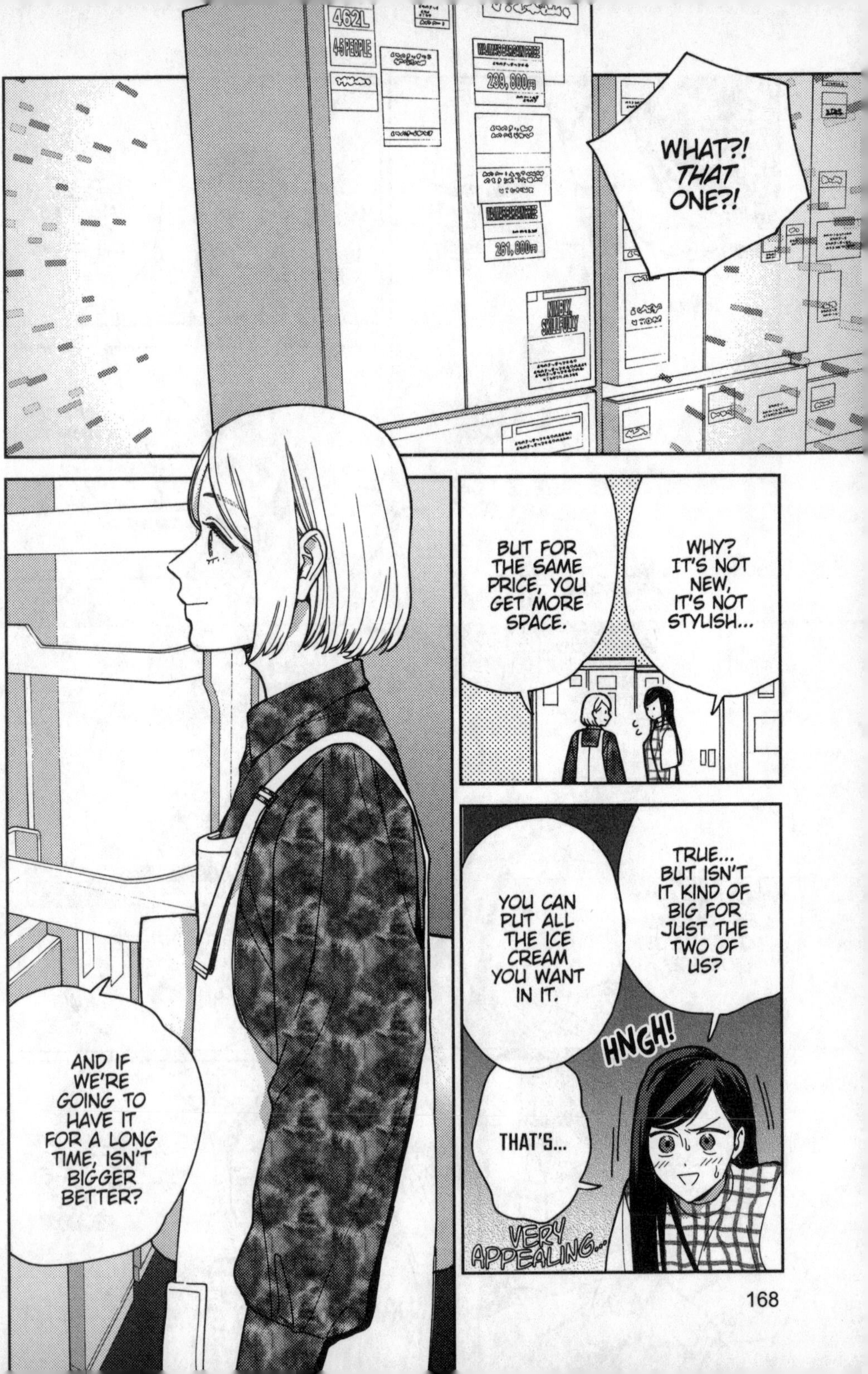
WHAT?! THAT ONE?!
462L
4-5 PEOPLE
WAJIMA'S BARGAIN PRICE
239,800円
261,800円
NIMBLY, SKILLFULLY
WHY? IT'S NOT NEW, IT'S NOT STYLISH...
BUT FOR THE SAME PRICE, YOU GET MORE SPACE.
TRUE... BUT ISN'T IT KIND OF BIG FOR JUST THE TWO OF US?
YOU CAN PUT ALL THE ICE CREAM YOU WANT IN IT.
HNGH!
THAT'S...
VERY APPEALING...
AND IF WE'RE GOING TO HAVE IT FOR A LONG TIME, ISN'T BIGGER BETTER?

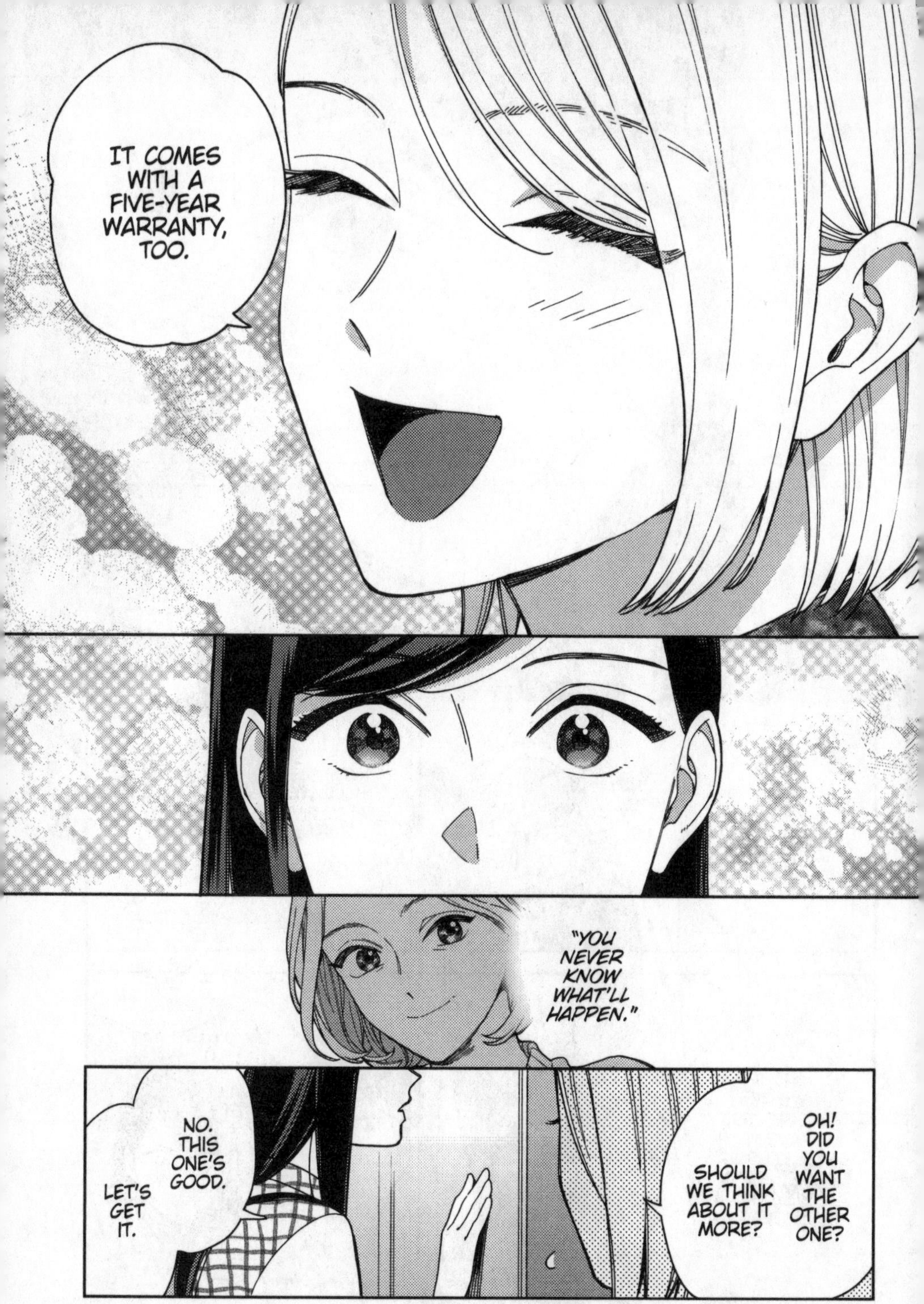
IT COMES WITH A FIVE-YEAR WARRANTY, TOO.
"YOU NEVER KNOW WHAT'LL HAPPEN."
OH! DID YOU WANT THE OTHER ONE?
SHOULD WE THINK ABOUT IT MORE?
NO. THIS ONE'S GOOD.
LET'S GET IT.

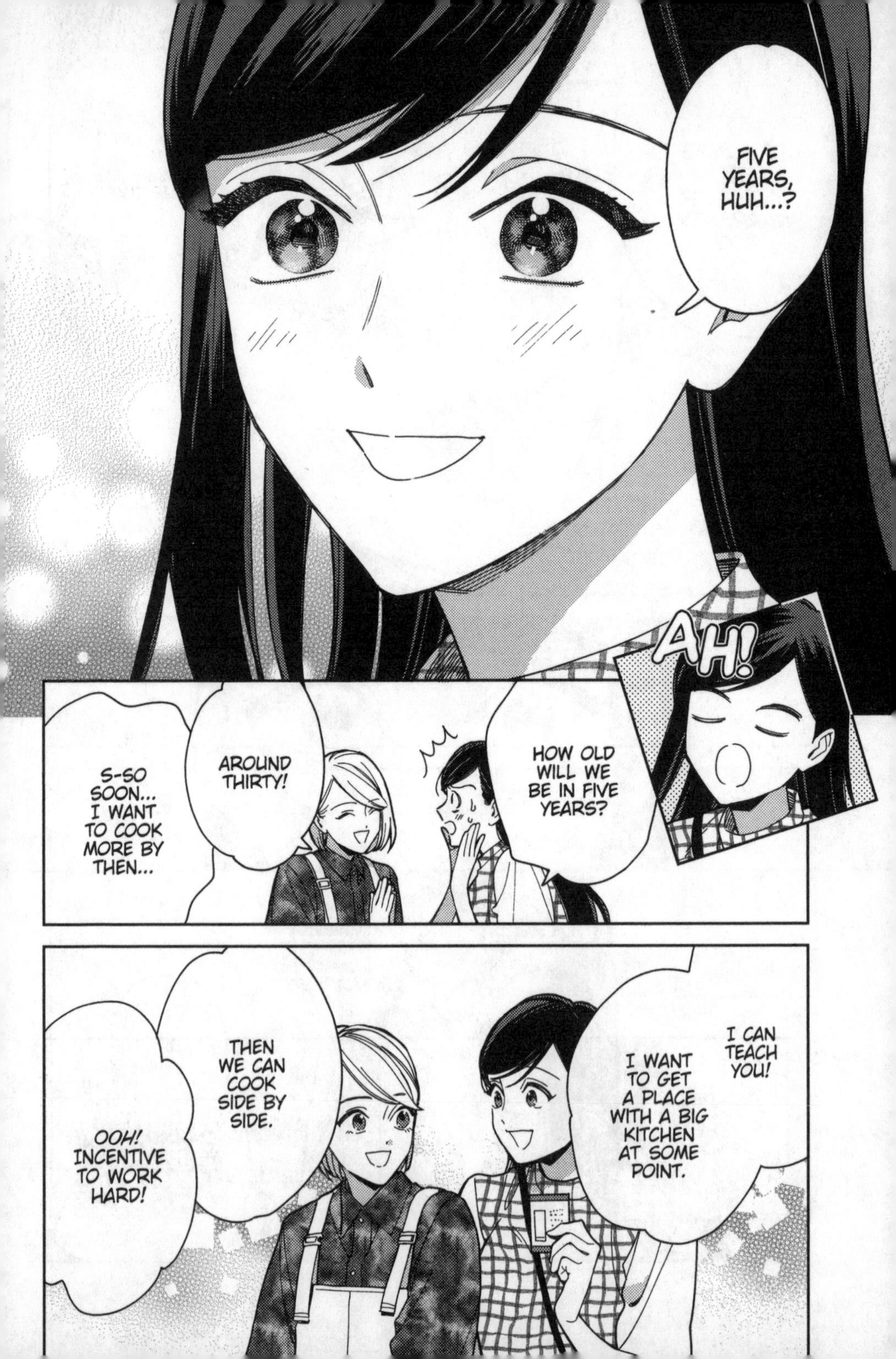
FIVE YEARS, HUH...?
AH!
HOW OLD WILL WE BE IN FIVE YEARS?
AROUND THIRTY!
S-SO SOON... I WANT TO COOK MORE BY THEN...
I CAN TEACH YOU!
I WANT TO GET A PLACE WITH A BIG KITCHEN AT SOME POINT.
THEN WE CAN COOK SIDE BY SIDE.
OOH! INCENTIVE TO WORK HARD!

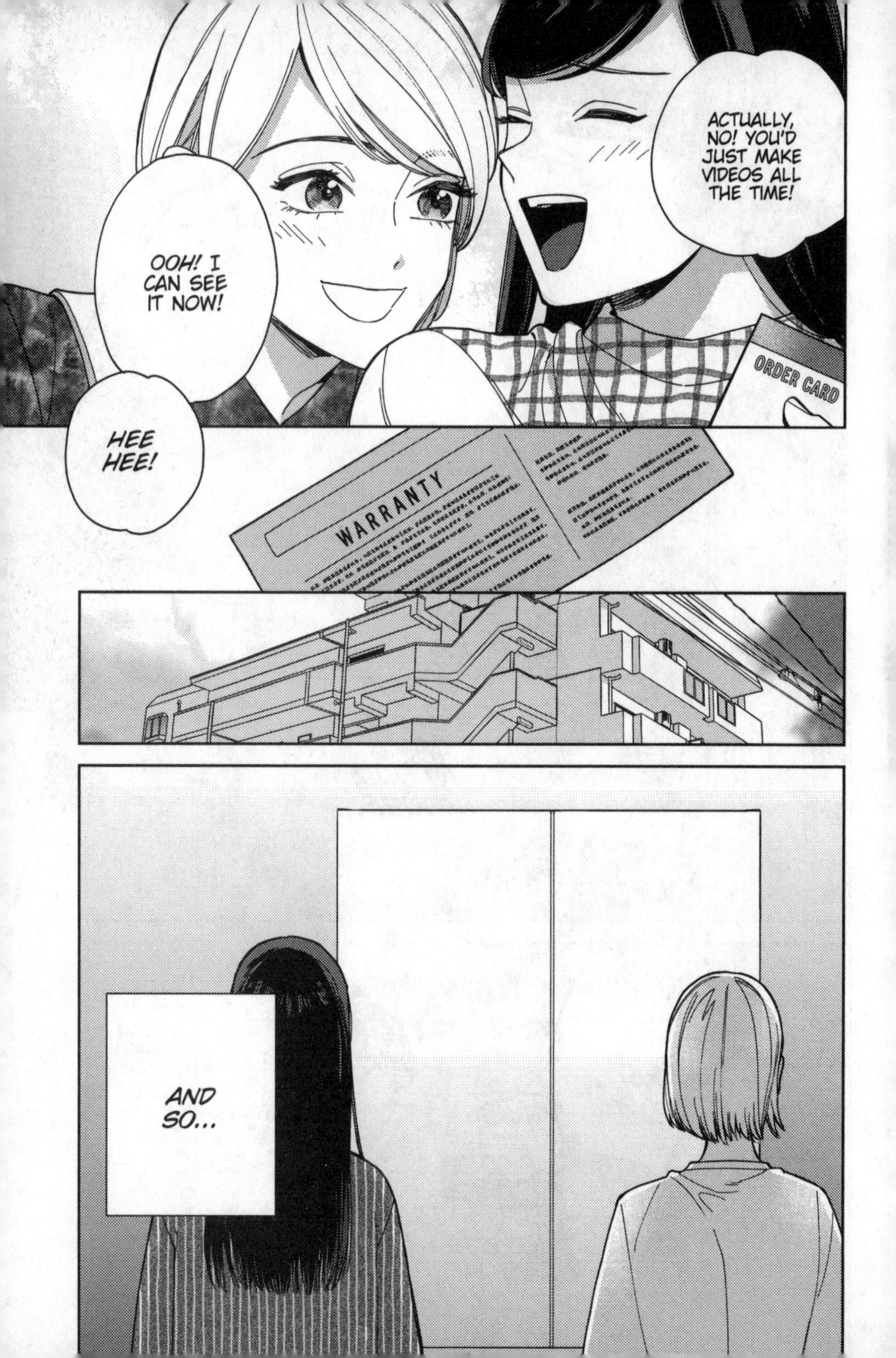
ACTUALLY, NO! YOU'D JUST MAKE VIDEOS ALL THE TIME!
ORDER CARD
OOH! I CAN SEE IT NOW!
HEE HEE!
WARRANTY
AND SO...

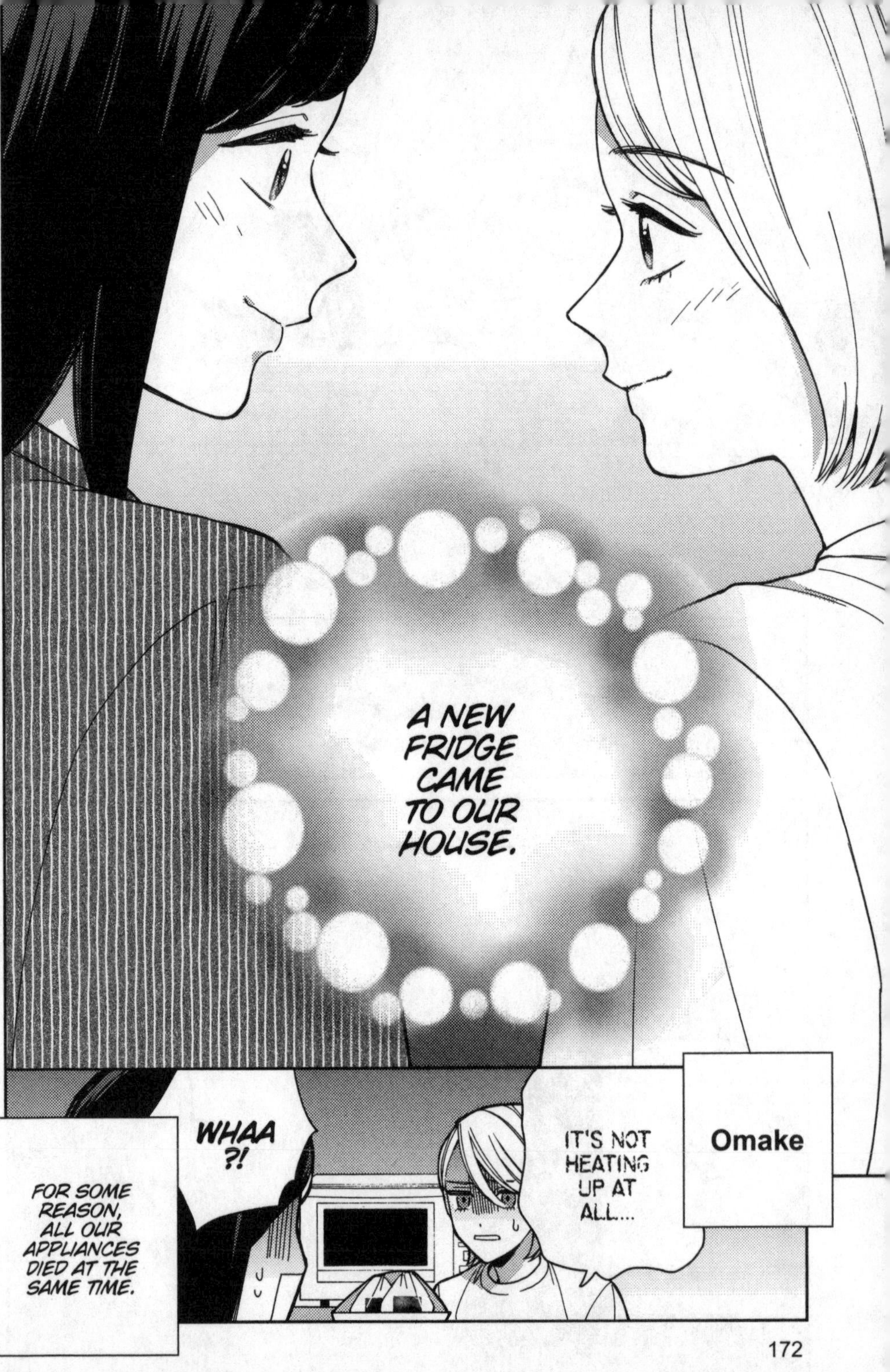
A NEW FRIDGE CAME TO OUR HOUSE.
Omake
IT'S NOT HEATING UP AT ALL...
WHAA ?!
FOR SOME REASON, ALL OUR APPLIANCES DIED AT THE SAME TIME.

To be continued ...

My Androgynous Boyfriend

SEVEN SEAS ENTERTAINMENT PRESENTS

My Androgynous Boyfriend

story and art by **TAMEKOU**

VOLUME 3

TRANSLATION
Jocelyne Allen

ADAPTATION
Lora Gray

LETTERING
Karis Page

COVER DESIGN
Kris Aubin

PROOFREADER
Kurestin Armada

COPY EDITOR
Dawn Davis

EDITOR
Jenn Grunigen

PREPRESS TECHNICIAN
Rhiannon Rasmussen-Silverstein

PRODUCTION MANAGER
Lissa Pattillo

MANAGING EDITOR
Julie Davis

ASSOCIATE PUBLISHER
Adam Arnold

PUBLISHER
Jason DeAngelis

GENDER LESS DANSHI NI AISARETEIMASU VOL.3
© Tamekou 2020
Originally published in Japan in 2020 by SHODENSHA Publishing Co., LTD.
English translation rights arranged through TOHAN CORPORATION, TOKYO.

Seven Seas press and purchase enquiries can be sent to Marketing Manager Lianne Sentar at press@gomanga.com. Information regarding the distribution and purchase of digital editions is available from Digital Manager CK Russell at digital@gomanga.com.

Seven Seas and the Seven Seas logo are trademarks of Seven Seas Entertainment. All rights reserved.

ISBN: 978-1-64827-931-7

Printed in Canada

First Printing: November 2021

10 9 8 7 6 5 4 3 2 1

FOLLOW US ONLINE: **www.sevenseasentertainment.com**

READING DIRECTIONS

This book reads from *right to left*, Japanese style. If this is your first time reading manga, you start reading from the top right panel on each page and take it from there. If you get lost, just follow the numbered diagram here. It may seem backwards at first, but you'll get the hang of it! Have fun!!

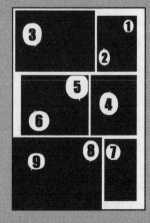